A Road is Made

Communism in Shanghai
1920-1927

Chinese Worlds

Chinese Worlds publishes high-quality scholarship, research monographs, and source collections on Chinese history and society from 1900 into the next century.

"Worlds" signals the ethnic, cultural, and political multiformity and regional diversity of China, the cycles of unity and division through which China's modern history has passed, and recent research trends toward regional studies and local issues. It also signals that Chineseness is not contained within territorial borders – overseas Chinese communities in all countries and regions are also "Chinese worlds". The editors see them as part of a political, economic, social, and cultural continuum that spans the Chinese mainland, Taiwan, Hong Kong, Macau, South-East Asia, and the world.

The focus of Chinese Worlds is on modern politics and society and history. It includes both history in its broader sweep and specialist monographs on Chinese politics, anthropology, political economy, sociology, education, and the social-science aspects of culture and religions.

The Literary Field of Twentieth-Century China
Edited by *Michel Hockx*

Chinese Business in Malaysia
Accumulation, Ascendance, Accommodation
Edmund Terence Gomez

Internal and International Migration
Chinese Perspectives
Edited by *Frank N. Pieke* and *Hein Mallee*

Village Inc.
Chinese Rural Society in the 1990s
Edited by *Flemming Christiansen* and *Zhang Junzuo*

Chen Duxiu's Last Articles and Letters, 1937–1942
Edited and translated by *Gregor Benton*

Encyclopedia of the Chinese Overseas
Edited by *Lynn Pan*

New Fourth Army
Communist Resistance along the Yangtze and the Huai, 1938–1941
Gregor Benton

A Road is Made
Communism in Shanghai 1920–1927
Steve Smith

The Bolsheviks and the Chinese Revolution 1919–1927
Alexander Pantsov

Chinatown, Europe
Identity of the European Chinese Towards the Beginning of the Twenty-First Century
Flemming Christiansen

Birth Control in China 1949–1999
Population Policy and Demographic Development
Thomas Scharping

A Road is Made

Communism in Shanghai
1920–1927

S.A. Smith

UNIVERSITY OF HAWAI'I PRESS
HONOLULU

© 2000 S.A. Smith

Published in North America by
University of Hawai'i Press
2840 Kolowalu Street
Honolulu, Hawai'i 96822

First published in the United Kingdom
by Curzon Press
Richmond, Surrey
England

Printed in Great Britain

Library of Congress Cataloging-in-Publication Data

Smith, S. A. (Stephen Anthony), 1952-
    A road is made: Communism in Shanghai, 1920-1927 / Steve Smith.
      p. cm. – (Chinese worlds)
    Includes bibliographical references and index.
    ISBN 0-8248-2314-1 (alk. paper)
      1. Communism–China–Shanghai. 2. Chung-kuo kung ch°n tang. 3.
  China–History–1912-1928. I. Title: Communism in Shanghai,
  1920-1927. II. Title. III. Series.

HX420.S485 S55 2000
324.251'132075'09042–dc21   99-048958

"Hope can neither be affirmed nor denied.
Hope is like a path in the countryside.
Originally, there was no path – but when many
people pass one way, a road is made."

Lu Xun, "My Old Home" (January 1921)

Contents

Acknowledgements	ix
Map	xii
Introduction	1
1 The Formation of a Communist Party in Shanghai	9
2 The Communist Party in Shanghai, 1921–22	31
3 The CCP and the United Front in Shanghai, 1923–24	51
4 The Communists Perfect a Labour Movement Strategy	74
5 The Shanghai Communists and the May Thirtieth Movement	89
6 The Shanghai Communists and the United Front, 1925–26	108
7 The CCP and the Labour Movement in 1926	130
8 The First and Second Armed Uprisings	145
9 The Third Armed Uprising	168
10 The 12 April 1927 Coup	190
Conclusion	209
Abbreviations	227
Notes	228
Bibliography	284
Subject Index	301
Name Index	310

Acknowledgements

I first began work on a study of labour and nationalism in Shanghai longer ago than I care to remember in 1986. The book I then planned to write was designed to shift the focus away from the Chinese Communist Party (CCP), by examining labour's relation to the nationalist movement from the turn of the century. However, since scholars in the PRC began to publish a vast amount of material relating to the early years of the CCP during the 1980s, I found myself collecting much more material on the history of the party than I needed for my book. The sudden opening of the Comintern archives to western scholars in 1991, following the collapse of the Soviet Union, made me reconsider my decision not to get involved in the history of the CCP, since my "other career" – as a historian of labour in late-imperial and early Soviet Russia – seemed to qualify me to try to integrate the new material on Comintern policy in China – most of which was in Russian – with the mass of material on the CCP in Shanghai. A visit to Moscow to the former archive of the Communist Party of the Soviet Union (RTsKhIDNI) confirmed that there was a indeed a huge amount of material relating to Comintern operations in China. Fortunately, I was spared the effort of wading through this by the discovery that a team of Russian and German scholars from the Far-Eastern Institute of the Russian Academy of Sciences and the East Asia Seminar of the Free University of Berlin, led, respectively, by Professors M.L. Titarenko and Mechthild Leutner, was already embarked on a massive project to publish all Comintern material relating to China. The first two volumes of their project, covering the years 1920 to 1927, appeared in 1994 and 1996 and greatly eased my work on this book. The result has been that I have ended up writing two books at once: the first is the book I always intended to write on labour and nationalism in Shanghai between 1900 and 1927, which is currently in the final stages of revision, and the second is the present volume which investigates the activities, ideas and internal life of the CCP in Shanghai during its formative years.

In writing this book I have accumulated many debts and I intend simply to list the names of most of those who have helped me. It would be discourteous, however, if I did not single out Greg Benton, formerly of the University of Leeds and now of the University of Cardiff, for giving me warm support and for reading this ms. with characteristic care and insight. In addition, I should like to thank Robert Bickers of the University of Bristol and Julia Strauss of the School of Oriental and African Studies, University of London, who served as exemplary publisher's readers, offering astute criticisms and suggestions for improvements. My sometimes flagging enthusiasm for the project was rekindled by invitations to participate in two major conferences, both of which turned out to be unusually stimulating. The first was the Third Medlicott Symposium, which took place in July 1995 at the University of Exeter, which was devoted to the history of the Comintern. I would like to thank Tim Rees and Andrew Thorpe, the organizers, for inviting me and Nina Fishman and Paul Wingrove for being stimulating companions. The second conference took place at the Free University of Berlin in October 1998 and was devoted to "New Research and New Perspectives on the Chinese Revolution in the 1920s". Again I would like warmly to thank the organizers, Professor Mechthild Leutner and Dr Tim Trampedach, and Konstantin Shevelev and Alexander Pantsov for sharing with me their matchless knowledge of the Comintern. Other participants from whom I learnt a great deal were Christina Gilmartin, Chen Yung-fa, Yu Minling and Li Yuzhen. Professor A.I. Kartunova deserves a special mention for graciously lending me a chapter of her unpublished doctor's dissertation, as does Professor Joachim Krüger, who gave me a copy of a rare Chinese poster from his personal collection. Finally, I must thank Elizabeth Perry, then of the University of California at Berkeley, and Hans van de Ven of Cambridge University for generously lending me materials to which I would otherwise not have had access.

It has been a pleasure to work at a number of libraries and archives in the course of this research and I would like to record my gratitude to staff at the library of Fudan University in Shanghai, the Shanghai Municipal Library, the Russian State Library in Moscow, the Hoover Institution at Stanford, the library of the University of California at Berkeley, the Public Record Office in London and, in particular, Cambridge University Library and SOAS library in London. My biggest debt, however, is to Paul Naish and Vanessa Coombe of the Interlibrary Loans department of the Albert Sloman Library, University of Essex, who have been unfailingly efficient in tracking down requests for obscure items over many years. I should also like to thank the University of Essex, for granting me various terms of study leave during the writing of this book; the British Council, for giving me a six-month scholarship to Fudan University in 1986; and the Humanities Research Board of the British Academy for one term's replacement teaching costs in 1996–97. Thanks, finally, to Chris Ward for his practical help and, last but by no means least, to Phil Jakes, to whom this book is dedicated.

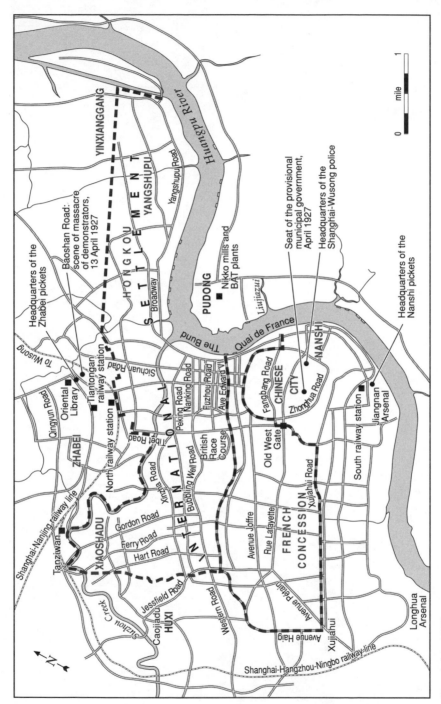

Shanghai in 1927

Introduction

With a population of three million by 1930, Shanghai was the third largest city in Asia, having more than doubled in size since 1910.[1] One of China's 'treaty ports', it was opened up to foreign trade as a result of the unequal treaties foisted on China after each of her defeats at the hands of foreign powers during the nineteenth century. The city was dominated by the International Settlement and the French Concession, both, in the words of John King Fairbank, 'traders' republics', each with its own administration, police force and judiciary.[2] In addition, there were three districts under Chinese administration – Nandao, Zhabei and Pudong – which were the object of contention between rival warlord factions, especially in 1924 when war flared up between Jiangsu and Zhejiang militarists.[3] Until 1949 the city was more important as a commercial than as an industrial centre. By 1919 the value of Shanghai's import-export trade was eight times its 1865 level, by 1920 ten times and by 1926 eighteen times as large.[4] Foreign capital dominated the import-export trade, banking, insurance, shipping and communications, but Chinese merchants participated enthusiastically in modern commerce from the late-nineteenth century.[5] Shanghai was also China's major centre of modern industry, with foreign capital dominant in sectors such as cotton textiles and tobacco, ship-building, ship-repair and public utilities.[6] With the First World War, Chinese industrialists took advantage of the weakening of foreign competition to make rapid advances in manufacturing and transportation. During the boom of 1919–22, the number of native and foreign-owned cotton mills grew from 26 to 51, with the Chinese-owned share of spindlage increasing from 42% to 47%.[7] Native manufacturers also dominated the expanding silk-spinning and food-processing industries and made inroads into tobacco.

With its western buildings and institutions, its department stores, its women with bobbed hair and make-up, its men in suits, Shanghai was a potent symbol of modernity. It was a city where traditional social categories, such as those of scholar-official, farmer, artisan and merchant, were breaking down, and new social categories, such as businessman, intellectual, clerk or worker, coming into existence. For conservatives

Shanghai's modernity challenged everything it meant to be Chinese, threatening to dissolve all social bonds and responsibilities. The city was perceived as a place where there was an unhealthy cult of novelty, where money talked, where morals were lax.[8] For others, by contrast, especially for educated youth, Shanghai was a site of emancipation from the crippling ties of the patriarchal family and traditional social order. These radically divergent perceptions were rooted in the contradictions of modernity itself. On the one hand, the advance of capitalist industrialization and urbanization created an alienated society, riven by exploitation and destructive of many of the values of community. On the other, the same onrush of developments brought in its train an enlarged sense of social possibility and the enhancement of the individual self, now increasingly released from the fixed status categories of the pre-capitalist past.[9]

Too unilateral an emphasis on Shanghai's modernity, however, is misleading, for the city combined elements of western culture and capitalism with much that was traditional. The vast mass of the population, for instance, were migrants, mainly young men, who had only recently arrived from the countryside: in 1930 only 22% of the population had been born in the city.[10] The constant influx of migrants, in addition to creating poverty and squalor on a hideous scale, served to reproduce traditional cultural forms within the modern urban space. In the eyes of the minority who considered themselves 'Shanghainese', the mass of impoverished and ignorant migrants were country bumpkins, likened to blocks of wood (*A Mulin*) or clods of earth (*A Tusheng*).[11] In the disorienting world of the city, migrants relied on social networks based on region of origin to find jobs and accommodation, on secret societies for protection, on relationships of clientelism with foremen, labour contractors or neighbourhood strong-men.[12] Seemingly atavistic networks were thus put to new uses in the urban and industrial environment while forming a bridgehead that linked the city's inhabitants to their relatives in the rural hinterland.

In view of this, Shanghai is best understood as the bastion of a hybrid culture – part urban, part peasant, part western, part Chinese – a matrix of sharp social and cultural contradictions that exerted a solvent effect on the traditional order.[13] Shanghai was an emblem of class exploitation and of consumer affluence, of foreign imperialism and patriotic resistance, of individualism and mass society; a city where high-rise buildings stood alongside shanty towns, limousines alongside rickshaws. Li Dazhao, co-founder of the CCP, writing in the journal *New Youth* (*Xin Qingnian*) in May 1918, captured the psychological dislocation that arose from living amid the confusing juxtaposition of old and new:

> The life of the Chinese today is completely contradictory... People across the nation pursue their lives amid contradictory phenomena and thus feel ill at ease and unhappy... A contradictory life is a life

in which new and old are not in harmony: here is new and there is old, countless things separated from one another, but gathered in one place, a life in which discrete things confront one another.[14]

Shanghai, more than anywhere else in China, seemed to promise the possibility of acquiring those forms of modernity created by the West, which alone seemed capable of saving China from national extinction. Yet at the same time, it bespoke the impossibility of ever doing so, when every step of progress seemed threatened by mounting economic misery and political failure. It was out of the sense of anxiety created by a situation 'in which new and old are not in harmony' that a layer of radical educated youth turned to Communism following the May Fourth Movement of 1919.

The end of the twentieth century is an appropriate point from which to reflect upon the significance of that century's most powerful political challenge to liberal capitalism. The century which saw Communist revolutions break out on a global scale witnessed during its last decade the demise of Communism in Russia, Eastern Europe, Yugoslavia, Cuba, Vietnam and, not least, in China itself. The present study, by investigating the political, social and cultural history of the Chinese Communist Party (CCP) in Shanghai during its formative years, seeks to trace the origins of that Communist regime which came to be second only to that of the Soviet Union; and to illuminate the ambivalent nature of Chinese Communism, which was at once a force for national liberation and social justice, offering hope to a country laid low by the collapse of government and the depredations of imperialism, and a force for despotism, that would eventuate in one of the most enduring authoritarian regimes of the century. By exploring the ideology and organization of the early CCP and, in particular, its relation to the social constituencies it sought to mobilize, this study shows how the ambivalence of the Communist project was inscribed in the party's operations from the first.

The tendency of much Cold War historiography of the national revolution which culminated in Chiang Kai-shek's reunification of China in 1927, was to ascribe paramount agency in the revolutionary process to Moscow.[15] With regard to the birth of the CCP, historians such as Conrad Brandt and Allen Whiting ascribed paternity to Moscow, but from early on historians such as Benjamin Schwartz and Maurice Meisner stressed its indigenous origins.[16] A more recent generation of scholars has followed the latter in playing down the importance of external influences in the formation of the CCP and in the national revolution more generally. In his admirable study Hans van de Ven traced the development of the CCP out of networks of friends, schoolmates and fellow provincials, each rooted in a particular regional and social environment.[17] In a similar fashion, Wen-hsin Yeh has elegantly traced the roots of radicalism in Zhejiang province – a crucial supplier of recruits to the early CCP – in the shifting spatial patterns of one of China's most commercially developed and culturally sophisticated regions.[18] Most recently, Patricia Stranahan's valuable study links the success of the Shanghai Communists in building an underground organization to withstand Guomindang (GMD) repression during the 1930s to the specificities of the urban context.[19] This book follows the lead of these innovative scholars, by setting the history of the CCP in Shanghai firmly in a domestic context, paying attention to the composition and inner dynamics of the party and to its relations with the city's workers, secret societies, students, women, businessmen and nationalists. But the study also challenges the recent tendency to minimize the influence of external forces in bringing the CCP into being. Using material that has become available since the opening of the Comintern archives in 1991, it assigns greater weight than many recent accounts to the role of the Comintern not only in bringing the CCP into existence but also in the national revolution at large.[20]

Franz Schurmann argued that the People's Republic of China (PRC) was held together by ideology and organization.[21] From the first, both these ingredients were recognized by the party leadership to be of vital importance. Ideology was central to the party's *raison d'être*, its strategy and tactics, its propaganda and agitation, its strategies of legitimation and to its internal allocation of power. This study, however, shifts the focus away from questions of ideology and strategy towards an analysis of the party's activities among different sectors of Shanghai society. In part, this is justified because there are now a couple of excellent studies of CCP ideology in this period. In a masterly account of radical ideas during the May Fourth Movement, Arif Dirlik resituated the CCP in a fluid field of political and ideological force, dominated by anarchism and state socialism.[22] And Michael Luk shed penetrating light on the emergence of a distinctive system of political thought among the Chinese Communists during the 1920s.[23] These studies render redundant any attempt on my part to traverse the same ground. Nevertheless, given the paramount importance attached by the party leadership to ideological questions, the debates on the nature of the Chinese revolution and the bitter disputes concerning strategy and tactics cannot be altogether ignored. The present study, therefore, confines itself to indicating the main theoretical and strategic issues that exercised the party and, where new material has come to light – particularly, in relation to united front policy – it dwells in greater detail on the issues. Vital matters such as agrarian policy or military strategy, however, are ignored, since they had little bearing on the party's activities in Shanghai. On the equally important matter of organization, I again have not tried to duplicate the fine account of van de Ven, who traced the structural and cultural transformation of the CCP into a leninist party, a process which he showed was not complete until 1927.[24] However, the present study does examine the organizational development of the

Shanghai regional committee of the CCP specifically, including its relation to the Central Executive Committee (CEC) which for most of the period was based in Shanghai.[25] It also looks at the relations of the CEC and Shanghai regional committee to the Socialist Youth League (later the Communist Youth League) in Shanghai and to the Shanghai General Labour Union, set up in May 1925. Moreover, it uses new material, particularly from the Comintern archive, to examine the interaction in policy-making between the Shanghai regional committee, the CEC, Comintern operatives based in Shanghai, the Executive Committee of the Comintern (ECCI) and the Soviet Politburo in Moscow. And it looks not only at the policy issues which provoked conflict at different levels of the Comintern hierarchy, but also at disputes over financial and organizational matters and at the implications for the smooth running of the party of conflicts between individuals. In showing that conflict was endemic, but always more complex than a two-party struggle between an indigenous Communist party and a foreign control-centre, the study confirms the perspective that emerges from Tony Saich's meticulous edition of the archive of Hendricus Sneevliet, which first revealed not only the depth of division within the Comintern, but the leeway which an individual such as Sneevliet could enjoy in making policy on the ground.[26] Finally, in this connection, the book examines the practical difficulties faced by the Comintern in seeking to control the CCP, and asks how far the policy carried out by the Communists in Shanghai accorded with the intentions and expectations of Moscow.

The main focus of the book, however, is on the practical activities of the party in Shanghai, particularly on its efforts to mobilize workers, students, youth, women, small traders and merchants and the patriotic public at large into a militant struggle for national liberation.[27] Substantial attention is paid to the activities of the SYL in the student movement and to the efforts to orient the city's women's organizations towards a class-inflected anti-imperialism. Throughout the period, however, except for a year when the united front with the GMD was being established, the party leadership was principally concerned with building a labour movement in the city. For this reason, this book pays particular attention to the party's efforts to organize the workers of Shanghai.[28] It examines the problems faced in seeking to overcome the particularist ties of native place, craft, secret-society affiliation, clientelism and gender that divided Shanghai's labour force. It traces the party's efforts to lead strikes, create labour unions and armed pickets, and its use of techniques ranging from education and agitation through to terror and armed insurrection. In its efforts to organize Shanghai's workers, the CCP-backed General Labour Union inevitably clashed with the Green Gang (*Qingbang*) and, to a lesser extent, the Red Gang, the city's principal secret-society networks. Lower-level bosses in the Green Gang were often labour contractors or foremen who controlled the system of labour contracting on Shanghai's waterfront and, increasingly, recruitment into jobs in transportation, manufacturing and public utilities.[29] The organizing efforts of the CCP threatened the lucrative operations of these elements and their hold over their worker clients. During our period, party leaders tried alternately to collaborate with and oppose the secret societies, a strategy that backfired in April 1927, when the "Big Three" who controlled the Green Gang turned dramatically against the CCP. Similarly, the CCP sought to cooperate with Shanghai's business community not only to further the struggle for national liberation but also in the hope of persuading the Shanghai General Chamber of Commerce to support labour unions and improve the lot of their employees. The business community, however, remained suspicious of the CCP after the May Thirtieth Movement and, eventually, joined the backlash against it.

The book attempts to fill a lacuna identified by Jeffrey Wasserstrom, who pointed out that we know far more about formal ideologies and high-level faction fighting in the CCP than we do about how its members lived and worked.[30] Christina Gilmartin's pioneering study did much to address these issues from the perspective of women inside and outside the CCP.[31] This study follows her lead, bringing a gendered perspective to bear on the internal life of the CCP, and seeks to broaden the focus to look at personal relations as a factor that shaped the character of the party. It reviews the backgrounds and orientations of intellectuals and workers who were drawn into the party, weaving into the narrative short biographies of individuals which pinpoint their family backgrounds and personal relationships, which were often highly unconventional by Confucian standards. It is now possible to do this because of the sterling work by historians in the PRC in reconstructing the lives of hundreds of early Communists, many of whom were cruelly cut down in their prime.[32] It also examines the tensions that existed between intellectuals and workers within the party, and the dynamics of empowerment and domination that governed the relationship between the CCP and the labour movement.

The book appears at a time when western historians of China are increasingly critical of narratives which axe the history of modern China around the theme of revolution, still more around the history of the CCP.[33] As the subject of the present study, the CCP necessarily dominates the narrative, but I have tried to situate the party's activities in a broader field of contesting social and political forces than is customary. In particular, the book seeks to emphasise the GMD as an independent political force rather than merely as an adjunct to the CCP. The united front policy has been much discussed by historians from the point of view of the ideological conflicts it inspired, but this study explores its operation in practice in one city. In so doing, it seeks to deepen understanding of what the united front actually meant and reveals the extent of opposition to the policy both within the CCP and within influential GMD circles in Shanghai.

The book does not offer a comprehensive account of the CCP's policies on all the issues which convulsed national politics in this turbulent period, but it does examine in depth the role of the CCP in the two major crises that erupted in Shanghai and which had a major bearing on national politics. The first of these was the May Thirtieth Movement of 1925, which may be regarded as the commencement of the national revolution in Shanghai, since it was at that point that radical anti-imperialist nationalism acquired a mass base. Through its influence in the mass movements, especially the labour movement, the CCP rose to become a key player in the city's nationalist movement. However, it was not until the second half of 1926, when Chiang Kai-shek led the Northern Expedition to overcome the warlords and create a national government, that the CCP became a major force nationally. Between October 1926 and March 1927 the CCP in Shanghai made three attempts, in loose alliance with the GMD, to seize control of the city from the warlords. The "third armed uprising", which culminated in the brief seizure of power by armed pickets of the GLU in March 1927, may be known to readers otherwise unfamiliar with the history of the CCP, since it was immortalized in Andre Malraux's gripping novel, *Man's Fate*. However, in retrospect it can be seen to have highlighted the weakness rather than the strength of the Communists in the city. On 12 April 1927 Chiang Kai-shek arranged for gangsters, backed by troops of the National Revolutionary Army, to ransack the headquarters of the pickets and liquidate hundreds of Communists and labour militants. This bloodbath, which brought an end to the united front between the CCP and the GMD, has ever since been the subject of impassioned political controversy, with some blaming the débâcle on the united front policy which had been foisted by Moscow on a reluctant CCP, others blaming the leadership of the CCP for failing to carry out the policy with sufficient vigour. The book looks afresh, in the light of new material that has become available, at the respective responsibilities of the Comintern and the CCP leadership for the dramatic events which brought an end to the first phase of the CCP's existence.

A vast amount of material on the CCP in Shanghai has been published in the PRC since the early 1980s, including memoirs, resolutions and statistics.[34] The resolutions and directives of the CEC are now available in their entirety, though not the minutes of its meetings (if these exist).[35] By contrast, the minutes of the Shanghai regional committee have only been published patchily, although they are fairly full for the period of the three armed uprisings.[36] This study draws heavily on the Comintern materials relating to China – including the minutes of the Chinese commission of the Soviet Politburo – which have now been published for our period by an outstanding team of Russian and German scholars.[37] In addition, this study draws on the files of the Shanghai Municipal Police and on consular and intelligence records in the Public Record Office in London. It is also based on a comprehensive reading of the CCP press for the period, supplemented by the key progressive newspapers of the 1920s, especially *Shenbao* and *Minguo ribao*. But if much has become available since 1991, there is undoubtedly still material which has yet to see the light of day – most obviously, in the party archives in the PRC itself and in the military archives of the former Soviet Union.

As anyone who has worked on the history of the Communist movement will know, its language is highly abstruse and littered with jargon. To the uninitiated, different resolutions and contributions to debate often appear to be saying the same thing, since they use the same recondite formulae and inhabit a single conceptual universe. One task of the historian, therefore, is to pick up subtle shades of difference in interpretation, the telling emphasis or silence, the marginalization of a particular issue within the discourse. Although the language of Communism, like its political practice, succeeded in internationalizing itself – becoming shared by militants from varied cultural backgrounds – I have been regularly struck by problems of translation between languages, by the gap that exists between, say, an ECCI resolution, drafted in Russian or German, and its Chinese translation; and by the further gap that is created as I attempt to convey it into English. I think productive work could be done in future in exploring these gaps, but I have not attempted to grapple with the problem of the incommensurability of language or of the part it may have played in the Comintern's failure in China.[38]

One final caveat. It is the aim of this study to demonstrate the substantial role played by the tiny CCP in the national revolution of 1925–27. It is in this period that a 'road is made', when the Communists get to grips with the problems of building a revolutionary movement in China, and establish themselves as a credible political option among those concerned to save the nation. Nevertheless in this period it succeeded in mobilizing tens of thousands, rather than millions. And it could easily have been wiped out at the end of the 1920s, to become no more than a footnote to China's twentieth-century history. In other words, there was nothing preordained about its later rise to power under Mao Zedong. Indeed subsequent history would prove that the CCP in its formative period was fundamentally marginal to the forces – the Red Army and peasantry – which would ultimately make the revolution in China.

Chapter 1 _____

The Formation of a Communist Party in Shanghai

In December 1919 Chen Duxiu, the future general secretary of the Chinese Communist Party (CCP), proclaimed that the task facing China was to create a society that was 'sincere, progressive, activist, free, egalitarian, creative, beautiful, kind, peaceful, full of universal love, mutual assistance, pleasant labour and prosperous for all', in contrast to current society, which was 'hypocritical, conservative, passive, constrained, class-divided, conventional, ugly, vicious, belligerent, disorderly, lazy and prosperous for only a few.'[1] Chen's clarion call was made in the journal, *New Youth*, which he had established in 1915, and it signalled a revival of interest in politics on the part of that journal. When first launched, this journal had reflected the mood of disillusionment then current among China's radical intellectuals, as president Yuan Shikai proceeded to dismantle the vestiges of the republican regime which had been founded after the 1911 Revolution. Repudiating politicians and political programmes, it embraced a project of radical cultural transformation of China, in the belief that profound change could come about only through the uncompromising rejection of Confucian tradition and the whole-hearted embrace of western democracy and science. *New Youth* thus gave rise to the New Culture Movement, which was to have immense influence on radical youth once they were energized by the May Fourth Movement of 1919.

Early in 1919 news began to filter through that the peacemakers in Versailles intended to transfer Germany's privileges in China to Japan, as a reward for her cooperation with the Allies in the First World War. At first, the patriotic public was incredulous, but as the feebleness of the government's response became clear, merchants, educationalists, journalists and students began to mobilize. On 4 May, after the government made clear its intention to acquiesce in the peace settlement, students took to the streets of Beijing, thereby launching a nation-wide protest against the 'national traitors' (*guozei*) in government and the injustice of the foreign powers (*qiangquan*). The May Fourth Movement greatly intensified interest in the New Culture Movement, but at the same time marked a revival of interest in politics among radically-minded patriots, as is evident in the new manifesto published by *New Youth* in December 1919: 'We advocate mass movement and social reconstruction. . . . We do not believe in the omnipotence of politics, but we recognize that politics is an important aspect of public life and we believe that in a genuine democracy, political rights must be distributed to all the people.'[2]

The manifesto encapsulated many of the elements typical of the politics engendered by the May Fourth Movement. Patriotic intellectuals, brought to political consciousness by a desire to save the nation, embraced a broad variety of political ideologies – from anarchism, state socialism, guild socialism to liberalism. But the predominant, if amorphous ideology of the movement has been characterized by Arif Dirlik as 'anarcho-communist'.[3] The students, teachers, journalists and others who gave ideological and organizational direction to the boycotts and strikes combined a passionate commitment to individual liberation with root-and-branch rejection of traditional values and institutions and a yearning for a radical reconstruction of society on the basis of democracy and equality. Casting themselves in the role of society's 'knowledgeable elements' – *zhishifenzi* – a neologism that was increasingly used to denote the emergent intelligentsia – they sought to save China by uniting their personal struggles for liberation with the struggle of the nation for justice, liberty and social renewal. Moreover, the May Fourth Movement popularized a conception of the nation as a community rooted in the common people. One of the most remarkable aspects of the May Fourth Movement had been the outbreak of China's first general strike, when up to 100,000 workers in Shanghai had struck between 6 and 11 June 1919 to demonstrate their concern to save China from national extinction. This largely spontaneous action had alerted radical intellectuals to the political potential of labour in the battle for national salvation, and following the strike, they threw themselves into the business of educating and organizing labour, discovering in the process personal fulfilment and a new political role.

Typical of the young intellectuals who came to political consciousness through participation in the May Fourth Movement was Yun Daiying, who later styled himself (in English) 'Freeman Yun'. Born in 1895 into a rather prosperous family in Wuchang, Hubei province, he studied literature at Zhonghua University in Wuhan. In 1915, when Japan placed Twenty-One Demands on the government of Yuan Shikai, he published an article denouncing Japan's aggression and the cravenness of the government. During the May Fourth Movement, he led student protests in Wuhan and formed a 'Benefit the Masses' publishing house and a 'Benefit the Masses' weaving workshop, where students were encouraged to combine manual work with study. In 1920 he moved to Huanggang, where he and like-minded fellow students formed the 'Common Existence Society' (*Gongcun she*), where they worked and lived as one, and the 'Educate the Masses' primary school.[4] Yu Xiusong was another product of the May Fourth Movement for whom personal and political liberation were inextricably united. Whilst a student at the Zhejiang First Normal School, he was known as 'Three W's-ism' (*San 'W'-zhuyi*) because of his habit of questioning everything, the 'W's' standing for the English words 'Who? Why? What?'. On 1 November 1919 he penned the editorial of the first number of *Zhejiang New Tide Weekly*, which proclaimed: 'The first objective is to seek a life of happiness and progress for humanity, i.e. all humanity . . .; the second is to reform society . . .; the third is to advance the consciousness and unity of labourers . . .; the fourth is to investigate and criticize the condition of students and labourers and offer guidance.'[5] At the end of 1919 he and three comrades set off for Beijing to join a Work-Study Mutual Aid Corps (*Gongdu huzhu tuan*) – a 'collective of learning, work and living' – which had been set up there by students at Beijing University.[6] After the commune dispersed through lack of funds on 23 March, Yu declared that henceforth he would be a revolutionary who would 'spit on the whole world' (*jushi tuoma*). 'I think the best means of reforming society is to stir up trouble. If we fear this method, we will not overcome the apathy of society.' Going on to express his determination to 'break with the outlook of an intellectual', to 'change my name and clothes', to 'throw myself into the world of labour', Yu moved to Shanghai, where he worked for a short time at the Housheng iron works in Hongkou. He was possibly drawn to the city by the fact that plans were afoot, backed by Chen Duxiu and others, to establish a Shanghai Work-Study Mutual Aid Corps.[7] 'Through the methods of part-work part-study and of mutual aid and cooperation' this aimed to enable 'the young men and women of Shanghai who have adopted new thinking' to 'uproot the economic foundations of the old society and the old family, to cast off the fetters on consciousness, and to bring into being a new way of life and new form of organization.'[8]

To young men like Yun and Yu, convinced that China faced national extinction (*wangguo*), the Russian Revolution seemed like a beacon of hope. At the time of the May Fourth Movement little was known about the situation in Soviet Russia, except for brief and often hostile reports in the foreign press. It was not until January 1920, when the Bolsheviks captured Irkutsk and established direct telegraphic contact with China, that the Chinese were exposed to Bolshevik propaganda about the society they were building. Indeed it was not until March of that year that news of Lev Karakhan's declaration of Russia's readiness to renounce the privileges enjoyed by the tsarist government in China finally reached the country. Dai Jitao, perhaps the most talented publicist in Sun Yat-sen's resuscitated Guomindang (GMD), hailed the Karakhan declaration as 'unprecedented in history and unsurpassed in spiritual nobility'.[9] Radical patriots increasingly regarded Soviet Russia with goodwill and respect. Between June 1919 and May 1920 eighteen articles about developments in Russia appeared in Shanghai journals, mostly in publications sponsored by the GMD, and a further ten explained the rudiments of marxism, including translations of Marx's *Wage Labour and Capital* and the *Communist Manifesto*.[10] By the spring of 1920 some of the study groups which had sprung out of the May Fourth Movement had begun to think that the Soviet model offered a way forward for China and, in particular, that a Bolshevik-style party might be exactly what China's divided, disoriented and dilettantish left required.[11]

In March 1920 a delegation of the Third Communist International (Comintern) arrived in China. In fact, it was technically a delegation of Bolshevik party members, since it had been despatched by V.D. Vilenskii-Sibiriakov of the Vladivostok section of the Far Eastern Bureau of the Bolshevik party. It was led by the 27-year-old Grigorii Voitinskii, son of a white-collar worker, who had worked as a type-setter and as an accounts clerk before setting off in 1913, at the age of 20, for the USA. There he joined the Socialist Party, returning to Vladivostok only in the spring of 1918. He joined the Bolsheviks, who packed him off to work against the Whites in Krasnoiarsk. After taking part in the uprising against Admiral Kolchak in Omsk, he was captured and made to do hard labour in Sakhalin. He returned to Vladivostok in early 1920, only to be sent at once to China.[12] Most sources agree that he arrived in April in Beijing and that he was accompanied by his wife, M.F. Kuznetsova, the 24-year-old I.K. Mamaev, and an interpreter, Yang Mingzhai. In Beijing Mamaev's wife, M. Sakh'ianova, a Buriat by ethnicity, joined the group.[13] There they held discussions with Li Dazhao, who had drawn around him a group of intellectuals interested in marxism. Armed with a letter of introduction to Chen Duxiu, the Russians (apparently with Sakh'ianova) set off for Shanghai in late April.[14]

Chen Duxiu (1879–1942) was one of China's leading intellectuals. Although a veteran revolutionary, he had never joined Sun Yat-sen's Alliance Society because of an aversion to nationalism. After the 'Second Revolution' of 1913, when Yuan Shikai disbanded the trappings of republican government, he fled to Japan where he had spent considerable time during the latter years of the Qing dynasty. He returned to Shanghai in 1915 to found the journal, *New Youth*, and when the great educator Cai Yuanpei was appointed chancellor of Beijing University in December 1916, he called on Chen to become dean of the School of Letters.[15] At the height of the May Fourth protests, on 11 June 1919, Chen was arrested in Beijing for distributing leaflets on the streets. Charged with 'Bolshevism', he was imprisoned for eighty-three days. Upon his release, he resigned his university post and set off for Shanghai, where his political views swerved sharply to the left. As late as December 1920, however, while already doubting the efficacy of capitalism as a solution to China's backwardness, he could still write that 'in implementing democracy, we must follow the

British and American models'. Only with his essay on Malthus of April 1920 did he for the first time draw upon marxist concepts.[16]

Voitinskii made a good impression upon the young radicals he met, being remembered variously as suave, taciturn, scholarly and informed about Chinese affairs.[17] With Voitinskii's encouragement, Chen set up an informal Marxist Research Society, which met at his house at No. 2 (old) Yuyang alley, off Huailong road in the French Concession, where the editorial office of *New Youth* was based.[18] Fourteen individuals are known to have participated in the Society, several of whom were leading intellectuals in the recently revived GMD, associated with the journal, *Weekly Review* (*Xingqi pinglun*).[19] They included its editor, Shen Xuanlu (Shen Dingyi), born in 1892 into one of wealthiest lineages in Xiaoshan county in Zhejiang province and president of the Zhejiang provincial assembly from 1916 to 1918; its co-editor, Dai Jitao (1891–1949), born in Wuxing county in Zhejiang, and one of Sun Yat-sen's personal secretaries; and Shao Lizi (1882–1967), born in Shaoxing in Zhejiang, and editor of its literary supplement, *Awakening* (*Juewu*). Other members of the Research Society not associated with the GMD were the novelist Shen Yanbing (later known as Mao Dun) and Zhang Dongsun, editor of the Shanghai newspaper, *Shishi Xinbao*, and formerly a member of the Research Clique and the Progressive Party. Two anarchists from Shaoxing also had dealings with the group: Shen Zhongjiu (1887–1968), the former editor of the journal of the Zhejiang Educational Association, and Liu Dabai (1880–1931), a talented poet and imperial-degree holder, who had served as personal secretary to Shen Xuanlu during his presidency of the Zhejiang Provincial Assembly.[20]

As this roll-call suggests, at the heart of the Marxist Research Society lay one of the study groups based on ties of common regional origin, friendship or schooling whose importance to the foundation of the CCP was stressed by Hans van de Ven.[21] A majority of its members hailed from Zhejiang province and several had been educated at the Zhejiang First Normal School in Hangzhou, described as 'one of the two most powerful provincial outposts of the new ideological movement', the other being Mao Zedong's alma mater, the Changsha First Normal School.[22] The Zhejiang First Normal School had been the scene of a *cause célèbre* in November 1919 when a student at the school, Shi Cuntong, published a 'Critique of Filial Piety' (*Fei xiao*) in the second issue of the *Zhejiang New Tide Weekly*. This drew a furious protest from the provincial authorities, but teachers at the school, including Chen Wangdao and the aforementioned Liu Dabai, supported Shi, prompting the military police to shut down the school.[23] Chen Wangdao (1891–1977), born in Yiwu county, Zhejiang, had studied in Japan; after his dismissal from his post at the First Normal School, he translated the *Communist Manifesto* before joining the *Weekly Review* in Shanghai. In September 1920 he was appointed to a post in the Chinese faculty of Shanghai's Fudan University, while continuing as an editor of *Awakening* and *New Youth*.[24] Shi Cuntong, instigator of the scandal at the First Normal School, accompanied his fellow student, Yu Xiusong, to Beijing where they joined the Work-Study Mutual Aid Corps; after it broke up, they moved to Shanghai and made contact with Chen Wangdao and fellow-provincials at the *Weekly Review*.[25] The Marxist Research Society thus functioned as much as a study group of friends and fellow-countrymen as one of a strictly ideological type.

Voitinskii, Kuznetsova and Mamaev – who left for Wuhan in the autumn – seem quickly to have decided that Shanghai was the best place on which to concentrate their efforts to form a Chinese Communist Party, in view of the presence of a large body of radical students and industrial workers. Yet not all members of the Marxist Research Society were happy with the increasing emphasis on party-building. Within a few weeks Zhang Dongsun quit the society since he believed that the creation of a socialist party was premature given the absence of a mature working class. Dai Jitao also dropped out because he was not prepared to dissociate himself from Sun Yat-sen and the GMD.[26] In June Voitinskii reported that lectures on Soviet Russia were being given to about thirty students and that it was hoped to hold a conference of socialists and anarchists in northern China in early July 'with the aim of coordinating and centralizing (the Chinese revolutionary movement, SAS)'.[27] There is no evidence that this conference took place, although a source from 1927 says that a meeting of Chinese activists was held on 19 July 1920 in Shanghai and that the 'foundations for the future CCP were laid'.[28] What is certain is that Russians active in China did hold a conference in Beijing from 5 to 7 July with Vilenskii-Sibiriakov of the Far Eastern Bureau, which discussed *inter alia* the 'forthcoming congress of Chinese Communist organizations and the formation of the Chinese Community Party'.[29] For various reasons, the inaugural congress of the CCP was delayed until July 1921.

On 22 August 1920 a Socialist Youth League (SYL) was formed in Shanghai. In May Yao Zuobing, a representative of the National Student Union, established in Shanghai in June 1919, had visited the Siberian Bureau of the Bolshevik party in Vladivostok to discuss how Russia might assist the Chinese revolutionary movement and help Chinese students go to Russia to study.[30] Three days before the inauguration of the SYL, Voitinskii wrote to the Siberian Bureau to explain that the purpose of the organization was to 'expose the utopianism of that section of democratic students which sees the salvation of the country in the possible growth of Chinese national capital via non-aggressive (American) foreign capital'; and to advocate that students 'carry out the struggle against Japanese militarism and foreign capital as a whole ... with the assistance of the labouring masses, who are being prepared for social revolution, since only the labouring masses by virtue of their very existence are interested in the independence of their country'.[31] It was to be two years before this linkage of labour to the anti-imperialist movement was to be heard of again.

There were eight founding members of the SYL, but they soon grew to thirty. The SYL was open to anyone aged 15 to 28 (later reduced to 25), and from the first aspired to recruit young workers, albeit with little success.[32] A key figure in the formation of the SYL was Zhang Tailei, a law graduate from Beiyang University in Tianjin, who spent the summer of 1920 in Shanghai. Tall and handsome, Zhang was born in 1898 in Changzhou, Jiangsu province, where Qu Qiubai would be born a year later.[33] His father, a petty trader, could not afford to establish his own household, so Zhang was brought up initially in his maternal grandfather's house. When he was three, the family moved to Anyuan, where his father got a job in the mines. Three years later, his father died; so Zhang, his mother and elder sister moved back to Changzhou, where his mother supported them by doing housework for one of the families in the Zhang lineage. Because Zhang Tailei was extremely bright, the lineage paid for his education. He studied at Changzhou middle school, where the head teacher was a supporter of the Alliance Society, and went to Beiyang University in 1916. In 1919 he was active in the May Fourth Movement in Tianjin.[34]

The network of Zhejiang fellow-provincials which formed the core of the Marxist Research Society also lay at the heart of the SYL. Both Yu Xiusong, its chair, and Zhang Qiuren, its secretary from 1921, hailed from Zhuji county. Zhang Qiuren, born in 1898, was a graduate from the Chongxin middle school in Ningbo.[35] Wang Yifei (1898–1928), also an early member of the SYL, was another of the alumni of the Zhejiang First Normal School. He became chair of the Moscow branch of the SYL and upon his return home in the autumn of 1924, became secretary of the Shanghai regional committee in September 1925 and a member of the standing committee of the Communist Youth League. Zhuang Wengong, an SYL member who had also studied at the First Normal School, was secretary of the regional committee from 1924 to 1925.[36] Another member of the Zhejiang network, who did not at this stage join the SYL, was Yang Zhihua (1900–73). Born into a small landlord-merchant family in Xiaoshan county, she was a graduate of Hangzhou Women's Normal School. In 1919 her father-in-law, Shen Xuanlu, arranged a summer job for her at the offices of *Weekly Review*. There she was tremendously impressed by the way that everyone took an equal part in the production of the journal, cooperating in a comradely way. The women, she recalled, looked like buddhist nuns, since they shaved their heads as an assertion of their equality with men.[37]

It is not easy to distinguish the SYL from the Foreign Languages School which the Russians had set up in order to recruit promising youngsters to go to Russia for training. It was located at no.6 (new) Yuyang alley, off Xiafei road in the French Concession. Most of the early Communists' ventures were located there, including the Chinese-Russian Press Agency (*Hua-E tongxun she*), the SYL and the mechanics' union. Between thirty and sixty students attended the Foreign Languages School, which operated until late 1921. Its principal instructors were M.F. Kuznetsova and Yang Mingzhai. Not surprisingly, Russian was the most popular foreign language, but Yuan Zhenying, a prominent anarchist close to Sun Yat-sen, and Shen Yanbing taught English, while Li Hanjun taught French and Li Da Japanese.[38] The biggest contingents of students came from Anhui, Hunan and Zhejiang, each provincial group tending to live as a separate unit. Tuition at the school was free, with classes occupying half the day so that students could work the rest of the time to support themselves. Not all the students were politically aware: one boy from a wealthy family was said to spend most days roaming Shanghai in his western suit.[39]

Yang Mingzhai, Voitinskii's interpreter, played a vital role not only as a teacher of Russian, but as a relatively sophisticated exponent of marxism and, above all, as someone who knew Russia and China intimately.[40] Born in 1882 to a poor peasant family in Pingdu county, Shandong, Yang had nevertheless had a fairly long classical education, going to school from the age of 7 to 16. In 1894, when he was 12, his mother and elder sister perished in the famine. After leaving school, he worked on the family farm and married shortly afterwards, but when he was 19, his wife died. In 1901 he thus decided to make a new life in Vladivostok where many people from his village had emigrated. There he took a factory job and learnt to speak Russian well. In 1908 he moved into Siberia, where he undertook a variety of jobs, apparently working for the tsarist Ministry of Foreign Affairs during the First World War. Following the February Revolution, he became active as a representative of Chinese workers in Russia and of Chinese volunteers in the Red Army, at some point joining the Bolsheviks. In late 1919 he moved to Tianjin, and it was there that he teamed up with Voitinskii.[41] Straightforward, rather stubborn by temperament, he was seen by Chinese as having become rather Russified during his years away from his motherland. Peng Shuzhi described him as 'a bit unmethodical, temperamental, inconsistent'.[42]

In August 1920 a 'revolutionary bureau' was established in Shanghai, intended to be a step towards creating a Communist Party. From this time, members of the Marxist Research Society are usually referred to as the Shanghai 'small group' (*xiaozu*) of the Communist party, although they clearly saw themselves as a political party.[43] Some fifteen people were involved with the small group prior to the First Congress, including Chen Duxiu, Li Hanjun, Shen Xuanlu, Chen Wangdao, Yu Xiusong, Yang Mingzhai, Li Da, Yuan Zhenying, Shao Lizi, Lin Boqu, Shen Yanbing, Li Qihan, Li Zhong and Shen Zemin. In addition, the two anarchists,

Liu Dabai and Shen Zhongjiu, appear briefly to have been members. The average age of members of the group was under 30, Chen Duxiu being the oldest at 41 and Shen Zemin the youngest at 19. All were intellectuals, who supported themselves modestly by teaching, editing and translating. Most had a university or college education, although only Li Hanjun had a higher degree.[44] The 'revolutionary bureau' consisted of Voitinskii plus four Chinese and evidently aspired to serve as a 'centre' for the entire Communist movement in China.[45] On 7 November it published a *Manifesto*:

> We wish to organize a revolutionary proletarian party – a communist party. Such a party exists to lead the revolutionary struggle of proletarians against capitalists, by taking political power from the hands of the capitalists and putting it in the hands of the workers and peasants, just as the Russian Communist Party did in 1917.[46]

The bureau had three sections for information and agitation, publications, and organization. The information and agitation section mainly provided translations of reports about life in Soviet Russia for release via the Chinese-Russian Press Agency. The publications section published *Labour World* (*Laodongjie*), the first 2,000 copies of which appeared on Sunday, 22 August 1920, at one cent each, and a theoretical journal, *The Communist* (*Gongchandang*), which circulated 'underground'.[47] In September 1920, with issue one of volume eight, *New Youth* took on the character of a Communist organ, publishing twenty articles on socialism and seven on marxism up to July 1921.[48] In the spring of 1921 the publishing section put out the full version of the *Communist Manifesto*, translated by Chen Wangdao. The organization section was responsible for recruiting students and organizing labour unions and tried unsuccessfully to make contact with local soldiers.[49] In January 1921 the 'small group' formed a labour movement bureau, consisting of Yu Xiusong, chair of the SYL, Li Qihan and others.[50]

These activities were loosely coordinated by the Comintern. In May 1920 an East Asian Secretariat of the Comintern had been formed in Shanghai with three sections responsible, respectively, for Comintern work in China, Korea and Japan.[51] From August it was formally accountable to a recently-formed Department for Peoples of the East, attached to the Siberian Bureau of the Bolshevik party in Irkutsk.[52] It was this Department which in December sent Liu Zerong (Liu Shaozhou) (1892–1970), chair of the Union of Chinese Workers in Russia and a delegate to both the first and second Comintern congresses, to Shanghai. Bela Kun described him as 'not a Communist, more like a populist or social democrat'.[53] The Chinese section of the East Asian Secretariat in Shanghai set to work with a will, publishing the Programme of the Russian Communist Party, the

Constitution of the RSFSR, the Soviet Codex of Labour Legislation and other official documents in Chinese. It also organized a press agency which served the Chinese, Japanese and Korean press.[54] It had no effective contact with the Siberian Bureau, however, although the latter did back a request from Voitinskii in December for $20,000.[55] On 15 January the Department for Peoples of the East was subordinated to a new Far Eastern Secretariat of the Executive Committee of the Comintern (ECCI) in Irkutsk. This was headed by B. Shumiatskii, and Zhang Tailei was soon brought in to head its Chinese section.[56]

The first of the future leaders of the CCP to travel to Soviet Russia did not go under the auspices of the Foreign Languages School. In October 1920 Qu Qiubai set off for Russia as correspondent of the Beijing newspaper, *Morning News (Chenbao)*. Born in 1899 into a scholar-gentry family in Changzhou, Jiangsu province, Qu had received a good classical education. His father was feckless, however, and squandered the family's wealth on opium and gambling, leaving his wife to raise six children in poverty. In 1915, worn out by the struggle, she killed herself by swallowing red phosphorus scraped from the heads of matches. Devastated by this loss, the 16-year-old Qu moved to Beijing and, because he had no money, enrolled in the Russian Language Institute, which had recently been established by the Ministry of Foreign Affairs, and which provided students with a small stipend during the five-year course. He proved to be a hardworking student who soon developed a love of Russian literature. At this stage, immersed as he was in Buddhism, he showed little interest in the Russian Revolution. It was the May Fourth Movement that awakened his interest in politics and led him to accept the job of press correspondent in Russia. 'I want to change the environment, to develop my individuality, to seek a proper solution to the "China problem" – to fulfil part of the responsibility of leading Chinese society to the path of a new life'. He claimed that an 'inner demand' compelled him to go to the 'first country in the world that had realised the socialist revolution'.[57] Yet he seems to have seen his journey very much as a Buddhist 'renunciation of the world' (*chushi*), as an experience of separation and death that would lead to rebirth. Calling Russia the 'Land of Hunger' (*Exiang*) – not just in the literal sense but by analogy with Mount Shouyang, where the brothers Boyi and Shuqi had died in the twelfth century BC out of loyalty to the Shang dynasty – he appears to have seen that country as a place where he would sacrifice himself for his ideals. His ultimate purpose was to bring back 'light' to China, which he called the Land of Slumber (*heitian xiang*, literally 'black sweetness').[58] Qu rose brilliantly to the journalistic challenge of informing the Chinese public about life in Russia. He wrote no fewer than two book and fifty-nine lengthy newspaper articles – fifteen of which never saw the light of day – which painted a rich account of Soviet socialism. By no means blind to the misery that abounded in Russia –

'dreams, illusions, rifles, jails' – Qu nevertheless depicted the revolution as a 'ray of light, red as blood, that illuminates the whole world.'[59] In summer 1921 he met Lenin at the Third Comintern Congress.[60]

On 29 March 1921 the first of three batches of students from the Foreign Languages School left for Russia. In all some twenty members of the SYL left Shanghai, including Liu Shaoqi, Ren Bishi, who was not quite 17, Luo Yinong, Xiao Jingguang, Peng Shuzhi and the anarchist, Hua Lin, the largest contingent coming from Hunan province.[61] In April the University of the Toilers of the East (KUTV) opened its doors to them in Moscow. Initially, its training course lasted only seven months, but in early 1923 this was lengthened to three years. All students were required to take courses in administration, economics, and politics. Later, in addition to Russian language, they generally took courses in dialectical materialism, marxist-leninist theory, world history, the history of the labour movement, the history of the Russian revolutionary movement, the Bolshevik party, political economy, mathematics, geography and the structure of the Soviet administration.[62] Those who went on to become important CCP leaders spent varying amounts of time in Russia. Liu Shaoqi returned to China early in 1922; Peng Shuzhi and Ren Bishi in August 1924; Luo Yinong and Wang Shouhua in early 1925.[63]

Organizing Labour

In spite of being intellectuals, the members of the 'small group' saw the task of labour organization as paramount. As Chen Duxiu explained, 'In industry the influence of the New Culture Movement must cause labourers to waken up to their position.'[64] In his report of 17 August 1920, Voitinskii wrote: 'This week our organization section is summoning ten local trade unions and guilds to send two representatives each to form a Central Bureau of Trade Unions, whose representative will go into our revolutionary bureau'.[65] Voitinskii drafted a resolution for the meeting in English, which was discussed and approved by the bureau, and then translated into Chinese.[66] In addition, the 'small group' brought out *Labour World,* which carried pieces about all aspects of the labour movement, including the conduct of strikes, the blacking of goods and boycotts, the principle of the closed shop, collective bargaining, social insurance and the history of strikes and trade unions in the West. The main message, which the Communists hammered out at every turn, was the need to form labour unions.

The Communists were very far from being pioneers of labour organization in Shanghai. The first attempts to create labour unions had been made in 1912 and the May Fourth Movement had led to a flurry of labour organizing by the GMD, anarchists and others. The most enduring of the May Fourth initiatives was the Shanghai Worker-Merchant Friendly

Society (*Shanghai gongshang youyi hui*) which was formed by a group of progressive businessmen in 1920. Like the labour associations backed by the GMD, it saw the organization of labour as vital to strengthening the nation. At its inaugural meeting in October, attended by 350 people, Shao Zonghui gave the keynote speech:

> First, there can be no question of eradicating nationalism, otherwise I am afraid we will be swallowed up by those with wild ambitions, and become slaves of slaves. Next I say that the two elements of workers and merchants must stand up and govern themselves; they must neither deceive nor flatter one another; they must assist one another and be fraternal (*bo'ai*). These things must characterise the spirit of the Worker-Merchant Friendly Society.[67]

The Society aimed to create one big union of journeymen (*huoyou*) and apprentices, first in the retail sector and then in the handicraft sector. Its chair was Tong Lizhang, the son of a shopkeeper turned commercial speculator, who during the May Fourth Movement had been a leading light in the Shandong Road street association and in the leadership of the 'national salvation teams of ten', which took the patriotic message to the common people through street-corner meetings.[68] Somewhat surprisingly, the Shanghai Communists decided to involve themselves in the Society, writing several articles for its journal, *Shanghai Shopclerk* (*Shanghai huoyou*). Their message of class struggle, however, was not to the liking of Tong Lizhang and his supporters and so the Communists were quickly expelled.[69]

Of the independent initiatives of the 'small group', the most successful was the mechanics' union (*Shanghai jiqi gonghui*), launched on 21 November 1920. The chair of the union was Li Zhong (Li Shengxie) (1897–1951). Born in Xiangxiang county, Hunan, where his father, a failed examination candidate, ran a government-sponsored school, Li learnt to read at an early age, studying the classics with his father. After the 1911 Revolution, he experienced the full force of the New Learning, though poverty forced him for a time to leave school and work on the family farm. In 1913 he passed the entrance examination to the non-fee-paying First Normal School in Changsha, where he met Cai Hesen and Mao Zedong. A successful student, he taught in a part-time workers' school until his graduation in summer 1918. He then went to Shanghai, where he worked in an antique shop. When Chen Duxiu moved to the city in spring 1920, Li got to know him, sharing his house for a time. Under his influence, Li took a job as an apprentice ironsmith at the Jiangnan arsenal, where he worked to build a mechanics' union. Since many workers of the workers hailed from the Li's home county, having originally been brought to the arsenal by Zeng Guofan, founder of the Hunan army and hammer of the Taiping rebels, Li was able to use his native-place connections to this end.[70] In 1921 he joined the CCP, and seems to have remained at the arsenal for some time thereafter. Active in Shanghai during the May Thirtieth Movement and later in Zhejiang, he dropped out of political activity after Chiang Kai-shek's coup of 12 April 1927, returning to Hunan to become a school teacher.[71]

On 30 October 1920 a preliminary meeting to form a mechanics' union took place at the Foreign Languages School, attended by seventy to eighty people, including mechanics from the electric-light factory in Yangshupu, the Housheng iron works and the Dongyang and Hengfeng textile mills. Yang Mingzhai gave a fighting speech in which he described how workers were under the thrall of capital which owned the banks, shops and factories. Workers needed to organize, he argued, in order to alleviate their suffering through their own efforts and 'save their own lives'. Li Zhong also gave a speech, urging workers to form pure working-class organizations that were neither regionally-based, nor under the control of employers, nor of mixed class composition, nor under the control of political opportunists and secret society bosses, nor purely 'signboard' unions. This list of 'five nots' formed the core of the union's constitution.[72] At the official launch of the union, Sun Yat-sen spoke for two hours, Chen Duxiu for rather less. Yet in spite of the rhetoric of class conflict heard at the preparatory meeting, the new union defined its aims in a way that suggested the influence of the guild tradition and of 'anarcho-communism'. They were: 'to promote common ideals, training and morality; to advance knowledge; to develop mutual aid of a class type; to join forces in an effective manner to reform our situation; to raise our standard of living and lessen our sufferings; to seek mutual peace and happiness and support one another in our common endeavour; to study the conditions of the labour market; to demand that the employers increase our pay, reduce our working hours, pay sickness and injury benefits and improve safety and health at work.'[73] The union seems to have gone out of its way not to alienate the mechanics' guild, for on 2 December it held a banquet for the general secretary and director of the latter. Also invited were Zhang Dongqing, a mechanic from the Xingfarong shipyard, Zhang Shilun, leader of the engineers, Zheng Xiaolan, leader of the coppersmiths, Wu Xiuhua, an engineer at the electric light factory, and Deng Yongyuan, the leader of the ironworkers.[74] These may have been heads of the workers' section (*xiaohang*) of the guild, or secret-society notables, or both. Soon the union had 370 members, each of whom paid a modest four cash a month in dues, and for a brief moment it became the most influential labour organization in Shanghai, publishing its own journal.[75] On 14 December 1920 it received a telegram of good wishes from Roy Brown of the Industrial Workers of the World in the USA.[76] Yet any hope on the part of the 'small group' that the mechanics' union might mark the onset of class-struggle trade unionism in Shanghai proved misplaced. Because a large number of mechanics in Shanghai were Cantonese, they soon turned to the 'southern party', i.e. the GMD, for leadership. Over the next years the mechanics' union came to model itself on its counterpart in Canton, and by 1924 was firmly in the anti-Communist camp.[77]

A second independent initiative by the 'small group' was far less successful. In December 1920 it helped set up a Shanghai printers' union, apparently by encouraging workers to break away from the printers' guild.[78] The union soon had a membership of 1,346 (another source says 1,600). At the heart of the union were some 300 typographers, with lithographers as the next best organised craft. The union produced a weekly newspaper, the *World Friendship Pictorial* (*Youshi huabao*), but after a couple of months, it became a casualty of the crisis within the Shanghai 'small group', which is discussed below.[79]

The early labour unions attached considerable importance to education. The mechanics' union provided English classes for its members, and the electricians' union ran a night school for workers aged 14 to 35, where Chinese language, book-keeping, abacus, the cultivation of moral character (*xiushen*), English, the principles of electricity, penmanship and arithmetic were taught. Open every evening from 7 pm to 9 pm, it provided free tuition although students were expected to buy their own materials.[80] In their effort to educate working people, the labour unions were acting in the spirit of the May Fourth Movement which had been vigorous in promoting common people's schools. But the electricians' union questioned the value of conventional education for working people: 'At present all education is the rich man's education, the aristocrat's education and is unsuitable for the worker.'[81] And the early Communists tended to shun the May Fourth rhetoric of 'enlightenment', insisting that the creative energies of the working class could be unleashed only through struggle. Their rationale for organizing schools was fundamentally pragmatic. According to the CCP's statement of aims of 1921, labourers' continuation schools were to be formed in every industrial enterprise 'as a preparatory step to organizing industrial unions.'[82]

In August 1920 Li Qihan established a workers' half-time school in Xiaoshadu, in the west of the city. Li proved to be the most able labour organizer in the early CCP. Born in 1898 in Jianghua county, Hunan, he was the eldest of six children in a downwardly mobile family. His father, a failed examination candidate, was bad-tempered and depressive and left the running of the household to his wife, who managed only by selling her dowry. From a young age, Li helped support the family by collecting firewood and herbs. After his father got a job as a teacher, Li went to school, finishing primary school in 1912. With a subsidy from the local county magistrate, he was able to enter the Yueyun middle school in Changsha in February 1917. In 1919 he became active in the May Fourth

Movement in Changsha, joining Mao Zedong's New People's Study Group. At the end of 1919 he came to Shanghai, soon enrolling in the Foreign Languages School and the SYL.[83] The half-time school which he set up was a dismal failure, partly because Li had trouble speaking Shanghai dialect. On 19 December the 'small group' decided to turn the school into the Shanghai Workers' Recreation Club (*Shanghai gongren youyi hui*) in the hope that this would prove more attractive to workers. Four hundred people attended its opening meeting, at which Yang Mingzhai gave a speech, clearly designed to assuage the fears of local employers. He argued that organization, far from fomenting unrest, would discourage it by helping workers tackle their problems collectively. The club, he said, would increase the knowledge and the vitality of the workers. According to its constitution, its aims were to 'use appropriate recreational means to promote lofty and pure knowledge and principles of beauty and happiness' While making provision for non-workers to join the club as supporting members, the constitution specifically excluded capitalists. In an attempt to draw in workers, Li Qihan bought a gramophone and organized football matches and other entertainments.[84] In the spring he made a second attempt to establish a school, but six months later it still had an enrolment of only twenty. Towards the end of 1921, its fortunes picked up, when the school, now named the Shanghai No.1 Workers' Continuation School (*Shanghai diyi gongren buxi xuexiao*), had around 200 pupils.[85]

Employers were suspicious of workers with aspirations to education. A young shop clerk wrote:

> I am a junior assistant in a foreign-goods store on Shanxi Road. Because I never had a high level of education, my knowledge is rather shallow, but I like to read books and newspapers in my spare time. Amid today's surging tide of New Thought, we seek to make new people by remaking society. We must read the New Thought Tide newspapers so that new knowledge can be dispersed. Yet in the shops all we can read are newspapers that have barely changed since the nineteenth century, such as *Xinwenbao*, which the old-style merchants enjoy. What is the slightest value of such newspapers to us? I refuse to read them, and took out a subscription to *Republican Daily*, which is like a dose of good medicine. But guess what, as soon as I began to read it, someone appeared on the scene like Cheng Yaojin to stop me. Who was this Cheng Yaojin? None other than the manager of the shop! He told me: 'You are a junior employee earning three jiao a month. You cannot possibly afford a subscription to a newspaper. It's obviously the extremist party (*guoji dang*) that wants you to read it, and no doubt you'll soon be joining them.'

23

He was made to wear a placard on his back saying 'I squander money' (*huihuo jinqian*), and his boss wrote to his father, who forbade him to read such dangerous stuff.[86]

If employer opposition was one factor that dogged the early efforts at labour organization, another was harassment by the police in the two foreign settlements in Shanghai, the International Settlement and the French Concession. In his report for March 1921 the police chief of the International Settlement reported:

> The special section of the CID has handled some twenty-seven papers, leaflets and handbills for the propaganda of anarchism and syndicalism ... circulated by persons who in all probability have the financial and other support of communist agents from other countries. Some of this literature made special appeals to the soldiers of the garrison ... but few are able to read it. The publications intended for the workers have been meeting with better success. The majority of the latter in their ignorance of letters probably do not fall far short of the soldiers but they can be ... reached through one or more of the recently formed associations and unions. Signs are not lacking that this propaganda has locally contributed its quota to the unrest in the labour world.[87]

On 14 April Li Qihan, described by the International Settlement police as 'a Hunanese and a follower of the notorious Chinese Bolshevik, Chen Duxiu', called together about a dozen labour organizations to arrange a May Day celebration, but a raid by the French Concession police, backed up with a ban by the Chinese Garrison Commissioner, meant that virtually no meetings took place.[88] Nevertheless, Shanghai's status as a divided city was one that the Communists were able to exploit, avoiding arrest by moving from the foreign settlements to the Chinese areas of the city – and vice versa – by paying bribes to police in the French Concession, and by having spies among Chinese employed as policemen in the foreign settlements.

The battle for discipline

It became axiomatic for the Comintern – an axiom parroted by the leaders of the CCP themselves – that those who joined the SYL and early CCP were inveterately petty-bourgeois in political orientation by virtue of their class background. A report on the Communist youth movement in China, written in 1926, summed up the character of the early SYL: 'they belonged to the petty bourgeoisie as regards their composition; they did not consider it necessary to take part in the political struggle; their studies bore a purely 'academic' or theoretical character; it was study of socialism along theoretical lines; their ideology was of a very confused character.'[89] There is a measure of truth in this, but it serves as a rather facile explanation of the problems faced by the radical intellectuals in their attempt to organize the masses. For, ultimately, these were rooted in the huge social and cultural gulf that separated the two. Xu Meikun, possibly the first worker to join the CCP in Shanghai, was acutely aware of this. Commenting on the intervention of students in the strike at the Nikko mills in April 1922, he wrote: 'Li Qihan, Zhang Guotao, Yang Mingzhai and others rented a room and bought a gramophone, thinking to draw in the workers with music. But the workers, seeing their western clothes, went home as soon as they had finished listening to the music.'[90] As this suggests, the failure of Communist intellectuals had less to do with dilettantism or academicism per se than with cultural westernization and their superior education. As products of the New Culture Movement, they embodied a style of individuality, expressed in dress, gesture, and deportment that was alien to working people. This cultural distance was to beset the internal life of the CCP throughout the 1920s.

In fact those drawn into the 'small group' and the SYL tended precisely to be those who wished to *do* something – those who were fed up with the tendency of the May Fourth intelligentsia to 'indulge in loud and empty talk' (*gaotan-kuolun*). They were stirred by the call of the Comintern to 'surrender to the proletariat' and to shun 'academic-type study which denies that theory is born of practice'.[91] Of course, they were hugely inexperienced – and some did lack seriousness – but if there was indeed something 'petty bourgeois' about their orientation to politics it was not expressed so much in a lack of commitment, as in a commitment that was essentially 'romantic' in character. Qu Qiubai wrote: 'I was born a romantic and always wanted to transcend the environment and accomplish some miraculous deed that would amaze and move people.'[92] Indeed it was precisely romanticism that was identified by a manual on party training, produced by the SYL in Moscow, as the besetting sin of these intellectuals.[93] By this was meant a style of politics that was individualist, idealist and emotional, typical of the anarcho-communist milieu from which so many of the Shanghai Communists came. It was the antithesis of everything the Comintern stood for.

Throughout the 1920s Moscow waged a battle against 'petty bourgeois' tendencies in the CCP. This began in the spring of 1921 when a sustained campaign began to distinguish 'Bolshevism' from the guild socialism of Zhang Dongsun and, especially, from the anarchism that was in vogue.[94] In Shanghai state-socialist ideology – as articulated by GMD publicists – was more influential than anarchism, but it was the latter which posed the most immediate threat to the creation of a centralized and disciplined Communist Party. From the beginning of 1921, *The Communist* and *New Youth* polemicized with anarchists, Chen Duxiu crossing swords with Ou Shengbai.[95] Li Hanjun, one of the two leaders of the Shanghai 'small group', also clashed with Chen over the issue of party organization, but from a social-democratic point of view.[96] The firmest expression of the determination to impose a more disciplined structure on the nascent party, and to demarcate Communism ideologically from non-marxist forms of socialism, came in May 1921 when the SYL was summarily disbanded. Hitherto acceptance of marxism had not been a condition of membership of the SYL or the Communist small groups, but now acceptance of the dictatorship of the proletariat was made binding on all members. The SYL was only revived in November after Zhang Tailei returned from the Soviet Union. He oversaw the imposition of a centralist structure on the SYL, which *inter alia* entailed a further purge of anarchists in January 1922.[97] It was not until the Second CCP Congress of July 1922, however, that the break with anarchism was complete.

The organizational regulations adopted by the Second CCP Congress declared that the party was neither a 'study association' (*xuehui*), a marxist discussion group, nor a group of abstract revolutionaries cut off from the masses, but a party fighting on behalf of the proletarian masses and seeking to root itself among them. The regulations stressed military-style discipline. 'Every comrade should sacrifice his own opinions, feelings and advancement to protect the unity of the party ... He should not possess any individual interest apart from that of the party.'[98] 'Even someone carrying out Communist work, but outside the control of the party, is guilty of complete individualism ... and anarchism.'[99] Given the sorry history of political parties in China up to that time, the severe tone was understandable; but it also reflected the authoritarian culture now in place within the Russian Communist party. Historically, the Bolshevik commitment to 'democratic centralism' had been tempered by some recognition of the right of expression of individual members and organized factions. By 1922, however, the trend within the Russian Communist Party was towards unrestricted centralism and monolithic unity. It is noteworthy that the organizational regulations of the CCP made no mention of the rights of party members, speaking only of their duties. Comrades who infringed party policy through their activities or views, who failed to abide by the decisions of central or local organs, who missed meetings twice in a row without cause, who failed to pay their party dues for three months, who failed to carry out party duties for four weeks, or who divulged party secrets were to be expelled.[100] It was in such exclusively negative terms that party membership was discussed.

The First Congress of the Communist Party

At the beginning of 1921, the Shanghai 'small group' fell into disarray. Voitinskii left the city in December to go to Irkutsk, where he helped

Shumiatskii set up the Far Eastern Secretariat of ECCI.[101] On 16 December 1920 Chen Duxiu left for Canton to head the education ministry of Chen Jiongming's government.[102] Li Da and Li Hanjun were the weightiest figures left in the 'small group'. Both were born in 1890, both had been students in Japan and both had a deeper knowledge of marxism than most of their contemporaries, including Chen Duxiu. Li Da, born in Hunan and said to have the forthrightness typical of those from that province, edited the party's theoretical journal, *The Communist*. Li Hanjun, born in Hubei, was a graduate of Tokyo Imperial University and a student of the Japanese marxist economist, Kawakami Hajime. He was fluent in Japanese, English, German and French and, whilst working on the *Weekly Review* from 1919, translated several of Marx's writings and wrote extensively on marxist theory. Neither was cut out for political leadership, both being, in Zhang Guotao's view, 'traditional scholar' types.[103] Li Hanjun allegedly advocated a cautious, gradualist approach to political change, and may have been expelled from the party as a 'legal marxist' in the summer of 1922, or left of his own accord the following year, because of his opposition to the United Front policy.[104] Lack of strong leadership in the Shanghai 'small group' was compounded by a shortage of activists. By the spring of 1921 many of the most promising recruits had gone off to the Soviet Union, Japan or France, or left Shanghai to set up 'small groups' elsewhere.[105] A further problem was finance. At the time of Voitinskii's departure, it was reckoned that the expenses of party work amounted to 200 Mexican dollars per month. Li Hanjun suggested to Chen Duxiu that the New Youth Book Company cover some of these costs, but received no answer. This appears to have caused the two men to fall out.[106] In January 1921 *Labour World* ceased publication after twenty-four issues, and in the spring production of *The Communist* was briefly interrupted, six issues appearing before it was wound up by the First Congress (in fact the last issue did not appear until September). *New Youth*, however, did continue, and in April was reportedly in receipt of a subsidy from the Soviet government.[107] A final factor in the travails of the Shanghai centre was that in the wake of the aborted May Day celebrations of 1921, the party office and Foreign Languages School were raided by the French police. At this point, Li Hanjun may have suggested suspending the party's activities and moving to Canton.[108]

The disarray of the Shanghai small group seems to have been the main factor which delayed the first party congress.[109] Only the arrival on 3 June of the Comintern delegate, Hendricus Sneevliet (Maring), expedited its foregathering. He and V.A. Nikol'skii (1898–1943), who was already in the city, liaised with Li Da and Li Hanjun to convene a congress as a matter of urgency.[110] Nikol'skii had been sent by the Far Eastern Secretariat of ECCI initially to attend a conference of Korean marxists, but he was soon designated representative in China of the Profintern, the Moscow-led international organization of trade unions which was not formally established until July1921.[111] Nikol'skii remained in Shanghai until the beginning of December when he left to attend the Congress of Toilers of the East which met in Moscow and Petrograd from 21 January to 2 February 1922.[112] The First CCP Congress opened on 23 July in a girls' school at 106 Wangzhi street in the French Concession, attended by thirteen delegates plus Sneevliet and Nikol'skii (for whom Li Hanjun and Liu Renjing translated the proceedings into English).[113] There were said to be fifty-three party members in China at the time, not counting the 350 who were members of the disbanded SYL.[114] In the wake of the Congress about half the delegates left the party, only three attending the Second Congress the following year.[115] Neither Chen Duxiu nor Li Dazhao was present, though Chen sent a draft 'party platform', outlining his ideas and proposals. In all, seven sessions of the congress were held, the last taking place on a boat in Jiaxing on 30 July, after police were apparently tipped off about the venue of the congress.[116]

The political perspective adopted by the First Congress was one of proletarian revolution rather than of national liberation:

> The revolutionary forces must together with the proletariat overthrow the political power of the capitalist class, must support the working class, with the aim of abolishing all class distinctions. We stand for the dictatorship of the proletariat until class struggle comes to an end and class distinctions are abolished. We stand for the abolition of capitalist private property, the confiscation of machinery, land, factory premises, semi-finished goods etc. and their transfer into public ownership.[117]

Given the presence of Sneevliet, this perspective is somewhat puzzling, since the Second Congress of the Comintern in July 1920 had passed 'Theses on the National and Colonial Questions' that outlined a perspective of a two-stage revolution for the colonial and semi-colonial countries. According to this resolution, the first stage of the national-liberation struggle would be waged by the bourgeoisie, with Communist parties actively supporting it while taking care to preserve their autonomy by organizing the working class and peasantry. How far Sneevliet tried to persuade the Chinese Communists to adopt this perspective is unclear. His authoritarian style may have alienated the Chinese since, according to Zhang Guotao, who was relatively well-disposed to him, he behaved like 'an angel of liberation to the Asian peoples'.[118]

The Congress witnessed heated disputes on the position to be taken towards other political parties. The line adopted, as set forth in the 'First Resolution as to the Object of the CCP', recommended 'an independent, combative and exclusive attitude' towards other parties: 'In the political struggle against the warlords and bureaucrats and for the freedoms of speech, the press and association, our party must staunchly defend the proletariat and must have no relations with any other political party or organization.'[119] On the issue of relations with the Guomindang, a minority argued, as the Comintern would do, that Sun Yat-sen should be supported, since the merits of his nationalism outweighed other defects in his ideology. But the majority shared the opinion of the Canton delegate that the 'attitude toward Sun Yat-sen must be the same as that toward the militarists, and even more negative, since he confuses the masses by his demagogy'. A compromise was reached whereby Sun Yat-sen was rebuked, but in milder terms than those applied to the northern warlords.[120]

It is clear, then, that the CCP saw its priority as to organize and educate China's workers. This task had been placed on the political agenda by the May Fourth Movement, and it was this element in the Comintern message, set within the wider perspective of a dictatorship of the proletariat (arguably, the element in marxism-leninism least appropriate to China), which appealed to that handful of intellectuals drawn into the ambit of the CCP. The flavour of thinking in the party at this time can be seen from a letter sent by Cai Hesen in France to *New Youth* on 11 February 1921, wherein he characterised China as a 'completely proletarian country'. 'If the Chinese proletariat does not take power as soon as possible, others will gain control over it. It will then be necessary for capitalism to set in, and we will not be able to start our revolution until social revolutions in the five great powers have taken place.'[121] By contrast, the idea of an alliance with the GMD in the interests of national liberation was much less appealing to these radicals, for they were deeply distrustful of conventional politicians and of parties of the GMD type. In that regard, the first cohort of Communists was probably untypical of Shanghai's radical intelligentsia, for whom the strengthening of the nation was the alpha and omega of political action. Communist intellectuals sought to go beyond the vague panaceas of the May Fourth Movement and to grapple with questions of organization and strategy.

Some recent accounts of the foundation of the CCP have downplayed the significance of the Soviet Union's intervention, stressing the indigenous roots of Chinese Communism. The foregoing discussion has sought to give due weight to the domestic political developments, catalyzed by the May Fourth Movement, which led small groups of intellectuals to embrace ideas of proletarian revolution and the leninist party. It is clear, for instance, that an orientation to the working class predated contacts with Soviet Russia, and that elements of class politics and sympathy for marxism were evident in the thinking of Chen Duxiu, Dai Jitao and others before the arrival of Voitinskii. Moreover, pre-existing study groups and informal networks of friends, fellow-provincials and classmates fed directly into the early CCP. Nevertheless, it is doubtful that internal developments would have led to the formation of the CCP without the intervention of the Comintern.[122]

It was the arrival of Voitinskii, a young man who had probably more experience of American socialism than Russian Bolshevism, which was crucial in providing the practical assistance – in the shape of money for publications and a Foreign Languages School to assist in sending youths to Soviet Russia – organizational experience and ideological clarity necessary to catalyze the formation of the CCP.[123] We have seen that Voitinskii was crucial in pushing for the creation of a party and his influence also shaped the way in which the 'small group' set about trying to organize labour. Yet even in this respect, the approach was not uninfluenced by previous efforts at labour organization – which had begun as early as 1912. More broadly, van de Ven is right to insist that there were no 'instant Bolsheviks': that prior to the First Congress, would-be leninists did battle with social democrats, who were well-represented in the Shanghai 'small group' (as the example of Li Hanjun shows), and in particular with anarchists.[124] Nevertheless, one is struck more by the speed than the slowness with which most early Communists embraced class struggle and the leninist party (however imperfectly). Those who did so were those who had been brought into politics by the May Fourth Movement but who had become disillusioned with peaceful strategies of social reconstruction, such as those of the work-study movement. The ideals of a disciplined vanguard party and a state organized as a dictatorship of the proletariat appealed to those who were sickened by the political opportunism and dilettantism which they saw around them. In Arif Dirlik's words, Bolshevism provided not just a social theory but a 'unifying principle for concerted action'.[125]

Chapter 2 _____

The Communist Party in Shanghai, 1921–22

The structure and operation of the CCP

The Far Eastern Secretariat (FES) of ECCI, formed in Irkutsk in January 1921, directed Comintern work throughout the Far East until February 1922. Shanghai was the nodal point (*uzlovoi punkt*) of its work, since the central bureaux of the CCP and the Korean CP and Japanese operations were all based there.[1] Hendricus Sneevliet was the principal agent of the Comintern in China, and was based in Shanghai from 3 June until 10 December 1921.[2] He met almost daily with Nikol'skii, the representative of Profintern, from whom he claimed to receive instructions.[3] V.V. Lidin (b.1895) arrived in the city in late October, having been sent by the FES on a mission to Canton. En route, however, he was told to remain in Shanghai so that he could take over from Nikol'skii once he had left in December.[4] During the first half of 1922, Sneevliet remained based in Shanghai, but he was only in the city periodically – from 7 to 19 February, 7 to 23 March, 29 March to 24 April – before leaving for the Netherlands and Russia. He arrived back on 12 August 1922.[5]

Communications between the FES and its agents on the ground were poor. In his report of July 1921, Sneevliet wrote: "After I had been in Shanghai for a time I was informed by courier from Irkutsk that the Executive had made me a member of the FES and that they had decided in Irkutsk to leave me in Shanghai. In truth I was a member in name only. . . . Because I never received any direct correspondence, I did not participate in deciding strategy or the work as a whole of the Secretariat".[6] The person with the most reliable link to Russia was S.L. Vil'de, who from September 1921 to March 1924 was chief accountant in the office of the Central Union of Consumer Associations (*Tsentrosoiuz*), whose office was in the compound of the Soviet Consulate on Huangpu road. However, it was Soviet policy to keep Comintern activities strictly separate from those of official soviet bodies, so Vil'de was forbidden to meet with Comintern agents. Even more confusingly, Comintern agents in Shanghai were forbidden to have contact with those who worked in the FES "nodal point".[7]

It was Sneevliet who had the most regular contact with the leadership of the CCP. Throughout the period covered by this study, the party's central organs were weak, although they steadily gained in strength after the Third Congress of June 1923.[8] The First Congress agreed that the party would not need a Central Committee until membership reached 500. Accordingly, a three-person central bureau was tasked with the day-to-day running of the party, its members being Chen Duxiu, who had been elected general secretary by the Congress in absentia, Zhang Guotao, who headed the organization department, and Li Da, who headed the propaganda department. Chen returned to Shanghai from Canton on 10 September 1921. Initially he did not get on well with Sneevliet, whom he considered overbearing, but on 4 October 1921 his house was raided and he and four others were arrested. When Sneevliet paid their fines of $100 and arranged for their release on 26 October, relations between the two appear to have improved. In 1922 relations became strained once more when Chen failed to show the requisite enthusiasm for the united front with the GMD which Sneevliet was busily promoting.[9] Whether because he did not get on with Sneevliet or because he despaired of the incompetence of local Communists, Chen Duxiu seems to have behaved capriciously at this stage.[10] Li Da, who never had the easiest of relationships with him, recalls: "His leadership style was very high-handed ... Once he came to my house and saw letters from comrades which spoke of difficulties in party work. When he saw them, he cursed, hurled a teacup and smashed it."[11]

In the early 1920s, regional organizations of the CCP retained far-reaching autonomy. Initially, however, there was little demarcation between the Shanghai organization and the central bureau. By the end of 1921, a shadowy Shanghai district committee had emerged, led by Chen Wangdao. According to Xu Meikun, Chen was an effective propagandist but poor at practical work – "all talk and no action" (*tukou shuo er bu xing*). He and his wife, Wu Shuwu, disdained to involve themselves in the day-to-day work of the committee, and consequently the party languished. Xu claims to have spoken to Chen Duxiu about this, and in May 1922 he replaced Chen Wangdao as secretary of a new Shanghai district and regional executive committee (*Shanghai difang jian qu zhixing weiyuan-hui*).[12] This had responsibility not only for Shanghai but for a large area of Jiangsu and Zhejiang provinces. By 1924 branches as far away as Hangzhou, Nanjing and Wenzhou were subordinate to the committee.[13] Shen Yanbing, who earned a good salary at the Commercial Press, rented the committee's premises.[14] Shen worked alongside Xu Meikun, and was in charge of propaganda.[15] After further elections in the first half of 1923, the executive of the Shanghai regional committee consisted of Xu as secretary, Shen in charge of propaganda, and Wang Zhenyi in charge of labour movement work.[16]

By June 1922 the CCP nationally had 195 members: of these just four were women and twenty-one workers. Shanghai had the largest regional organization with fifty members, followed by Canton with thirty-two members, Changsha with thirty, and Beijing and Hubei each with twenty.[17] The party's activities were almost entirely dependent on Comintern funding. Of 17,500 dollars (*yuan*) spent by central organs between October 1921 and January 1922, no less than 16,655 came from the ECCI.[18] However, Lidin complained that the amounts of funding received fluctuated and were unpredictable in their timing, which adversely affected the party's operations.[19] The largest element of party finances was spent on propaganda, which included leaflets, periodicals and the People's Publishing House, set up on 1 September 1921. An official party organ, the *Guide Weekly* (*Xiangdao zhoubao*), commenced publication on 13 September 1922, under the editorship of Cai Hesen. Two-hundred and one issues appeared before it was closed down in July 1927. Its print-run grew from 1,000 to 5,000 in 1923, and later may briefly have touched 20,000.[20] A subsidy was also paid by ECCI to *New Youth*, but once taken over by the CCP it became a much less lively journal and fast lost influence in progressive circles. It appeared intermittently until July 1926 when it ceased publication.[21]

Labour Organization Secretariat in Shanghai, 1921–22

Non-Communist organizations dominated the labour movement in Shanghai. Yet the key development of 1921 was the setting up by the CCP of the Chinese Labour Organization Secretariat (*Zhonghua laodong zuhe shuji bu*) on 11 August.[22] The idea of establishing a national centre to represent the labour movement had been mooted before the First CCP Congress, but there is no record of the Congress formally deciding to set up the LOS.[23] The decision to go ahead and establish a national centre appears to have been Sneevliet's.[24] He wrote the declaration announcing the formation of the LOS and chose a name for the organization, which some felt unduly obscure, since it was neither Chinese nor western in character. Curiously, in view of the fact that within a year Sneevliet would emphasise the immaturity of the working class in China and the impossibility of a proletarian revolution, the declaration made no mention of imperialism or the struggle for national liberation, simply likening the position of Chinese workers to 'slaves' of 'Chinese and foreign capitalists'.[25] It is clear from the declaration that the CCP hoped to give the LOS a 'non-party' image, since among its twenty-six signatories, members of the CCP and SYL were in a minority.[26] In practice, however, it was under the tight control of the party, its president, Zhang Guotao, being one of the three members of the party's central bureau. Zhang was also editor of the LOS journal, *Labour Weekly* (*Laodong Zhoukan*), which was published in Shanghai from August 1921 to June 1922 and which had a print-run of 4,000.[27] Sneevliet secured funding for the LOS from Profintern, so overall policy must have been approved by the Far Eastern Bureau of the Profintern and, ultimately, by ECCI.[28] After some initial in-fighting, the LOS began work in mid-October. Soon, however, Zhang Guotao left for Irkutsk in order to attend the Congress of Toilers of the Far East.[29]

The main aim of the Shanghai section of the LOS, which was headed by Li Qihan, was to form a city-wide federation of trade unions. At the beginning of November it announced the creation of a Shanghai Trades Union Representative Council (*Shanghai geye gonghui daibiaotuan*) to 'bring together representatives from the labour unions in each industry and lay the foundations for a Shanghai General Labour Union (*zonggonghui*)'.[30] The constitution was drawn up by Li Zhenying, who went on to serve as director of the No.1 Workers' Continuation School in Xiaoshadu.[31] Twelve organizations responded to the call, including the Shanghai mechanics' union, the printers' union, the textile union, the tobacco workers' union and the electricians' union. Two organizations founded during the May Fourth Movement, the Worker-Merchant Friendly Society and the All-China Association for the Progress of the Workers' Section of Society (*Zhonghua quanguo gongjie xiejinhui*), neither of which was strictly a labour union, also affiliated.[32] At the preparatory meeting the latter proposed that the planned federation take the name of Shanghai Federation of Syndicates (*Shanghai gegongtuan lianhehui*), but Li Zhenying and Li Qihan persuaded the meeting to reject that name on the grounds that such a broad title would invite organizations dominated by merchants and teachers to affiliate. They argued that a General Labour Union could be formed only after real labour unions had been established at the grass roots.[33] This assertion rankled, and one merchant wrote to *Republican Daily* to say that the LOS's claim to be the 'true' representative of labour was spurious.[34] At its first formal meeting on 12 November Tong Lizhang of the Shanghai Worker-Merchant Friendly Society, who had not been at the drafting meeting, put forward an alternative constitution for discussion, provoking protests from the Communist delegates and from Mr Tao of the Labour Federation (*Laodong lianhehui*). The chairman of the meeting, Zhu Dingyi, a representative of the China Industrial Association (*Zhonghua gongye xiehui*), agreed that a vote should be taken and delegated Yang Huaping to vote by proxy on his behalf. The vote split evenly, five against five, whereupon Zhu insisted on his right to a further casting vote as chairman and opted to allow discussion of the constitution to be reopened. Uproar ensued and the Communists walked out.[35]

In January 1922 Tong Lizhang sent a letter to labour associations proposing the establishment of a new Labour Alliance Society (*Laodong tongmenghui*) 'to lend one another a helping hand and cooperate in improving society.' He made it clear that mixed-class bodies could affiliate and reminded them that his own organization, the Friendly Society, was 'a partnership of the labouring and commercial classes, both of whom belong to the workers' section of society (*gongjie*).'[36] In May the Executive Committee of Shanghai Syndicates (*Shanghai gegongtuan zhixing weiyuan-hui*) was formed to which more than thirty non-Communist labour organizations affiliated.[37] It did not achieve a great deal, though it backed the strike by women in the Japanese cotton mills of Pudong. The Communists, however, had even less success with their attempt to form a representative council. Only four labour unions – those of textile workers, tobacco workers, printers and mechanics – responded to the LOS's invitation to attend an inaugural meeting, though the electricians' union, which still retained its link with the non-Communist Executive Committee, also sent a representative. Li Zhong, Communist chair of the mechanics' union, was elected president of the representative committee, and Zhang Ruixuan, the non-Communist chair of the tobacco union, its secretary.[38] In the event, it achieved little.[39]

The CCP intervention in strikes.

It was an ideal time for the CCP to try to organize Shanghai workers, since there was an unprecedented wave of labour militancy, inspired by a surge in rice prices and a rapid depreciation of the copper currency. In the thirteen months between January 1922 and February 1923 there were no fewer than fifty-four strikes in Shanghai, involving over 85,000 workers, sixteen of them involving 1000 workers or more, and five lasting twenty days or more.[40] The CCP intervened in the biggest of these stoppages with some success, but the most important lesson it learnt was about the difficulties of unifying a workforce that was so profoundly divided by particularistic ties. Shanghai labour was imbricated by a dense network of solidarities based on native place, craft, clientelism and the secret societies, and these posed a huge obstacle to the CCP's attempt to build a broad and inclusive class movement.[41]

The Shanghai Communists encountered the might of the secret societies, in particular of the Green Gang, in the very first strike in which they intervened. The wealth and influence of the Green Gang were based principally on its domination of the opium trade, but at lower levels small-time bosses, such as foremen and labour contractors, made a comfortable living from their control of the job market, especially on the docks and in shipping. In order to get a job or to enjoy the protection and patronage which a foreman or contractor could provide, workers had to pledge allegiance to them as their disciples. Although these gang bosses milked their 'disciples' for all they were worth, they nevertheless provided them with a degree of security that the nascent CCP could not hope to match.

Li Qihan quickly discovered the necessity of cultivating good relations with foremen and contractors who were bosses in the secret societies, when seeking to promote his night school in Xiaoshadu. He met a woman textile worker who was a member of the Green Gang, and through her he pledged discipleship to a high-ranking master in the Green Gang, in the hope that this would facilitate his efforts at labour organization.[42] The first test of this strategy came on 20 July 1921, when a strike broke out at the two British-American Tobacco plants in Pudong, a district on the east bank of the Huangpu river that was cut off from the rest of Shanghai on the opposite bank.

The strike began at the old BAT plant in protest at the conduct of a foreign supervisor who had beaten men under his authority and made deductions from their wages.[43] The foremen at BAT were all members of the Green Gang, and the Communists realised at once that they would make no headway unless they won the confidence of these gang bosses. Li Qihan sought to bring them over to the side of the strikers by 'drinking cock's blood wine' with them and using his connections with Green Gang notables. He was partially successful, although one of the most influential gang bosses at BAT actively recruited strike breakers on behalf of the company. Nevertheless after twenty-one days, the workers won a modest victory and in late August the Communists helped to set up a tobacco workers' union (*Shanghai yancao gongrenhui*). The company was not prepared to tolerate this and members soon began to leave the union.[44] However, the sacking of the vice-president of the union, together with a mechanic, infuriated the workers and on 26 September they began a second stoppage in order to demand their reinstatement. Once again, Li Qihan appealed to the foremen for support by invoking the secret-society tradition of fighting for justice on behalf of the common people. Using the language of the sworn brotherhoods of the 'rivers and lakes', he proclaimed: 'Foremen you are all elders (*lao touzi*) in the gang. Can you tolerate behaviour that goes against the code of brotherhood?'.[45] His appeal worked and 100 foremen, mechanics and machinists met secretly and pledged to support the strikers. After two days, the company agreed to reinstate the two men but refused to recognize the union.[46] Out of their experience of these two strikes, the Communists learnt a good deal about how to cultivate the secret-society bosses who carried such influence in workplaces and in working-class neighbourhoods. The relative success at BAT turned out, however, to be connected to the fact that the strikers were pitted against a foreign company. Soon they would discover that foremen and contractors in native enterprises could not be relied upon to support workers. Indeed by April 1922 gang bosses had grown irritated by Li Qihan's activities and betrayed him to the police.[47]

An even bigger impediment to labour organization was posed by the social networks based on common native place (*bang*) that also served to provide workers with employment and protection through their domination of particular sectors of the job market. The workforce of Shanghai was far more diverse in terms of its regional origins than those in Canton, Beijing or Hunan.[48] And from the first, the Communists had few illusions about the difficulties of uniting workers whose loyalties were first and foremost to those who came from the same region as themselves, who spoke the same language, ate the same food, practised the same customs. The Manifesto of the LOS called for the rooting out of regionalist parochialism: 'It will not do for labourers to divide themselves into so-called Ningbo societies, Guangdong societies, Subei societies etc. This is a way of creating disunity among ourselves.'[49] One of the sectors of the labour force where regional *bang* were most firmly entrenched were the seamen, whose number in Shanghai may have reached 30,000, if those who plied inland waterways are included. The first test of the Communists' ability to deal with regionalist divisions came when the seamen of Hong Kong went on strike.

On 13 January 1922 against a background of rocketing prices, seamen in Hong Kong launched a well-organized strike, which was to last fifty-six days and was to involve 120,000 seamen at its peak.[50] The strikers in the south were mainly Cantonese and throughout its course the strike was threatened by the importation of strike breakers from Shanghai. Among Shanghai seamen the largest regional grouping was the Ningbo *bang*, to which native Shanghainese also belonged. The next largest was the Cantonese *bang*, followed by smaller *bang* from Tianjin and Hankou.[51] The foreign shipping companies in Hong Kong encouraged Ningbo seamen from Shanghai to break the strike, something which the Jun'an guild, an organization of Ningbo seamen in Shanghai, and the LOS sought to prevent.[52] With organizational and financial support from the GMD government in Canton, the seamen's union led the Hong Kong strikers to victory. This much impressed Sneevliet, who was briefly in Canton during the strike, and he concluded that the strike was 'undoubtedly the most important event in the young history of the Chinese labour movement.'[53] Even prior to the strike, he had had talks with Sun Yat-sen in Guilin from 23 to 25 December 1921 about cooperation between the GMD and CCP, but the backing given to the strike by the GMD government convinced him that the way forward lay through a united front.[54]

The success of the seamen's union in Hong Kong spurred the LOS and the Jun'an guild to try to form a Shanghai branch of the union. Zhu Baoting (1880–1947), a member of the Jun'an guild, was instrumental in this. Born in Ningbo, Zhu was the son of a soldier who had fought in the Taiping army and died in the Sino-French war in 1884. At the age of 5, the orphan Zhu entered a non-fee-paying school, but two years later had to give up his studies when his mother moved out of the area. In 1893, at the age of 13, he went with his older brother to Shanghai and worked for a few

37

months as a cabin boy for the Butterfield and Swire company, although it was to be several years before he began to work full-time on ocean-going steamers. When the Jun'an guild was formed in 1914, Zhu became active in it and in 1919 he helped bring out the seamen in support of the May Fourth Movement. In July 1921 he met Li Qihan, and even before the Hong Kong strike, he and Dong Chuping of the LOS started to try to organize seamen, using the slogan 'all workers under heaven are one family' as a way of trying to overcome the ingrained mistrust between different regional *bang*.[55] In May 1922 the Shanghai branch of the LOS sent Zhu as a delegate to the First National Labour Congress in Canton, where he met two leaders of the Hong Kong seamen's strike, Su Zhaozheng and Lin Weimin, both of whom would, like him, go on to join the CCP. Zhu persuaded Lin to come to Shanghai and set up a branch of the seamen's union.[56]

No sooner had the branch been established, than it launched a strike to demand that crews of Chinese-owned ships be paid the same rate as had been won by the crews of foreign companies as a result of the Hong Kong strike. The Shanghai strike involved 1500 seamen on thirty-seven ships, and lasted from 5 to 26 August, 1922.[57] However, unity between Ningbo and Cantonese seamen proved tenuous. The Ningbo native-place association (*tongxianghui*) denounced the seamen's union as a Cantonese plot, pointing to the fact that its president, Lin Weimin, was Cantonese. In fact, the strike committee was carefully constructed to reflect the preponderance of Ningbo seamen in the shipping trades of Shanghai.[58] In spite of these tensions, the strike was largely successful, since the seamen gained a 20 per cent wage increase, backdated to 1 May.[59] This victory should have spurred the consolidation of the union – and membership did briefly reach 2,700 – but cracks between the regional *bang* soon began to show. Within a few months, most Ningbo seamen had left the union, and the Shanghai branch turned into a bastion of the Cantonese minority and of the GMD.

During the 'first strike high tide' the CCP also gained experience of organizing handicraft workers and of the problems of dealing with the guilds. There were up to 2,000 gold- and silver-smiths in Shanghai, employed in thirty-four firms, most of them Cantonese. They had been the first group of artisans to try, with the help of the Labour Party in 1912, to form a union separate from the guild. On 16 September 1922 Yuan Dashi, who had recently returned from Russia to take up the post of head of the Shanghai branch of the LOS, organized a club for gold- and silversmiths which opened in premises inside the Old North Gate of the Chinese City.[60] Within a couple of weeks, the club sent a letter to the guild, asking for a pay rise and various improvements in conditions. The guild directors failed to respond, but ordered the sacking of the chair of the club, Zhang Jingxuan, who went on to join the CCP in 1923, along with two others. This prompted the gold- and silver-smiths to go on strike from 6 October, declaring that the club was 'their second life', which they would die in order to protect (*shisi hanwei*). The guild directors stated that the club was being used by outsiders to stir up trouble, and refused to negotiate.[61] A bitter stoppage ensued, which culminated on 20 October in a riot at the Qinghua store, whose employees were working in spite of the strike. The riot led to twenty-two arrests.[62] Three days later, the club was shut down and twenty-five militants were arrested. The club was not revived, although after twenty-eight days the strikers did win significant concessions in respect of wages and conditions.[63]

Cotton workers comprised by far the largest group of factory workers in Shanghai, and the LOS was eager to unionize them. On 19 March 1922 it organised a meeting in Pudong, attended by 300 workers, addressed by Li Qihan, Chen Duxiu and Shao Lizi. It led to the formation of the Pudong weavers' union.[64] On 6 April the union put forward a demand for a 20 per cent wage increase to the Nikko company, whose two mills in Pudong employed 3,800 workers. The company turned down the demand, so on 16 April the union launched a well-organized strike which ended nine days later with workers gaining rises of between 10 and 15 per cent. Membership of the union grew to 500, drawn mainly from the male weavers and machine-setters, rather than from the female spinners who comprised the bulk of the workforce.[65] The company determined to crush the union, engineering the arrest of its president, Zhang Yizhang, and two others. In response, the entire workforce walked out on 20 May.[66] The LOS worked hard to garner support for the strikers, putting out 3,000 leaflets to textile workers in Yangshupu and Xiaoshadu – respectively, the eastern and western districts of the city – calling on them to support their comrades in Pudong.[67] In Xiaoshadu, where there was a heavy concentration of Japanese mills, Li Qihan sought in vain to use his Green Gang connections to win support for the strike.[68] After sixteen days on strike the workers in Pudong won a partial victory, but the company refused to recognize the union or to reinstate the three men whose dismissal had caused the stoppage.[69]

In the course of the summer, the LOS began to lose influence in the Pudong weavers' union. The anti-Communist Executive Committee of Shanghai Syndicates backed the strikers, and in early June the International Settlement police reported that one of its leaders, Xu Xilin, a postal worker, was now the leading light in the union.[70] The Nikko company continued to oppose the union and finally managed to persuade the police to close it down on 28 September. The Executive Committee petitioned the Jiangsu Military Governor to lift the ban but without success. Eventually, the weavers' union decided to call a strike, starting on 1 November, which was energetically backed by the LOS.[71] Three days later, a remarkable turn of events transpired, when 7,000 workers at the neighbouring BAT plants came out in support of their fellow workers at Nikko. The background to this unprecedented show of solidarity lay in efforts by the LOS to revive the union at BAT, which had been in the doldrums since the end of the strike the previous September.[72] Guo Jingren of the LOS used his Ningbo connections to call a meeting of 1,000 people at the Ningbo *tongxianghui* on 1 October. This resolved to set up a Pudong Tobacco Printers' Club (*Pudong yancao yinshua gongren julebu*) in the same premises as the weavers' union and it was this which helped to bring the BAT workers out in support of the textile workers.[73]

The managements at Nikko and BAT were determined to smash the strike. On 15 November BAT implemented a lockout, the first example of a tactic that was to become standard during the next five years. It also cultivated a rival to the tobacco workers' club in the shape of the Pudong Industrial Society for the Advancement of Morality (*Pudong gongye jindehui*), whose founder, Shao Bingsheng, was almost certainly a gang leader. It was reported to have 300 to 400 members, and actively encouraged strikers to return to work.[74] At Nikko the management resorted to similar tactics, bribing male workers in the packing department to end their strike and bringing in priests to persuade the women, many of whom were Roman Catholics from Shandong, to return to work.[75] As the strike dragged on, Pudong witnessed scenes of unprecedented violence which prompted the authorities to send in forty police and 100 troops to reinforce the local police.[76] After three weeks, facing mounting debt and hunger, the workers returned to work. Two-hundred employees at BAT were fired and the club was shut down. Forty-eight 'agitators' were fired from the Nikko company.[77]

This defeat marked the beginning of the decline of the LOS in Shanghai. It had been wrong-footed by the tactics of the two companies, both of which had exploited divisions among the workers, imported strikebreakers and, in the case of BAT, promoted a pliant alternative to the tobacco workers' club. In addition, it had had to compete with non-Communist labour leaders who, though willing to back a stoppage against foreign companies, utterly rejected the class-struggle tactics of the LOS. As the strike ran into the sands, these non-Communists did not hesitate to exploit the growing unpopularity of the LOS.[78]

Before the scale of the failure of the LOS became evident, however, the Communists did enjoy some small success among the city's printers. Two previous attempts to unionize printers had come to grief, but in late 1922 Xu Meikun, secretary of the Shanghai regional committee, was elected chair of a Shanghai printers' federation (*Shanghai yinshua gongren lianhehui*). A printer at the Commercial Press, Xu claimed to be the first worker to join the CCP in Shanghai.[79] He had come to Shanghai from Hangzhou in 1920 and found a job at the small Guangming print works. Joining the SYL, he became one of the Zhejiang network at the heart of that organization, his views at that time being the 'anarcho-communist' ones then in vogue. At Chen Duxiu's suggestion, he contacted his fellow-provincial, Shen Yanbing, who worked in the publishing department of Commercial Press; he arranged a job for him. In 1921 Xu joined the CCP. At the party's behest, he also became head of the Zhejiang workers' *tongxianghui*, where he met Zheng Futa, who became his deputy in the Shanghai printers' federation.[80] Zheng, born in 1904, hailed from Zhuji county, whence Yu Xiusong, Zhang Qiuren and others also sprang.[81] Using their native-place ties, Xu and Zheng established strong branches of the printers' federation at the Commercial Press and the China Book Company.

The CCP formed its first workplace branch at the Commercial Press, a bastion of the New Culture Movement and also the city's most enlightened employer. Shen Yanbing was the lynchpin of the branch. Born into a scholar family in Tongxiang county, Zhejiang, in 1896, Shen graduated in 1916 from the preparatory course at Beijing University and became editor of the Fiction Monthly (*Xiaoshuo yuebao*), one of the most popular of the Commercial Press imprints. His brother, Shen Zemin (1900–33), who had studied at Henan Engineering College and been a leader of the May Fourth Movement in Nanjing, also worked at the Commercial Press for a time. During 1922 Shen Yanbing recruited a group of intellectuals into the party, who included Dong Yixiang, a dictionary editor, and Yang Xianjiang, editor of the *Student Miscellany* (*Xuesheng Zazhi*). Yang Xianjiang (1895–1931), born into an artisan family in Yuyao county, Zhejiang, was, like so many others, a graduate of the Zhejiang First Normal School.[82] By the summer of 1923, the Commercial Press had a party branch of thirteen members, at a time when there were still only fifty-three Communists in the entire regional organization.[83]

The CCP and rival labour unions

Non-communist labour organizations far outnumbered those instigated by the LOS. Some estimate that there were as many as fifty such organizations in the city (including Wusong), although most were small and fragile.[84] Organizations such as the Worker-Merchant Friendly Society and the All-China Association for the Progress of the Workers' Section of Society, which united workers and employers in common organizations, were no longer typical, since most non-Communist labour organizations now catered solely for workers. Some were regionalist in character, such as the unions of Sichuanese, Anhuinese, Hunanese, Cantonese or Jiangxi labourers. Others more closely approximated to trade unions, such as the electricians' union. By far the most influential such associations down to 1926 were the Shanghai Women's Industrial Progress Union, formed in March 1922 by Mrs. Mu Zhiying, which catered for silk workers, and the Nanyang tobacco workers' friendly society.

The Nanyang tobacco company, founded in 1905 by the Jian brothers in Hong Kong, set up its first Shanghai plant in 1916 in Broadway, Yangshupu. A second plant was opened in Pudong, which was the most modern of the company's four plants. By the second half of the 1920s, the company produced 20 per cent of the total output of cigarettes in China, a considerable volume, but far less than its rival, BAT.[85] By 1930 5,494 workers were employed at the Broadway plant and 2,500 at the Pudong plant, of whom over two-thirds were young women, engaged in piece work.[86] Most of these were employed on short-term contracts (*sangong*) and hired through foremen and recruiting agents.[87] In October 1922 a number of white-collar workers and skilled male craftsmen established a union, whose aim was to raise the standing of the labourer in society, maintain the safety of labourers' livelihood, and promote social happiness through the spread of mutual aid.[88] Its initiators were A Zhongmin, an inspector, and Guan Minsheng, head of the general office. Since skilled workers at Nanyang were Cantonese, the union appealed mainly to Cantonese workers who were well-represented in the skilled trades of Shanghai. In addition to 500 employees of the Nanyang company, including forty to fifty women, the union embraced 200 metal workers, ships' stokers, shop assistants and thirty to forty tram conductors from Wayside. Twenty of the twenty-one committee members were Nanyang employees, and nineteen were Cantonese.[89] The company refused to recognize the union, allegedly offering $2,000 to anyone who succeeded in smashing it.[90] On 5 November the union called out the workers on strike in pursuit of union recognition and a wage increase. But a settlement was reached within two days when the company offered to recognise a Nanyang tobacco employees' friendly society (*Nanyang yancao zhigong tongzhihui*) if the union disbanded. In return for the right to appoint the officials of the society, the company agreed to provide it with premises and a monthly subsidy of $300.[91] Kuang Gongyao, a senior clerk, was appointed its first chairperson. The friendly society was dominated by white-collar employees, permanent employees (*changgong*) being required to join the society whereas temporary workers were not. Yet in spite of being a company union, the society commanded the support of staff and workers for about two years.[92]

So far as the CCP was concerned, unions such as the Nanyang friendly society were 'signboard' (*zhaopai*) unions, i.e. facades behind which politicians, capitalists and intellectuals manipulated the working class for their own ends. The LOS poured scorn on the claims of their leaders to be genuine representatives of labour, dubbing them *gongfa* ('labour barons'), a word analogous to the term for 'warlord' (*junfa*).[93] Initially, the CCP tried to work with such unions, with a view to 'exposing' them and winning over 'class-conscious elements' within them. It thus collaborated with the non-Communist unions in protests against the Washington Conference (11 December 1921 to 6 February 1922); the execution of two labour leaders in Hunan in March 1922; and the shooting of unarmed demonstrators in Macao by Portuguese troops.[94] This, however, did nothing to overcome the mistrust felt by the non-Communists unions towards the CCP, which they called the 'extremist party' (*guoji dang*) and accused of exploiting workers' sufferings for its own political ends. The charges seem to have struck a chord among many workers since, according to the Communist-authored 'Brief History of the CCP' of 1926, 'the labouring masses, though greatly agitated, regarded the party's actions as dangerous and radical ... The workers feared being utilized by others as instruments of violent struggle.'[95] In September 1922 over thirty non-Communist organizations, led by the All-China Association for the Progress of the Workers' Section of Society, thwarted an attempt by the LOS to organize a conference to discuss a labour law, accusing it of making fraudulent claims to represent the working class.[96]

Jean Chesneaux argued that the non-Communist unions emphasised 'mutual aid, technical training and recreational activity' and favoured class collaboration rather than militant defence of workers' living standards.[97] This is broadly true, but one needs to draw distinctions between different types of union. For all that the Nanyang tobacco workers' friendly society had a cosy relationship with management, it subsequently proved to be far less of a docile instrument of the employers, than, for example, the Pudong Industrial Society for the Advancement of Morality, set up by the BAT company. And some organizations, such as the silk women's association, which engaged in a militant strike in August 1922, were heartily detested by the employers. Even a mixed-class organization such as the All-China Association for the Progress of the Workers' Section of Society acted vigorously in support of the Hong Kong seamen (though this may have been connected to the fact that it was supporting fellow Cantonese). Similarly, the Executive Committee of Shanghai Syndicates supported the Nikko strike of November 1922, even if half-heartedly. The crucial difference between the non-Communist unions and the LOS, then, was not so much that the former abstained from the struggle to improve wages and working conditions, but that they repudiated class struggle as a political principle. That said, we may note that the constitutions of unions under Communist influence seldom espoused class struggle explicitly and revealed a surprisingly enduring commitment to the anarchist ideal of mutual aid.

The end of the LOS

On 18 July 1922 International Settlement police raided the office of the LOS and shut it down. Henceforth it was forced to operate clandestinely.

43

The national headquarters moved to Beijing, where Deng Zhongxia became president and Liu Renjing his deputy.[98] By this time, the LOS had established itself as a nation-wide organization, making its greatest impact in central China – in the Hanyeping mines, in Changsha and Wuhan. It also had effective branches in Canton, Beijing and, later in 1922, in Jinan.[99] Its main achievement was to convene the First All-China Labour Congress, which took place in Canton from 1 to 7 May 1922, and which marked an important step in forging a national strategy for the nascent labour movement.[100] Judged against the national picture, the record of the LOS in Shanghai was not impressive. In addition to the huge obstacles posed by the particularistic ties of Shanghai workers and the prevailing mistrust of 'extremism', the LOS faced unremitting harassment by the British and Chinese authorities. Thanks to a well-organized network of spies and informers, routine reading of correspondence, and periodic raids on its headquarters, the International Settlement police were well-informed about the doings of the LOS. In August 1922 for a second time they raided the home of Chen Duxiu, whom the Acting Consul described as 'an ardent ape of Russian extremism'.[101] But it was the arrest of Li Qihan that dealt the foulest blow to the LOS. In February 1922 Li was briefly imprisoned for mobilizing support for the Hong Kong seamen, but it was his agitation during a brief strike by employees of the Chinese Post Office in late April that particularly alarmed the International Settlement authorities. On 9 June he was charged with 'inciting strikes' and with publishing articles 'likely to cause a breach of the peace'. After three months in jail, he was handed over to the Chinese Garrison Commissioner, in the knowledge that he could expect little mercy at the hands of the Anfu militarist, He Fenglin. In the event, Li was luckier than some of his comrades later, in that he escaped summary execution. But he was sentenced to a further stint in a military prison of two years and four months.[102] After Li's arrest, Yuan Dashi took over as head of the Shanghai branch, but he had less charisma, and since the LOS was now forced to work underground, its pool of activists was diminished.[103]

Nationally, the first phase of CCP labour organization came to an end when the northern warlord, Wu Peifu, abruptly smashed the Beijing-Hankou railway union on 7 February 1923. Once declared by Sneevliet to be a 'class ally', Wu had permitted the LOS to organize in the areas under his control in return for Russian support against his adversaries. His sudden *volte-face* signalled the onset of a nation-wide reversal for the CCP's labour-movement activities. Deng Zhongxia states that the CCP ceased to 'make use of' the LOS, although in June 1923 the Third CCP Congress appointed Wang Hebo to head the organization.[104] For the next eighteen months, however, little was heard of the LOS, and it is even possible that it was successfully infiltrated by right-wing GMD labour leaders.[105] In October 1924, when the CCP's fortunes finally began to revive, the LOS put out a new journal, *The Chinese Worker* (*Zhongguo Gongren*), which was published first in Shanghai and then in Canton.[106] Yet despite this shaky revival, the LOS was disbanded for good in the run-up to the Second National Labour Congress in May 1925.[107]

The Socialist Youth League and the Anti-Christian Movement

If the CCP's priority was to organize labour, its second most important task was to organize the city's youth. In this sphere it enjoyed decidedly more success than in the labour movement. When the SYL was refounded in November 1921, Zhang Tailei drew up a new constitution on the orders of the Communist Youth International (KIM), which declared its aims to be 'the study of marxism, the implementation of socialist reconstruction and the upholding of the authority of youth.'[108] Though a partial gesture towards leninism, this formula suggests that the SYL had still not sloughed off the ideology of the May Fourth Movement, a supposition confirmed by the editorial of the first number of its journal, *Pioneer* (*Xianqu*). This defined the aim of the SYL as being to: 'strive to awaken the consciousness of the citizens, to smash persisting habits of slavishness, laziness and dependence and, as a result of fighting these, to call forth a spirit of creativity.'[109]

The First National Congress of the SYL, held in Canton from 5 to 10 May 1922, was attended by twenty-five delegates, representing fifteen organizations and a national membership of 5,000, although the latter figure was much exaggerated.[110] The delegates from Shanghai were Yu Xiusong and Shi Cuntong. Shanghai served as the national centre of the SYL; but with a membership of only 200, its local organization did not compare with that of Canton, which had 800 members.[111] Six resolutions were passed, including one to join KIM. In line with the Comintern belief that countries such as China faced a democratic national revolution, the SYL now defined its principal aim as being to fight warlordism and imperialism. Yet it continued to stress the longer-term goal of proletarian revolution. 'On the one hand, it fights to improve the living conditions of young workers and peasants and for the interests of young women and students. On the other, it fosters a youthful revolutionary spirit and follows the path of struggle for the emancipation of the proletariat as a whole.'[112] The Congress elected Shi Cuntong national secretary, but until September 1923 he also continued to be secretary of the Shanghai organization, at which point Zhang Qiuren replaced him.[113] Following the Congress, growth of the SYL in Shanghai was sluggish. In January 1924 there were still only nine branches, with a total membership of 160 (forty-nine of whom were at Shanghai University).[114]

In spite of this, the SYL was successful beyond its wildest dreams in launching a nation-wide anti-Christian movement. This began as a response to the World Christian Student Association conference that was scheduled to open at Qinghua University in Beijing on 4 April 1922. Hostility to Christianity, and antagonism to religion generally, had long been a staple of the 'New Thought Tide' that had been advancing since the turn of the century. In Beijing the Anti-Religious Federation responded to the announcement of the conference with a telegram which vowed to 'sweep the poisonous fog from mankind' and to 'show the light of human progress through the spirit of science.'[115] But the contribution of the SYL was to articulate hostility to Christianity in the new language of anti-imperialism. At its instigation, an Anti-Christian Student Federation (*Fei Jidujiao xuesheng tongmeng*) was set up on 9 March, which proclaimed:

> In capitalist society there are the plundering and oppressing classes, on the one hand, and the classes that are plundered on the other ... Contemporary Christianity and the Christian churches are demons that assist the former to plunder the latter ... The capitalists of every nation have set up churches in China solely to entice the Chinese people into welcoming capitalism. Christian youth organizations have been established in China to rear well-behaved running dogs (*shanliang zougou*) of the capitalists.[116]

The publication of this manifesto in *Republican Daily*, together with telegrams sent to the major cities, precipitated a nation-wide, albeit highly localised anti-Christian student movement.[117] And since the Chinese authorities showed greater tolerance of this movement than they did of the labour movement, it provided a facade behind which the party could carry out its political propaganda.[118] The LOS, for example, seized the opportunity to 'expose and refute the pro-imperialist propaganda' of Jian Hanwen, a professor of theology, who preached in working-class districts of Shanghai.[119] Lidin, the Comintern agent, contrasted the 'miserable' influence of the CCP on the labour movement with the party's vigorous leadership of the anti-Christian movement, arguing that this was 'indisputable proof ... that these circles can draw into a broad movement significant masses of students and the radical intelligentsia in circumstances where the basic direction of the movement touches on issues that are most relevant for contemporary China.'[120]

Organising Women

The early CCP displayed considerably more sympathy towards the feminist movement than did its antecedents in Europe. This was because the New Culture Movement, out of which it was born, viewed the subordination of women as one of the corner-stones of the edifice of Confucianism. The 'anarcho-communist' ideology of the 'small groups' took it as axiomatic that there was a tight nexus between the subordination of women and the subordination of labour. During his brief time in Canton in 1921, for example, Chen Duxiu was closely associated with the journal *Women and Labour* (*Funü yu laodong*), which linked the liberation (*jiefang*) of workers to that of women:

> Labourers are demanding liberation, and the proper way to demand this is through uniting in organization. The wrong way is to beseech the capitalists to liberate you. Women are demanding liberation, and the proper way is for women to demand this for themselves. The wrong way is to beg men to liberate you ... The practical existence of labourers and of women is obviously different, and labourers and women will each strive to follow a path appropriate to their different circumstances. But both groups suffer economic oppression under the class system, so labourers and women are similar.[121]

Chen Wangdao, first secretary of the Shanghai regional committee, edited *Women's Review* (*Funü pinglun*), a supplement of the *Republican Daily*, which was published from August 1921 until 1923. Here and in the more mainstream *Women's Magazine* (*Funü zazhi*), founded in 1915 by the Commercial Press, he and other male party members, such as Shen Yanbing, Li Da and Shen Zemin, wrote articles on the gamut of issues affecting women, including their subordination in the family, arranged marriage, the sexual double standard, their right to education, female suffrage and civil rights.[122] Increasingly, these issues, first raised by the New Culture Movement, were framed by a marxist analysis that stressed the primacy of economic independence for women's emancipation.

In late 1921 the CCP inaugurated a women's programme under the leadership of Wang Huiwu, wife of Li Da, and Gao Junman, partner of Chen Duxiu. Gao was of an older generation to Wang, having studied at Beijing Women's Normal Institute in the last years of the empire. She was the younger sister of Chen Duxiu's illiterate wife, from whom he had separated, and in 1910 she took the unconventional step of going to live with her sister's husband. Wang Huiwu, born in 1898 in Jiaxing, Zhejiang province, was the daughter of an impoverished schoolteacher and his illiterate wife. She studied at the Jiaxing Women's Normal School and the Hujun Academy for Girls, where she became a Christian. Radicalized by the May Fourth Movement, she published an influential article against arranged marriage in *Young China* (*Shaonian Zhongguo*). After moving to Shanghai in 1920, she met and married Li Da. In late 1921 she and Gao, together with Huang Zonghan, the chair of the Shanghai Federation of Women's Circles (*Nüjie lianhehui*) and erstwhile comrade of Huang Xing, a prominent leader of the 1911 Revolution, launched a periodical, *Women's Voice* (*Funü sheng*). This journal appealed to women with 'consciousness' to support the struggles of working-class women. Only ten issues of the journal appeared before it ceased publication in June 1922. In contrast to the other journals for women, however, it was written mainly by women themselves.[123]

The most significant initiative of the women's programme was to create a Common People's Women's School (*Shanghai pingmin Nüxuexiao*), with backing from the Shanghai Federation of Women's Circles. Wang Huiwu ran the school, but her husband, Li Da, was formally the school principal.[124] The school, which opened after Chinese New Year in 1922, aimed to offer young women a modern education. It attracted both lower-class illiterate women and educated women, some of whom were fleeing arranged marriages, among them Ding Ling, who later became China's foremost woman writer. When Yang Zhihua visited the school, she was shocked to see Ding Ling wearing a sleeveless singlet of grass cloth and men and women socializing freely.[125] In keeping with the May Fourth ethos, it sought to combine study with work and social involvement. The students supported themselves by making clothes and socks, ran a night school for women workers and supported striking cotton workers in Yangshupu. Most of the middle-class students left in disgust at the poor quality of the teaching, and at the end of 1922 the school closed down.[126]

In July 1922 the Second Congress of the CCP established a women's bureau, which formally marked an upgrading of the party's women's programme. At the same time, a certain hardening of attitude towards 'bourgeois' feminism was detectable. According to Ding Ling, the decision to close *Women's Voice* was motivated by displeasure in the party leadership at the anarchist tenor of some of its articles.[127] Under its head, Xiang Jingyu, the women's bureau stayed aloof from the Women's Rights Alliance (*Nüquan yundong tongmenghui*). Founded in October 1922, this campaigned for a broad legislative programme designed to ease the lot of all women, particularly those of the common people.[128] The *Guide Weekly* criticized the Alliance for failing to recognize that the prerequisites to women's emancipation were the abolition of feudalism and private property, and said that the Alliance's stress on equal rights reflected the preponderance of upper-class women in the organization. It insisted that the women's movement could only succeed if it were aligned to the working class.[129]

As head of the women's bureau, Xiang Jingyu crafted a women's programme that was feminist yet rooted in class politics. Born in 1895 in Xupu in Hunan, she was the ninth daughter of a well-to-do merchant. At 17, she entered the Zhounan Girls' School where, together with six other students, including Ding Ling's 30-year-old mother, she pledged to devote herself to study in order to achieve equality between the sexes and the salvation of the nation. In 1915 she graduated, having written a highly commended essay which lamented China's decline and advocated reliance on the people, hard work, innovation and education as the means to create a new citizenry.[130] For a couple of years she returned to Xupu to teach in a girls' school, but in 1918 she went to Beijing to attend French classes, run by the Franco-Chinese Society, with a view to going to France on the work-study scheme which had been established by the Paris-based anarchist, Li Shizeng. During the May Fourth Movement she met Cai Hesen as a result of her involvement in the New People's Study Group in Changsha.[131] Refusing an arranged marriage, she set off for France with Cai in December 1919, accompanied by his mother and sister. His mother, Ge Jianhao, who had bound feet, had left her ineffectual husband shortly after the birth of her sixth child; his younger sister, Cai Chang, had gone to the same school as Xiang. In June 1920 Xiang and Cai married in Montargis. In their wedding photograph they are shown sitting side by side, holding a copy of *Das Kapital*. In late 1921 they returned to Shanghai after she and Cai were expelled from France for their involvement in a student protest at Lyon University.[132] Xiang was said to be learned, pretty, competent and an excellent speaker. As head of the women's bureau, she devoted herself full-time to party work, her two children being sent to Hunan to be cared for by her mother-in-law.[133] Despite her commitment to personal emancipation, she was said to detest romantic politics, and other women comrades feared her severity, especially Yang Zhihua. Fond of lecturing people, she was nicknamed 'Granny' or 'Granny of the Revolution'.[134]

A good reflection of Xiang's thinking on the woman question is provided by an article of 1923. This was a critique of the feminist movement, sharp in its exposure of its shortcomings, yet not ungenerous in its appreciation of its strengths. Her main point was that a working-class women's movement was now fact rather than fancy, in so far as Shanghai had witnessed fourteen strikes in 1922 by women workers. Yet neither the Women's Suffrage Association nor the Women's Rights Alliance had as wide an audience among working women as the YWCA. She argued that consciousness was determined by social existence and that education did not necessarily led to clarity of vision. Many educated women, slaves of their fathers and husbands, thought that liberation meant no more than the right to go out in the park, to shoot sparrows or play poker. They would not tolerate 'maiden aunt' jokes, yet were openly condescending towards poorly-dressed, uneducated women. She concluded that it was useless to seek influence within the present political system: only a militant alliance with working women would make feminism effective.[135]

The record of achievement

In his report to the ECCI of 30 June 1922, Chen Duxiu said that the Communists in Shanghai had taken part in six strikes (tobacco, seamen, postal workers, and the two Pudong strikes); had contacts with five unions (tobacco, mechanics, printers, weavers and postal) and had taken part in five political campaigns. He also mentioned that in Zhejiang peasant associations to oppose the landlords had been formed in eighty villages, but had been smashed and several leaders had been killed and wounded.[136] This was not a bad record for a tiny party, but it was much less than the Comintern expected. Reporting to the ECCI on 11 July 1922, Sneevliet dismissed Shanghai, saying that it was too inhospitable a terrain for labour organization. 'In Shanghai I acquired a totally pessimistic view of the Chinese movement and its potential for development, but in the South I discovered that prospects are bright, and would even say that success is inevitable.'[137] In response, the ECCI sent a hectoring report criticising the party for having so few links with the workers, for 'completing neglecting the needs of the workers' in its propaganda, and for 'standing quite outside the movement' during the Hong Kong seamen's strike: none of which was fair. It also called on the party to begin propaganda aimed at women, especially working women, and to raise the interest of young workers and intellectuals in the activity of the party.[138] Sneevliet may have deliberately painted a negative picture to convince the ECCI of the correctness of his plan to make the Communists join the GMD. Certainly, he played up for all it was worth the support given by the GMD in Canton to the Hong Kong seamen's strike.[139]

But Sneevliet was not alone in doubting the strategy oriented towards proletarian revolution. Lidin claimed that the Communist organizations had the character of 'circles', small and cut off from the masses, insufficiently oriented towards public activity, fixated on their own internal affairs, dominated by individuals and with a weak ability to undertake practical activity.[140] Like Sneevliet, he was struck by the potential of the politics of nationalism rather than the politics of class. 'With the forces which we have to hand in China there is now a possibility of regulating the national-revolutionary movement to a significant extent and placing our organizations at its head.'[141] In May 1922 he complained that 'several times the central bureau at my insistence issued a declaration about the necessity in certain circumstances of cooperating with the GMD, but this was never put into effect'.[142] The reorientation of the party away from an exclusive 'proletarian' orientation was to prove psychologically painful. Yet it was only by reorienting towards the nationalist movement that the CCP would prove able to build itself as a serious political force.

Chapter 3 _____

The CCP and the United Front in Shanghai, 1923–24

Sneevliet first proposed that the CCP ally with the GMD at the end of March 1922, but the CCP refused. On 6 April 1922 Chen Duxiu wrote to Voitinskii, explaining that the aims and principles of the two parties were quite dissimilar; that outside Guangdong the GMD was seen as a party scrambling for power and profit; that the consequence of such an alliance would be a loss of face for the CCP, particularly in youth organizations; and that Sun Yat-sen would not tolerate a challenge to his principles from newcomers.[1] When Sneevliet left China on 24 April the dispute was still unresolved. Sergei Dalin, the KIM representative, repeated the proposal, but it was again rejected.[2] Although no Comintern delegate attended the Second CCP Congress, which took place in Shanghai from 16 to 23 July 1922, the party tempered its hostility to the GMD, albeit at the cost of exposing the depth of its divisions. The 'Resolution on the Democratic United Front' declared:

> Our Communist Party should unite with all the nation's revolutionary parties and organise a democratic united front to bring about the overthrow of the feudal militarists and imperialist oppression and establish a real democratic, independent nation. We must call on all workers and peasants to join the struggle under our party's banner ... The proletariat must not forget its own independent organization during the struggle.[3]

What the CCP evidently envisaged was what became known as a united front 'from without', i.e. joint action between the CCP and GMD (and with 'other revolutionary parties'), with each retaining its autonomy. Even this relatively limited form of cooperation was not acceptable to Zhang Guotao, who may have had the majority of the congress behind him. According to Sneevliet, four out of the five members of the newly-created Central Executive Committee (*zhongyang zhixing weiyuanhui*) of the CCP supported Zhang, causing Chen Duxiu to proffer his resignation.[4]

In his report of 11 July 1922 Sneevliet played up the revolutionary character of the GMD, suggesting that it was an alliance of various popular classes rather than a 'bourgeois' party.[5] Claiming that the formation of a Communist Party in China had been premature, he proposed that Communists join the GMD on an individual basis, a tactic that became known as a 'bloc within'. The ECCI agreed to back the united front strategy, but it is not clear that it endorsed the 'bloc within'.[6] In instructions, dated August 1922, which Sneevliet took back to China, the CCP was told to support the GMD, especially its proletarian elements, and to create groups of supporters within the GMD and the trade unions. But the paramount task of the Communists was said to be the organization of labour unions.[7] Moreover, in a letter to the Central Executive Committee (CEC) in August, Voitinskii only mentioned in passing that that the party should 'enter into close contact on agreed principles to form a single democratic front' with the GMD.[8]

Upon his return to Shanghai, Sneevliet convened the first plenum of the CEC in Hangzhou on 29–30 August. He informed the Chinese that the ECCI Instructions which he bore required them to join the GMD on an individual basis.[9] Chen Duxiu objected, arguing that the GMD was a 'bourgeois' party and that the class independence of the CCP would be compromised by a 'bloc within'. Only when Sneevliet raised the issue of Comintern discipline did a majority agree to the proposal. They did so, however, on condition that the GMD was reorganized on democratic lines and that Sun Yat-sen waive the requirement that new members pledge personal allegiance to him.[10] In spite of this, when Chen Duxiu attended the Fourth Congress of the Comintern, which met in Moscow from 5 November to 5 December 1922, he spoke out against the 'bloc within' tactic, arguing that cooperation with the GMD was necessary in the struggle for democracy and national unification, but that it was vital for the CCP to retain independence.[11] Thereupon Zinoviev referred the matter to the Politburo of the Russian Communist Party.

We now know that ECCI itself was deeply split over the issue. Only after Sneevliet was summoned back to Moscow from 23 December to 11 January did the Politburo approve a proposal from him and A.A. Joffe for 'full support for the GMD' on 4 January. On 12 January the ECCI presidium adopted a resolution, drafted by Bukharin, which argued that since the Chinese working class was insufficiently differentiated as an independent social force and had a direct interest in the success of the national revolution, members of the CCP should 'remain' members of the GMD, which was described as a coalition of four social groups: the liberal-democratic bourgeoisie, the petty-bourgeoisie, the intelligentsia and the workers. At the same time, the resolution insisted that the CCP retain its own organization, complete with a strictly centralized apparatus, in order to organize labour unions and educate the working masses under its own banner.[12] In January 1923 A.A. Ioffe held discussions with Sun Yat-sen in Shanghai during which he reassured Sun that there was no question of introducing a Communist system in China or even soviets; and that the 'most essential and important task for China is national unification and the achievement of full national independence.'[13] On 8 March the Politburo agreed to send around two million Mexican dollars' worth of aid to Sun, but rejected his request for the Red Army to intervene in Manchuria. Trotsky, G.V. Chicherin and Karl Radek prepared instructions for Ioffe, which ordered him to press Sun to undertake more political and ideological work in the nationalist movement and to create a centralized party apparatus.[14] Meanwhile Sun's allies in the southwestern armies drove the warlord Chen Jiongming out of Guangdong, allowing Sun to return there in February.

Opposition to the united front persisted within ECCI. Neither Voitinskii nor G.I. Safarov, head of the Eastern Section of the ECCI, approved of help being given to Sun Yat-sen, since they considered that he underestimated the importance of mass organization and agitational-propaganda work, was inclined to intrigue with reactionary militarists, and to compromise with the imperialist powers. They accused Sneevliet of covering up the true politics of the GMD and demanded that he be withdrawn from China. In contrast to the ECCI resolution of 12 January, which stated that the 'independent labour movement in the country is still weak', they insisted that labour had become the key factor in the nationalist movement and urged the CCP to pursue an independent policy in relation to it.[15] However, Wu Peifu's assault on the Beijing-Hankou railway union on 7 February 1923 seemed to vindicate Sneevliet's gloomy prognosis for the Chinese labour movement; he now demanded that the CCP make work within the GMD its priority, going so far as to propose that it recruit workers directly into the GMD.[16] In an irate letter to Bukharin on 31 May he complained that 'in ECCI the connection between our people and the KMT is still sharply criticised and ... people still revel in fantasies about a mass party.'[17]

On 24 May ECCI issued a directive intended to guide the Third Congress of the CCP, which was due to meet in June. Based on a draft written by Voitinskii, it glossed the ECCI resolution of 12 January in a way that was far more acceptable to left-wing critics of the united front. In its first paragraph the draft stated that the 'basic task' of the CCP was the 'consolidation of forces, organization and education of the working masses', the creation and centralization of labour unions and the establishment of a mass Communist party. The second paragraph stated that the events of the previous six months had shown that the labour movement was a 'significant factor' in the nationalist movement, which suggests that the ECCI had not grasped the implications of Wu Peifu's treachery. Rather confusingly, the next paragraph stated: '(we) stand by the position we took earlier that the "central task for China is the national revolution against imperialism and its internal feudal agents"'. The general tenor of the resolution, however, suggested that the CCP should make the labour movement, not the GMD, its priority. Indeed Voitinskii's suspicion of the GMD was made explicit in paragraph five, which declared that 'we must struggle by all means within the GMD against military combinations by Sun Yat-sen with the militarists, behind whom stand Anglo-American or Japanese imperialism.'[18] Confusion was compounded when, at Bukharin's insistence, four new paragraphs were added to the beginning of the directive. These laid down that the 'central question of our entire policy is precisely the peasant question' and that the national revolution could be victorious only if the peasantry were drawn into the movement.[19] Though Bukharin is known to have been more enthusiastic about the united front than Voitinskii, the effect of his amendment was to weaken still further the united front strategy in favour of a stress on the role of the peasantry and its alliance with the working class. Voitinskii's original paragraph, expressing suspicion of Sun Yat-sen's militaristic proclivities, was left largely unmodified, and leadership in the national revolution was said to belong to the 'party of the working class.' The resolution thus exemplified all the contradictions that were to beset united front policy in the following years. It did not explain how proletarian leadership of the national revolution was to be reconciled with support for the GMD; and in calling on Sun Yat-sen to carry out land confiscation and other revolutionary measures in areas which fell under his military control, ECCI displayed illusions in the GMD that were to dog the united front policy up to its sanguinary end in the summer of 1927.[20]

In the event, this muddled directive arrived too late to have any influence on discussions at the Third Congress, which took place in the Tongshan district of Canton from 12 to 20 June 1923. Instead, Sneevliet and Chen Duxiu took the ECCI resolution of 12 January as the basis of the resolution on the national question. The latter stated that since the proletariat was not yet capable of acting as a strong independent social force, the CCP should join the GMD, while maintaining its own organization, with a view to drawing workers and left-wing elements into the GMD. It also required the CCP to work within the GMD in order to draw it away from its fixation on military matters towards revolutionary propaganda, thereby helping to forge a left wing of workers and peasants.[21] The resolution was passed by only twenty-one to sixteen votes, an indication of the continuing opposition in the CCP to the united front.[22] Zhang Guotao and Cai Hesen, in particular, were incensed by Sneevliet's readiness to see labour movement work conducted within the framework of the united front.[23] And because of the depth of the split, little was done to implement the resolution until the November plenum of the CEC, by which time Sneevliet had left China for good.[24]

On 31 July Stalin proposed to the Politburo that M.M. Borodin be sent as Soviet envoy to Sun Yat-sen to work in the 'interests of the national liberation movement in China' and 'not to be distracted by the aims of sowing Communism.'[25] He arrived in Canton on 6 October. Under Borodin's stewardship the military, political and ideological reorganization of the GMD proceeded apace. His success appears to have silenced doubts about the united front in both the CCP and ECCI. At its plenum of 24–25 November, which Voitinskii may have attended, the CEC agreed that all Communists who were not yet members of the GMD should join the party; that all should assist in expanding the GMD where conditions permitted; that both the CCP and SYL should organize secret fractions within the GMD to expand their political influence; that CCP members should strive for central positions in the party, but not by force; and that those in central positions should be financially accountable to the GMD.[26] In a resolution of 28 November ECCI, too, was far more positive than it had been at its meeting on 24 May. Its declared that the 'revolutionary elements headed by Sun' were aware of the necessity of moving closer to the labouring masses, and expressed confidence that it would encourage and support the growing labour movement. It sketched a political programme for the GMD that differed little from the minimum programme of the CCP.[27] By 1 January 1924 when Borodin addressed a joint meeting of the CCP and SYL in Shanghai he could express broad satisfaction with the political line of the CEC, whilst warning that Communists should not strive for positions on GMD committees and commissions, but allow their influence to grow naturally as a result of the increasing strength of the left.[28]

It looked as though Borodin's efforts to transform the GMD into a revolutionary nationalist party had been crowned with success at the First National Congress of the GMD, which met from 20 to 30 January 1924. This committed the party to lead the struggle against imperialism and warlordism and to carry out far-reaching economic, social and political reforms. It centralised the party structure according to a five-level hierarchy, capped by a CEC of twenty-four members of whom three were communists. On 9 February 1924 Lev Karakhan wrote to Chicherin that the congress marked a turning point: 'The GMD is turning into a really vital, active, correctly organized national-revolutionary party, such as we do not have in any other country.' He criticised 'doubters' in Moscow who were intent on cutting funds to Sun Yat-sen.[29] Yet it is notable that the architect of this transformation did not share his optimism. In a private letter of February, Borodin expressed frustration at the 'complete ideological and organizational confusion' of the GMD; at its tendency to compromise with imperialism and to neglect the mass movements; and at the utopianism and opportunism of Sun Yat-sen himself.[30]

Following the victory of the 'left' at the First GMD Congress, the plenum of the CEC of the CCP, meeting at the end of February, adopted its most accommodating policy to date towards the GMD. Its resolution would later be seized upon as evidence of Chen Duxiu's 'right-wing opportunism', though if there were an aberration in that direction, it proved to be a temporary one.[31] Nevertheless the resolution was enough to cause Voitinskii concern that the CEC had now gone too far in subordinating work among the masses to the reorganization of the GMD; and he left Moscow for China with a view to rectifying policy.[32] By the time he arrived in April 1924, however, opposition to the united front among CCP leaders had once again flared up, as a consequence of fierce attacks from the GMD right wing. At the enlarged plenum in Shanghai from 10 to 15 May, Chen Duxiu called for withdrawal from the 'bloc within' and demanded that Borodin cease to support the military activities of the GMD. Voitinskii managed to assuage the opposition by drafting a resolution which called for intensification of the struggle against the right wing and the strengthening of the CCP through an expansion of its base in the labour movement.[33]

The right wing of the GMD grew ever more vociferous. In April 1924, after a GMD member complained about statements in the SYL journal such as 'We must find ways to guide GMD meetings and work', three of the five members of the central supervisory commission of the GMD demanded the formal impeachment of the Communists. Borodin prevailed upon Sun to resist the demand, but it was a straw in the wind.[34] Once Voitinskii was back in Moscow, Chen Duxiu bombarded him with criticism of Borodin's policy, going so far on 21 July as to order party organizations to prepare to withdraw from the GMD.[35] Meanwhile at the GMD plenum from 15 to 30 August the conservatives who dominated the central supervisory commission demanded the expulsion of the Communists, whilst centrists accused them of having 'secrets' and of being intent on 'monopolising the Chinese revolution'.[36] Sun Yat-sen vigorously defended the alliance with the CCP, and a resolution passed at Borodin's behest tried to defuse tension by stating that as ordinary members of GMD, Communists were subject to normal party discipline.[37] The resolution was disingenuous, since in September the CEC sent out a circular repeating its call for the creation of secret party fractions within the GMD.[38] Borodin also proposed an international liaison commission subject to the Political Council of GMD to oversee relations between the two parties.[39] The CEC majority was still unhappy, accusing Borodin and his ally, Qu Qiubai, on 8 October of being too eager to appease the 'centre' instead of going on the attack against the right.[40] 'In view of fact that at present the GMD is full of reactionary right-wing elements and a wavering centre, and that the only commanders in the army are from the reactionary right, the GMD is absolutely unable to carry out military operations of a revolutionary character.'[41] Voitinskii felt impelled to return to China in November to sort out the trouble. He persuaded Chen Duxiu to withdraw a fresh demand that the CCP leave the GMD, in return for allowing the

CCP to concentrate on 'greater penetration of the worker-peasant masses' and on 'more open struggle with the right wing'.[42]

In fact, the Fifth Congress of the Comintern, which met in Moscow from 17 June to 18 July 1924, had prepared the ground for a shift towards a more worker-oriented policy.[43] Against a background of intensifying struggle within the Russian Communist Party, Stalin had demanded that the resolution on the national and colonial questions be reworked, since it made no mention of 'smashing the compromising bourgeoisie' or of striving for proletarian hegemony in the national revolution.[44] Stalin was now moving away from the 'stageist' conception of the national revolution that had been enunciated by the Second Comintern Congress in 1920, which had assumed that the national bourgeoisie would be the leading force in the revolution against imperialism.[45] Peng Shuzhi attended the Fifth Congress prior to leaving the Soviet Union and, upon his return to China, became the most ardent advocate of the new perspective, claiming – in a phrase that would return to haunt him – that hegemony 'naturally' (*tianran*) belonged to the proletariat, since the Chinese bourgeoisie was so feeble.[46] What remained unclear, however, was whether the proletariat was already capable of exercising hegemony in the national revolution or whether this was something to be striven for – possibly in the very long term.[47]

The Fourth CCP Congress met in Shanghai from 11 to 22 January 1925. It endorsed Voitinskii's policy of reorienting the party away from collaboration with the GMD towards independent work in the labour movement.[48] The resolution, which he drafted, characterized the GMD as 'only one'- albeit the major – element in the national liberation movement, and defined the principal task of the CCP as being to develop the labour and peasant movements. Whilst calling on comrades to build the GMD by massively strengthening its left wing, the resolution stressed the importance of exposing and isolating the right wing and of criticising the vacillating centre ('i.e. the revolutionary elements of the petty-bourgeoisie and intelligentsia').[49] The congress also ratified the new perspective of proletarian hegemony: 'The national revolution cannot win unless the most revolutionary class shares in it with all its might and leads it.'[50] What the practical implications of this perspective were remained unclear, as is evident from the fact that both defenders and opponents of the united front policy welcomed the congress as a victory.[51]

This review of Comintern policy towards the united front reveals a shift over three years. Initially, ECCI had assumed that the revolution against imperialism and warlordism would be carried out under bourgeois auspices; indeed it was because the proletariat in China was weak that the CCP was told to enter the GMD and lend support to the bloc of bourgeois and petty-bourgeois forces. By 1924 the aspirations of the Comintern had become more ambitious: now the national bourgeoisie was depicted as vacillating, whereas the proletariat was seen having the capacity to achieve hegemony in the national revolution.[52] This shift also entailed an increasingly optimistic evaluation of the GMD itself. From Sneevliet's bloc of four classes, it was increasingly seen as a radical leftist party in embryo. In a speech to students at the University of Toilers of the East (KUTV) on 18 May 1925, Stalin went so far as to speak of turning the GMD into a 'worker-peasant' party – a fatuity that reflects how little the leaders of the international Communist movement understood the complexity of class forces in China.[53] Yet in spite of this shift or, more probably, because of it, the majority of the CCP leadership never overcame its innate mistrust of the GMD. Comintern prognostications concerning the political potential of the GMD and the proletariat might have become more optimistic, but this had not eased the fundamental dilemmas of the CCP. How far should it subordinate its activities to those of the GMD and how much autonomy should it retain? How far should it seek to preserve unity in the interests of the revolution against imperialism and warlordism and how far should it actively promote social revolution?

Structure and membership of the CCP

In his report to the Third CCP Congress of June 1923, Chen Duxiu stated that national membership during the past year had risen from 195 to 420 members (of whom forty-four were abroad).[54] It may have fallen during the summer of 1923 as a consequence of divisions over the 'bloc within' policy; but it rose again during 1924 to reach 994 by the time of the Fourth CCP Congress in January 1925.[55] Membership growth was more sluggish in Shanghai. In July 1923 there were forty-four members, of whom ten were said to have left the party, been arrested or vanished.[56] On 1 June 1924 there were fifty-six members, organized into five cells, the largest being at Shanghai University with sixteen members, followed by Zhabei district with ten; Nanshi with six; the French Concession with seven; and Hongkou with five.[57] Only in the fall of 1924 did party membership in Shanghai begin to rise. By November there were 109 members organized into eight cells, of which the largest was at Shanghai University with twenty-three members.[58]

The CCP remained an organization of men (there were only a handful of women) from gentry, intellectual or merchant families with modern education. But the proportion of worker members slowly grew. At the Second Congress in June 1922 only twenty-one (10.8 per cent) out of 195 members were workers.[59] By the Third Congress in June 1923, there were 164 workers in the party, representing 39 per cent of national membership. At this date there were thirty-seven women in the party, representing 9 per cent of the membership.[60] In the Shanghai organization in May 1924 of forty-seven members, twenty-three were teachers, journalists or other professionals, thirteen were students, eight workers, and three merchants.[61] A high number of members were without regular employment which meant that many spent only a short time in Shanghai before moving on, one reason that was cited to explain why Communists had relatively few contacts with nationalist circles in the city.[62] Later in 1924, the proportion of workers began to rise, and Shanghai may have moved into line with the national picture by early 1925, when it was reckoned that 30 per cent of the approximately 1,000 party members and 9,000 Communist Youth League members were workers.[63] In late 1924 seven out of 109 members of the Shanghai regional organization were women.[64]

The CEC, set up by the Second Congress, consisted of five full members and three candidate members. Its presidium (*zhongyang ju*), which was based in Shanghai, consisted of Chen Duxiu, as party secretary, Zhang Guotao, in charge of organization, Cai Hesen, in charge of propaganda, and Xiang Jingyu, in charge of women's work.[65] In his report to the Third Congress Chen Duxiu said that the CEC did not wish to be enlarged, but the Congress nevertheless expanded it to nine full members and five candidates.[66] In May 1924 the CEC was divided into departments: Mao Zedong was put in charge of the organization department; Luo Zhanglong of the propaganda department; Wang Hebo of the worker and peasant department; Xiang Jingyu of the women's department. The CEC also had representatives in the major regions.[67] The Third Congress also set up a central bureau to preside over the day-to-day running of the party, which had its headquarters in a building known as the "three household mansion" (*Sanhulou*) in Zhabei district.[68]

The Comintern was not impressed with the way the Communists conducted business. In an article published in the Soviet Komsomol journal in 1923, Sergei Dalin described his recent experiences in China, commenting inter alia on the inability of the Chinese to drink hard liquor, the 'despairing squeal of antediluvian musical instruments' and the 'intolerable stench of bean oil'. He was particularly scathing about the conversations – 'conversations, precisely, rather than formal sessions' – through which party business was transacted:

> Matters are discussed without a chairperson or secretary and everyone speaks whenever they like or feel it necessary. Only on the following day does the secretary record decisions in the minute book. Having talked for hours it seems as though they are just about to reach a final decision when suddenly someone slaps down a small amendment, which touches on no issue of principle, and everything is once again thrown into disarray, matters of substance as well as amendments.

On one occasion, Dalin proposed that they end the discussion, allowing each side five minutes to sum up, followed by a vote.

>They fell silent, opening their eyes wide at me, so that I looked in the little mirror hanging on the wall to see if there was dirt on my face. Suddenly, they all began to laugh. I asked the interpreter what the matter was. His face expressed some surprise but he could tell me nothing ... Evidently, no one had ever made such a proposal in thousands of years of Chinese history. Later I learnt that Chinese refrain from a final decision until everyone is in agreement. It can happen that discussion goes on for days because someone has not made up their mind, but to resolve the question by voting or by limiting the time that anyone may speak is absolutely not done in China.

Dalin vowed to 'put an end to such Chinese ceremonial'![69]

It was in order to inculcate 'Bolshevik discipline' that promising members of the CCP and SYL were brought to the KUTV in Moscow for training before being sent back to take up leadership positions in the CCP. Qu Qiubai returned to China as early as January 1923, having spent two years in Russia, but he was unusual in having had no formal training. At the Third CCP Congress he was elected to the CEC.[70] According to Zheng Chaolin, although Qu was only 24, he was 'clever, learned and popular with students' and used to regale his comrades with witty anecdotes, as well as keep them au fait with literary trends. He always wore a western suit, a hat and leather shoes.[71] At the Fourth CCP Congress in January 1925, when 'proletarianization' was the *mot d'ordre*, Li Weihan asked in all seriousness how they could contemplate this when Qu Qiubai was sitting on congress presidium, dressed so suavely.[72] But let this not suggest that Qu was a dilettante. In October 1923 the writer, Xu Zhimo, was shocked to see how ravaged he had become by the tuberculosis that had dogged his health since 1919, noting how punishing was his self-imposed work regime.[73]

It was not until 1924 that most of the so-called 'Moscow branch group' returned to China to take up leading positions in the CEC and Shanghai regional committee. The two most important returnees were Peng Shuzhi and Luo Yinong, both of whom had been groomed for high office at the KUTV, where they were known by the Russian names of 'Bukharov' and 'Petrov'. The two had been the unelected leaders of the CCP branch in Moscow, lording it over their less experienced comrades. Apparently, Peng would tell new Chinese students: 'You won't be here long. Russian is not an easy language. Fortunately, there are already people among the Chinese students who know Russian well, who know theory well, and who are experienced. It's enough to learn from them.'[74] In August 1924 Peng returned to Shanghai and took over the running of the CEC propaganda department. Born in 1895 into a small landlord family in Shaoyang county in south-west Hunan, he had passed from liberalism to anarchism to

Communism in a period of little more than five years, while studying and teaching in Changsha. He was among the first group of SYL students to go to Russia in the spring of 1921, where he stayed for three-and-a-half years.[75] Short, swarthy and short-sighted, he wore a leather jacket and leather flat cap. He spoke with a thick Baoqing accent, and was nicknamed 'Confucius' by students in the Moscow group because of his habit of lecturing them at length. Later comrades in the Shanghai organization would dread his speeches, since they were always tedious, hackneyed and self-important.[76] In September 1924 Zhuang Wengong, returned from the Soviet Union and took over as secretary of the Shanghai executive committee (now renamed *Shanghai difang zhixing weiyuanhui*), which after April 1924 was theoretically responsible only for the cells within Shanghai, though it continued to oversee cells in Nanjing and Hangzhou.[77] Zhuang (real name Han Baihu), born in Shaoxing, was another alumnus of the Zhejiang First Normal School. According to Zheng Chaolin, 'he was like a primary school teacher – loyal and hardworking, but with little real ability. After the expansion of the party as a result of the May Thirtieth Movement, he was unable to cope and was replaced.'[78]

When Zheng Chaolin returned from Moscow in late summer 1924 to edit *Guide Weekly*, he moved into a house on Moulmein Road in the International Settlement which was shared by Cai Hesen and Xiang Jingyu; Li Lisan and his wife Li Yichun; Zhang Tailei's mother, wife and child; Qu Qiubai, who had recently been widowed; Peng Shuzhi and two maidservants. Zheng was struck by the transformation in Cai Hesen, whom he had known as a work-study student in France. Born in 1895 to a merchant family in Xiangxiang, Hunan province, Cai had grown up in extreme poverty after his mother left her husband. Having served as an apprentice in the family business for three years, he entered elementary school at the age of 16. Two years later, in 1913 he enrolled in the Hunan First Normal School, graduating as a teacher in 1917. After going to France in December 1919, Cai quickly developed a rather sophisticated understanding of marxism, and his correspondence with Chen Duxiu prior to the First CCP Congress was crucial in strengthening the latter's grasp of marxist theory, just as it was for Mao Zedong.[79] Cai had a stern personality, but in Paris was renowned rather for his eccentricity: 'he never washed his face, cut his hair, changed his clothes or paid attention to women.' Now Zheng Chaolin noted that his appearance had completely changed. 'His face was clean, his hair was not particularly long, and he was dressed like a country *xiucai*, quite the opposite of Qu Qiubai, who looked like one of the talented scribblers in the foreign settlement.'[80]

In January 1925 the Fourth Congress elected a new CEC which comprised nine full members and five candidates. Chen Duxiu was re-elected general secretary and also headed the CEC's organization department until Zhou Enlai took over in November 1926, followed by

Chen Qiaonian in the spring of 1927. Other members of the presidium included Zhang Guotao, Peng Shuzhi, Cai Hesen and Qu Qiubai. Zhang Guotao headed the peasant and worker department along with a new labour movement commission (*zhigong yundong weiyuanhui*), whose vice-secretaries were Li Lisan and Liu Shaoqi.[81] The Congress urged local branches to establish labour movement commissions, though nothing may have happened, since the CEC plenum of October 1925 repeated the call.[82] Chen Duxiu, Cai Hesen and Peng Shuzhi each received forty dollars per month in salary in 1924, compared with the thirty earned by Zheng Chaolin, Xiang Jingyu and others.[83] This was not high compared to the average salary of a professional, but it was still roughly double the average worker's wage.[84]

The CCP continued to rely overwhelmingly for its finances on the Comintern. In his report to the Third CCP Congress in June 1923 Chen Duxiu said: 'Party finances – practically all is received from the Comintern. Party membership dues are very little. This year expenses received from the Comintern are 15,000. Of this, 1,600 has been used for this congress.'[85] In 1923 ECCI earmarked 12,000 gold rubles for the CCP, which included 210 rubles per month for the publication of *Guide Weekly* and sixty rubles per month to pay for three full-time organizers in Shanghai (Beijing was assigned four organizers, Canton just one).[86] This compared with two million gold rubles promised to Sun Yat-sen in May 1923.[87] The CCP complained that a monthly income of 1,200 gold rubles was insufficient, and put in a request to ECCI for 1,400, 630 to cover labour movement work and 770 political and propaganda work. In addition, on 1 July 1923 it asked the Profintern for 1,000 rubles a month for labour-movement work.[88] The Comintern paid the CCP in quarterly instalments, the money being channelled through Vil'de, chief accountant of the Shanghai office of Central Union of Consumer Associations, but it often arrived late, causing the CCP severe embarrassment.[89] It could not rely on membership dues. According to a letter of Sneevliet of 20 June 1923, less than one-tenth of CCP members paid dues, since most had no jobs.[90] A report on the Shanghai region in November said that since the Third Congress, payment of dues had improved, and over half the local membership were now paying them.[91] Nevertheless in its June 1924 report the regional committee reported that in May it had received only $30 in dues instead of $130.[92]

The Shanghai Guomindang, 1923–25

In Shanghai the GMD was much weaker than in the south. On paper there were about 700 GMD members in the city in 1923, making it the second largest organization after Canton.[93] A Shanghai bureau of the Central Executive Committee existed, but it was ineffective and the infrastructure of party branches was weak. Nevertheless Sun Yat-sen's closest supporters in the party reorganization, such as Liao Zhongkai, Hu Hanmin, Wang Jingwei and Dai Jitao, were all relatively young men of letters with strong links to Shanghai.[94] In December 1923 Liao Zhongkai arrived in the city to assist in the reconstruction of the CEC, and quickly established a Shanghai executive bureau (*zhixing bu*).[95] At the time of the First GMD Congress in January 1924 there were 1,023 members in Shanghai.[96]

Following the Congress, individual Communists rapidly achieved positions of authority within the local GMD apparatus. Two Communists from Shanghai, Shen Xuanlu and Shao Lizi, were elected candidate members of the CEC, although both had a semi-detached relationship to the CCP. Neither was active in party work, albeit with the blessing of Chen Duxiu – Shen resigning officially in July 1925 and Shao in August 1926.[97] Mao Zedong occupied a powerful position in the Shanghai executive bureau, as secretary of the organization department from February to December 1924. Ye Chucang, head of the propaganda department, evidently feared his influence and schemed to have him removed. Mao's closeness to Hu Hanmin, head of the organization department – Li Lisan dubbed him 'Hu Hanmin's secretary' – may have aroused suspicions in the CCP, since he was not elected to the CEC at the Fourth Congress.[98] Other Communists with positions in the Shanghai executive bureau included Yun Daiying and Shi Cuntong in the propaganda department, which was headed by Wang Jingwei; Luo Zhanglong in the organization department; Deng Zhongxia, Wang Zhongyi, Wang Hebo and Liu Bolun in the worker-and-peasant department. In May 1924 a special labour department was set up under the chairmanship of left-leaning Yu Youren, president of Shanghai University; this fell under Communist control when Li Lisan was appointed its secretary. Communists in the women's and youth department included the secretary, Chen Bilan, who was the wife of Peng Shuzhi, Xiang Jingyu, Yang Zhihua and Wang Yizhi.[99] Considering how small the number of Communists in Shanghai was, their influence in the GMD apparat was considerable. Yet it is noteworthy that the highest positions they achieved in general were as secretaries rather department heads.[100]

During 1924 growth of the GMD in Shanghai was slow. The absence of precise membership figures reflects a general laxness in the organization. Party branches, hobbled by lack of personnel and finance, did not meet regularly, keep track of members, or train recruits.[101] At the beginning of the year, the Shanghai executive bureau presided over a city committee, seven district committees and thirty-three local branches. The largest district organization was in Zhabei, which had responsibility for six local branches, the biggest of which was at Shanghai University with 122 members. All six of the local branches were dominated by Communists. The majority of GMD members in Shanghai were students and 'cultural workers', employed in bookstores, printing houses or educational institutions.[102] The Nanshi district organization, which like the Zhabei district committee was controlled by Communists, was typical, with local branches at Qingxin middle school, a Japanese-language school, the Chinese Vocational School, the Shanghai Bookstore, the state-funded Nanyang College and the Number Two Normal School.[103] There were some worker branches, notably at the Nanyang Tobacco Company, which had over 200 members, the Commercial Press, the China Book Company, the Zhonghua iron works, the Dazhong cotton mill, the tramworkers' union, the Lingsheng printing ink company and the gold- and silver-smiths' union and the Shanghai-Hangzhou railway.[104] Many of these were under the influence of the left. In the French Concession, however, more conservative elements were well-represented. By the end of 1924, the French Concession district committee had a membership of 300, divided into twenty branches. Branches like the No. 18 branch, which consisted of fourteen military officers from Anhui, mostly in their thirties and forties, tended to support the right of the party, though Communists dominated the branch at the New Construction publishing house.[105]

Despite the dominance of Communists in many local branches, the so-called 'right wing' of the party was fairly strong in the higher echelons of the Shanghai GMD organization. The ink was barely dry on the ratification of the united front policy by the First GMD Congress when the powerful party affairs bureau (*dangwu bu*), whose premises were in Route Vallon in the French Concession, publicly opposed the new policy.[106] Prominent in the campaign against the alliance with the Communists was the secretary of the bureau, Ye Chucang, who was the prestigious editor of *Republican Daily*. In retaliation, Mao Zedong and nine other Communists issued a telegram denouncing Ye Chucang, relations reaching their nadir in September when *Republican Daily* refused to support the strike at the Nanyang tobacco company.[107] By early summer 1924, Xie Chi and the anarchist Zhang Ji, both members of the Shanghai executive bureau as well as of the central supervisory commission, had announced their opposition to Communists forming fractions in the GMD, Xie publishing the *Protect-the-Party Journal* (*Hudang tekan*).[108] In July no fewer than fifteen anti-Communist petitions were sent to Sun Yat-sen or the CEC by GMD organizations in Shanghai and Zhejiang. Typical were complaints by sixteen members of the GMD branch at Shanghai University at alleged Communist vote-rigging, and by fifty-one members at the Southern (*Nanfang*) University at the party's manipulation of the GMD for its own sectarian ends.[109] By the autumn of 1924, however, opponents of the united front had withdrawn from the executive bureau, leaving the Communists in control but the GMD considerably weakened.[110]

The CCP divided the GMD into a left wing, right wing and a centre, basically according to orientation towards the Soviet Union and the united front. These labels obscured the complexity of factional alignments inside the GMD, which to a great extent remained personalistic in character, even though Borodin's reorganization of the party did enhance the importance of ideology as a basis of factional alignment. The Communists were probably right in their view that the united front policy and the pro-Soviet orientation of Sun Yat-sen constituted the most potent source of ideological cleavage within the GMD. But they underestimated the significance of other ideological issues.[111] One such was that concerning the role and extent of mass mobilization within the national revolution. The First GMD Congress declared mass organization to be at the heart of the national revolution, and singled out five groups – peasants, workers, merchants, youth and women – for mobilization. Broadly speaking, the more conservative members of the GMD opposed the 'socialization' of the national revolution through the mass movements adhering to the traditional stance of the Alliance Society which saw the party and army as the key instruments of revolution. By contrast, those who leaned to the left believed that mass mobilization was essential if the GMD was to become a popular party capable of eradicating the social roots of warlordism and imperialism.[112] Other issues which caused ideological dissension inside the GMD concerned the relative order of importance of Sun Yat-sen's Three People's Principles and the extent to which social reform could be carried out prior to national unification, issues which for the Communists were ludicrously recondite.[113] In view of the complex interplay of ideological disagreements and personalised factions in producing political alignments inside the GMD, it is difficult – and of limited analytical value – to quantify the balance of forces inside the Shanghai GMD at this time along a simple right-left axis. In general, the effect of the ratification of the united front policy was to increase the influence of the "left" in base-level GMD branches and to give the Communists substantial influence within the Shanghai executive bureau and the Jiangsu provincial bureau. The downside for the Communists, however, was that the upsurge in their influence merely served to harden the opposition of conservative elements, some of whom had long-standing influence in the city.

The Socialist Youth League and Shanghai University

By the time of its Second Congress in August 1923, national membership of the SYL had dropped to 2,000.[114] This fall appears to have been due to activists having to go underground, following the massacre on the Beijing-Hankou railway, and to their channelling their energies into the reorganization of the GMD. Membership failed to grow substantially during 1924, standing at 2,365 in January 1925.[115] In Shanghai by May 1924 there were 180 members of the SYL, organized into eleven branches, the largest of which was at Shanghai University with seventy-seven members.[116] In spite of sluggish growth, the membership of the SYL was still five times that of the CCP and, although intended to be an ancillary body of the latter, it continued to overshadow its parent party until well into 1925. It also remained an overwhelmingly student body, with workers comprising less than 10 per cent of members.[117]

During the years 1922 to 1923 the national student movement was in the doldrums. However, the influence of the SYL within it was out of all proportion to its numbers. The National Student Union (NSU) was the first of the mass organizations in China to adopt a radical nationalist programme committed to anti-imperialism and anti-warlordism, at the fourth national student congress in Shanghai on 15 March 1923. It may have been this action which prompted the warlord authorities to close the NSU office shortly afterwards.[118] Yet Moscow was unimpressed by the SYL's achievements in the student movement. On 31 May 1923 the executive of KIM sent a letter to the SYL in advance of its Second Congress, complimenting it on organizing solidarity action in the wake of the massacre of railway workers on the Beijing-Hankou railway, but criticising it for doing too little to mobilize working-class youth, and calling on the forthcoming congress to make its priority the organization of SYL cells in factories and SYL fractions in all labour organizations. However, it also ordered the SYL to press for a national student congress in the near future and to ensure that it had fractions in all local student associations.[119]

At the Second Congress of the SYL, which met in Nanjing in August 1923, delegates backed the 'bloc within' tactic. Members of the SYL were ordered to join the GMD as individuals, and to form SYL fractions inside the GMD accountable to the CCP and SYL. The congress decided to replace its journal, *The Pioneer*, twenty-five numbers of which had appeared, with *Chinese Youth* (*Zhongguo qingnian*), under the editorship of Yun Daiying in Shanghai, the first issue of which came out in November 1923. Unlike *The Pioneer*, whose project was still in part influenced by the ideology of the May Fourth Movement, *Chinese Youth* was a typical organ of Communist propaganda.[120] The congress elected Liu Renjing secretary of the SYL, Deng Zhongxia head of organization and Yun Daiying head of propaganda. Upon his return from the Soviet Union in the summer of 1924, Ren Bishi, one of the 'Moscow branch group', was quickly thrust to prominence, despite never having been elected to the CEC. Born to a scholar family in Xiangyin county in Hunan, Ren, who was still only 20, looked like a young boy since he was slight of stature with a high-pitched voice.[121] In January 1925, when the SYL was transformed into the CYL, he was picked by Moscow for the job of general secretary, since Zhang Tailei had fallen into disfavour because of an affair with Wang Yizhi, the wife of Shi Cuntong. In the event, however, Zhang was re-elected secretary and Ren became head of the organizational bureau.[122] Zhang Qiuren remained secretary of the Shanghai regional committee.

In Shanghai the student movement was also in relative abeyance in the years 1923–24, with the singular exception of Shanghai University, which is discussed below. After 1920 the Shanghai Student Union (SSU) fell into desuetude and, despite several attempts to revive it, failed to become a significant force until early 1925. The NSU, whose headquarters were in Shanghai, continued to be more active but suffered periodic harassment by the authorities.[123] At its fifth congress in Canton in August 1923 the NSU passed an SYL resolution calling on all local student organizations to make the overthrow of foreign imperialism their principal task, and Yu Zhenhong, Li Shixun, He Chengxiang and Guo Bohe were among the SYL members elected to the executive.[124] Increasingly, the SYL used the women's and youth department of the Shanghai executive bureau of the GMD as the medium through which to influence the political direction of the student movement. At its sixth congress in August 1924 the NSU called for a radical overhaul in the structure of the student movement, based on strong local and regional organizations. After Shanghai became embroiled in the war between Jiangsu and Zhejiang militarists in September 1924, the campaign for a national assembly grew apace, and the NSU played an active part in popularizing this among local student organizations.[125] Finally in December seven colleges, led by Shanghai University, seized control of the moribund SSU, electing Liu Yijing of Shanghai University to be its chair.[126] In that month, however, Voitinskii complained that the SYL was losing respect by too obviously seeking to control the city's student movement.[127]

1924 also saw a revival of the anti-Christian movement which had been flagging since 1922. In August 1924 the SYL formed the Shanghai Anti-Christian Alliance, headed by a committee of five persons, including Zhang Qiuren and two other Communists. Its constitution was written by Wu Zhihui, quondam anarchist and increasingly a force on the GMD 'right'. The Alliance published a short-lived journal and Zhang penned a number of anti-religious broadsides in *Republican Daily*, *Awakening*, and *Chinese Youth*.[128] The focus of the campaign was now upon missionary schools and colleges, which were denounced for their denial of freedom of thought and action, their spiritual terrorism (their resort to the threat of eternal damnation), their victimization of non-believers and their reprisals against students who participated in the patriotic movement. At Christmas 1924 and Chinese New Year demonstrations were organized and cards were printed with messages such as 'Christianity is a tool of world imperialism'.[129]

Throughout these rather quiet years the torch of student protest was held aloft by Shanghai University, which from its inception proved to be the most successful example of the united front in action in the city.[130] It originated in student unrest at the Southeast Higher Normal School in October 1922. After ten months of deliberation, the GMD agreed to take

67

over the college as a 'party school', although it was not until 28 December 1923 that it was placed on a stable financial footing by Hu Hanmin.[131] Its president was Yu Youren, formerly a professor at Fudan University. The aim of the new university was declared to be to 'nurture human talent for the construction of the nation in accordance with the Three People's Principles.'[132] Most of the staff were GMD members, mainly on the left of the party, but Communists enjoyed a colossal influence.[133] In April 1923, Deng Zhongxia, with backing from Li Dazhao, was put in charge of university administration, and because Yu Youren spent relatively little time at the university, was able to stamp his mark upon the institution, at least until the summer of 1924 when he resigned to concentrate on full-time party work. Qu Qiubai was made dean of the social science faculty, which quickly established itself as the hub of the university's intellectual life, teaching a syllabus with a strongly contemporary and revolutionary cast. At various times its lecturers included Cai Hesen, Yun Daiying, Zhang Tailei, Peng Shuzhi, An Ticheng, Li Da, Shen Zemin and Ren Bishi. Chen Wangdao headed the Chinese Literature Faculty, where Shao Lizi, Shen Yanbing and Zheng Zhenduo taught.[134] When Communist students in the social science faculty demanded the removal of He Shizhen, a GMD rightist, as dean of the English faculty, his students retaliated by demanding that Qu Qiubai be removed as dean of the social science faculty. The resulting feud eventually led to He removing the English faculty from the university in the fall of 1924, but not before he had forced out Qu from his position. Shi Cuntong took over as dean of social sciences, a rumour circulating to the effect that he had helped engineer Qu's ouster.[135]

In February 1924 the university moved from its cramped premises in Zhabei into the International Settlement. By that date it had nearly 400 students, over twenty departments and a fair-sized library. Most students came from public high and normal schools in Sichuan, Hunan, Zhejiang and Jiangsu, and already had some experience of political activity. Women were in a minority among the students, but there was a women's student association. SYL and CCP members dominated the student union.[136] The university, which did not register with the Ministry of Education, was looked down upon by other colleges in the city as a 'pheasant [i.e. third-rate] university'. And it appears that, with the honourable exception of Li Ji, most lecturers who were also members of the CCP approached their teaching duties in a perfunctory fashion.[137] Deng Zhongxia conceded that the university had little in the way of an academic reputation, but said that students were inspired by its militant patriotism.[138] Dubbed the 'Shanghai School of Bolshevism' by the International Settlement authorities, it became the chief centre of revolutionary activity in the city between spring 1924 and the May Thirtieth Movement, supporting the strikes by silk women, the Nanyang tobacco workers and the workers in the Japanese cotton mills. Its students also undertook investigations into the social conditions of the poor.[139] On 9 December the University was raided by the International Settlement police, who seized over 700 books. 'The officers conducting the search remarked that ... the students had the walls of their sleeping apartments decorated with photos of the Russian Communist revolutionaries.' Shao Lizi, acting president of the University, was arrested, but the case against him was dismissed.[140]

The CCP and the Women's Movement

The united front policy implied a more positive orientation to progressive forces of all kinds, including the middle-class women's organizations. At the Third CCP Congress in June 1923, Xiang Jingyu drafted the resolution on the women's movement, which was more positive with regard to the latter than that passed by the Second Congress. Communist women were summoned to unify the different strands of the women's movement – for women's rights, suffrage, social reform – by forming a national centre and by publishing a feminist journal. The resolution dealt with the panoply of issues relating to women's political rights, right to education, equality before the law, concubinage, the sale of women, and prostitution. Of particular note was the resolution's condemnation of male chauvinism in the labour movement. Comrades were warned not to slight the women's movement as being one of 'ladies and young misses' (xiaojie taitai) or of female politicians on the make. They were also warned not to emphasize class issues too stridently, so as to avoid alienating middle-class women. The key task was to be the integration of the women's movement into the broader nationalist movement.[141]

From January 1923 the Shanghai regional committee of the CCP had its own women's committee, chaired by Xiang Jingyu.[142] From September 1923 she channelled all CCP women's work through the GMD. In April 1924 she became head of the newly-formed women's-movement committee of the Shanghai executive bureau of the GMD, whose membership quickly grew from thirty to more than sixty members. At its core was a group of Communists who, in addition to Yang Zhihua and Li Yichun, included Zhang Jinqiu, the wife of Shen Zemin, He Baozhen, the wife of Liu Shaoqi, and Wang Yizhi, the wife of Shi Cuntong. The influence of the committee was mainly confined to students and intellectuals, since night schools failed to attract significant numbers of working-class women.[143] Xiang Jingyu also became editor of *Women's Weekly* (*Funü zhoubao*), which was published as a supplement of the *Republican Daily* from August 1923 to January 1926. It carried articles on love, sexuality and morality, and called on feminist groups to orient towards the working class in order to create a mass women's movement.[144] Xiang spearheaded intervention by the women's movement on a wide range of issues, her greatest achievement being to initiate the Committee to Promote Women's Participation in the National Assembly (*Funü guomin huiyi cuchenghui*), after Sun Yat-sen warmed to this idea in 1924. Its aims were to 'resolve national affairs (*jiejue guoshi*) and to liberate women.'[145] By 21 December 1924 at least ten women's organizations had responded to the initiative. On 5 January 1925 the committee declared: 'We women are citizens too. We must, of course, bear the same responsibility as men in solving (the problems of) the country ... However, because we women have suffered thousands of years of inhuman treatment, our position is seen as special. We have no choice but to insist that the only progressive policy is for women's organizations to be represented among the popular organizations in the National Assembly.'[146] The campaign went into overdrive in February when Duan Qirui, chief executive of the Beijing government, adopted draft regulations which gave only men the right to vote. The Shanghai branch of the committee put out a hard-hitting statement on 28 February condemning him for 'insulting the dignity of women'. 'We swear to fight for justice, for women's rights and for the right to participate in the National Assembly.'[147] On 22 March some 200 women from forty organizations met to form the Shanghai women's citizens' assembly. Xiang Jingyu gave the main report and the meeting ended with shouts of 'Long Live Women's Rights, Long Live the Rights of the People'.[148] When the constitution of the Assembly was finally published, the committee contemptuously dismissed it as the 'men's national assembly'.[149]

The Communists retreat from the labour movement, February 1923 to fall 1924

The 7 February massacre created a climate of repression which made labour organization extremely difficult for at least eighteen months. In his report to the Third Congress in June 1923 Chen Duxiu described workers' organizations in Shanghai as 'very backward'. He said that the party had links with a small group of workers in the metal trades (*wujin*), which probably refers to the mechanics' club, but implied that the GMD, with a base among the seamen and the Nanyang tobacco workers, was much stronger.[150] During June and July Communists tried to revive the postal workers' club, but their success in recruiting seventy to eighty members caused the postal authorities to close it down. At the May 1924 CEC plenum the report on the Shanghai district said that 'the labour movement we have organized up to now did not penetrate the mass of workers, it remained on the surface. Therefore we failed every time. Up to now the results have been nil.'[151]

During this period the number of labour unions in Shanghai grew, even though most were tiny. It was the influence of the right wing of the

GMD, however, rather than that of the CCP, which proved all-important. Estimates of the number of labour associations vary. Deng Zhongxia reckoned that in 1923 a couple of dozen labour organizations were active, with a membership of 16,300, of whom 5,000 were industrial workers. This compared with 32,300 organized workers in Wuhan and 50,000 in Canton and Hong Kong.[152] With the establishment of the Shanghai Federation of Syndicates (SFS) (*Shanghai gongtuan lianhehui*) in 1924, however, the number of organized workers in Shanghai may have grown to 84,000.[153] The SFS, which was formally inaugurated on 8 March 1924, was the brainchild of GMD members hostile to the united front with the CCP. Thirty-two labour organizations affiliated to it, the most significant being the mechanics' union, the silk women's association and the Nanyang tobacco company friendly society.[154] The SFS was defined by its animosity towards the CCP, but it campaigned to improve wages, working conditions and the educational level of the working class, and was instrumental in the formation of several unions, particularly in the handicraft sector. Since it believed that the interests of workers and employers were fundamentally similar during the national revolution, it had little enthusiasm for strikes.[155]

In a report of 1 June 1924 the regional committee of the CCP declared the SFS a dangerous influence in the Shanghai labour movement, both organizationally and politically. It agreed to send a dozen labour organizations into the Federation with the aim of undermining it.[156] Predictably, since the party did not have a dozen labour unions to send, this policy came to nothing. The SFS failed to support the strike at the Nanyang tobacco company in September 1924, since the company was owned by national capitalists loyal to the GMD, causing the CCP to condemn it as a band of 'scabs' (*gongzei*).[157] The difficulties of deciding how best to respond to the Communist-led strike in the Japanese cotton mills in February 1925 led to divisions in the leadership of the SFS and wavering among some of its affiliated organizations. Nevertheless in the spring thirty-three organizations associated with the SFS denounced the Communists for taking it upon themselves to organise the Second National Labour Congress. The fact that it went ahead in May, however, underlined the waning influence of the SFS.[158]

At the CEC plenum in May 1924 the regional committee decided to try to make contact with local workers by setting up common people's schools. Deng Zhongxia, former president of the LOS, played a pivotal role in this. Born in 1894 in Yizhang county, Hunan province, into a gentry official family, his mother died when he was seven years old, and his step-mother treated him cruelly. At the age of 15, his parents arranged for him to be married; but two years later, in 1915, he left his wife to enrol in the Hunan higher normal school in Changsha. In 1917, he entered the literature faculty of Beijing University. In 1919 he was active in the common people's education movement in that city and in October 1920 became a member of the Beijing Communist 'small group'. He gained considerable experience as a labour organizer at the Changxindian workers club on the Jing-Han railway, but after this was crushed in February 1923, he fled to Shanghai where, with Li Dazhao's help, he became head of administration at Shanghai University.[159] At Deng's instigation, on 15 April teachers and students at Shanghai University set up a people's school (*pinmin xuexiao*), which offered free tuition to workers and their children, plus night classes in English.[160] Bu Shiji, a Communist active in the Zhabei district committee of the GMD, was the first principal of the school. Yang Zhihua, partner of Qu Qiubai, taught at the school, though Communists were in a minority on the staff. The school asked local millowners for financial support, arguing that the strength of the nation was determined by the educational level of its people.[161] The initial enrolment consisted of 280 pupils, of whom one-fifth were children, including factory workers, shop clerks, apprentices, bookstore and printing house employees, newspaper proof-readers and elementary school teachers. They were divided into classes for literate and illiterate adults, literate and illiterate children, and for adult women. By November the school had 460 pupils.[162]

Students were eager to volunteer as teachers in the common people's schools. Soon eight schools were operating in Shanghai and Wusong, all funded by the GMD.[163] On 1 June 1924 students from Shanghai University set up a school in Yangshupu district. It had 150 students, all mill-workers, divided into a class for men and a class for women. They studied Chinese, arithmetic, history, geography and English at twice-weekly classes.[164] The No.2 People's school in Zhabei had an initial enrolment of 500, which soon fell to around 100. Teachers were drawn from the Shanggong college and from the Commercial Press. The curriculum included tuition in 1,000 basic Chinese characters, plus public speaking and a weekly choir.[165] Women outnumbered men in all five classes. Given the prejudice against female education, the number of women who enrolled in the common people's schools was impressive. One satirical account suggested that the only reason men enrolled was to find a girlfriend.[166]

Through the common people's schools the Communists hoped to stimulate class consciousness and the will to fight.[167] To this end, they experimented with new methods of teaching. Xiang Jingyu wrote militant songs for her pupils about the condition of women.[168] Li Lisan, who arrived in Shanghai in April 1924, had developed a system for teaching one-thousand characters during his time among the miners of Anyuan in Hunan, which began by showing that if one placed the character for 'labour' on top of the character for 'person' it made the character for heaven; and if one divided the second character in the word for 'gentleman' (*xiansheng*), it consisted of a cow (*niu*) on the ground (*tu*).[169] It should be noted that knowledge of 1,000 characters was quite insufficient to read a newspaper, still less a novel.

The people's schools allowed the Communists to make contact with activist workers, with a view to reviving the labour unions, since their ostensibly non-political character meant that they were tolerated by the authorities. Moreover, the GMD banner under which they were organized served as a magnet for patriotic workers. After two years of gloom, the CEC plenum of December 1924 could report that the party was at last making headway. It said that it had organized illegal 'unions' among textile workers, mechanics and tobacco workers with a total membership of 2,000 (in fact, these were 'cells' of two workers' clubs); that it was publishing a weekly paper, the *Shanghai Worker*; and that the *Guide Weekly*, whose print-run had increased from 4,000 to 6,000 per week, was managing to circulate openly.[170]

The picture which emerges of the operation of the united front in Shanghai is complex. To some degree, the alliance operated according to plan: Communists took up positions within the GMD apparat, and in sectors such as the student and women's movements the parties cooperated rather successfully. In both parties, however, there was strong opposition to the policy, which meant that the 'bloc within' was only ever applied partially. Just as the Communists preserved their independent organization, so opponents of the united front within the GMD created bases outside the official party structures, even as they continued informally to carry influence in the highest reaches of the party. With regard to the labour movement, the Communists in Shanghai never tried to carry out the policy agreed at the Third CCP Congress in June 1923, of 'joint control' (although the Communists in Canton did).[171] And the May 1924 CEC plenum reaffirmed the correctness of the policy of working in the labour movement as an independent party.[172] It is true that in setting up common people's schools the Communists benefited from their alliance with GMD, but in general work in the labour movement was characterised by rivalry rather than cooperation. The Communists were trounced by GMD labour leaders opposed to the united front, who succeeded in creating the first effective federation of labour unions in the city precisely as a bulwark against Communism. The SFS did not last long, yet the conflict between two opposed perspectives for integrating labour into the national revolution proved to be enduring.

Chapter 4 _____

The Communists Perfect a Labour Movement Strategy

The Fourth CCP Congress met in Shanghai from 11 to 22 January 1925. It discussed the relationship between the labour movement and the nationalist movement in detail. Its resolution started from the premise that in a semi-colonial country 'the working class not only fights for its own class interests, but at the same time participates in the national revolution, and indeed must assume the leading role in the national movement.'[1] It went on to call for the unification of 'all types of industrial workers in independent organizations of a pure-class type and under the leadership of our party.'[2] It emphasised the need to build independent trade unions outside the framework of the united front, but it qualified this by stating that 'if within the Guomindang there develops a left-wing force based on the labouring masses, we must at the right time and to the right degree lead workers in large-scale industry into the Guomindang so as to give the party a decisively revolutionary character.'[3] 'As regards those labour organizations that already exist under the banner of the Guomindang, we must make every effort to get involved in them, to acquire leadership of them, to absorb the conscious elements and to organize party branches within them .... Above all, when economic conflicts break out between workers and employers, we must use them to raise the class consciousness of the workers and reveal the nature of the Guomindang, and develop a trend towards the workers' own political party – the CCP.'[4]

The Congress also discussed the tactics of creating labour-union cells (*xiaozu*), tactics first outlined at the CEC plenum of May 1924.[5] The resolution stated: 'In the present situation there is more opportunity for open work, so we must hasten to implement the policy of factory cells, so that we can genuinely penetrate the masses, ensure victory over the reactionaries within the labour unions, and establish a real base for ourselves in the labour movement.'[6] Cells were to be limited to a single workshop and each cell was to elect a delegate to a factory committee, which was to operate as the highest organ of the labour union in the enterprise. 'Where open activity is impossible, the cells must operate in absolute secrecy. In labour unions that are under the control of the reactionaries this form of organization is most suitable.'[7] The decision to opt for cells as the *points d'appui* of union organization – rather than factory or district branches – was influenced not only by security concerns, but also by the fact that organization at the level of the shop-floor cell alone could hope to supplant the dense network of social ties that existed among rank-and-file workers.

Workers' Clubs

In the fall of 1924 the Communists began to form workers' clubs out of the common people's schools. On 1 September the West Shanghai Workers' Club was formed out of two evening classes that were being run by Ji Zhi and Xu Wei at the No.1 Workers' Continuation School in Xiaoshadu. Initially, the club had about thirty members, mainly workers from Naigai Wata Kaisha (NWK) mills Nos. 4, 5, 8 and 9. It served as a social centre where workers could chat, play chess or table tennis, play musical instruments, sing songs or *tanhuang* (Shanghai regional opera), watch *shuanghuang* (an entertainment in which one person stands behind another so that he is invisible and speaks or sings, while the person in front acts out the content of the speech or song). Much of the content of the singing or drama was political and satirical. A lecture society proved especially popular.[8] Education continued to be a central element in the club's activities but Jiang Weixin, a worker at NWK No.5, said that he learnt less than he had done at the half-time school, since lessons were little more than political propaganda, and much time was spent distributing leaflets.[9] The constitution of the club defined its aims as being: 'the cementing of fellow-feeling (*lianluo ganqing*), the exchange of knowledge, the promotion of mutual aid and the common pursuit of happiness.'[10] The club was open to any man or woman willing to accept its rules, subject to recommendation by an existing member. The rules required compliance with collective decisions, the dissolving of selfish interests into the collective, the avoidance of any word or action that might disrupt the organization, the rejection of internal strife and mutual antagonism between members, and the prompt payment of subscriptions, fixed at ten coppers per month for those earning less than $10; one jiao for those earning $10 to $15; and two jiao for those earning $15 to $25.[11] That this was not a club in the conventional sense is shown by the fact that it sought to create cells in the principal factories as embryonic labour unions.[12]

Although intellectuals were the key organizers of the club, its chair was Sun Lianghui, a textile worker of Manchu origin, who in 1921 had helped set up the Pudong weavers' union. As a result of his union activities, he lost his job, and by 1924 was working as a guard at a bank. He joined the CCP in that year, the first worker in Xiaoshadu district to do so.[13] Liu Hua soon became secretary of the club. Born in 1899 into a tenant-farmer family of five children in Yibin county, Sichuan, Liu had a primary education in the Baofeng temple school. In August 1920, through a contact in Chengdu, he was taken on as an apprentice lithographer at the China Book company in Shanghai. After three years' apprenticeship, he enrolled on a part-time basis at the middle school attached to Shanghai University. On 23 November 1923 he was recruited into the CCP and by January was chair of the Shanghai University branch, whose sixteen members comprised students and teachers.[14] Because of his good looks and effective speaking style, it was said that he could hold a working-class audience in the palm of his hand.[15]

In Yangshupu, the eastern district of the city, Cai Zhihua set up the Workers Moral Progess Society (*Gongren jindehui*) in premises behind the Yong'an mill. Cai was born in 1898 in Huarong county, Hunan, and had been a part-time work-study student in France and then at the KUTV from 1923–4.[16] Teachers at the club included Wu Xianqing (1904–37), a woman 'with short hair' from Hangzhou, and Zhou Jinjiang, said to have been an instigator of the February mill strikes, but not, apparently, a Communist.[17] The Society put on literacy classes, lectures and plays and began to forms cells in local factories. That at the Ta Kong (Dakang) mill soon had over a hundred members. Communists, however, soon lost influence in the cell to secret-society bosses.[18] There was also a strong branch at the Toyo (Yufeng) mill. By early 1925 there may have been as many as 1,100 in the 'cells' around the Moral Progress Society.[19] Although it had fewer members than the latter, the West Shanghai club had a stronger core of seventy to eighty activists, who formed 'cells' in nineteen cotton mills with up to 1,000 members. The main ones were at the NWK Nos. 3, 4 and 9 mills and at the Doko (Tongxing) mill, where there were forty active members and several dozen less active ones.[20]

The Japanese Mills Strike

In the wake of the Fourth Congress, the West Shanghai Workers' Club looked for an opportunity to test its strength in battle with the employers.[21] The chance came when trouble broke out at the NWK No.8 mill on 2 February 1925, after a girl of twelve was caught napping at her fly-frame on the night shift. The Japanese supervisor flew into a rage and kicked the girl, whereupon an 'elder sister' complained to the manager and was herself slapped in the face. The incident infuriated fifty men who worked in the roving shop, notwithstanding the fact that their own position was being undermined by girls such as the one who had been slapped, since the company had since 1922 gradually been replacing adult male workers with girl apprentices (*yangchenggong*). As soon as the men protested, they were fired *en masse* for being 'trouble makers' (*bu an fen*). Some had connections with the Workers Club.[22] Two days later, when six of the sacked men came to claim their deposit money, they were accused of returning in order to stir up a strike and were promptly arrested.[23] The average age of the men was twenty-five, and four were married. All came from Subei, the northern part of Jiangsu province above the Yangtze river, which was an impoverished and declining region, prone to flooding. Immigrants from Subei faced considerable prejudice in Shanghai, where they tended to be concentrated in the least skilled and worst paid jobs.[24] One was given three weeks imprisonment, the other five were cautioned.[25] It was this sequence of events that led to the largest strike yet seen in Shanghai – discounting the strikes in support of the May Fourth Movement – and it was to mark a turning-point in the relationship of the CCP to the city's labour force.

From the first, the leaders of the West Shanghai Workers' Club were determined that the NWK company should not get away with such high-handed action. They were anxious, however, that a strike should not begin before the workers had been paid. On 8 February rumours reached the International Settlement police that a strike was to start the next day. The club took the precaution of moving out of the International Settlement into derelict premises in Sande alley, Tanziwan in Zhabei, adjacent to a piece of waste ground. This had the advantage of being on the north bank of Suzhou creek, opposite NWK nos.5E and 5W, 7, 8 and 12 mills in Ichang / Macao Road on the other side of the creek. On the morning of 9 February about 9,000 workers at these mills stopped work to hold a mass meeting. As they streamed out, they threw down their company hats and stamped on them, shouting 'We will no longer wear East Asian hats!' Placards at the meeting read: 'We resolutely oppose East Asians beating people'. Ten arrests were made. Speaker teams were formed to publicize the strikers' cause and handbills printed containing the strikers' demands.[26] That evening a meeting of representatives from the five mills set up a strike committee, which drew up the following demands: 1) an end to beatings; 2) a 10 per cent wage rise and no deduction of wages without reason; 3) the reinstatement of workers who had lost their jobs and the release of those in detention; 4) prompt payment of wages once every two weeks; 5) payment for the period of the strike; and 6) no dismissals without due cause.[27]

Force was used to bring out workers in the remaining mills belonging to the NWK company. By 13 February all ten mills were at a standstill, with some 15,000 workers on strike.[28] On the 14th the strike extended to the Nikko (Rihua) nos.3 and 4 mills at 98 Robison Road, also in the western part of the city.[29] On the same day the strike spread to the Doko mill in Yangshupu district at the other end of the city. The next day in the far west of Shanghai a party set out from Jessfield village for the Toyota (Fengtian) cotton mill, led by secret-society members who ruled the roost in the workers' settlement at Zhoujiaqiao.[30] Thirty youths scaled the walls of the mill and lit a fire, apparently as a signal to those outside to break down the factory gates. The marauders did considerable damage and it was with difficulty that they were evicted by Japanese supervisors and International Settlement police. Outside a crowd of 700 men and women, led by the woman teacher, Wu Xianqing, brandishing a white flag, worked itself into a frenzy. Chinese police arrived and fired shots in an effort to disperse it. Supposing the shots to have been fired by the Japanese staff, the crowd tried to storm the factory gates. When a car carrying seven Japanese drew up, it was pounced upon, and the passengers were savagely beaten up with sticks. Mr Harada, the mill manager of Toyota, who had allegedly once kicked a woman in the stomach, subsequently died of his injuries. Another passenger was shot through the chest and a third was beaten and thrown into the Suzhou Creek.[31] The International Settlement police, who had authority to operate only on the road itself, arrested nine people, complaining bitterly of the laxity of the Chinese authorities.[32] The average age of the nine men arrested, mainly employees of the Toyota mill, was just under twenty. Significantly, all bar one were from Subei and had been in Shanghai for three years on average. All lived in the same workers' settlement.[33] On 18 February the strike reached its zenith, with 30,800 workers in twenty-two mills belonging to six different Japanese companies in Xiaoshadu and Yangshupu at a halt. Half-a-dozen Japanese mills outside the western district of the city, employing about 12,500 workers, continued to work normally, including the two Nikko mills in Pudong.[34]

Leadership and organization in the strike

The strike was the first test of the CCP's new strategy. In overall charge were Li Lisan and Deng Zhongxia, both Hunanese and both recently elected to the CEC labour movement commission at the Fourth Congress. The head of the commission, Zhang Guotao, did not arrive in Shanghai until 16 March when the strike was over.[35] Voitinskii was also in the city at this time, and he and Chen Duxiu was consulted on all important matters.[36] Li Lisan, aged twenty-five, was the eldest son of a poor rural school-teacher in Liling county in Hunan. After his expulsion from France in late 1921 for his involvement in the occupation of the dormitory at Lyon University, he went to Anyuan in his native province to organize miners. Arriving in Shanghai in April 1924, he became head of the worker-peasant bureau of the Shanghai regional committee. He was tall and strong with flashing eyes, heavy red lips and rather white skin. He had a loud, clear voice. He lacked a sense of humour and was easily provoked.[37] His rival as a labour organizer was Xiang Ying, the driving force behind the West Shanghai Workers' Club. Born in 1898 in Wuchang in Hubei province, Xiang had been an active labour organizer in Wuhan, forming a mechanics' union and promoting the Beijing-Hankou railway workers' union. After joining the CCP in 1922, he became chair of the Hubei provincial general labour union, a member of the executive of the National

General Labour Union and secretary of the CEC's labour movement committee.[38]

Li Lisan and Deng Zhongxia brought together the leaders of the West Shanghai Workers' Club, including Liu Hua, Sun Lianghui and Liu Guanzhi, to form a central strike committee. Yang Zhihua was also brought on to the committee, since her speeches were said to thrill the mill women. She dressed as a mill worker and took a close interest in the women's personal as well as working lives, meeting them at the Jade Buddha Temple, where they would act like pilgrims to avoid provoking suspicion. When teased by male comrades for being a believer, she would retort: 'Isn't it a good thing to be a rebel believer?'[39] In Xiaoshadu and Yangshupu there were also district strike committees, the latter led by Cai Zhihua, secretary of the Workers' Moral Progress Society.

In all, only four to five Communists, plus about ten members of the CYL, were involved in the strike, so they relied heavily on sympathetic students.[40] According to the *North China Herald*, 'In the riots of last Tuesday and again on Sunday, students were seen among the ranters and flag-waggers, one or two of them even being girls . . . And although the boy or girl who runs out to shout for the strikers, in a spasm of deluded self-righteousness, may be an object more pathetic than blameable, at the back of them is often a teacher of vituperous malignity.'[41] One such student was Dai San, described by the International Settlement police as the 'number one leader of the strike'. He was a student at Daxia University and was not yet a member of the CCP; he was sentenced to twenty-five days in prison for his part in the unrest.[42] At factory level the leaders of the strike were often foremen and interpreters, who commanded authority on the basis of clientelist or secret-society ties. If we look at those for whom the International Settlement police issued arrest warrants, of the eleven named as instigators of the troubles at Toyota, no fewer than eight were foremen (several from Subei) and one an interpreter. And those wanted in connection with inciting the strike at the Nikko mills included six foremen, a forewoman, three mill clerks and an interpreter. The picture at the NWK mills was similar.[43] During the strike, however, there also emerged a small layer of worker militants, some already groomed by the West Shanghai Workers' Club, who would go on to become activists in the cotton workers' federation. The average age of forty-nine workers and employees, who were arrested for riot, intimidation and other offences, was 23.6. Of those for whom we have information, fifteen were single and eight were married. No fewer than twenty-seven were from Subei, not counting six from Yangzhou (on the southwestern corner of Subei), three from Shanghai and three from Nanjing.[44] In Yangshupu, where twenty-one were workers were arrested, of sixteen whose address is known, no fewer than thirteen lived in mill accommodation, suggesting that collective residence, too, was an important factor in generating cohesion and purpose.[45]

In each of the six companies affected by the stoppage a strike committee was formed to organize pickets to maintain order and prevent strike-breaking. These were formed on a traditional decimal basis, with a team (*xiaodui*) of ten pickets electing a representative to a team of ten at the next highest level, and so on up to a supreme coordinating team of ten.[46] At NWK sixty-seven teams of pickets were formed, including fourteen consisting of women.[47] Some were stationed at the landing stages on the north bank of Suzhou creek, where NWK employees crossed each day to go to work. Pickets confiscated the work books of those suspected of trying to break the strike.[48] At the Doko mill, which employed 500 men, 3,000 women and 100 girls, mostly from Subei, there were sixty teams of pickets.[49] And the Nikko and Toyota strike committees jointly formed sixty-four teams of pickets to maintain order in the Jessfield area.[50] The picket at Toyota was said to consist exclusively of secret-society members.[51] In addition, a body called the volunteer corps (*yiyongdui*) was set up, whose job was to defend the strike against outside attackers and to smash up factories when necessary.[52]

The strike committees were subordinate to the central strike committee at general headquarters (*zong zhihui chu*) at the West Shanghai Workers' Club in Tanziwan. The latter had a secretariat and sections responsible for propaganda, communications, news and printing; it was also responsible for fund-raising and for forming a defence corps. It was able to function more or less openly, since it was within Chinese jurisdiction and the authorities were told by the new Beijing government not to be too heavy-handed towards the strikers.[53] The leaders at general headquarters worked hard to keep up the momentum of the strike, to ensure effective coordination, to see that mass meetings were held regularly, to convey news, keep up spirits, and check that the factory delegate system functioned properly. On the north bank of Suzhou creek there were virtually non-stop demonstrations designed to maintain morale. 'Banners were waved, inflammatory leaflets distributed and would-be peaceful work people interfered with.'[54] Much of the energy of activists, especially students, went into winning public support and raising funds for the strikers.

At the start of the strike the workers were promised two jiao ($0.2) per day for the duration of the strike, on condition that they registered their names with the strike committee.[55] This was a paltry sum, but the West Shanghai Workers' Club had no funds of its own, so payment did not begin until late into the strike.[56] Thirty-thousand rubles was said to have been sent by the Profintern (half of it coming via the All-Union Central Council of Trade Unions of the USSR), but it is unlikely that it reached the city during the strike itself, for after ten days it was reported that all funds had dried up. The International Settlement police, however, claimed that some funds also came from the USSR via Daxia university.[57] The strikers relied mainly on contributions from the public, including donations from Chinese Millowners Association (*Huashang shachang lianhehui*) and owners of public utilities in Zhabei.[58] In an attempt to break the strike several companies offered to pay employees 30 per cent of their daily wage if they signed in for work. The strike leaders urged workers not to do so, but to little avail.[59] On 13 February the NWK company announced that 39.6 per cent of the day shift and 45.4 per cent of the night shift had reported for duty.[60] By 16 February this had risen to 62 per cent and 72 per cent; by 18 February to 72 per cent and 77 per cent; and by the 19th to 84 per cent and 88 per cent.[61] These figures may be exaggerated, but they suggest that the majority of strikers at NWK felt they could not live on promised subventions from strike headquarters. However, in spite of these numbers, the NWK company was not able to resume production, so signing on may not have reflected workers' desire to go back to work – as the company and the International Settlement police insisted – as a canny desire to ensure that they were not saddled by debt once the strike ended. At other mills, however, the percentage of workers registering for work was smaller than at NWK.[62]

In the course of the strike, the CCP played the anti-imperialist card for all it was worth. Zhang Guotao was shocked at the intensity of nationalist passion among the strikers. 'Even women and child workers with relatively low levels of awareness, on hearing about 'anti-Japanese' action, were roused to take a righteous position. I considered that this indicated a new direction to be taken in the labour movement in Shanghai.'[63] The leitmotif of all propaganda on behalf of the strike was the insults suffered by Chinese workers in the Japanese mills. One appeal for solidarity from other workers, however, modulated the nationalist refrain by drawing explicitly upon the language of class: 'We, like you, are impoverished Chinese who only eat if we work'. But it went on to suggest that it was particularly unfortunate to be the employee of a Japanese company:

> Japanese capitalists are truly hateful. They treat us Chinese workers like slaves of a conquered nation, beating and cursing us whenever they like, making deductions from our wages, giving us the sack. The time has come when we can stand it no longer, and so we have all risen up to go on strike (*yaoban*). ... All capitalists think only of making money and stubbornly exploit us; but foreign capitalists, relying on the might of their governments, oppose us Chinese workers even more. We, Chinese workers and compatriots, must unite on a grand scale to resist them. Workers of all trades, our strength lies in the fact that we are a million people of one mind![64]

On 12 February the Shanghai Citizens' Association (*Guomin huiyi*), a broad umbrella organization founded in December 1924 and representing nearly 200 student, merchant, women's and labour organizations, formed a strike support committee, which was active in publicizing the strike and raising funds. It was said that even old women came to the strike headquarters to stick up handbills and to make flags.[65] The SFS set up a rival strike support committee which proclaimed its aim as being to 'draw the workers on to the right track' and to avoid 'the spread of agitation and act in favour of order'. This had the backing of the Chinese authorities who supported its efforts to restrain the workers and to bring about a negotiated settlement.[66] Although the committee supported the strikers – unlike the 'Protect-the-Party' (*hudang*) faction of the GMD, which informed the North China Herald that the strike was subsidized by $40,000 from 'Bolshevik sources' – the SFS had little impact on the strike.[67]

The end of the strike

On 17 February a procession in Caojiadu, policed by pickets and yelling 'Oppose the Foreign Capitalists' and 'Chinese Should Help Chinese', clashed with International Settlement police, causing demonstrators to invade the International Settlement in protest. Among those arrested were Deng Zhongxia and Sun Lianghui.[68] On the 19th police in the eastern district adopted similar tough tactics. Cai Zhihua, secretary of the Workers' Moral Progress Society, and his female colleague, Wu Xianqing, were arrested while speaking to an open-air meeting. Cai was said to have been badly beaten up by International Settlement constabulary.[69] Several thousand workers set off and surrounded the police station, the police firing twenty to thirty rounds to disperse them.[70] The following day, the police closed down the headquarters of the Yangshupu district strike committee.[71] In a statement they said that workers were ignorant, but basically good-hearted people (*liangmin*), who were being led astray by thugs. They warned that they would deal mercilessly with anyone breaching martial law.[72] In all, the disorders saw a total of fifty-six people brought to court for disturbing the peace, the great majority of them workers. The most severe sentences imposed were two terms of six months' imprisonment. Fines levied by the courts totalled $2,175. On 26 February the cotton workers' union telegraphed the British Labour Party to ask it to protest the fact that fifty-six strikers were still in the custody of the International Settlement police.[73]

Police repression made a settlement of the strike urgent. The Western District Four Roads Street Association and the Five Roads Street Association of the International Settlement – both organizations representing merchants and traders – together with the Chinese Millowners' Association had been striving to broker a settlement for some time, but had achieved little.[74] On 25 February six workers' delegates presented themselves to the Shanghai General Chamber of Commerce (GCC) to ask it to mediate. Its vice-chair, Fang Jiaobo, agreed to do so, but the terms he initially proposed were flatly rejected by the Japanese millowners.[75] The following day, he did reach a settlement, but it was one which conceded little to the workers: the owners promised that if workers reported cases of ill-treatment, they would investigate them impartially (*binggong banli*); that law-abiding workers who returned to work could work on the old conditions; that wages would be paid promptly every two weeks and that savings would be paid out after five years. They refused to grant any increase in wages or strike pay and, crucially, refused to take back the workers whose dismissal had caused the strike. Finally, they declined to intervene on behalf of those arrested.[76] The International Settlement police rightly observed that the settlement was 'nothing more than a reiteration of conditions under which the employees formerly served.'[77]

Although the outcome of the strike was hailed publicly by the CCP as a 'victory' – and is still so described by historians in the PRC – it was clearly a defeat.[78] The employers had coordinated resistance through the Japanese Millowners' Association and, though the market for cotton goods was relatively favourable, had opted not to make concessions to what they considered an anti-foreign movement, one – *horribile dictu* – backed by the Soviet Union.[79] The tactic of offering workers who registered for work one-third of their wages had proved fairly effective, since workers worried about sinking into debt or losing their jobs. From the first, there were reports of workers trying to return to work and of many more staying at home, frightened by rumours that the strike would end in mass sackings.[80] Yet though the strike ended in failure, workers returned to work in an atmosphere of carnival, with songs, banners and firecrackers, to the vexation of the International Settlement police.[81] For if the material gains of the stoppage were trifling, its impact on workers' morale was huge. For three weeks, they had sustained the largest ever economic strike in Shanghai, in the course of which they had learnt much about the organization of industrial action. In particular, the strike had given a boost to trade unionism in the city that was to prove long-term.[82]

The CCP gained invaluable experience from organizing such a large strike and from successfully laying the foundations of trade unionism in the city's largest industry. In particular, by putting into circulation a class-inflected discourse of anti-imperialism, it discovered a powerful tool to mobilize the city's workers. At the same time, the strike exposed the limits of its influence, since it was forced to rely on business representatives to end the stoppage on terms over which it had no control.

The formation of the cotton workers' union

In the course of the strike the cells established over the winter by the two workers' clubs transformed themselves into the branches of a cotton

83

workers' union.[83] On 4 March Liu Hua claimed that sixteen branches of the union existed.[84] On 12 March an office of the cotton workers' union was formally opened at the West Shanghai Workers' Club in Tanziwan. Its twenty or so members were mainly Communists. Xiang Ying was in charge of the office, assisted by Liu Hua. Sun Lianghui was in charge of organizational affairs, assisted by Li Ruiqing, an interpreter at Nikko and part-time student at Shanghai University. Liu Guanzhi, who had lost his job at the Doko mill as a result of the strike, was in charge of general administration.[85] A solitary woman Communist, Kong Yannan, described variously as an employee at NWK No.3 mill and as a student, headed a section for women workers.[86] The twenty-five-year-old Liu Hua was driving force of the union. Hard-working, courageous and hot-headed, he was held in high esteem by the cotton workers.[87] Among the cotton workers on the executive were the deputy secretary, Guo Jianxia, a foreman at NWK No.9 mill, Tao Jingxuan, Zhang Zuochen and Zhang Yinglong.[88] Tao Jingxuan was typical. A worker at the NWK No.15 mill, he had come to prominence in the West Shanghai Workers' Club and been invited to join the CCP. Born in 1890 in Jiangling, Hubei province, he came to Shanghai in 1923. A key figure in the Anhui bang, at the start of the strike he used his native-place and secret-society connections to bring together the leaders of the Anhui, Hubei, Subei, Shandong and Shaoxing bangs in order to pledge brotherhood. Meeting at a small temple behind the mill, they drank wine mixed with cock's blood and recognised Tao as their 'elder brother'. During the summer of 1925 Tao rose to become deputy head of the accounts section of the GLU and was later sent by the CCP to organize dock workers into the Pudong dockers' union, where he again put his secret-society connections to good effect. For his part in organising an armed picket of dock workers during the first armed uprising of October 1926, he was shot by troops of Sun Chuanfang, the Zhejiang militarist.[89]

In the course of the strike, membership of the cotton unions rose to around 6,000 in Xiaoshadu and 3,000 in Yangshupu, but it proved difficult to sustain this number, not least because many militants were fired when they tried to return to work.[90] On 20 March 1925 Chen Duxiu reported to ECCI:

> Because the workers were not successful, they no longer have much confidence in the labour unions. The Japanese employers make every effort to prevent the workers from joining the unions, and so no more than 10,000 have joined the unions, although the majority of workers' leaders have joined. The unions, though not officially recognized by the authorities, in effect exist legally. More than fifty of the strikers joined our party, including three women, and two cells have been created.[91]

Six days later, a report from the Shanghai committee of the CYL said that it was proving difficult to consolidate the nascent unions for want of cadres.[92] Whether membership grew or fell during March is unclear. Certainly, union branches were formed at most Japanese cotton mills, the exception being the Nikko mills in Pudong and a few hemp mills. On 31 March there were said to be 2,000 members at NWK No.12 and 1,600 at NWK No.15.[93] Yet early in April the International Settlement daily police reports stated that only 5,000 workers were members of the cotton unions – almost certainly an underestimate, but closer to the truth than the claim that there were 20,000.[94]

There are telltale bits of evidence that the sway of the Communists over the union was by no means firm. Both the GCC and the Federation of Street Associations were represented at the celebration to mark the end of the strike on 1 March. Pan Donglin, a leading figure in the FSA, who had played a major part in bring the dispute to an end, called on workers to join the union in order to help one another and improve the state of society. Pan was photographed alongside the banners of four mill unions and the International Settlement police even reported that the workers had elected him president of the cotton workers' union.[95] Though this seems unlikely, nationalist businessmen did broadly support trade unions at this stage of the national revolution, seeing them as a means of strengthening the self-organization of the Chinese people and as a means of introducing order and rationality into industrial conflict.

If workers returned to the Japanese mills in a mood of optimism, it soon turned sour. Militants were fired, the 30 per cent of wages promised to strikers who registered for work was not always paid and, crucially, the companies refused to recognize the union. To compound difficulties, rice prices stayed high and the copper currency continued to depreciate. The result was a plethora of brief stoppages, go-slows and disturbances throughout the spring, which affected the NWK company particularly badly. On 7 May, National Humiliation Day, the Japanese Millowners' Association announced that it was imposing a ban on trade-union membership in all its mills and the Japanese Chamber of Commerce published a list of 'seditious' unions said to be under Communist control. The millowners agreed that in the event of further unrest, they would implement a policy of lockouts.[96] On 14 May management at the NWK No.12 mill sacked two workers for 'unreliability', causing a brouhaha in which five workers beat up a Chinese foreman. They were arrested by the International Settlement police, and promptly dismissed. The night shift responded by mounting a go-slow. In accordance with the policy announced, the management at No.12 mill declared a lockout. The next day, workers who turned up for work at No.7 mill were told that they, too, could not work since their mill relied on yarn spun at No.12 mill.[97] At 5 pm when the night shift arrived at No.7 mill to find the gates locked, a group of forty men and thirty women smashed down the gates and swarmed into the factory compound.[98] Some got into the mill itself, causing considerable damage to machinery. In panic, Japanese guards opened fire, wounding seven workers, including one woman.[99] One of the wounded, Gu Zhenghong, a twenty-year-old from Funing in Subei, later died of his injuries.[100] It was the protest movement triggered by this incident that led to the May Thirtieth Movement.

The next day, 16 May, an Association to Wipe Out the Disgrace of the Japanese Atrocity (*Riben cansha tongbao xuechi hui*) was formed. The CEC of the CCP sent out directives calling on all party organizations to develop a 'big anti-Japanese movement' throughout the country.[101] Three days later, the Shanghai regional committee decided to mount a large memorial service for Gu Zhenghong to broadcast the political significance of his murder. On the afternoon of Sunday, 24 May, some 10,000 people, 90 per cent of them said to be workers, met behind the Dafeng mill in Zhabei. In the middle of open ground hung a portrait of Gu Zhenghong, flanked by elegiac couplets written by Liu Hua – 'The Man May Be Dead, But His Spirit Lives On' – and topped by a tablet reading 'Vanguard Worker'. Beneath this was a curtain behind which stood his coffin covered with white silk, on which was written in black ink: 'East Asians Beat Chinese to Death'. Sun Lianghui presided and Liu Hua read the order of service.[102]

The Shanghai CCP on the Eve of the May Thirtieth Movement

The effect of the February mill strike and the ensuing troubles was to boost the fortunes of the CCP in Shanghai. In November 1924 membership of the regional organization had stood at 109, organized into eight cells; by May it stood at 220, organised into fifteen branches, not counting members in branches outside Shanghai. Significantly, the largest district organization was now in Yangshupu, with forty-six members; the next largest in West Shanghai, with thirty-two members; followed by the Shanghai University branch, with twenty-five members.[103] For the first time, the party had a number of industrial branches, including those of shop employees' (*dianyuan lianhehui*), with eight members; the Nanyang tobacco company, with eighteen; seamen, with five; gold- and silversmiths, with thirteen; printers, with eight; and postal workers, with six.[104] On the eve of the May Thirtieth Incident the Shanghai regional organization had twenty-six branches with a membership of 297.[105] Despite this growth, the CCP was still chronically short of activists. In his report to ECCI on 20 March 1925, Chen Duxiu begged it to send back students from KUTV in Moscow as soon as possible.[106] He also complained about the crippling shortage of funds: in the first three months of 1925 the CCP had received only 3,423 US dollars, equivalent to 5,887 yuan, which had left it with a deficit of 863 yuan. He asked for an increase in monthly subsidy from 2,250 to 3,650 yuan, in view of the quickening tempo of party activities.[107]

Meanwhile the death of Sun Yat-sen on 12 March strengthened the determination of right-wingers in Shanghai to rid the GMD of Communist influence. A group tried to promote Tang Shaoyi, veteran of the 1911 Revolution, as Sun's successor, and Tang and Zhang Taiyan set up the Xinhai comrades clubs as a focus of this campaign. On 1 April 1925, Feng Ziyou and other veterans issued a manifesto opposing the CEC, the Guangdong government and the CCP. On 14 April the group, which later became known as the 'old right' – to distinguish it from the 'new right' which emerged in the second half of 1925 – was expelled by the CEC.[108] By May it was clear that the CCP was losing influence in the Shanghai executive bureau and the Jiangsu provincial committee of the GMD. On 5 May the party leadership called on members to step up the fight against the right by forming speaker teams to encourage the masses to join the GMD; to strengthen training within the GMD; to elect Communists and left-wingers to the propaganda bureaux of GMD branches and to ensure that they met once a week.[109] On 29 May the Shanghai regional committee, alarmed at the decline in its influence within the GMD, set up two 'guidance committees' to work inside the Shanghai executive bureau of the GMD and the Jiangsu provincial committee.[110]

During the protests that followed the murder of Gu Zhenghong, the Communists, notably Yun Daiying, worked mainly through the GMD-led Shanghai Student Union, rather than the Shanghai executive bureau of the GMD. On 23 May two students from Wenzhi university were arrested in the International Settlement while collecting money for Gu Zhenghong's family. They reported that the Chinese police who dealt with them expressed sympathy for their cause.[111] The next day four more students, including the Communist Zhu Yiquan and a schoolboy who was only thirteen years old, were arrested for carrying flags supporting the Association to Wipe Out Disgrace.[112] All six came before the Mixed Court on 25 May, charged with disturbing the peace, and were remanded to await the Japanese assessor on 30 May.[113] This denial of bail infuriated the Shanghai Student Union, which had revived since December 1924, partly as a result of the activities of the SYL. On 27 May Yun Daiying, in his capacity as secretary of the propaganda department of the Shanghai executive bureau of the GMD and editor of *New Construction* magazine, addressed a meeting of representatives of some twenty different colleges. The meeting agreed to set up a committee to campaign for the release of the students in custody and to link the strike at NWK to protests by businessmen against the Municipal Council's plans to introduce four by-laws concerning the increase in wharfage dues, the licensing of stocks and produce exchanges, restrictions on the publication of printed matter and limitations on child labour.[114]

On 28 May the CEC and Shanghai regional committee held an emergency meeting which decided to support a mass infiltration of the International Settlement on 30 May to protest the trial of the students. It agreed that the demonstration should have a clear anti-imperialist character, protesting not only the killing of Gu Zhenghong and the arrest of students, but also the proposed by-laws.[115] Yun Daiying reported to a joint meeting of CCP and GMD propaganda workers that he had arranged for students at Shanghai University, accompanied by workers, to go to schools to gather support for the demonstration.[116] A detailed plan was drawn up to infiltrate the International Settlement in small groups at appropriate signals ('It's raining' and 'Let's eat').[117] The next day, Yun reported to the propaganda department of the GMD executive bureau about the plan for the next day's mass civil disobedience, but discovered that many had misgivings, fearing to break the law.[118] The same day a big meeting was held at Shanghai University to drum up support for the demonstration. He Chengyi, a 23-year-old student from Sichuan, spoke enthusiastically in support of the protest inside the International Settlement. The following day he was one of those gunned down.[119]

Chapter 5 _____

The Shanghai Communists and the May Thirtieth Movement

On Saturday, 30 May, students and workers protesting about the ongoing conflict in the Japanese mills and the trial of student protestors infiltrated the International Settlement, distributing leaflets. Scores were arrested and taken to Louza police station. By the afternoon an angry crowd surrounded the station, and when police proved unable to disperse it with batons, Inspector Everson ordered that they open fire on the crowd.[1] Twelve were killed and seventeen injured as a result.[2] Such action by the International Settlement police was not without precedent, yet it proved to be a turning-point in the fortunes of imperialism in China. Within hours, representatives of the National Student Union (NSU), the Shanghai Student Union (SSU) and the Shanghai Federation of Street Associations met and agreed to convene an open meeting at 3 pm the following afternoon. At the GMD party affairs bureau in route Vallon a meeting took place at which student and SFS representatives met with GMD right-wingers Ma Chaojun, Ye Chucang and Liu Luyin, the prominent Cantonese merchant, Feng Shaoshan, YMCA leader, Yu Rizhang, and Du Yuesheng and Zhang Xiaolin of the Green Gang.[3] Later, Yun Daiying told a meeting of the CEC and Shanghai regional committee of the CCP at Zhang Guotao's house how indignant the mood of GMD right-wingers was.[4] The Communist leaders resolved to call a general strike, or three-fold stoppage (*sanba*), of workers, students and businessmen to protest the atrocity and to demand proper compensation.[5] According to Zhang Guotao, it was agreed that the merchants' strike should aim to inconvenience foreigners but not cause losses to Chinese business and that workers' strikes should be confined to foreign concerns.[6] The Communists sent a request to the Shanghai General Chamber of Commerce (GCC) and other public organizations to meet the next day to consider a joint response.[7] They also decided to launch immediately a Shanghai General Labour Union (*zonggonghui*) (GLU), which had been under discussion for several weeks, in order to lead the workers' strike.[8]

The following morning the office of the GLU was opened in Nandao at No.2 Baoshan alley, off Baoshan Road. The new body was led by Li Lisan as president; Liu Shaoqi, as head of administration; Chen Xinglin as head of communications; Liu Guanzhi as head of propaganda; Fu Yuanxiong as head of accounts; and Wu Min, as head of organization.[9] Although neither Chen, Fu nor Wu were Communists, the CCP exercised paramount influence over the GLU through Li Lisan and Liu Shaoqi, and through the many deputy heads of departments who were Communists.[10] In its inaugural proclamation the GLU declared: 'Foreign imperialism is oppressing our country, it is riding roughshod over us. We are like slaves without a country. The savagery which we have seen recently is getting worse by the day.'[11]

The open meeting of merchants' and students' representatives met on Sunday afternoon at the headquarters of the GCC at the Queen of Heaven Temple (*Tianhou gong*) in Zhabei. As they were meeting. deputations arrived to demand that business leaders support a three-fold stoppage by workers, students and traders. Fang Jiaobo, vice-chair of the GCC, was reluctant to give his backing to the proposed action; but eventually, under mass pressure, he complied, while secretly informing the Municipal Council that he had signed the order under duress.[12] The meeting, which had grown to more than 1,500 people by the end of the afternoon, passed a resolution calling on the Municipal Council to punish the murderers; pay compensation to the victims; offer an apology; abolish the proposed by-law on printed matter, and return the Mixed Court to Chinese control. It called on Chinese to boycott British and Japanese goods, not to use foreign bank notes, not to travel on trams belonging to the Municipal Council, to oppose foreign-run schools and not to wear foreign clothes.[13] Thus was the May Thirtieth Movement launched.

On 1 June the Shanghai executive bureau of the GMD issued a declaration, penned by Dai Jitao, which rehearsed the past 'insults against China's dignity' and explained that that the GMD would 'help the country's patriots to struggle for freedom, equal rights and independence and to restore the rights and dignity of our country.'[14] The same day, the NSU, the SSU, the Federation of Street Associations and the GLU each sent two representatives to a meeting to discuss the setting up of a citizens' assembly. The GLU delegates were Guo Jianxia and Zhu Guoping, both textile workers who had risen to prominence during the mill strikes in February. This meeting decided to form a Union of Labour, Commerce and Education (*Gongshangxue lianhehui*) to coordinate the triple stoppage. It was agreed that the Union (ULCE) should comprise six representatives each from the GCC, the Federation of Street Associations, the NSU, SSU and GLU.[15] On 4 June the ULCE held a preparatory meeting, attended by twenty-two delegates.[16] In the absence of its president, Yu Xiaqing, who was in Beijing, the GCC refused to join the new body.[17] On his return, Yu made it clear that Shanghai's merchants, bankers and industrialists would have no truck with the union. On 6 June a bomb exploded at his home and a threatening letter was left there by the 'Blood and Iron Corps', no doubt a secret-society front.[18] On 6 June the ULCE set up a commission to draw up a comprehensive set of demands to put to the Beijing government as a basis for negotiation with the foreign powers.[19] It comprised four people, of whom Lin Jun, Mei Dianlong and Li Lisan were either Communists or sympathisers. Two days later, the commission produced a set of seventeen demands that were intended to serve as the aims of the May Thirtieth Movement. They consisted of four preliminary demands, which included the cancellation of the state of emergency by the Municipal Council, the withdrawal of landing parties, the release of those under arrest and the reopening of schools and other institutions occupied by the Volunteer Corps of the International Settlement. They were followed by thirteen formal demands, the most important of which included the handing-over to the Chinese courts of the officer and policemen who fired on the crowd on 30 May; indemnities to the families of the deceased and wounded; a formal apology for the incident; freedom of speech, publication and association in the International Settlement; better treatment of workers in foreign factories, the rights to strike and form unions and no dismissals because of strike action; cancellation of the proposed by-laws; the return of the Mixed Court to Chinese control; the abolition of extraterritoriality; and full Chinese representation on the Municipal Council.[20] This was a far-reaching anti-imperialist programme, though it fell short of calling for the total abolition of the unequal treaties and the return of all foreign settlements.[21] The demands were endorsed by the GMD.[22]

The ULCE was formally inaugurated on 7 June and held more than thirty meetings before its liquidation on 18 September. It took energetic steps to direct and coordinate the triple strike, raising funds for the strikers, publishing a newspaper, the *Hot-Blooded Daily* (*Rexue Ribao*), and campaigning to rouse the public to press the Beijing government to accept the seventeen demands as the basis of negotiation with the Diplomatic Body.[23] However, the ULCE was quickly outflanked politically by Yu Xiaqing, who set up a rival May Thirtieth Committee to assist Duan Qirui's government in effecting a settlement with the foreign powers.[24] This committee immediately scaled down the seventeen demands to thirteen, dropping the more radical ones. On 11 June the ULCE tried to foil this move by holding a huge meeting at the Public Recreation Ground in Nanshi, attended by nearly 100,000 people. Chaired by Lin Jun, it tried to rally public support for the original anti-imperialist programme. In a dramatic gesture, Sun Jindong slashed his hand and wrote in blood on a banner the six characters: 'We do not fear death. We are fighting for our dignity.'[25]

The CCP enjoyed extensive but not overwhelming influence in the ULCE. Perhaps the most important conduit of influence was the *Hot-Blooded Daily*, which the party launched on 4 June under the editorship of

Qu Qiubai. Through Li Lisan, too, the most authoritative of the GLU representatives on ULCE, the party also exerted influence in formulating the latter's policy. GLU representatives attended ULCE meetings assiduously, though they rarely chaired its meetings, tending to defer to representatives of the students and street unions. This may have been a calculated bid to give the ULCE a 'united front' rather than 'class' character. The most publicly visible leader of the ULCE was Lin Jun, one of the NSU representatives, who does not appear to have joined the CCP until June 1926.[26] Born in 1896 in Chuansha county, Jiangsu, he began work as an apprentice in a weaving shop at the age of fourteen. In July 1924 he entered the sociology faculty of Shanghai university.[27] Lin was a somewhat inflammatory presence on the ULCE, and the Communists did not always see eye to eye with him. The CCP had far less influence among the delegates from the Federation of Street Associations and the SSU, who looked to the GMD for political guidance. However, the double representation of students (through the SSU and the NSU) may have worked to the Communists' advantage, since the NSU generally took a more left-wing stance than the SSU.

On 13 June two battalions of troops belonging to Zhang Xueliang, son of the Fengtian warlord, Zhang Zuolin, occupied the Chinese areas of Shanghai. Lin Jun led a delegation to ask Zhang to occupy the International Settlement. They were courteously received, Zhang expressing the hope that the patriotic movement would keep up pressure on the government during negotiations with the foreign powers. Ominously, however, he reminded the delegation that his mission was to restore order. As this suggests, student representatives seriously entertained the idea of defeating the foreign powers by force of arms, Lin Jun and the NSU delegates proposing the formation of a student army, a merchant army and a workers' army.[28] At a meeting of ULCE on 18 June, a representative of the Federation of Street Associations proposed that students go into the International Settlement to distribute leaflets and that Zhang Xueliang's troops occupy the International Settlement in the event of their arrest. The meeting turned down the proposal, but agreed that preparations be made for the forcible recovery of the International Settlement.[29] The following day, Lin Jun berated the ULCE for its circumspection, insisting that the time had come for an immediate armed uprising. Backed by his NSU comrade, Lei Rongpu, he called on the GLU to launch the slogan 'For a popular armed uprising.' The GLU delegate, however, demurred, pointing out that conditions were far from favourable, and that any such adventure could only end in failure. He argued that the priority must be organization, and proposed the slogan: 'Everyone must organize!'[30]

The Diplomatic Body refused to accept even the May Thirtieth Committee's thirteen demands as a basis for negotiation with the government. Consequently, GCC leaders decided that the continuation of the business stoppage had little point and proposed that it be replaced by a boycott of British and Japanese goods and services. Since there was a widespread feeling that the stoppage was damaging Chinese businesses more than foreign ones, it succeeded in persuading the Federation of Street Associations to back this policy. Meanwhile the onset of the summer vacation meant that the student boycott of classes also came to an end, leaving the workers to pursue their strike alone. At a meeting on 20 June, attended by 130 delegates from sixty unions, the GLU discussed the implications of the shopkeepers' decision to go back to work. Zhang Guotao called for the continuance of the workers' strike and for pressure to be put on the GCC to ensure that it carried out the boycott and supported strikers financially.[31]

The workers of Shanghai displayed impressive resolve during the May Thirtieth Movement. One estimate suggests that 201,978 workers in 206 enterprises or trades stopped work at some point in protest at the action of the International Settlement police.[32] Initially, many workers in Chinese-owned enterprises halted work, despite the decision of the CCP to confine the stoppage to foreign enterprises.[33] The initial rush to join the stoppage was largely spontaneous, but it was not long before there were reports of the GLU using force to keep the strike solid. Strike breakers and 'traitors' were abducted, taken to the headquarters of the cotton workers' union and beaten up. On 8 June a man called Shen, accused of spying for the Japanese millowners, was seized.[34] On 2 July a gardener at the Nikko mill was taken off to Tanziwan where he was beaten and had his fingerprints taken.[35] On 7 July Li Lisan was said to have admitted that there were as many as 100 strike breakers being held by the GLU. He said that ten had just been released on payment of a surety of $50.[36] On 12 July a party of soldiers came to Tanziwan to warn Liu Hua that the cotton workers' union was breaking the law, but he dismissed their 'empty threats'.[37] The appalling news of the Shamian massacre on 23 June, when police in the British concession in Canton opened fire on demonstrators, leaving fifty-three Chinese and one foreigner dead, stiffened the determination of the strikers. On 25 June 1925 the Soviet Politburo decided to send Voitinskii to China at once: 'it is vital to push (the movement) forward, without fearing to accentuate tensions'.[38] At the same time the CCP was advised to deter participants from undertaking actions that might provoke armed intervention by imperialists.[39] According to the estimates of the International Settlement police, which only cover the International Settlement, the number of strikers actually rose during the month of July from 80,000 to 96,000.[40]

The fundamental problem faced by the GLU was not that of strike-breaking but of the rapid depletion of the strike fund. The GCC, as a gesture of support for the May Thirtieth Movement, had helped set up a relief fund (ji'anhui) to provide strikers with a modest subvention. Up to 2

July it claimed to have disbursed $450,000 in 'big money', plus a few thousand in 'small money'.[41] By the end of July, according to Liu Shaoqi, no less than 1.7 million dollars had been given to strikers, a figure that is repeated in other sources.[42] The problem was that the longer the strike continued, the harder it was to pay the strikers. A turning point came on 6 July when the Municipal Council cut off supplies of electricity to all 'non-essential' bulk users, i.e. to those Chinese-owned enterprises, mainly textile mills and tobacco factories, that were still working normally. The result was that thousands more workers – at least 40,000 – were laid off.[43] This massively compounded the financial difficulties of sustaining the strike. On 20 July the GLU was forced to cut the dole from $4 – it had once been $5 – to $3 for a half-month period.[44] Moreover, as the money dried up, criticism of the way the relief fund was managed intensified. On 4 July, following charges of inefficiency and red tape, the three commissioners of the relief fund resigned, and it was reorganized to include representatives of the GLU and the ULCE. However, the GLU, which published no accounts until 12 August, itself soon faced accusations of corruption.[45] At the end of July, the GLU proposed that strikers be encouraged to return to their native places, and offered a $4 travel subsidy to this end.[46] On 10 August it received a report that $1,200,000 would be needed to support the strikers for a further month.[47]

It is often claimed that the Soviet Union bankrolled the strike, but this needs to be kept in perspective. On 11 June the Politburo ordered the All-Union Central Council of Trade Unions to send 50,000 rubles to Shanghai, and on 16 June it earmarked another 50,000 rubles to this end. On 5–7 August it assigned a further 100,000 rubles, but sent it via the International Class-War Prisoners' Aid (*Mezhdunarodnaia organizatsiia pomoshchi revoliutsioneram*).[48] Ivan Lepse, who led a Soviet trade-union delegation to Shanghai, said that 300,000 rubles were raised for the May Thirtieth strikers in Russia. If true, this would represent 17.5 per cent of the 1.7 million dollars said to have been disbursed to the strikers by the end of July, since one gold ruble was roughly equivalent to one Chinese silver dollar.[49] Voitinskii was thus probably correct when he claimed that 'the general strike in Shanghai, in particular, but elsewhere too, was nine-tenths supported by material contributions from the bourgeoisie'.[50] In reality, this meant the patriotic public and overseas Chinese.

To add to the difficulties, on 22 July General Xing Shilian, whose 7,000 Fengtian soldiers had been in control of the Chinese areas for a month, caved into pressure from the British Consul and moved to quell the anti-imperialist movement, closing the offices of the ULCE, the SSU, the seamen's union and the foreign employees' union (*yangwu gonghui*).[51] General Xing also suppressed the levy on cargo unloaded by the waterfront unions which the GCC had agreed should go to the strikers' relief fund.[52] Yu Xiaqing, Fu Xiaoan and the circuit intendant protested Xing's action, even though by now their enthusiasm for the labour movement was waning rapidly. To the annoyance of the British Consul, the seamen's union was unsealed on the 25th, flinging open its doors to the sound of music, fireworks and speeches from the five leaders who had briefly been imprisoned.[53] Three days later, ULCE, too, reopened, although the foreign employees union remained closed. On 9 August six members of that union who had been under arrest were finally released.[54] Even as Yu Xiaqing played the patriotic card, by defending the unions against the warlords, however, he was putting out feelers towards the foreign powers, since there was mounting pressure from Chinese millowners to end the strike.[55]

On 28 July the Chinese commission of the Soviet Politburo agreed that it was time to work out a series of demands on the basis of which the strike could be wound down.[56] On 4 August 1925 Voitinskii wrote to Moscow to confirm that he had received the commission's telegram and to report that he was in Beijing to discuss with ambassador Karakhan tactics for 'braking' the strike. The CEC of the CCP had discussed ending the strike several times, but each time had rejected the idea, believing that there was still a chance that the movement would flare up again. On 10 August the CEC agreed that the anti-imperialist demands of the triple strike should be sidelined in favour of concrete economic demands which could be put to the employers. It agreed that such demands should be put first to the Japanese millowners.[57] Five days earlier, sixty representatives from all thirty-two Japanese mills in Shanghai had met with GLU leaders to draw up a list of eight mainly economic demands to serve as a basis for winding down the strike.[58] The CEC was thus not pleased when on 10 August a 200-strong meeting of GLU delegates drew up a new list of nine conditions for a return to work that went well beyond the economic demands previously agreed, to include calls for the return of the Mixed Court, Chinese representation on the Municipal Council and the repeal of the four by-laws.[59] Relations between the CEC and the GLU became strained. In May 1926 a report of the CEC labour department accused the GLU at this time of pursuing a 'disastrous course' and of failing to liaise with the party.[60] It also accused Li Lisan of favouring some 'gesture of despair', such as an armed uprising.[61]

After much soul-searching, terms for a settlement of the strike in the Japanese cotton mills were agreed. The Japanese Millowners' Association agreed to pay the entire wage in 'big money', by incorporating fractions of a dollar, which had hitherto been paid in 'small money', into the following wage packet. They also agreed that guards would not 'normally' carry arms on factory premises. With respect to the central demand for trade-union recognition, they promised to abide by any labour law enacted by the government, but added a rider that their observance of the law would depend on order being restored.[62] They agreed that there should be no dismissals without just cause, but reserved the right to determine what constituted a just cause. They refused to commit themselves to any pay increase, but agreed to 'take pity' (a phrase which stuck in the craw of the GLU activists) upon 'well-intentioned' workers who had suffered because of the strike. Finally, they made a very modest contribution to the strikers' compensation fund.[63] This was hardly a ringingly favourable outcome for the strikers, but the CCP put the best complexion on it. On 25 August, when Japanese mills that did not rely on the Municipal Council for their electricity supply recommenced operations, the GLU congratulated the strikers: 'We upheld the nation's code of brotherhood ... but we have still not regained face (*timian*).'[64]

The terms for settling the strike by seamen employed by Japanese companies, the lay-off in the Chinese mills, and the strikes in British mills and shipping companies were essentially similar – if anything, slightly less favourable to the workers. But what in objective terms might have counted as a defeat was packaged by the GLU as a commendable victory. Thus when the employees of Japanese shipping companies returned to work on 21 August, they held a meeting, addressed by speakers who included Yu Xiaqing and the Chinese manager of the Nisshin company. They then processed around the Sixteen Shops docks in Nandao, led by officials of the seamen's union, bearing a republican flag and the union banner, plus leaders of the various seamen's guilds, a delegation of seamen employed in British companies, a military band and a traditional music ensemble (*chuidayue*). When the procession reached the waterfront the men were greeted by blasts of ships' whistles and banners, proclaiming 'Seamen on Japanese Ships are Returning to Work' and 'Seamen on British Ships Persist in Their Strike'. Firecrackers were set off, cries went up of 'Long Live the Seamen's Union' and cigarettes were given out by delegates from a Chinese tobacco factory.[65]

The explosion of labour unions

In one vital respect the May Thirtieth strikes marked a huge stride forward for Shanghai labour, in that the GLU brilliantly capitalized on the triple strike to promote the unionization of the city's workers. By 28 July the GLU claimed to have 117 affiliated unions with 218,859 members.[66] The rush to organize was as much an expression of anti-imperialism as of class consciousness, the GLU advertizing its aim as being 'externally to resist imperialism, internally to uphold national government authority (*guoquan*).'[67] A statement on behalf of rickshaw pullers was typical in declaring: 'the whole country has mobilized to fight imperialism, so we must form a labour union to strive for vengeance (*litu fuchou*) and bring the strike to a satisfactory conclusion'.[68] Nevertheless in spite of the predominance of nationalist themes, Communist propaganda also sought to foster a rudimentary class consciousness: 'The union is an organization that will defend our interests. If it asks us not to go to work, then we must not go to work'. 'The strike is the workers' weapon in the struggle against the capitalists. Without weapons the soldier cannot fight the enemy.' 'Make no mistake, the labour union is neither a Jade Emperor come down from Heaven nor a Guanyin dispensing bounteous charity; it is an organization created by the workers themselves'.[69] A favourite metaphor was that of rice straw: one rice straw was easy to break, but rice straw bound into a rope was impossible to break.[70] As in 1921–2, Communists also argued for labour unions in terms that made sense to members of the secret societies, urging workers to uphold the code of brotherhood (*bao yiqi*).

The biggest industrial federation that was established was that of the cotton workers, which was launched on 20 August by 124 delegates, representing thirty-six mill unions with a membership of 120,000. Xiang Ying was chair and Zhang Weizhen, a worker from Hunan who had only arrived in the city in May, was made secretary.[71] Its aims encapsulated the class-inflected anti-imperialist nationalism popularized by the May Thirtieth Movement: 'to concentrate our forces, to resist imperialist oppression and to struggle for the sovereignty of the race (*minzu*) and seek the emancipation of the working class'.[72] Its more particular aims were: '1) to improve the lives, raise the status and promote the welfare of all textile unions in Shanghai; 2) unify sentiment, practise mutual aid, eliminate all localist, craft and sexual discrimination and seek the unity of all workers; 3) to increase knowledge, set up schools, speaker teams, libraries, reading rooms and clubs, in order to promote the class awareness of workers; 4) to lead the activities of the labour unions in Shanghai mills and to lay down common objectives.'[73] Here the echo of certain anarchist and May Fourth themes was still audible, while the theme of class struggle was deliberately muted. Printers, ironworkers and dockers also managed to establish industrial federations (*zonggonghui*) – the printers with pronounced success – but other sectors failed to make headway before General Xing ruthlessly shut the GLU down.

Well over a hundred individuals held positions in the GLU as heads or members of its functional sections, only a few of whom were paid officials. Two lists of office holders are extant, drawn up only six weeks apart from one another, yet they fail to correspond in most respects. The first, consisting of fifty-four names, was published in *Republican Daily* on 16 June; the second, consisting of ninety-nine names and bearing no date, was drawn up in late July.[74] Only twenty-two names on the first list appear on the second, which suggests a very high level of turnover among GLU personnel. Because so many were active for so short a period of time, it is impossible to identify the majority of people on either list; and the problem is compounded by the fact that some office-holders used aliases, since the legal status of the GLU was uncertain and they risked arrest or even death

97

for their trade-union activism. The difficulty of identifying individuals makes it hard to measure the extent of Communist influence within the GLU. Of 131 names on the two lists, only about twenty can be positively identified as party members. Of course, the leading positions were monopolised by Communists, Li Lisan being chair and Liu Shaoqi head of administration. Liu's two deputies, Xie Wenjin and Sun Lianghui, were also Communists. Xie Wenjin (1894–1927), born in Yongjia in Zhejiang, studied at the Zhejiang First Normal School in Hangzhou. He went to Russia in 1921, accompanied by Wang Shouhua, who was an alumnus of the same school; upon his return in the winter of 1923, Xie served as an interpreter for Borodin and as chair of the CCP in Wenzhou.[75] Wang Shouhua did not return to China until 1925 but was soon appointed to head the propaganda department of the Shanghai GLU. Like Yu Xiusong and Zhang Qiuren, Wang hailed from Zhuji county, Zhejiang. He was twenty-four and had spent more than three-and-a-half years in Russia, mainly in Vladivostok, where he and Liang Botai, another alumnus of the Zhejiang First Normal School, had gained valuable experience organizing Chinese workers through the May First Club.[76] Zhang Guotao was said to be impressed by his ability.[77] But if the most influential positions were the preserve of Communists, they were in a minority among office holders as a whole. A few non-Communists held important offices, such as Yang Jianhong, chair of the union of foreign employees, who was in charge of the public relations section, and Wu Min, head of the organization section.[78] The great majority, however, were ordinary members of GLU sections – at best, deputy heads of sections, rather than full heads. Typical were two members of the liaison section, Xu Zaizhou, chair of the offset printers' union, who was thirty-four and hailed from Zhejiang, and Yu Xianting, a leader of the dockers' union.

From a list of chairs of individual unions, which dates from late July, it is possible to sketch a social profile of the emergent layer of working-class activists. It transpires that the average age of 111 leaders for whom we have information was 32.4, older than the average for the workforce as a whole. Of 109 for whom we have information on region of origin, thirty-one (28.4 per cent) came from Zhejiang province, including no fewer than thirteen (11.9 per cent) from Ningbo; seventeen (15.6 per cent) came from Jiangnan, including three from Nanjing; and fourteen (12.8 per cent) came from Subei; twelve (11 per cent) were from Shanghai and its environs; nine (8.3 per cent) from Anhui, seven (6.4 per cent) from Hubei and six (5.5 per cent) from Guangdong.[79] There are no data on the regional origins of the Shanghai labour force as a whole, but figures for the cotton workforce for 1928 suggest that workers from Subei made up the biggest contingent (40 per cent), followed by natives of Jiangnan (30 per cent); those from Hunan and Hubei together formed 15 per cent of the workforce; while those from Jiangxi, Anhui and Shandong together formed a further 15 per cent.[80] Given that Subei migrants comprised an even bigger proportion of the workforce in transportation (though not of the workforce of the handicraft sector, which, however, was under-represented in the 1925 unionisation drive), it is clear that workers from Subei were under-represented among labour leaders. This would tally with the prevalent perception of Zhejiang and Jiangnan as areas where the populace was better educated and more prosperous than in Subei. Curiously, however, trade-union leaders born in Shanghai and its immediate environs also appear to have been underrepresented.[81]

The GLU under attack

The success of the CCP in launching the GLU drastically worsened its relations with those labour leaders who detested the GMD's united front policy. That some kind of confrontation was on the cards even before the May Thirtieth Movement was shown by the Second National Labour Congress in May 1925, which condemned leaders of the SFS by name as 'scabs'.[82] The SFS was galvanised into protest by the May Thirtieth shootings. On 1 June it called a meeting of fifty representatives from over twenty organizations which appealed to fellow-countrymen to mobilize in protest and to the government to resist the foreign powers.[83] Three days later, at the first delegate meeting of the GLU, 200 representatives denounced the SFS and launched the slogan 'Down with Fake Unions'. The following day, Chen Guoliang, leader of the SFS-affiliated China Labour Union, and Li Shiliang, leader of the dock warehouse workers' union (*Shanghai chuanwu zhanfang gonghui*), were beaten up at a meeting in Nanshi when they claimed that the 1,000-plus foreign employees who were meeting in the same building were members of the SFS.[84]

The SFS backed the efforts to create a counterweight to the ULCE, by affiliating to Yu Xiaqing's May Thirtieth Committee. On 8 June Tong Lizhang of the Shanghai Worker-Merchant Friendly Society chaired a meeting, attended by 4,000 people, at which he called on Chinese enterprises to continue working in order to support the strike financially. Calls were made for the retrocession of the foreign concessions, the abolition of extra-territoriality and the unequal treaties.[85] Leaflets were circulated, accusing the Communists of 'taking advantage of our present patriotic movement by driving our students into the fighting zone thus causing them to be shot dead. For one death they obtain $50,000 from the USSR.'[86] On 10 June forty representatives of twenty-two unions affiliated to the SFS demanded that the GCC-backed relief fund provide the SFS with monies to distribute to striking members of its affiliated unions.[87] The fund apparently agreed, but then stopped when the fund was reorganized in early July. On 19 July four unions – the dock warehouse workers' union, the electricians' union at the Deluo company, the union at the British

Longgongmao weaving mill, which claimed 1,463 members, and the Pudong textile workers' union – issued a protest, accusing the relief committee of infringing the liberty of workers to join whichever union federation they chose.[88] A couple of days later, in a letter to the Martial Law Commander, the GLU claimed that the SFS had no base among the workers and was chaotically organized. It denied that it controlled the relief fund and said that it dispensed money to all strikers regardless of whether their unions were affiliated to the GLU.[89]

Although the broad outline of the conflict between the GLU and SFS can be reconstructed, there is much that remains obscure. Basically, the SFS seems to have encouraged the secret societies to try to subvert the GLU from within, causing the GLU leadership to undertake a purge of labour leaders whose first loyalties were suspected to be either to the SFS or to the secret societies.[90] This may explain the high turnover among GLU officeholders between the two lists of 16 June and the end of July, the second list having been drawn up after the 'purge'. Certainly at the end of July the GLU announced that any unions seeking affiliation with it would publicly have to repudiate the crimes of the 'scabs' in SFS; announce that they had severed all ties with the SFS; and restructure their constitutions in accord with GLU principles.[91] It also launched a blistering salvo of denunciations of the SFS, accusing it of being a 'lair of a small band of scum, who bluff and swindle, who stop at nothing, who are not only bitterly hated by all workers but also held in contempt by every section of society.'[92] In response, on 11 August, twenty-two individuals published a statement in which they accused the GLU of embezzling strike funds.

> This time we have no choice but to stand up. The hoodlum Li Lisan and his ilk under the false signature of the GLU are deceiving the workers in every possible way and injuring us workers through crimes as numerous as the hairs on our heads. They are using the workers' movement for their own ends, and are lining their pockets with money that has been collected to assist the workers. ... They are a bunch of gangsters who spoil their wives and indulge their concubines, who ride around in cars. Since the May Thirtieth strike the GLU has received over 1,700,000 dollars but has published no accounts. Meanwhile we workers face starvation. We have no influence in the movement and are expected simply to obey orders. They even beat us up or detain us. How long must we endure their cruel injuries and their deception! We cannot stand by and let these national traitors (*maiguo zei*) bury this great movement of ours. We have no choice but to stand up and drive them out.[93]

The signatories claimed to represent the West Shanghai foreign employees' union, the Dafeng, Hengfeng, NWK Nos.3, 5E, 5W,7, 13, 14, Nikko,

Ewo, Weitong, Hongzhang spinning, Hongzhang weaving, the Tongyi, Shenxin, Puyi Nos.1 and 2 mill unions, the Bailishi candle factory union and the Yangshupu workers' union (*Yangshupu gongren gonghui*).[94] Among them, two can be identified as chairs of unions, namely, Dai Jinan, aged 33 from Tianjin, who was chair of the Hongzhang union, and Li Fengchi, aged 44 from Hubei, who was chair of the Dafeng union. We know, albeit from a hostile source, that at least two of the signatories had been expelled from the GLU: Zhou Deming and Sun Guangren, both former workers at NWK No.5 mill, were alleged to have been expelled for bad behaviour.[95]

The SFS set 22 August as the date for an attack on GLU headquarters in Nanshi. The preceding night, according to the International Settlement police, they arranged a break-in during which documents were stolen.[96] On the 22nd Sun Guangren, one of those allegedly expelled from the GLU for bad behaviour, went to the headquarters, where he kept Li Lisan in long conversation. At 5.30 pm he left the building and was seen to give a signal, whereupon a truck carrying some forty Green Gang hoodlums drew up. Wielding revolvers, knives and iron bars, they smashed their way into the headquarters, injuring eight people, five of them seriously. Two may later have died. However, Li Lisan, their target, managed to escape. On the same day, the mobsters also wrecked the headquarters of the seamen's union and those of the relief fund.[97] There were also reports of attacks on the union at the Hengfeng cotton mill and on the Xiaoshadu district cotton federation.[98] The GLU publicly blamed the SFS for the attack, singling out Zhou Zhonghua for condemnation. Zhou, whose nickname was 'Slippery Fellow' (*Xiao Huatou*), was known to be a Green Gang notable.[99] But it was Sun Guangren and Yuan Youcai, both leaders of the SFS, who were actually arrested.[100] A report in the *North China Herald* linked the attack to the contemporaneous demonstrations that were taking place by wharf coolies against 'the unfairness of the GLU in distributing strike pay'.[101] And the mobsters involved in the attack on the GLU may also have been dockers, linked to the Thirty-Six Sections of the Green Gang and hired by the SFS.

The GLU and the secret societies

The situation would seem to be straightforward: on the one hand, the GLU; on the other, the SFS, backed by the Green Gang. In fact, things were more complicated, since the GLU itself had links with the Green Gang. So what appears to be a contest between two ideologically opposed labour federations, undoubtedly also had roots in rivalries between secret-society and native-place networks battling for control of the world of labour. We have seen that since 1921 Communists had joined the secret societies in an effort to win their support for labour organization or, at least, to neutralize them, a policy that later was known as the 'red heart, white skin' policy. The problem acquired new urgency during the February 1925 mill strikes when the Green Gang attempted to mediate between the embryonic cotton unions and the employers. Chang Yuqing, chief of the guards at NWK No.5 mill and the Fengtian mill and owner of a bath-house close to Xinzha bridge, refused to back the strike. Other gang bosses, however, were drawn into supporting the stoppage, approving the slogan 'Stop the Japanese beating people'.[102] Similarly, in May Shi Jinkun, another boss with considerable clout in Xiaoshadu district, called a strike at the Tongyi mill in protest at the killing of Gu Zhenghong, and brought the Tongyi cotton workers' union into the GLU when it was set up.[103]

Following the May Thirtieth Incident, a majority of secret-society leaders seems to have backed the GLU's efforts to organize a general strike in protest at foreign imperialism. But as the number of affiliated unions grew, the GLU necessarily found itself encroaching on Green Gang turf.[104] Zhang Weizhen recalled how the unionization drive by the GLU office in Xiaoshadu district was blocked by local gang boss, Ma Lianghui, who was a Muslim. Ma was unmoved by both the blandishments – a banquet in a mutton restaurant – and the threats of the GLU activists. "Later, the leadership allowed me, Wang Kequan, ten of us in all, to kowtow and pledge ourselves as sworn brothers to Ma Lianghui. After that our work proceeded smoothly, with no more trouble from the gangsters."[105] No less a figure than Li Lisan became the disciple of Chang Yuqing, a man of great prestige in Xiaoshadu district, in order to expedite the unionization drive.[106] And the International Settlement police attributed his soaring influence in labour circles to his links with the secret societies.[107] There is circumstantial evidence that secret-society leaders succeeded almost at once in taking control of the new unions from within. Certainly, by July the GLU was seriously concerned that secret-society elements were seeking to disrupt its operations, possibly with connivance of the SFS.[108] On 16 July it put out a statement warning that many gangsters were sullying the honour of the labour movement by encouraging workers to steal and do damage and that some, pretending to be members of the propaganda section, were inciting workers to undermine the discipline of the GLU.[109] Several officials in the district offices of the GLU were accused of being involved in protection rackets.[110] This might explain the large turnover in GLU officials between 16 June and late July, when the two aforementioned lists of GLU officials were drawn up, for the Communist leadership may have taken steps to weed out those whose principal loyalties were to the secret societies. It would also explain why by August the secret-societies were ready to assist the SFS in its war against the GLU.

To further complicate the picture, some secret societies were in the pay of the Japanese Millowners' Association. At the beginning of July Chinese police tipped off the GLU that Japanese companies were hiring gangsters to disrupt the unions.[111] Gu Xueqiao, a distant relation of the murdered worker, Gu Zhenghong, and an influential gang boss in Xiaoshadu, was reported to have been offered 10,000 dollars by the Japanese to bring the mill strike to an end. Forty pickets kidnapped Gu, beat him up and made him sign a statement of repentance.[112] In addition, the GLU claimed that the Japanese millowners were behind the SFS's attack on its headquarters, alleging that the Japanese had paid fifty gangsters $100 each.[113] Certainly, the Japanese millowners used secret societies to break the unions after the return to work. In Yangshupu district 500 gangsters were said to be employed by the Japanese mills. At the Doko mill in the western district the GLU claimed that management hired fifty gangsters to beat up strike leaders.[114] Also in the western district, Shi Jinkun, who had brought the Tongyi mill union into the GLU, was said to have been bought off and to now be undermining the GLU.[115] The May Thirtieth Movement thus once again revealed how limited were the advances the Communists could make without the cooperation of foremen and secret-society bosses. It also revealed how determined the latter were to ensure that their control of the job market and shop floor relations was not challenged by the new labour unions.[116] It had become crystal-clear that the CCP's policy of cultivating and utilising secret-society bosses was highly risky. As Hans van de Ven notes, 'it made the CCP dependent exactly on the people and institutions, such as foremen and the Green Gang, it sought to fight.'[117]

The labour unions in retreat

The attack on the headquarters of the GLU on 22 August, instead of increasing sympathy for the union, as the closures by General Xing a month earlier had done, marked the point at which respectable public opinion began to turn against it. The severance of electricity by the Municipal Council increased the desire for a settlement of the strike, and the charges of embezzlement and extremism made by the SFS against the GLU began to stick. Finding itself on the defensive, the GLU several times argued to the martial law authorities that its function was to diminish rather than augment industrial unrest, by diverting spontaneous labour conflict into organized channels. But businessmen and members of the educated public who, two months earlier, had seen the GLU as strengthening the capacity of the nation to fight imperialism, now saw it as disrupting social order and weakening the already feeble competitiveness of Chinese industry. The Chinese Millowners' Association complained to the government in Beijing that industry was stagnating and that disorder was rife in the mills. It said that there had been mob fights at Hengfeng; machine-breaking at Hongyu; a gate-keeper beaten to death at Puyi; and coercion at the Shenxin mill. Whilst it was careful not to pin the blame explicitly on the GLU, it called on the government to uphold order, saying that even if the British restored electricity, the future of Chinese industry would remain bleak unless firm management were restored.[118] The GLU publicly rejected these allegations, saying that the incidents cited were fabricated.[119] The GCC, for its part, having condemned the closure of unions in mid-July as a blow against the patriotic movement, now made oblique signals to General Xing that it would not be averse to seeing him repeat his action. Publicly, however, Yu Xiaqing was careful not to condemn the GLU.[120]

Once the strikers were back at work, General Xing was swift to pounce. Speed was of the essence, since rival warlord, Sun Chuanfang, was threatening Shanghai, and Xing feared that the GLU might give aid to his enemy. On 18 September, acting on orders from Duan Qirui, chief executive of the Beijing government, he closed the GLU down. His order declared that the GLU was the creation of 'politicians, Bolsheviks, students and unemployed drifters, who use the good name of labour union to cheat the people and cause them untold sufferings in order that they themselves might benefit.'[121] It alleged that the GLU was coercing workers into striking, disrupting law and order and embezzling strike funds.[122] Liu Guanzhi and Yang Jianhong were taken into custody, and released on bail only on 21 October. In December, having served his prison term, Yang announced that he had severed all connection with the GLU.[123] A warrant was issued for the arrest of Li Lisan, but he escaped to Zhengzhou and thence to Moscow in late November. Liu Shaoqi, ill with overwork and not fit enough to leave Shanghai, managed to flee to Changsha in early November. He was nevertheless arrested in December, and only the action of a well-wisher helped him to escape from custody, whence he made his way to Canton.[124] All unregistered labour unions were ordered to dissolve, and a ban was placed on meetings and demonstrations. The Federation of Street Associations liquidated the ULCE on its own initiative, and the Commissioner of the Shanghai-Wusong police ordered the suppression of sixteen cotton mill unions in foreign and Chinese mills and the arrest of some twenty leaders.[125] On 5 October the Shanghai Tramway Workers' Union 'voluntarily' dissolved itself, having managed to hang on for almost a month after being ordered to close.[126]

On 24 September, 117 organizations protested the closure of the GLU, saying that it was at the forefront of the patriotic movement, had provided protection for workers against all manner of abuses, and had always sought to prevent conflicts between workers and other sections of society. They rejected the allegations against Li Lisan, saying that if he was guilty of embezzlement, he should be charged. A few days later, twenty unions in Yangshupu put out a similar statement, saying that what was good for the workers was good for the nation.[127] The National General Labour Union put out a statement saying that the GLU was a 'patriotic organ' which had 'restored the nation's face and rescued Shanghai from disorder'[128]

Militants in the Japanese mills were fired as soon they returned to work. But what particularly incensed the GLU was the insouciance with which Chinese employers also sacked activists and suppressed labour unions. Unions at the Shenxin No.5 and Housheng mills were closed down on 10 September.[129] On 16 September it was reported that Chinese mills had refused to take back twenty to thirty union activists.[130] At the Hengfeng mill workers struck successfully against similar dismissals from 23 to 26 November, although their success was untypical.[131] Finally, still smarting from a victorious strike in August, the management of the Commercial Press fired forty employees at the beginning of December.[132] In all, it was estimated that 1,600 workers had been fired by the end of October, 2,000 by the end of December, and 2,700 by the end of January 1926, most of them for union activities. The sackings decimated the emergent cadre of working-class labour leaders.[133] The CCP was powerless to do much except try to provide some financial assistance to those who lost their jobs. On 20 September it set up the China Relief Society (*Zhongguo jinan hui*), affiliated to the International Class-War Prisoners' Aid, under the chairmanship of Yun Daiying. It aimed to offer financial assistance, solidarity and legal aid to victims of the employer counter-offensive.[134] The party also helped people go south to find work or join the National Revolutionary Army. The International Settlement police reported that by the end of September 600 had gone to Canton.[135] From the underground, the GLU denounced the GCC for failing to halt the victimizations.[136]

Until the beginning of October Shanghai remained under the occupation of 7,000 to 8,000 soldiers of the Fengtian clique. On 10 October, however, Sun Chuanfang's troops sprang a surprise attack, and by 16 October the Fengtian forces had fled the city without a fight. Sun then installed a garrison of 4,200 Zhejiang soldiers, 2,720 of them at Wusong.[137] The GLU hoped that Sun would practise a more liberal policy; but when it tried to reopen near the West Gate on 30 October, the police moved swiftly to shut it down.[138] According to the British Consul-General, Sun showed himself determined 'to suppress bolshevism and disorder by the free use of the executioner's sword.'[139] On 25 November the International Settlement police captured Liu Hua, a warrant for whose arrest had been issued in September. As head of the Xiaoshadu office of the GLU and vice-chair of the GLU, Liu had been at the centre of the unrest in the Japanese mills. In July bandits robbed his family in Sichuan, killing his younger brother, capturing his father and wounding his mother. His family telegraphed to demand his return home, but he replied: 'The nation is feeble. Its strong neighbours insult it. Sacred labour is like meat on a chopping board. I am an activist for the nation. I am an activist for labour. My responsibilities are heavy. How can I be of use to my family? You must know that the nation too is my family.'[140] Exhausted by the May Thirtieth strike, Liu Hua was eventually prevailed upon to go into hospital. Whilst there, he penned a verse which would serve as his own epitaph: 'One who is willing to give his hot blood/ like spring rain or wine/ that sacred labour may blossom.'[141] Following his capture, he was brought before the Mixed Court on 30 November, handed over to the new Martial Law Commander, Yan Fangong, and summarily executed on 17 December. He was just 26 years old.[142] There was outrage at his execution, for he had been immensely popular, yet the ability of the labour unions to protest was severely circumscribed. Only workers at the British-owned Ewo and Oriental mills dared openly to call for his release. Mill hands in Xiaoshadu wore black arm bands, but there was no coordinated protest.[143]

Meanwhile the GLU battled to relaunch itself. On 6 December, after the Zhabei citizens' assembly gave it 'permission', the GLU reopened its office. It speedily summoned a second delegate conference on the 10th, attended by some forty representatives, which elected a new executive. The conference vowed to advance the patriotic cause by fighting for the abrogation of the unequal treaties and the attainment of customs autonomy. It pledged to support the struggle against Duan Qirui and Zhang Zuolin, and called for the creation of a representative government.[144] On 12 December the authorities again sealed the GLU office. On 20 December twenty GLU delegates met, but their call for a general strike to protest against the execution of Liu Hua met with little response.[145] Against all the odds, however, the GLU survived. In the difficult months ahead it worked mainly underground, yet it maintained an office in Zhabei and continued to publish a newspaper.[146] In the nine months after September 1925, the number of members of unions affiliated to the GLU who paid dues fell by half; yet in mid-1926 workers were still far better organized than they had been a year previously.[147]

The CCP's Assessment of the May Thirtieth Movement

Despite setbacks, the May Thirtieth Movement established the CCP in Shanghai as an influential party with a working-class base. The growth of its working-class membership, combined with the dramatic demonstration of the power of organized labour, reinforced the leadership's belief in 'proletarian hegemony' during the national revolution. At its plenum of October 1925, the CEC concluded that the May Thirtieth Movement had proved that the working class was the 'vanguard and driving force' of the national revolution.[148] Yet as early as the plenum of July 1926, the CEC would be forced to concede that 'in fact the May Thirtieth Movement was led by the General Chamber of Commerce and not by the General Labour Union.'[149] Cai Hesen accused the CEC – at a time when it was politic to do so – of concluding from the May Thirtieth Movement that 'almost the entire bourgeoisie is counter-revolutionary'.[150] The charge was too unnuanced, but it was not unfair. The May Thirtieth Movement did indeed deepen the leadership's suspicion of the 'bourgeoisie', rather paradoxically given the GCC's support – however hedged in with qualifications – for the anti-imperialist movement. Yet the compromises of the GCC – and perhaps simple pique at the adroitness with which Yu Xiaqing had marginalized the CCP – fuelled the party's mistrust of Chinese capitalists en bloc, even though it continued to maintain the ritual, but utterly unreal distinction between 'national' capitalists and 'compradore' or 'bureaucratic' elements. As early as 20 June the *Truth Daily* thundered:

> The GCC has neither the heart nor the spirit of true Chinese people. They have tagged along behind the mass movement and reluctantly supported the strike by traders. But apart from that, they have done nothing to support the movement. Everyone knows that they have strength, everyone has hoped that they would use it for the benefit of the movement, but they have remained as quiet as a dead mouse.[151]

For similar reasons, the May Thirtieth Movement tended to intensify opposition to the united front, not least because in Shanghai, in contrast to Canton, the CCP managed to acquire a position of dominance in the movement without too much reliance on the GMD. Moreover, the resurgence of the triple stoppage as the basic tactic of the anti-imperialist movement – a tactic that had first emerged during the May Fourth Movement of 1919 – suggested that the united front model, which presumed that an alliance of two parties would lead the mass movement, might not be altogether appropriate to Chinese realities. Without minimizing the leadership exercised by the CCP, particularly through the GLU, the May Thirtieth Movement proved fundamentally not to be a party-led movement; instead it assumed the form of an alliance between three different *jie*, or sections of society, under the aegis of a non-party coalition (the ULCE). There is no evidence that the CEC reflected upon this paradox, yet the vigour and spontaneity of the mass movement seem to have strengthened its distaste for politicking in the GMD – the unavoidable corollary of the 'bloc within' strategy – and hardened its conviction that social classes, not political parties, would make the national revolution.

Chapter 6

The Shanghai Communists and the United Front, 1925-26

The Shanghai Guomindang

The May Thirtieth Movement caused the Shanghai GMD to grow, but it continued to lack the mass base which the party had in Canton and the south. Over 2,000 joined the Shanghai organization in the second half of 1925, but the drop-out rate was high, and by May 1926 membership still stood at only 1,200, of whom half were Communists.[1] There are no data on the social composition of party members, but at least half were students. We know, for instance, that there were over 300 members in the GMD branch at Shanghai University and seventy in the branch at Daxia University at this time.[2] During the summer of 1926 membership grew rapidly to reach 2,266 by October, 1,300 of whom were students, one-third allegedly 'rightists'.[3] Workers probably formed the next largest contingent of members, followed by merchants, who in May 1926 numbered 300.[4] Roughly the same size as the local CCP (for a brief period around May 1926, Communists outnumbered GMD members), the growth of the Shanghai GMD was pitifully slow. When measured against a national membership of 183,700, according to the far from complete figures given to the Second National GMD Congress in January 1926, the GMD in Shanghai was small.[5]

Although left-leaning elements were always stronger in the Shanghai GMD than the 'right wing', the latter acquired a firm hold over certain organs of the regional party apparatus. Particularly worrying for the Communists was the emergence after the death of Sun Yat-sen of a so-called 'new right', led by Dai Jitao, a member of the CEC of the GMD and of the Shanghai executive bureau (*Shanghai zhixing bu*). The latter briefly became a stronghold of his supporters, issuing, together with the executive committee of the Zhejiang provincial organization (dominated by Shen Xuanlu), a directive to propaganda organs urging them to repudiate class struggle and 'awaken' capitalists and landlords to their responsibility to exercise benevolence (*ren'ai*).[6] So grudging was support offered by the bureau to the May Thirtieth Movement that the CEC cut off its funding.[7]

In July 1925 Dai Jitao published *The National Revolution and the GMD*, in which he argued that the national revolution was one in which all classes should unite, and that class struggle violated the 'mutual social responsibility' (*shehui liandai zeren zhuyi*) at the heart of Chinese culture. He contended that membership of a party other than the GMD was incompatible with the principles of the national revolution, and accused the Communists of monopolizing posts, poaching members, and undermining confidence in the leadership through their remorseless criticism.[8] Dai's second work, *The Philosophical Basis of Sun Wenism*, proved even more controversial, since it offered the first systematic exposition of Sun Yat-sen's philosophy. Dai argued that whilst Sun had sought to modernize political institutions, his philosophy was rooted in traditional Chinese morality: in the benevolence which inspired man's will to knowledge and action.[9] The Three People's Principles were thus the antithesis of Communist materialism. The success of Dai's brochure caught the CCP napping. In September Qu Qiubai counterattacked, arguing that it was 'pure utopianism' to suggest that the 'benevolent and loving nature' of the bourgeoisie could replace a mass revolution of the proletariat and peasantry.[10] Chen Duxiu supplied reinforcements, defending class struggle as a necessary element in the national revolution, and insisting that whilst the latter required a measure of consensus (*gongxin*) between classes, each class within the GMD should retain its own identity (*bie xin*).[11]

Even more fervently opposed to the alliance with the Communists were those the CCP dubbed the 'old right', such as the Xinhai comrades club, led by Zhang Taiyan and Tang Shaoyi. The 'old right' consisted of various networks of GMD elders, most of whom had their roots in the Alliance Society, founded by Sun Yat-sen to topple the Qing dynasty. By the time of the May Thirtieth Movement, the 'old right' was marginalized; but it found a new focus after 23 November 1925 when an unofficial 'Fourth CEC Plenum' convened at Sun Yat-sen's bier in the Western Hills, north of Beijing.[12] The Western Hills group, united by its rejection of the united front with the CCP, was initially supported by the network of GMD activists from Zhejiang, which included Dai Jitao, Zhang Jingjiang and Wu Zhihui. After Dai and Shen Xuanlu were beaten up at the start of the Western Hills gathering for being too pro-Communist, Dai withdrew from the group. By December Ye Chucang and Shao Yuanchong, in solidarity with their Zhejiang compatriots, had also distanced themselves from Western Hills irreconcilables. The Second GMD Congress, which took place in Canton in January 1926, chose to treat Wu Zhihui, too, as a 'loyal comrade'.[13] Since the Western Hills group did not recognise the legitimacy of the Second Congress, it organized its own in Shanghai. Opening on 29 March, it was attended by seventy-one participants, including Shen Xuanlu, Xie Chi and Zou Lu.[14] By May, virtually all members of the Zhejiang network had been reconciled to Canton, their members looking to their fellow-provincial, Chiang Kai-shek, for leadership. Ye Chucang was appointed director of the secretariat of the CEC and Shao Yuanchong head of the youth department in Canton.[15]

Despite the relative strength of the GMD right in Shanghai, the Shanghai party bureau (*Shanghai tebie shi dangbu*) and, to a lesser extent, the Jiangsu provincial bureau (*Jiangsu sheng dangbu*) remained under the control of those who approved the united front. In July 1926 there were nine Communists on the executive of the Shanghai party bureau. Luo Yinong, secretary of the Shanghai regional committee of the CCP, headed the party fraction within it.[16] Although no more than a couple of dozen Communists worked predominantly in the GMD, they constituted the core of the so-called 'GMD Left'. There were able left-leaning GMD members in the Shanghai bureau, such as Yang Xianjiang and Yang Xingfo, but the GMD failed to develop a 'left wing' with a separate political identity. In July 1926 the Shanghai regional committee of the CCP told the enlarged plenum of the CEC that it was meaningless to speak of a GMD left in the city. Voitinskii blamed this situation on the fact that Borodin had imposed an inappropriately 'Bolshevik' structure on the GMD, characterised by lack of local autonomy and organizational flexibility, which made it hard to draw in the petty-bourgeois masses who were assumed to be the social base of the party's left wing.[17] The July plenum urged Communists to give up their majority on the Shanghai party bureau and work to draw the medium and small merchants, the progressive gentry, university teachers, students, artisans and professionals into the GMD, so that a genuine left wing could develop.[18] But the resolution had little effect: on 4 November 1926 Chen Duxiu confessed that in Shanghai, as in Canton, Communists still controlled the key committees in the local GMD. He recounted how comrades had tried to persuade Liu Yazi, a leading left-winger in the local GMD, to take greater responsibility, but in vain. Chen concluded that much as GMD leftists might resent the tendency of the CCP to monopolise (*baoban*) activity inside the GMD, they were unable to survive without the Communists.[19]

The Growth of the CCP and CYL

The May Thirtieth Movement, together with a loosening of restrictions on admission to the CCP, led to a rapid growth of the party. In May 1925 national membership was a little over 1,000, a year later it stood at 11,257.[20] It then rose to 13,281 in August 1926, and to 18,526 by December 1926.[21] The Shanghai regional organization, which covered much of Zhejiang and Jiangsu, grew substantially, but not so fast as national membership. During the May Thirtieth Movement local membership more than trebled from 297 in May to 1,080 in September.[22] By November 1925 there were 1,350 members in the Shanghai region, and by

April 1926, 2,500; but this figure masked the fact that 800 had left the party in the intervening period.[23] Thereafter the party entered a period of stagnation. In May 1926 membership in the region dropped to 2,241, and to 2,223 by late August.[24] Repression by Sun Chuanfang's troops and the police of the foreign settlements, combined with victimization by employers, meant that neither the CCP nor the GMD grew as rapidly in Shanghai as in some other areas. Whereas in October 1925 the Shanghai region had the largest share of CCP members, by April 1926 it had been outstripped by Guangdong, and by September 1926 by Hunan also.[25] The significance of this was not lost on the British. In its annual report for 1926, the Municipal Council observed:

> Police action has considerably curtailed the activities of Commu-
> nists in Shanghai by prohibiting all political demonstrations,
> handbill distribution and street lectures. During the year no fewer
> than 125 persons were prosecuted for rioting, intimidation,
> distribution of literature and kindred offences. On six occasions
> successful application was made to have the headquarters of
> agitators closed. Similar prohibitive measures were adopted in
> Chinese territory, where the General Labour Union and the
> National Students Union were closed. In Chinese territory
> proclamations were issued prohibiting meetings and the distribu-
> tion of inflammatory literature.[26]

Following the failure of the strikes in the Japanese mills in the summer of 1926, membership reached a nadir of 1,380 in September, a fall of 45 per cent on the April level.[27] During the last three months of 1926, however, the setbacks of the summer were dramatically reversed, as Chiang Kai-shek's victorious National Revolutionary Army swept northwards. By December membership in the Shanghai region had doubled to an all-time high of 2,688.[28]

If the growth of the Shanghai CCP was not as impressive as elsewhere, the party could feel proud of its record in transforming itself into a working-class party. Already in May 1925 57.3 per cent of the 297 members were workers, but during the May Thirtieth Movement workers were recruited directly into the CCP – without dual membership of the GMD – so that by September their proportion had increased to 78.5 per cent (out of 1,080 members).[29] At the October 1925 plenum the CEC cut the probationary period of workers and peasants entering the party to one month, compared with three months for intellectuals, stating that for class-conscious workers neither extensive practical experience nor theoretical understanding were necessary for full membership.[30] By August 1926, of 2,223 members no fewer than 84.32 per cent were said to be workers – vastly more than in Guangdong (42.68 per cent), the north (63.7 per cent) or Hunan (46.9 per cent).[31] By contrast, there were only 165 students in the party, seventy of them at Shanghai University, and a paltry eighteen 'merchants', most of whom were in fact shop assistants. Around this time, eight-seven of the 119 branches under the regional committee were workplace branches, no fewer than forty-seven of them in cotton mills.[32] Perhaps the most remarkable feature of the Shanghai organization was the extent to which it became a party of cotton workers (though significantly of male cotton workers rather than of females, who comprised the majority of the industry's labour force). In December 1926 cotton workers formed 54 per cent of the regional membership.[33] In April 1926, when there were forty-four branches in the cotton industry, the largest were at Shenxin No.1 mill (thirty-one members), Toyoda (thirty members) and NWK No.7 (twenty-three members).[34] Nevertheless some of the strongest workplace branches in the CCP were rooted among more skilled workers. The largest such branch was at the Commercial Press, where membership rose from thirty in May 1925 to around 100 in September.[35] The Shanghai power station branch, set up in March 1926, had a membership of almost sixty by March 1927, and there was a flourishing branch at the Compagnie Française de Tramways et d'Eclairage Electrique.[36] The proletarianization of the CCP in Shanghai did not alter the fundamentally male character of the party, even though a majority of the factory workforce in the city was female. Nevertheless, the proportion of female members in the Shanghai organization was considerably higher than the national average. In March 1926, 22 per cent of members in the region were female (25 per cent in Shanghai itself), though this fell in April to 18.5 per cent (21 per cent in Shanghai).[37]

In January 1925 the Fourth CCP Congress decided to turn the SYL into the Communist Youth League (CYL). At that stage, there were still only 200 members in the Shanghai SYL. As a result of the May Thirtieth Movement, however, membership of the CYL increased to 518 in August 1925. Like the CCP itself, the May Thirtieth general strike led to the CYL becoming more proletarian in composition. In August 1925 it had twenty-eight worker branches, eleven student branches and three mixed branches, and workers were estimated to make up 53.7 per cent of membership and intellectuals 45.6 per cent.[38] By January 1926 there were sixty-eight branches of the CYL in Shanghai, with a membership of 1,074; but the CYL did not expand as fast as the CCP (indeed at this point the latter was briefly larger than its youth wing). By March, however, the CYL had once again slightly overtaken the parent party, with ninety-four branches and 2,285 members.[39] Thereafter membership of the CYL fell as did that of the CCP. By June there were 1,713 members in the city, the strongest district organizations being in Xiaoshadu (354 members), Yinxianggang (209 members), Yangshupu (194 members), Zhabei (171 members) and Shanghai University (175 members).[40] Membership continued to fall during the summer and autumn, only picking up towards the end of the year. By the end of 1926 there were eight-five CYL branches in Shanghai with 1,897 members.[41]

United Front Policy

Following the May Thirtieth Movement, ECCI became anxious that Communists in Canton were sidelining work in the mass movements in favour of capturing positions of power within the GMD. The second enlarged plenum of the CEC of the CCP, which met in Beijing from 28 September to 2 October 1925, was designed to rectify this deviation.[42] In the event, the plenum fell into what Moscow considered to be another deviation, when Chen Duxiu used the occasion to call once again for the party to prepare to leave the GMD and not be 'tied down' (*qianzhi*) by the united front when organizing the masses.[43] Thanks to Voitinskii, Chen's call was not endorsed by the plenum; but Voitinskii must have approved the change in policy, which prescribed that 'except where necessary, new comrades should not join the GMD nor engage in its work, especially in the work of higher party organs'. Indeed Voitinskii frankly reported to Moscow that 'we are planning to shift our relations with the GMD from a union to a bloc.'[44] This was definitely not what the Politburo wished to hear. The new policy, combined with the plenum's categorization of Dai Jitao's supporters as 'rightists' rather than 'centrists', convinced Moscow that the CEC was in the grip of a 'leftist deviation'.[45] From the ground in China, however, it appeared to Voitinskii and the CEC majority that it was Borodin and the comrades in Canton who represented a 'leftist deviation'. Fearful that their aggressive strategy within the GMD was likely to provoke a right-wing backlash, Voitinskii in mid-December persuaded Chen Duxiu and others to hold private talks with the more tractable supporters of the Western Hills faction. Ye Chucang, Shao Yuanchong and Sun Ke, the son of Sun Yat-sen, were assured that the CCP had no ambition to monopolize GMD affairs and that it would be content to receive a maximum of one-third of the places on GMD committees at the forthcoming Second GMD Congress. At the same time, Chen urged these less intransigent 'rightists' to make peace with the party, participate in the congress, and take up party and government posts in Guangdong.[46]

The Second GMD Congress, which took place from 4 to 19 January 1926, suggested to some in the CCP that Voitinskii's fears were unfounded, since it resoundingly approved the alliance with the CCP and condemned the Western Hills faction. In the face of overwhelming support for the left, Borodin and the comrades in Canton pressed for an all-out assault on the right wing, demanding the expulsion of Dai Jitao and Sun Ke. Voitinskii and the CEC majority, however, insisted on a more moderate line. In the event, the Second Congress expelled only seven 'old rightists'; and only seven Communists were nominated for the thirty-six places on the CEC and one for the seven places on the central supervisory commission. Some historians in the PRC have characterized these concessions as unnecessary appeasement of the GMD right, a policy of 'strengthening the right, boosting the centre and isolating the left', i.e. the exact opposite of the official Comintern line.[47] Yet events were soon to show that, notwithstanding these concessions, the Communist leadership had overplayed its hand.

Despite his well-grounded fears of the strength of opposition to the united front within the GMD, Voitinskii fully shared the illusions of the Comintern concerning the nature of that party. In a report to ECCI on 20 February 1926 he described it as a 'popular-democratic party' and claimed that the 'CCP in fact directs the GMD'.[48] Such illusions were shattered by the events of 20 March, when Chiang Kai-shek ordered two gunboats to train their sights on the Huangpu Military Academy, the arrest of Soviet commissars of the Canton garrison, and the surrounding of the residence of Soviet advisers in Canton by troops. It happened that a special commission of the Russian Politburo, led by A.S. Bubnov, secretary of the Central Committee of the Russian Communist Party and director of the Chief Political Administration of the Red Army, was in Canton at the time. Bubnov immediately resolved to play down the significance of the incident, which he described as a 'small semi-uprising directed against Russian advisers and Chinese communists', on the grounds that Soviet advisers had brought the action on themselves by behaving insolently towards the officers corps of the National Revolutionary Army (NRA). In a bid to appease Chiang Kai-shek and to 'win time', he ordered the removal of N.V. Kuibyshev, director of the group of military advisers, and two others.[49] In the light of Bubnov's reassurances, ECCI decided that the March 20th Incident had not altered the balance of forces within the national revolution. Indeed it insisted even more clamorously that Chiang Kai-shek was a representative of the 'centre' of the GMD, and not of the right wing, who could be pushed in a more leftward direction under mass pressure.[50]

Chen Duxiu heard of the March 20th Incident while he was in hospital, suffering from the typhoid fever which plagued him for most of 1926. Typically, he had not bothered to inform leading comrades of his whereabouts, and they were anxious that he had 'gone missing'.[51] 'Depressed' by the news of the incident, Chen's immediate response was to propose resistance to Chiang Kai-shek; on second thoughts, however, he decided that only substantial concessions could prevent Chiang siding decisively with the right.[52] In mid-April he changed his mind once again, after learning more about the incident from his son, Chen Yannian, leader of the Canton Communists and Zhou Enlai. Refusing to play along with the Comintern whitewash of the incident, he called for the CCP to withdraw from the GMD and proposed that the 2nd and 6th Armies be strengthened in readiness to resist Chiang Kai-shek. He may also have suggested that 5,000 rifles be sent to the peasant associations of Guangdong. Peng Shuzhi and Zhang Guotao were sent south to investigate the incident, where they stayed for almost two months.[53]

The new demand for withdrawal from the GMD could not have come at a less favourable moment, since within the Russian Communist Party the United Opposition was on the point of proposing the same course of action. Karl Radek, a member of the opposition, had already suggested transforming the 'bloc within' to a 'bloc without' at the VI ECCI plenum in March, but had been soundly rebuffed.[54] At a Politburo meeting on 29 April he and Zinoviev repeated the proposal, to which Voitinskii also gave cautious backing, but were denounced by the majority who supported Stalin.[55] Matters came to a head in July at a joint plenum of the CC and Central Control Commission of the Russian Communist Party when the proposal of the United Opposition was described as right-wing capitulationism and 'inadmissible defeatism'.[56]

Borodin had been in Russia at the time of the March 20th Incident. On his return on 29 April, he went to great lengths to placate Chiang Kai-shek, so much so that GMD left-wingers began to taunt the Communists with being Chiang's 'running dogs'.[57] At the 2nd plenum of the CEC of the GMD, which met from 15 to 22 May, Borodin acceded to Chiang's demands that Communists should not head GMD bureaux; that they should not comprise more than one-third of the personnel of any party organ; and that a list of CCP members should be given to the chair of the CEC.[58] In a letter to Karakhan of 30 May, he justified these concessions by arguing that the Communists were depriving the right wing of a stick with which to beat them, and reassuring 'honourable' GMD members that they did not wish to devour their party. He claimed that the left still controlled most departmental directorships, and made light of the fact that 'centrists', such as Shao Yuanchong and Ye Chucang, were now in key positions. He even contended that the arrest of Wu Tiecheng, the chief of police in Canton, was evidence that Chiang was carrying out a purge of rightists in return for the concessions which the CCP had made. The analysis was wholly self-deceiving, and Borodin, while insisting that Chiang was a 'centrist' whose course of action would be determined by the overall balance of forces within the party, was forced to concede that the NRA was becoming Chiang's 'personal army'. And having begun his letter by suggesting that Chiang was repaying his dues to the left, he ended by admitting that 'notwithstanding all his protestations that he is and remains a revolutionary . . . he has been forced to make concessions to the right and centrists.'[59] The CEC of the CCP was unpersuaded by Borodin's diagnosis. On 4 June 1926 it backed a call from Chen Duxiu to withdraw from the GMD in favour of a 'bloc without'.[60] The same day, Chen sent a letter to Chiang Kai-shek, published in the *Guide Weekly*, which strongly hinted that he was a 'rightist'. According to PRC historian, Gui Xinqiu, this 'undoubtedly showed contempt for the Comintern'.[61]

ECCI was not amused. Voitinskii was ordered back to China once again to bring the CEC into line. On 1 July he despatched a report from Shanghai stating that the March 20th Incident had done grave damage to the left and that Chiang Kai-shek was bent on personal dictatorship.[62] Yet he also described Chiang as a 'centrist' who could not afford to sever his ties with the left.[63] At the third enlarged plenum of the CEC, from 12 to 18 July, Chen Duxiu and Peng Shuzhi formally proposed that the CCP withdraw from the GMD. Voitinskii used his diplomatic skill to persuade a majority, led by Qu Quibai, that withdrawal would be unwise. According to the resolution passed, which was drafted by the Far Eastern Bureau of ECCI which Voitinskii had just set up in Shanghai, the CCP agreed to stay in the GMD and to follow the approved formula of expanding the left, uniting with the left to handle the centre, and attacking the right.[64] Forced 'to lower the banners and muffle the drums' (*yanqi-xigu*), Chen Duxiu now proceeded to adopt a policy of substantial compromise towards the GMD, which he maintained until early 1927, captured in the slogan 'engage but don't monopolise, make concessions but don't withdraw' (*ban er bu bao, tui er bu chu*).[65] Yet despite Voitinskii's success in persuading the CEC to abide by the Comintern line, it continued tacitly to deny that there was a 'centre' grouping within the GMD, referring in its pronouncements to Chiang Kai-shek as the 'new right', but always making sure that each such reference was followed by a parenthesis containing the words, 'the centre faction'.[66]

Another 'error' which Voitinskii was sent to correct was the support given by the CEC plenum in February 1926 to Chiang Kai-shek's plans for a Northern Expedition, which envisaged that the NRA would defeat the warlords and achieve the political reunification of China. As adviser to the Canton government, Borodin did not oppose the Northern Expedition, although he criticised the plan for being too narrowly military in character.[67] Moscow, however, regarded any campaign to reunify China as premature and likely to have undesirable diplomatic repercussions. At Voitinskii's urging, Chen Duxiu published an article criticising the Northern Expedition on 7 July, to the chagrin of Chiang Kai-shek.[68] Yet the CEC resisted demands from the newly-established Far Eastern Bureau of ECCI that it oppose the expedition outright. Instead a compromise was reached, whereby the CEC agreed not to orient the activities of the CCP towards the Northern Expedition as such, but to use it as a way of expanding its own forces.[69] In the event, the policy had little practical import, since local party organizations everywhere, especially in Guangdong, mobilized vigorously in support of the NRA after it set out to reunify the country on 9 July.

Organizing Youth

Following the Fourth CCP Congress, the Third Congress of the SYL convened in Shanghai, from 26 to 31 January 1925. It agreed to change the name of the organization to the Communist Youth League, to join KIM and to adopt a new constitution. It also affirmed a perspective of concentrating on the labour movement and recruiting working-class youth. Zhang Tailei was elected general secretary of the new Central Committee, which was based in Shanghai. Yun Daiying, Ren Bishi and Wang Yifei were its most prominent members. Wang, born in 1898 in Shangyu county, Zhejiang, was another alumnus of the First Normal School in Hangzhou. As a member of the SYL, he had gone to the Soviet Union, where he had learned to speak and write Russian well and become chair of the Moscow committee of the SYL. According to Zheng Chaolin, he 'was short in stature and mediocre in personality'.[70] Upon his return in autumn 1924, he joined the CC of the SYL; from September 1925 he served as secretary of the Shanghai regional committee of the CCP. The Third SYL Congress appointed Zhang Qiuren secretary of the Shanghai regional committee of the new CYL.[71] In September 1925 he was replaced by He Chang, who remained in that office until December 1926. He Chang was born in Liulin, Shanxi, in 1906 and graduated from the No.1 Middle School in Taiyuan. He joined the SYL in 1921 and the CCP in 1923, moving to Shanghai to enrol at Shanghai University. He soon became a member of the CC of the CYL and head of its worker-peasant bureau.[72] The Shanghai regional committee of the CYL had nine functional bureaux, and its student and women's committees were jointly responsible to the regional committee of the CCP.

In the course of the May Thirtieth Movement, several CYL members sprang to prominence in the student movement. Li Shuoxun, the chair of the NSU, had joined the SYL in 1922 and the CCP in 1924. Born in 1903 in Qinfu, Sichuan, he was brother-in-law of Zhao Shiyan.[73] Another prominent activist, also born in Sichuan in 1900, was Guo Bohe, a student at Shanghai University and a member of the CCP.[74] Such leaders were crucial in orienting students towards the labour movement. At its seventh conference, which opened in Shanghai on 26 June 1925, the NSU pledged support for the workers on strike and called on students to propagandize on behalf of labour unions, set up night schools, establish periodicals for workers, and call on the government to institute protective legislation and help the unemployed.[75] The chair of the conference, Yang Shannan, a student from Beijing who had been born in Shanghai in 1904, was a CYL member. The conference also exhorted student unions to 'induce Christians to leave the Church', to infiltrate the YMCA and to encourage students in mission schools to recover their educational rights.[76] This was partly in response to the recent showdown at St John's University, when nineteen teachers and 580 students had withdrawn after the principal forbade them to fly the flag at half-mast in honour of the victims of the May Thirtieth Incident.[77]

Yet while CYL and CCP members attained high-ranking positions in the student movement, especially in the NSU, the political sway of the CYL did not expand accordingly at the grass roots. There were several reasons for this. One was the loss of Shanghai University as a base for left-wing activity. On 4 June 1925 the International Settlement police occupied and sealed the university, causing many militants to leave the city. The university soon reopened in new premises in Shishou lane, off Qingyun road, Zhabei, on 10 September; and by 1926, it had a larger CCP branch than ever, consisting of 130 members. Yet Shanghai University never regained the standing it had once enjoyed.[78] Secondly, the failure of the CYL substantially to increase its sway in the student world was a consequence of its decision to concentrate on the labour and peasant movements. On 23 December 1925, for instance, the CEC ordered the CYL to send its members into the countryside to start elementary schools as a way of spreading 'revolutionary thought.'[79] In this way, some potential leaders were lost to the labour and peasant movements, though it must be said that most CYL members were singularly ill-fitted for work outside the student milieu. Thirdly, a sizeable minority of students, especially in the SSU, resented what they considered to be the duplicity and manipulativeness of the Communists, and came to sympathise with those who opposed the united front. Some were drawn towards the Sun Yat-sen Three People's Principles Study Groups (*Sun Wen sanminzhuyi xuehui*), which had been set up Dai Jitao. Activists from the study groups, such as Chen Chengyin and Duanmu Kai, acquired influence in the SSU, though failed to displace the leftist majority.[80] Others, such as Zuo Shunsheng, a standard bearer for the work-study movement in 1919, proselytized on behalf of the Young China Party, a nationalist group seduced by the authoritarian nationalism then in vogue in Europe. It had supporters at the Southeastern University and University of Political Science and Law.[81] Opponents of the Communists sought to create a counter-pole to the SSU, in the form of the Shanghai All-University Association (*gedaxue tongzhihui*), whose watchwords were 'Save the Nation through Study' and 'Cooperation between Students and Teachers'.[82]

By 1926 the Communist leadership was alarmed by the decline of its influence in the student movement, but chose to blame this on defective work by the CYL. On 17 January 1926 the CEC of the CCP and CC of the CYL prescribed that future work be carried out under the joint control of the two organizations, with party cells in student organizations taking orders directly from local CCP organization.[83] This intensification of party control failed, however, to stem the steady decline in the CYL's fortunes. In July 1926 the third CEC plenum observed that 'reactionary ideas and organizations resulting from class differentiation are daily expanding and exerting a strong influence on the masses of youth.'[84] The response was again the standard one of stepping up party control still further: 'the party should hereafter direct the CYL in earnest'. Yet in keeping with the Comintern's desire to have its cake and eat it, the resolution also warned party cadres against 'assigning work arbitrarily to responsible comrades of the CYL'.[85] The fortunes of the CYL did revive in the second half of 1926, but this had more to do with a general revival in the student movement that got underway from the spring of 1926. However, the success of the summer schools organized by the SSU, to which assorted leftists lectured, undoubtedly helped.[86]

In the spring of 1926 the student movement in Shanghai took on a new lease of life. The 18 March massacre, when forty-seven student protesters in Beijing were killed and many more wounded by troops of Duan Qirui, provoked the SSU into calling students out on strike for four days. Beginning on 24 March, most but not all schools in Shanghai took part, flying flags at half mast and holding memorial meetings for the victims. The inflexible response of the authorities further intensified student discontent. At Tongji University, the Commercial University and some smaller colleges students were ordered to sign a 'vow of repentance', promising that they would refrain from any further boycott of classes or face expulsion. When the entire student body at Tongji University refused to do so, the police were called in and the campus was sealed off. Some eighty students left in protest and many student associations sent messages of solidarity and funds for those who had been victimized.[87] Students also protested boisterously on the first anniversary of the May Thirtieth Movement, though the International Settlement police were struck more by the participation of 'young boys and girls from the mills'.[88]

Meanwhile the number of young people sent to the Soviet Union for training increased substantially. Following the death of Sun Yat-sen, the Soviet Politburo decided to establish a university for 500 students in Moscow, named after the founder of the GMD. Karl Radek was appointed rector of the Sun Yat-sen University, which was intended to exist alongside the Chinese section of the KUTV, to which all students had hitherto been sent.[89] On 17 September 1925 the Politburo assigned 550,000 rubles to the new university, but it did not open its doors until January 1926, owing to a lack of interpreters.[90] In the autumn of 1925 two distinct groups of students left China to study at the Sun Yat-sen University. Of the 103 students who left from Shanghai, twenty-four were members of the CCP, sixty-seven of the CYL and twelve were members of both organizations. They included Zhang Liang, a woman worker from the NWK mills, and a male worker, Zhu Huaishan. They were led by a group of eight students who had previous experience of the Soviet Union, including Yu Xiusong and Dong Yixiang.[91] By contrast, the Canton contingent consisted of

GMD members, many of whom were on the right of the party. Of this group of 147 (chosen from a pool of 1030 applicants), 31 per cent were married, 65 per cent were unmarried and the marital status of 4 per cent was unknown. Only 5 per cent were women. Twenty-four per cent were aged twenty or less; 59 per cent were aged twenty-one to twenty-five; 14 per cent were aged twenty-six to thirty; and 3 per cent were of unknown age. Forty-eight per cent were from Guangdong; 19 per cent from Hunan;10 per cent from Jiangxi; 5 per cent from Yunnan; 5 per cent from Sichuan; 3 per cent from Hubei; 2 per cent from Zhejiang; 2 per cent from Guizhou etc. Only eight-two responded to the question about their occupation, and ten replies were unclear. Of the remainder, fifty-five were classed as students, seven as teachers, two as journalists, one as a farmer and seven as 'miscellaneous'. Each person had to provide 150 dollars towards their fare, the other 100 dollars being paid by the GMD.[92] On 20 June 1926 the CEC of the CCP decided not to send any more Communists to the Sun Yat-sen University on the grounds that they merely aroused the antipathy of GMD students.[93] On 28 September Radek complained to the Politburo about this decision, but ECCI said that it had already instructed the CEC to reverse it.[94] Nevertheless the Sun Yat-sen University continued to cater largely for GMD students – that is until 26 July 1927 when the GMD withdrew all students – whereas KUTV received students who were mainly members of the CCP and CYL.[95]

Organizing Women

The May Thirtieth Movement brought about a modest revival of the women's movement. On 5 June, eighty representatives of twenty-three organizations, including the Women's Suffrage Association (*Nüzi canzheng hui*) and the Committee to Promote Women's Participation in the National Assembly, met to form the Shanghai Association of Women of all Sections of Society (*Shanghai gejie funü lianhehui*), under the presidency of Song Qingling. The association defined its aim as being to 'seek complete and genuine equality for women in society and practical liberation at a personal level'.[96] It backed a list of anti-imperialist demands put forward by Xiang Jingyu, including ones relating to labour, and agreed to organize street collections and street corner meetings in support of the victims of the May Thirtieth Incident. Kong Dezhi, a student at Shanghai University and wife of Shen Yanbing, organized groups to tour the mills of Pudong to speak to mill women, and a woman from Xiada university organized similar groups in the Xiaoshadu mill district.[97] On 10 June the Shanghai GMD women's committee held a well-attended seventh meeting which planned a large meeting for women in the city, to be backed up by street collections and speaker teams.[98] Through such activities the number of female activists in Shanghai increased substantially, and their bobbed hair and student attire became potent symbols of the new gender order associated with the national revolution.[99]

In December 1925 Xiang Jingyu was sent to Moscow. Her former father-in-law, Shen Xuanlu, who had by this time left the CCP and joined the Western Hills faction, seized the opportunity to install his wife as chair of the women's movement committee of the GMD party bureau in her stead.[100] Xiang's post as director of the CEC women's bureau was filled by Yang Zhihua, who had enjoyed great success as an organizer of women workers during the May Thirtieth Movement. Liu Zunyi headed the women's bureau of the regional committee of the CCP until April 1926. Born in Sichuan, she had studied in Beijing and sworn sisterhood with ten other women in the party. However, she broke her vow of celibacy to marry He Luo, a student at Shanghai University.[101] In April she asked to be relieved of her post so that she could concentrate on work in the Shanghai Association of Women of all Sections of Society which was planning a women's congress with a view to creating a national women's organization.[102] In December 1925 this Association had begun to publish a journal, *Chinese Women* (*Zhongguo funü*), which the CCP financed.[103] In August 1926 the regional committee divided responsibility for women's work between Chen Bilan, who was put in charge of work in the women's movement, and Wang Yazhang, a student at Shanghai University, who was put in charge of work in the labour movement.[104] Chen was born in 1902 in Hubei and had joined the SYL as a student in Wuhan in 1922. In 1924 she went to Moscow, where she separated from her husband and became amorously entangled with Luo Yinong. In August 1925 she returned to China, just as Peng Shuzhi was recovering from a short, unhappy affair with Xiang Jingyu. When Xiang left for Moscow, Peng became melancholic and started to drink. Chen brought him out of his misery and they lived together for the rest of their lives.[105]

In June 1926 Chen Bilan bemoaned the fact that the women's movement in the city was not keeping pace with the other mass movements.[106] In July the CEC plenum criticized party organizations for failing to make inroads among the mass of peasant and working women. It suggested that the success of Communists in gaining control of GMD women's bureaux and other women's organizations had actually militated against this, since the radical statements put out by these organizations had alarmed ordinary women.[107] Whether the party deliberately chose to downgrade its women's programme is unclear, but there is circumstantial evidence that it no longer regarded it with the earnestness it had once shown. During the summer of 1926, for example, the CEC told the women's department that it had three months to find funding from civic organizations for the journal *Chinese Women*. When it failed to do so, the journal was allowed to fold.[108] And on 20 September 1926 at a joint session of the CEC and the FEB, Voitinskii complained that no sum had been set aside in the budget for work among women, to which Chen Duxiu replied that there were simply no funds.[109]

Party Life

The Shanghai regional committee found it hard to cope with the expansion of membership and of activity caused by the May Thirtieth Movement. Li Lisan was technically a member of the committee, but rarely attended meetings, and its other leading members, Zhuang Wengong and Xie Wenjin, were both mediocrities.[110] Yin Kuan, secretary of the committee and head of propaganda, was able but valetudinarian. Born in 1897 in Tongcheng, Anhui province, his name – which means "broad" – belied his appearance, which was tall and thin. He had a sardonic wit. As a work-study student in France and a founder member of the European branch of the CCP, he had made a name as a skilled polemicist against anarchism. In the late summer of 1923 he went to Moscow. On returning to China, he was assigned to work as secretary of the Shandong provincial committee, where he fell in love with Wang Bian. After his transfer to Shanghai, Wang's father – who was a prominent member of the CCP in Shandong – denounced him to the CEC, threatening to come to Shanghai with a dagger to track him down.[111] The work of the Shanghai regional committee only began to pick up in December when Luo Yinong arrived to take up the post of secretary. Born in 1902 into a poor peasant family in Xiangtan, Hunan province, Luo had joined the SYL in 1920 and gone to Russia in 1921, where he stayed until 1925. He soon caught the eye of Russian officials, who made him secretary of the Moscow branch of the CCP and a member of the presidium of the KUTV branch of the Russian Communist Party. Tall and thin, with a pale complexion, he too 'loved to tell people that he was in bad health'.[112] Yet he acted vigorously to resuscitate the Shanghai regional committee.

In May 1926 Zhao Shiyan was sent to Shanghai to take charge of organizational work, thereby inaugurating what has been called the 'golden age' of the regional committee.[113] Born in 1901 in Youyang, Sichuan province, Zhao was the last of five sons of a landlord and businessman, with three older sisters and one younger sister. After graduating from elementary school in 1914, Zhao accompanied his next older brother to attend secondary school in Beijing. Of boundless energy, he not only excelled in his studies, especially English, but became the moving force behind the Youth Study Society. In 1920 he went to France, where he worked at the Schneider engineering works at Le Creusot, becoming secretary of the European branch of the CCP. In March 1923 he led the first cohort of work-study students from France to the KUTV. Returning in 1924, he became secretary of the Beijing committee and head of propaganda of the Northern regional committee.[114] Zhao was a born leader, a good speaker, a magnetic personality, someone who was adept at getting on with people.[115] He and Luo Yinong made an excellent team. Luo ran the Shanghai organization in a less bureaucratic fashion than the Canton organization, preferring meetings of activists to formal conferences.[116] He kept in contact with important members of the Shanghai GMD, Yu Xiaqing and other 'national capitalists' and with Green Gang bosses. To that end, he lived with his wife, mother-in-law and brother-in-law in a luxurious residence – shared by Zhao Shiyan, who lived much more frugally – and wore a long gown and a mandarin jacket, looking every inch the family patriarch.[117]

Several members of the CEC, including Peng Shuzhi, Cai Hesen and Xiang Jingyu, lived collectively after October 1925 in a three-storey lane house on Fusheng Road, not too far from the secretariat of the CEC and the office of the GLU in Zhabei. Zhang Guotao and Chen Duxiu often took meals there.[118] Such collective living arrangements were inspired partly by considerations of economy, and partly by a desire to create an alternative to the repressive 'feudal' family from which most of them had fled. Party members were, of course, expected to subordinate family loyalty to political loyalty. After Shao Lizi refused to back the Wuhan government against Chiang Kai-shek, his son wrote to him from Moscow, saying: "You are a counter-revolutionary; you are no longer my father and henceforth shall be my enemy."[119] Such repudiation of family ties was not unusual, and the party provided a setting in which intellectuals could experiment with new, freer alternatives to the patriarchal family and traditional marriage. Some spurned marriage in both its traditional and 'civilised' (*wenming*), i.e. western, forms, on the grounds that they would not act as 'performing monkeys' for the sake of convention.[120] The marriage ceremony between Yang Zilie and Zhang Guotao, for example, consisted of a solemn meeting of comrades before whom they vowed to share joy and sorrow, where they exchanged a slip of paper on which was written the word 'trust', instead of a ring.[121] When Ren Bishi married a girl from Hunan there was no ceremony or banquet.[122] He Baozhen resisted Liu Shaoqi's entreaties to marry him, ignoring pressure from her family and his complaints that she was uncaring, insisting on a free union.[123] Not all comrades, however, rejected marriage. In 1925 Wang Shouhua voluntarily entered an arranged marriage which was celebrated with all the pomp of the customary wedding feast.[124]

For women in the CCP, in particular, the struggle for personal liberation continued to be at the heart of their revolutionary commitment. After Hu Shi, the doyen of Chinese liberalism, translated Ibsen's *A Doll's House* into Chinese in 1918, an entire generation of educated young women strove to emulate the example of the play's heroine, Nora, by slamming the door on the patriarchal family – that bastion of selfishness, slavishness, hypocrisy and cowardice, in the words of Hu Shi – and affirming Nora's words that 'My sacred duty is to myself'.[125] Yang Zhihua was typical. She had married Shen Jianlong, the ne'er-do-well son of Shen Xuanlu, but he was in love with a Korean woman. When Yang gave birth to his daughter, she named her Duyi ('only she'), since the daughter was all she had. After she became a student at Shanghai University, she fell in love with Qu Qiubai, who had recently been widowed. In 1924 three curious notices appeared in *Republican Daily*, stating, respectively, that Shen Jianlong and Yang Zhihua had 'formally stopped being a couple'; that Qu Qiubai had formally begun to live with Yang; and that Shen and Qu had 'formally become friends'. Her father-in-law, Shen Xuanlu, seems to have approved the divorce.[126] In Jiang Guangci's novel, *The Party of Sans-Culottes*, a thinly fictionalized Yang Zhihua is told by Chen Duxiu to look after Qu Qiubai, who is stricken with tuberculosis. Angrily, she reflects: 'Did he really say that it is the special task of women to look after men?' She tells herself that she is not cut out to be a 'virtuous wife' and that she is no less important to the party than Qu; however, she ends up taking care of him out of love.[127]

If Chen Duxiu did indeed say this to Yang, it reminds us that male chauvinism was alive and well within the CCP, in spite of a broadly permissive attitude to experimentation in personal relationships. Chen was older than the majority of party leaders formed by the May Fourth Movement, and as a young man was said regularly to have frequented brothels. As general secretary of the CCP he continued to womanize.[128] His second wife, Gao Junman, alleged that he boasted to her that he had had women from every province in China except Gansu.[129] She and Chen finally split up in 1924 after he embarked on a liaison with Shi Zhiying, a woman doctor. Gao took their two children to Nanjing, where the cost of living was cheaper than in Shanghai, since she could not rely on financial support from Chen. He lived with Shi Zhiying until March 1927 when she left to marry someone else. She bore Chen a daughter whom he later refused to recognize.[130] Li Lisan was another party leader who had a reputation for philandering. His wife, Li Yichun, claimed that every time she went into hospital, he 'ran wild'.[131]

Experimentation in personal relationships could have deleterious effects on the political operations of the party. When Shi Cuntong's wife, Wang Yizhi, eloped with Zhang Tailei, Shi chased the couple to Changsha and Qingdao, creating havoc in local party ranks. Shi, who was dean of the social science faculty at Shanghai University, had hitherto presided over a household at Moulmein Road noted for its bourgeois respectability, guests being invited for decorous games of mahjong.[132] Similarly, domestic concord at the household on Fusheng Road was shattered when Xiang Jingyu took up with Peng Shuzhi, causing Cai Hesen, her husband, to file a complaint to the CEC. The latter determined to send both Cai and Xiang to Moscow out of harm's way, a decision which provoked bitter enmity between Peng and Cai. En route to Russia, however, Cai fell in love with Li Yuchun, wife of Li Lisan, causing relations between him and Li also to break down irrevocably. Both quarrels would have subsequent political repercussions.[133]

Experimentation in personal relations was a luxury that only intellectuals in the party could afford. Worker comrades lived in a world where arranged marriages were taken for granted, where extramarital affairs were unthinkable and where social pressures to conform to patriarchal norms remained intense.[134] As the proportion of workers in the party grew, tolerance of sexual liberalism and bohemianism within the party may have diminished. Certainly, the leadership was not prepared to tolerate party members remaining single, apparently because people living alone attracted public suspicion. It did not hesitate to indulge in matchmaking. In early 1926 when Zhang Shuping, aged 29 and still unmarried, arrived in Shanghai, the local leadership ordered Fan Jiebao, a woman worker at the Ewo mill, to move in with him, along with her sister and brother-in-law. In due course, Zhang and Fan got married, as the leadership had hoped.[135]

Another sphere in which the politicization of the personal was evident was in the tendency of intellectuals in the party to give political meaning to their experience by writing about it, either in the form of private diaries or of short stories and novellas that were barely fictionalized autobiography.[136] Typical was Jiang Guangci's novella, *Young Wanderer* (*Shaonian piaobozhe*), published in January 1926. It takes the form of 125-page letter describing the travails of Wang Zhong, who becomes a strike leader and dies a hero, fighting alongside cadets of the Huangpu Military Academy. The novella, which may be seen as the first comprehensive example of revolutionary romanticism, is characterized, in the words of one critic, by its 'hypertrophy of feelings', the hero, Wang, being clearly modelled on Byron, another "wanderer".[137] In April 1927 Jiang – whom Qu Qiubai – dismissed as 'talentless' – published another novella, *The Party of Sans-Culottes*, which succeeds in conveying something of the heroism, self-sacrifice and emotionalism of party life in Shanghai at the time of the third armed uprising.[138] Perhaps the greatest novel of the 1920s, Mao Dun's trilogy, *The Canker* (*Shi*), also takes the inner life of these romantic revolutionaries as its subject-matter, the first part of the trilogy, *Disillusion* (*Huanmie*) [1927], being set in Shanghai in early summer 1926. It features a young student, Jing, who is deeply dissatisfied with her life and whose faith in the future, rekindled during a stay in Wuhan, is gradually eroded as a result of her political and personal experiences.[139]

In spite of growing conservatism in matters sexual, a dominant feature of the party in the 1920s, which distinguished it from the party after 1927, was that it continued to function as a subculture in which educated youth could seek to free themselves from the fetters of 'feudal' society. For the generation forged by the New Culture Movement, the personal was political; and a commitment to free and equal personal relationships remained central to its vision of revolution. That said, from the first, the party defined itself in opposition to the anarchism and individualism of the May Fourth Movement, and considerable effort was expended in pressurising intellectuals to purge themselves of petty-bourgeois traits. Yet it remained true up to 1927 that many intellectuals in the party continued to 'ride on the tempestuous storm of romanticism', as Zheng Boqi vividly characterized the May Fourth generation.

Intensifying Comintern control

Some of best scholarship on the later CCP has shown the vital importance of party organization in consolidating Communist power.[140] During the 1920s, however, the CCP was very far from being an "organizational weapon".[141] For the Comintern, the fact that energy was squandered on the struggle for personal freedom was evidence of the incomplete internalization of marxist-leninist norms. Since 1921 the CCP had achieved a great deal by way of strengthening its own organization and the discipline and ideological training of its members. As the party grew, it developed an increasingly elaborate organizational structure. Yet the number of full-time party functionaries was still rather low. In July 1926 'barely 120' persons were working full-time for the party – mostly in Shanghai, Guangdong and Hunan – at a time when it was reckoned that the party needed 35 full-time organizers at regional level, 160 at area level and 160 at branch level.[142] In Shanghai by 1926 the regional committee was better organized than ever before. However, it is probably true to say that compared with later periods, internal organizational matters were a relatively low priority of the party leadership, compared with efforts to build influence in the mass movement. So in Moscow's eyes, there was little cause for complacency and it was with a view to exerting tighter control over the CEC that the Soviet Politburo on 25 March 1926 decided to establish a Far Eastern Bureau (FEB) of ECCI in Shanghai, it being agreed on 29 April that this should consist of Voitinskii, as chairman; M.G. Rafes, as secretary; L.N. Geller, as Profintern representative; N.A. Fokin, as representative of the KIM, and representatives from the Chinese, Korean and Japanese Communist Parties.[143] Although intended to make sure that the CEC toed the Comintern line, the FEB was told only to give general direction to the leadership and not to involve itself in the detailed determination of tactics.[144] Yet if the FEB was intended to demonstrate the wonders of Bolshevik discipline, it singularly failed to do so. From its first meeting on 19 June, it was torn by personal and political dissension. Rafes and Fokin were invariably at loggerheads, but united in their contempt for Voitinskii. Geller, Voitinskii's ally, was soon compelled to leave China because of illness, leaving the chairman to fend for himself.[145] A key cause of strife on the FEB was Voitinskii's handling of relations with the leadership of the CCP, Fokin and Rafes accusing him of preferring to square things directly with Chen Duxiu and of misleading Moscow with reassuring bromides. More generally, they accused him of avoiding political discussion at all cost.[146] At the behest of the FEB, the CEC at its July plenum endeavoured to create a more centralized organizational structure by shifting emphasis from the creation of party cells to the consolidation of territorial organizations: 'Now as before (sic!) the basis of our party remains the territorial unit and not the cell'.[147] The CEC felt that in the prevailing inhospitable political conditions individual cells tended to work in isolation, with the result that party members seldom had opportunity to share experiences. The work plan for Shanghai, drawn up by the plenum, spoke of involving all members in the work of the party and of ensuring that they received party publications. It proposed that the functional departments of party committees and base-level party branches experiment with limited democracy. Members of functional departments should be partly appointed but also partly elected by the committee to which they were attached; similarly, the secretary of a party branch (*zhibu de shuji*) should continue to be appointed by the Shanghai regional committee, but its executive officers (*zhibu de ganshi*) should be elected by the branch.[148] Meanwhile the regional organization should take steps to raise the level of party culture (*dang de wenhua chengdu*) by setting up party schools, training courses for members of functional departments and meetings of activists.[149]

Ideological correctness had by now become increasingly central to political decision-making and to individual status within the CCP.[150] Yet in Shanghai the average level of political education of party members was low, and must have declined as a result of the influx of worker members after 1925. In February 1926 the regional committee established a rather grandly named 'higher party school' to run an eight-month course, taught by Luo Yinong and Yin Kuan, on marxist theory, marxist economics, history of class struggle and Leninism.[151] It was intended for advanced members of the party and the key text used was the *ABC of Communism* by Bukharin and E. Preobrazhenskii.[152] Zheng Chaolin translated it into Chinese, and was delighted by its success. In 1927 it came second in a list of the year's best-sellers published by a Shanghai newspaper, beaten into first place by Sun Yat-sen's *Three Peoples' Principles*, most copies of which were printed at official expense and distributed free, and followed by Zhang Jingsheng's notorious *Xing shi* (Stories of sex lives).[153] Zheng opined that its success was due to the fact that it was one of the few marxist classics that tries to describe what Communist society would be like, though it should also be mentioned that at twenty cents it was relatively cheap. It was not, however, a book that most worker members of the party could read. In *The Party of Sans-Culottes* the silk worker Xing Cuiying is shown struggling to read it, but consoling herself with the thought that her husband, also a Communist militant, has trouble reading even a leaflet.[154] Political education for worker members of the party amounted to little more than slogans and spoon-feeding. Qu Qiubai claimed that rank-and-file members were never encouraged to ask questions and were told simply that 'this is what Lenin said'.[155] In January 1927 ECCI declared that since the 'overwhelming majority' of members were illiterate, the CCP should, wherever possible, organize workers' clubs and reading rooms, using student members and sympathisers as teachers. 'We must guarantee, however, that in those cases where the literacy teachers have not had the appropriate training, they do not play a leading political role by virtue of their higher intellectual development.'[156]

In December 1926 the VII ECCI plenum condemned the CCP's shift to a territorially-based structure: 'the obligatory basis of a correct structure and of Bolshevization is the cell – more precisely, the factory cell.'[157] It declared that the transformation of the CCP into a proper leninist organization could be delayed no longer. On 19 January 1927 ECCI issued a draft resolution on the organizational tasks of the CCP, which claimed, not unfairly, that a small circle of leading comrades were monopolizing decision-making; that there was no collective leadership at any level of the party; that there were no effective bureaux to direct the everyday work of committees; and that there were no regular plenary sessions of committees. At lower levels of the party hierarchy, ECCI claimed, matters were even worse. There were virtually no provincial, county or city committees, regional committees, appointed by the CEC, substituting for these.[158] It declared: 'Party discipline in communist organizations should not be mechanical discipline, such as one has in religious organizations, nor discipline based on blind submission to members of the party committee and other leading officials.'[159] It recommended that where political conditions allowed, there should be regular meetings of members of cells and higher-level committees, and that matters which were not urgent or secret in character should be discussed by lower organs, with the party press keeping comrades informed of the issues.[160]

Given that the CCP left so much to be desired in Moscow's eyes, it is hardly surprising that its persistent appeals for money met with resistance.[161] In June 1926 Voitinskii reported to Moscow that the CCP's monthly budget of 6,000 rubles was quite inadequate, and asked that it be raised to 14,000 rubles (of which at least 1,000 rubles should be earmarked for Manchuria).[162] In addition, it appears that the party received 3,000 rubles a month from Soviet ambassador Karakhan in Beijing; when Karakhan was recalled to Russia in October, Voitinksii asked ECCI to continue paying the extra subsidy.[163] Planned expenditure for the first half of the year 1925–6 for the CCP as a whole was US$93,863, of which $11,700 were earmarked for the central party apparatus and its ten employees, and no less than $50,000 for the upkeep of the military advisers attached to the CEC.[164] These sums were large, yet considerably smaller than the millions of rubles which Moscow was pouring into the national armies in China. In the 1925–6 budgetary year planned expenditure on military assistance was costed at eleven million rubles.[165] Nevertheless the size of the subsidy to the CCP strongly suggests that without 'Moscow gold' the CCP would have perished.

Chapter 7

The CCP and the Labour Movement in 1926

The non-Communist labour organizations

On 29 September 1925 General Xing ordered the closure of the SFS, an act from which – unlike the GLU – it never fully recovered.[1] Leading lights within the SFS continued to be active: Tong Lizhang remained popular among coal hauliers, masons and carpenters until 1927 and Wang Guanghui participated in the Western Hills faction.[2] In March 1925 Sun Zongfang had formed the Male and Female Labourers' Anti-Communist Alliance (*Nannü laogong fan gongchan tongmenghui*), with backing from some Subei politicians. During the May Thirtieth Movement the Alliance displayed as much hostility to Pan Donglin as it did to the GLU. In June 1926 upon his return to Shanghai, Sun formed the Workers' and Merchants' Association (*Gongshang xiehui*), again to combat Communism in the labour movement.[3] Other initiatives by GMD members opposed to the united front were a Workers' and Peasants' Club and a Women's Club.[4] All these anti-Communist organizations were tiny, and although one should not underestimate the potency of anti-Communism as an element in the political culture of the labour movement in Shanghai, the efforts of the GMD rightists to reassert their influence enjoyed only limited success.

In the wake of the May Thirtieth Movement, the leaders of the GLU, now consigned to working underground, appear to have been more concerned about labour unions they called 'reformist' than they were about the outrightly anti-Communist labour organizations. In his report to the Third National Labor Congress in May 1926, Li Lisan asked:

> 'Who are the reformists? We can say they are new-style scabs. But these new brigands are a million times more dangerous than their predecessors. Why exactly? Because the old labour brigands carried signs around their neck, so that as soon as you saw them you knew them for the traitors they were. But the new labour brigands wear attractive masks but have daggers concealed in their hearts, and are ever ready to help the capitalists find ways of killing us.'[5]

Li singled out two 'dangerous' reformist organizations in Shanghai, including the Workers' Section of Society Support Association (*Gongjie weizhihui*), which was active among seamen and which had the backing of two major shipping owners, Yu Xiaqing and Li Zhengyu, and the more considerable Workers' Thrift and Morality Society (*Gongren jiande hui*).[6] This had been set up by Pan Donglin, as part of the settlement of the May Thirtieth strike in the Japanese cotton mills. Pan was the Ningbonese chair of the Boone Road street association and a leading figure in both the FSA and the GCC. He was well-connected to the secret societies. During the May Thirtieth Movement he supported the GLU, rather than the SFS, and helped to defend the foreign employees' union against repression. He was popular among cotton workers because of his mediation in the Japanese mill strike of February 1925, and his prestige was further boosted when he played a similar role in August in bringing an end to the strike in the Japanese mills.[7] His skills as a mediator may have impressed the Japanese millowners for there is evidence that they gave him covert backing in setting up the Workers' Thrift and Morality Society. In addition, the Communists claimed that the GCC diverted $40,000 to $50,000 into the Society's coffers.[8] The Society was specifically aimed at women mill hands, who played a passive role in the male-dominated unions of the GLU, and it enjoyed its greatest success in the Nikko mills in Pudong, where Xu Xilin's weavers' union had been influential since 1922. The leaders of the Society there were two forewomen, Yang Damei and Tang Jinda, whose dismissal the GLU union insistently demanded.[9] In September 1925 a bruising month-long strike broke out, which culminated in a riot in which Fengtian soldiers shot and wounded seven workers.[10] Pan Donglin battled to bring the strike to an end, and succeeded in getting the strikers a 10 per cent wage increase, $2 strike pay and the dismissal of a Japanese overseer and two Chinese foremen.[11] This, however, made him even less popular with the GLU. Some twenty women smashed up his house, claiming that he had given the police information which led to the arrest of the GLU activists.[12]

There were other unions which set out to challenge the GLU. The postal employees' association, though dominated by senior staff, had wide influence among the city's 3,000 postal workers. It sponsored a wide range of activities, including evening classes, a library, a gymnasium, a music society and concerts, an educational society, a dramatic society and a consumer cooperative. It was accused by the GLU of being the fiefdom of a class-collaborationist 'labour aristocracy'.[13] Du Yuesheng was influential within the association, since he relied on its cooperation to intercept mail.[14] On 17 July 1926 it organized a one-day strike to demand a special rice bonus of $7 for postal apprentices and $4 or $5 for other categories, plus payment in customs taels (this had been a demand of the strike in August 1925, and the postal administration claimed that it was equivalent to a demand for a 50 per cent wage rise). The Postal Commissioner refused to negotiate with the association, and only a rumour that Sun Chuanfang intended to execute the leaders of the strike caused seventeen of the twenty members of the strike committee to call off the stoppage.[15]

The GLU continued to enjoy little influence among Shanghai's silk women.[16] Yet dissatisfaction with Mu Zhiying's association was welling up, since it had turned into little more than a tool of the Silk Guild. In late June 1926, against a background of unusually high temperatures and unprecedentedly high rice prices, an estimated 90 per cent of silk workers – 6,900 women in Hongkou and 13,400 in Zhabei – walked out in pursuit of a wage increase and an end to the payment of compulsory membership dues to Mu Zhiying's association (employers automatically deducted two fen from every worker's wages). The women claimed that Mu was appropriating these funds for her own use.[17] On 27 June 500 women, armed with choppers, iron bars and scissors, ransacked the headquarters of the association and beat up six of its leaders.[18] The filature owners demanded that the police arrest eight-nine named troublemakers, including the Communist, Zhu Yingru.[19] On 28 June representatives from thirty filatures, brought together by the GLU, published a set of conditions for a return to work, which included the disbandment of the association.[20] The following day the Silk Guild agreed to this demand. Mrs Mu 'retired' and on 1 July was arrested for appropriating funds, whereupon director of the Guild put up bail for her.[21] Yet although it was instrumental in killing off Mu's association, the GLU failed to establish a viable alternative. Only after the successful third armed uprising on 26 March 1927 did the GLU succeed in summoning a meeting of 3000 silk workers which set up a labour-union preparatory committee of thirty-five – twenty of them women – but the initiative was soon snuffed out by the 12 April coup.[22]

The Shanghai GLU under pressure, January to June 1926

The destruction of the silk women's association proved a pyrrhic victory, since it stirred the authorities into closing down the GLU office once more. In March the GLU had tentatively opened premises in Shuncheng alley in Zhabei under the ever watchful eye of the Chinese police.[23] On 4 April it published demands which called inter alia for the legalization of trade unions and strikes. Four days later, the Zhejiang militarists stepped in and arrested Wang Jingyun (1877–1952), the Communist chair of the GLU. Born in Shandong province, Wang was considerably older than the average union militant, having worked in the warehouse of the Commercial Press for many years. On 31 May he was released at the request of the management of the Commercial Press.[24] Despite being hemmed in by police and troops of Sun Chuanfang, the GLU struggled to maintain a semi-public presence. On 16 June it summoned a delegate meeting, attended by more than fifty union representatives, at which Yan Huiqing condemned the Beijing Government for preparing to strike a secret deal with foreign powers to settle the May Thirtieth Incident.[25] On 23 June an emergency meeting, chaired by Kong Baisheng (a pseudonym of Wang Shouhua), discussed the frightening spurt in the price of rice.[26]

Because it was forced to work mainly underground, it is difficult to assess the effectiveness of the GLU in the first half of 1926. The July plenum of the CEC of the CCP painted a rather sombre picture: 'Although the Shanghai GLU is supported by all Shanghai workers, its foundation is built only on a portion of the printers and textile workers. Henceforward our most important task is the organization of seamen, railway workers, postal workers, electrical workers, longshoremen and street transportation workers.'[27] In July the GLU produced statistics which purported to show that membership of affiliated unions stood at 105,137 – 48 per cent down on the total for September 1925.[28] This figure must include many whose membership had lapsed, for two months earlier Liu Shaoqi had told the Third National Labour Congress that only 79,740 of the 207,400 trade unionists affiliated to the Shanghai GLU were paying dues.[29] Even the figure for the number of dues-paying members may be inflated, since a year later, in 1927, the GLU reported that in June 1926 the dues-paying membership slumped to a low of 42,410 members, compared with 217,000 in June 1925.[30] This is more or less confirmed by Rafes, secretary of the FEB, who in October 1926 reported to I.A. Piatnitskii, secretary of ECCI, that there were 'up to 40,000' members of labour unions in Shanghai.[31]

The membership figures for July 1926 thus exaggerate the size of the GLU by a factor of more than two; yet they do provide a reliable indication of the distribution of membership. Notwithstanding a steep decline in membership of the cotton workers' federation, cotton workers by July comprised a larger proportion of the overall membership – 79 per cent – than they had at the end of the May Thirtieth Movement. The shares represented by printers and seamen had also increased to 5.4 per cent and just over 3 per cent, respectively. Conversely, dockers' share of membership had fallen from 16 per cent to 1.6 per cent.[32] Curiously, the Shanghai regional committee reported on 2 June that dockers were fairly well organized, though it admitted that they lacked proper union branches and needed to learn that a union was not a welfare organization.[33] The perception that they were organized must have been due to the extensive presence of the secret societies in their ranks. In this instance, the fall in membership of the dockers' federation suggests that the secret societies had withdrawn cooperation with the GLU, but in other industries the Communists were concerned about the extent to which the Green and Red Gangs had succeeded in infiltrating GLU unions. The work plan for Shanghai, endorsed by July 1926 CEC plenum, noted that many GLU-affiliated unions in the city were under the control of the secret societies and were thus not genuine mass organizations. It advised comrades to join the Red and Green Gangs in order to facilitate labour organization and prevent strife between groups of workers. It also called on them to reorganize the pickets, since many had fallen into the clutches of gangsters and 'scabs'.[34]

The union federations (*zonggonghui*), which had emerged rather late during the May Thirtieth strike, were generally in poor shape. The federations of dockers, railway workers, seamen, handicraft workers, shop workers and postal workers existed on paper, but were either weak or, as in the case of the postal workers, outside the control of the GLU.[35] Only the cotton union federation, under the chairmanship of Zhang Zuochen, was healthy, despite losing many activists through mass sackings; but it suffered, in particular, from a lack of organizers capable of working with women and youth.[36] Born in 1906 in Pinghu county, Zhejiang province, Zhang worked from an early age at the Dakang mill as an inspector. As the first worker to the join the union in 1924, he naturally came to the attention of the CCP. By the time of the Japanese mill strikes of February 1925, he was already a party member. In May 1925 he attended the Second National Labour Congress as one of the delegates from Shanghai. By August, he was conspicuous in the cotton workers' federation, known as 'Zhang of the Big Song', and was a candidate member of the Shanghai regional committee. In spring 1926 he was elected by the Third National Labour Congress to the executive of the NGLU. After Chiang Kai-shek's coup in April 1927, he returned to Shanghai, only to be arrested and killed in June. He was just 21 years old.[37] The other federation which was in reasonably good shape was that of the printers, although its membership was overwhelmingly concentrated at the Commercial Press and China Book Company, which together claimed 3,200 members in June 1926.[38] Its chair, Wang Jingyun, was briefly president of the GLU until his arrest.[39]

On 27 June 1926 the GLU was again sealed by order of Sun Chuanfang. Zhao Shiyan, who headed the CCP fraction in the GLU, opined that Sun was 'only tamely carrying out the orders of imperialism', and declared that the imperialists would never break the union.[40] The GLU issued a statement saying that it had 'tried to lessen the sufferings of the workers and done its best to foster the development of national industries' and that it had made every effort to mediate in industrial disputes in order to bring about peaceful settlements.[41] It appealed to public organizations to bring pressure on the warlord authorities to allow it to reopen.[42] A woman who went to petition the civil governor (*duban*) as part of a workers' delegation told him that the workers loved the GLU 'like their own mother', and that since merchants, craftsmen and students had their own federations, it was unfair to deprive the workers of theirs.[43] The GLU did not meekly submit to the militarists. On 11 July it summoned a third delegate conference, attended by 132 labour activists, which was held in secret, but widely reported in the press. Liu Shaoqi addressed the conference on the subject of the recent Third National Labour Congress, and it endorsed a list of eleven demands around which labour unions were called to rally. These were for a minimum wage of $15 a month; annual wage increases in line with inflation; a ten-hour working day; a paid Sunday holiday; no ill-treatment or arbitrary deductions from wages; no dismissals without due cause; compensation to families of workers who died at work; payment of medical expenses and at least half pay during periods of sickness; improved treatment of women and child workers and one month's paid maternity leave; freedom of association, speech and publication; and improved health and safety conditions at work.[44] The conference elected a new EC, consisting of thirty-one people, including Wang Shouhua, Zhang Zuochen, Li Baizhi, Li Lisan and Ye Dagong.[45]

The long hot summer

June 1926 saw the highest number of economic strikes ever recorded in Shanghai in a single month, with the police recording forty strikes and 53,306 strikers in the International Settlement alone.[46] Zhao Shiyan, distrustful of 'imperialist' strike statistics, made his own meticulous calculation in the *Guide Weekly*. He counted a total of thirty-five joint or individual stoppages throughout the city, involving 69,556 strikers and affecting 107 enterprises.[47] In July the number of strikers grew still further. The International Settlement police counted only thirty-one, including four that were in progress at the start of the month, involving a total of 35,430 workers, of whom 19,563 were in the cotton industry. But the *Guide Weekly* counted no fewer than fifty-four joint or single stoppages, affecting 70,494 workers.[48] In August the strike wave broke, though stoppages remained at a higher than normal level. The four different estimates for the number of strikers in that month (among which the *Guide Weekly*'s was not the highest) average at more than 32,000. According to the International Settlement police, there were fifteen strikes, four of which were in progress at the start of the month, involving 25,111 strikers, 20,689 of whom were mill workers.[49] Throughout the summer the epicentre of the strike wave lay in the Japanese cotton mills, and it is on these that we shall concentrate, although it should be borne in mind that many other trades were affected.

The principal cause of the strike fever was the massive rise in rice prices. From February 1926 prices began a dizzying ascent which did not stop until September 1927. By August 1926 the price of first-quality rice had reached an unprecedented $19.7 per picul (*dan*) and the average price for rice was $17.87.[50] In addition, the rate of exchange of the silver dollar against the copper cent was at an all-time high, averaging around 260 cents.[51] To make matters worse, the summer was one of the hottest on record, with temperatures well over 100F.[52] Finally, because the market for textiles was depressed, Japanese and British manufacturers felt little inclination to make concessions. After a fairly promising start, therefore, the number of strikes ending in defeat rapidly began to increase. *Guide Weekly* calculated that of 180 strike demands raised in July, sixty were successfully attained; and of sixty-two wage demands, thirty-four were attained.[53] The usefulness of a purely economic analysis of the strikes, however, is limited, since in the Japanese mills, where the largest stoppages occurred, wages formed only one element in strikers' grievances. According to Zhao Shiyan, the rallying cry of all strikers was: 'We can't take any more inhuman treatment.'[54] This newly-asserted sense of dignity and self-respect had developed since the May Thirtieth Movement and the employees of Japanese mills, in particular, were no longer prepared to tolerate 'humiliation' at the hands of foreigners. This psychological change was one of the deepest well-springs of militancy. It also allowed the Communists rather easily to forge ideological links between the heightened sense of dignity, burgeoning nationalist sentiment and class consciousness.

A month of disturbances at the NWK mills culminated on 24 June in a riot. Women in the carding room at NWK No.4 mill went on the rampage after an assistant forewoman, with whom they had no native-place ties, was imposed on them by management. The women smashed machines and set fire to yarn. Management announced that it would shut the mill until the machinery was repaired. This proved to be the beginning of a thirty-day lockout. That evening, delegates met to decide how they might secure the release of sixteen workers arrested for their part in the riot and, according to the *North China Herald*, agreed that 'twenty more axes and twenty more iron bars be purchased for the use of the corps of heroes (*yiyongdui*, SAS), to enable them to defend themselves against labour brigands'.[55] They also agreed to donate 15 per cent of union dues to the GLU.[56] Soon the No.3 mill, too, was subject to a lockout which lasted a month and was only lifted on 24 July, after mediation by Yu Xiaqing, who had recently been ousted as president of the GCC. The GLU later accused him of selling out the workers, but at the time it and the federation of cotton workers ratified the terms brokered by Yu, however reluctantly.[57] The union at No.3 mill gave written undertakings that it would not seek severance pay for those dismissed and that it recognized management's right to hire whomever it wished. In return, the company promised that there would be no unjust dismissals; that no police would enter the mills without grave cause; and that every worker would be lent $5 to pay off debts incurred during the lockout.[58] On the very day that a settlement was reached at NWK, Hao Huoqing, a worker at the Nikko mills in Pudong, was electrocuted. The two mills had been in a state of high tension throughout June and July, and the workers immediately occupied the mills to demand compensation for Hao's family and a special rice bonus of five cents a day.[59] The following day, management fired twenty-two alleged ringleaders and imposed a lockout. After twenty-seven days, the lockout was finally lifted on 28 August, and 1,300 of the 1,700 workers returned to work with nothing to show for their pains.[60] The Nikko management systematically implemented the policy of lockouts adopted by the The Japanese Millowners' Association. Other lockouts imposed at this time included one at the NWK No.9 mill, where 2,300 workers were laid off for nineteen days, the Doko mill, where 3,000 workers were laid off for three days, and the British-owned Ewo mill, where a strike turned into a lockout in September.[61]

On 3 August, a hawker, Chen Atang, was found dead in the hold of a Japanese steamer, the Manri Maru, berthed at Pudong. The captain said he had been caught stealing a watch from the crew's quarters and had fallen into a coal bunker while trying to escape. The Chinese press furiously countered this version of events, insisting that he had been gagged, taken to open ground, beaten up, stuffed in a sack, taken back on board the ship, and thrown into the hold to die of suffocation.[62] Labour, student and merchant organisations rallied to demand the detention of the steamer, the handing over of the assailants to the Chinese authorities, an apology from the Japanese consul, the severance of economic relations with Japan, the recall of Chinese students in Japan and a general strike in the Japanese mills.[63] On 13 August hundreds of mill workers gathered on vacant ground close to Suzhou creek, with banners reading 'Let us fight the Japanese and insist on justice'; 'Let us revenge the wrong done to Chen Atang and demonstrate that the spirit of May 30th is still alive'; 'Let us assist the workers at the NWK No.9 mill and demand that the lock-out be ended'; 'We demand freedom to hold meetings, organise unions and strikes'.[64]

This turn of events raised the hopes of the CCP leadership that the setbacks of June and July might be reversed. On 17 August, with a lockout at NWK No.9 dragging on, the Shanghai regional committee agreed to broaden the stoppages at several NWK mills into a strike across the entire company. They were under no illusion that conditions for such an action were favourable, but they hoped that public outrage over Chen Atang's murder would transform the hitherto isolated workers' protests into a broad pan-class anti-Japanese movement.[65] On 20 August they set up a special body to lead the NWK strike, consisting of the most experienced CCP labour leaders: Luo Yinong, Zhao Shiyan, Wang Shouhua, Li Lisan and Xiang Ying.[66] The Communists played the anti-imperialist card for all it was worth. In its appeal for public support, the NWK strike committee proclaimed:

Fellow countrymen! Japanese imperialism is the Chinese people's greatest enemy. We can never forget the various incidents of cruelty against our Chinese fellow-countrymen. Last year's May

Thirtieth battle commenced with the slaying of Gu Zhenghong in the Japanese mills. In the first half of this year a whole number of Japanese mills arrested workers' leaders and subjected them to brutal torture, including the electrocution of Hao Huoqing; and apart from these leaders, it has threatened ordinary workers with the sack. Everybody knows that the plunder and oppression of Chinese workers in Japanese mills is a hundred times worse than in other factories.[67]

The strike began on 20 August, and was aimed, initially, at mills Nos. 4, 5E and 5W, 7, 8 and 12, which were considered to be the best unionized in the NWK company. Only No.4 mill failed to respond to the summons of the cotton federation. NWK mill No.15 and the day shift of No.13 did not join the stoppage until the 25th.[68] The strike was well organized, the central strike committee, based at the headquarters of the Xiaoshadu federation of cotton unions, consisting of nearly 200 delegates from the different NWK mills. A forty-strong protection corps and twelve teams of pickets, each comprising fifty workers, were formed to maintain order. A daily strike bulletin was published, and speaker teams organized, including ones consisting of women only, to win public support.[69] By 26 August 13,980 workers at the NWK mills were on strike. The following day, Nos. 3 and 4 mills, the first to be locked out, joined in, leaving only No.9 mill still working.[70]

Inspired by this apparent success, on 24 August the Shanghai regional committee decided to try to extend the strike to all Japanese enterprises in the city.[71] Three days later, the GLU issued a call to all Japanese enterprises to strike in protest at the conduct of the Chen Atang case. An article in *Guide Weekly* hints that the GLU had misgivings about the strike in view of the unpropitious economic circumstances.[72] But vigorous efforts were made to bring out workers in all Japanese mills, wharves and steamships.[73] Workers at the Nikko mills in Pudong and at the Doko mill in Yangshupu walked out, but elsewhere the response was poor.[74] Meanwhile, the last days of August saw the strike at the NWK mill begin to crumble, becoming concentrated once more on the Nos.5E, 5W, 7 and 8 mills.[75] The GLU and the CCP milked the murder of Chen Atang for its propaganda value. Zhao Shiyan declared that the strike was about national autonomy, and warned that the strikers would fail unless they received the ardent backing of all patriots. Demonstrations took place on 28 and 29 August, in spite of preventative measures by the authorities. In what the police described as a well-organized manoeuvre, workers and students infiltrated the International Settlement in dribs and drabs and then unfurled banners, scattered leaflets and made speeches. Thirty-four people were arrested, consisting of a roughly equal number of workers and students (including nine from Guangdong and some women).[76] Yet failure was staring the Communists in the face. According to the International Settlement police, only 15,479 workers were on strike in Japanese mills during September.[77] On 7 September demonstrations to mark National Humiliation Day – in commemoration of the infamous Boxer Indemnity paid by China to the foreign powers – were, according to the International Settlement police, a miserable flop, although they were sponsored by the GMD, the SSU, the Federation of Street Associations and the GLU. The Chinese authorities prohibited all meetings and the police commissioner called on Sun Chuanfang to send in military reinforcements.[78]

The attempt to use the Chen Atang case to generate a 'second May Thirtieth Movement' failed.[79] How far the regional committee was acting under its own volition in spreading the strike across the entire Japanese-owned sector, how far it was overriding the reluctance of the GLU, and how far the latter acceded to pressure from militant activists in the NWK company is uncertain. Later, when it was clear that the strike had been an error, the Shanghai regional committee alleged that it had been reluctant to authorize the strike but had been pressured into doing so by the GLU. It claimed that Chen Duxiu's continuing illness, combined with the absence of several members of the CEC and FEB from Shanghai, left the local leadership powerless to resist.[80] A year later, at the Fourth National Labour Congress, the GLU conceded that it had been forced into calling the strike against its better judgement but suggested that it had had little choice in the face of 'workers' anger'.[81]

The desperation of the CCP

As the strikes of the long hot summer foundered on the rock of lockouts, dismissals and plummeting morale, the Shanghai regional committee searched for ways to break the impasse. Since the spring of 1926, the CCP had become increasingly excited by the prospect of armed uprising; and, in particular, of creating a permanent armed force at the disposal of the GLU. In March the regional committee formed a body, consisting of Gu Shunzhang, He Jingru, Xu Meikun, Yuan Dashi and three workers, charged with setting up a standing army (changbei jun) of 1,500 pickets, along with three reserve units.[82] In April Voitinskii wrote to Chen Duxiu that thirty comrades had completed special military training courses in the Soviet Union and were returning to China.[83] In May the Shanghai regional committee set up a military commission, headed by Luo Yinong. In the same month the labour department of the CEC called for the creation of a secret workers' self-defence corps (gongren ziwei tuan) to defend unions against 'fascists' and 'scabs' and prepare for an armed uprising at some unspecified date.[84] In the early summer six workers, including Shi Liqing, who had worked as an oiler at Shenxin No.1 mill since 1918, were sent in secret to Guangzhou for military training. Doubtless, others went too.[85]

Whether any body of armed and trained men existed separate from the pickets, i.e. a 'workers' self-defence corps' as opposed to the 'standing army' of 'pickets' (*jiuchadui*) is by no means clear. Terminology was loose and it is unclear how far at this stage the party distinguished between pickets, whose function was principally to maintain order in industrial disputes and demonstrations, and a more offensive group that was being trained for armed insurrection. The notorious difficulty which the Communists had in procuring arms – though they were easily available – together with the difficulties of putting any such group through serious military training, given the dangers of arousing the attention of the police – suggests that basically only a loose group of untrained pickets existed.

On 2 June Liu Zhongmin, a member of the regional committee's military commission, reported that 1,000 workers had enrolled in eight self-defence corps. He said that those in Nandao and Zhabei, which each consisted of 160 men, were the best organized of the eight. These 'self-defence corps' were simply pickets, who did little more than steward demonstrations and protect public meetings, though even these tasks they performed with little distinction, often arriving late or proving unable to control crowds.[86] During the NWK strikes of July and August the pickets were a constant thorn in the side of the strike committee. On 31 August spies reported to the International Settlement police that Guo Jianxia, a worker Communist active in the cotton workers' federation, 'heard complaints from pickets that they were receiving only 16 cents a day, whereas those fired from their jobs were getting 20 cents'. On 1 September Zhang Zuochen, chair of the Xiaoshadu district committee of the GLU, explained to the pickets that the difference was due to the fact that strikers had left work voluntarily whereas those fired had no prospect of returning to their jobs, but he agreed that they, too, would henceforth be paid 20 cents a day.[87] At a meeting of the regional committee on 7 September, Zhao Shiyan denounced the pickets for being 'scroungers' (*kaiyou*).[88] By October 1926 there were said to be 2,000 pickets – though this may be an exaggeration – but only a handful of them had arms or any idea of how to use them.

A sign of the growing desperation of the Communists was their increasing reliance on terror. The use of terror emerged gradually. It was axiomatic for the Comintern that terror represented one of the highest forms of class struggle, and from its inception the CCP dabbled in armed attacks on its opponents. During the Shanghai seamen's strike of 1922, the CMSNC company employed thugs to intimidate strike leaders, and after Zhu Baoting was beaten up, he and others formed a gang to exact revenge on 'running dogs', known colloquially as the 'dog-beating squad' (*dagoudui*). Inter alia, this cut off the ear of one of Fu Xiaoan's retinue.[89] Acts of terror multiplied during the May Thirtieth Movement. On 2 July 1925 a subcontractor at the Shanghai Water Works, recruiting scabs, was shot down in the street by two unemployed workers, who later confessed that they had been paid $300 by a high-ranking member of the GLU.[90] On 18 July two tramcar employees, who were breaking the strike, narrowly escaped injury when they were shot at with a .32 calibre revolver.[91] In Xiaoshadu in the west of the city Bao Xiaoliang headed the 'dog-beating squad'. Born in 1901 in Anhui, Bao was of slight build and had a limp. In 1923 he got a job as a piecer at NWK No.15, where he became leader of the Anhui *bang*. In April 1924 he joined the West Shanghai Workers' Club and at the beginning of 1925 the CCP. During the February 1925 strike he helped create a cotton union at NWK no.15 mill, which became one of the best organized in Shanghai, and the dog-beating squad which he led originated out of the volunteer corps (*yiyongdui*) created to protect the strikers. During the May Thirtieth Movement his squad was said to have attacked some thirty scabs in West Shanghai. Bao himself perished in the coup of 12 April 1927.[92]

Following the suppression of the GLU in September 1925, and the sacking and even killing of hundreds of activists, the CCP raised terror to official policy. In December 1925 the Shanghai regional committee gave permission to Jiang Weixin, Li Jianru, Liu Huaiqing (a worker at NWK, No.9), Tao Yihe (a worker at NWK, No.5), the brothers Wang Si and Wang San, both employed at No.7 mill, Xie Dejin and later Yang Fulin, to form a 'dog-beating squad.' In the course of 1926 this squad axed to death an interpreter at Nikko and killed a policeman, Dai Dingchen.[93] A separate squad apparently existed at NWK No.9. Both operated under only the loosest of party controls.[94] In response to the lockouts of the late summer, the party leaders decided to step up terrorist attacks on those who were seeking to undermine the workers' cause. On 17 August the Shanghai regional committee launched an all-out offensive on 'running dogs'. Wang Shouhua, however, did point out that in Xiaoshadu an offensive against running dogs had been in progress for more than a year and had achieved little. He said that attacks needed to be accompanied by propaganda and to take place when workers were feeling angry.[95]

On 25 August 1926 two brothers, both foremen at the Doko mill, were shot – one fatally – on their way to work by a Chinese 'in a long gown'.[96] On the same day, a gang of five or six broke into the house of a sub-foreman in Yangshupu and set about him and his wife with axes. Both were overseers at the British Ewo mill, where the workers had been on strike for a month. On 1 September Chen Maomao, a foreman in the fly-frame room at the Ewo mill, was killed while recruiting scabs.[97] On 16 October another mill foreman in Yangshupu was murdered for the same reason.[98] Dong Yaoxian at NWK No.9 mill also succumbed to assassins around this time. It is likely that some, if not all, of these foremen were secret-society bosses. We know, for example, that Shi Jinkun, murdered for allegedly helping the International Settlement police to smash trade unions in late 1925, was a gang boss at the Tongyi mill.[99] Yet the paradox was that the dog-beating squads could only operate with the support of local gang bosses. Jiang Weixin, active in the NWK squad, was protected by Green Gang leader, Gu Zhuxuan, as the younger brother of Gu's niece's husband, and at least one other member of the squad, Xiao Asi, was in the Red Gang.[100] Given the complex networks of protection and predation within which the "dog-beating squads" operated, it is hardly surprising that most acts of terror were carried out without the knowledge or sanction of the Shanghai regional committee. As a result, in November 1926 the committee determined to replace the unruly squads with a Red Terror Squad (*hongse kongbu dui*). Gu Shunzhang, who had been given responsibility for the GLU pickets in October, was put in charge of it. It may have been around this time that Gu joined the Green Gang.[101]

Another example of the desperation of the CCP was its readiness to indulge workers' proclivities to smash up factories (*dachang*). Such proclivities were evident among all workers, male and female, skilled and unskilled, and they had surfaced during the February 1925 mill strikes, when pickets had formed teams (*dachang dui*), armed with axes, iron bars and sticks, to force their way into factories and break windows and machinery, in the hope of exerting pressure on the employers.[102] It is not clear whether at that time the CCP encouraged such destructiveness. However, on 17 August 1926, the regional committee resolved that if the Nikko management tried to reopen the mills with scab labour, party members should break in and destroy machinery.[103] On 3 September it agreed that if it proved to be the case that NWK No.9 worker, Shi Wancai, had died of a beating, then activists should incite the workers to go on the rampage.[104] At a meeting on the 7th, however, it heard that not even the pickets at NWK No.9 mill were willing to go on the rampage, only the women workers being so inclined. They, too, lost interest, however, when male workers refused to get involved.[105]

The end of the strike and the consequences for the CCP

By the second week of September, it was clear that the NWK strike had failed, so the strike committee asked Pan Donglin of the FSA – whom Li Lisan had denounced as recently as May as a 'new-style scab' – to mediate. He agreed to put to the Japanese authorities demands for the trial of Chen Atang's alleged murderers in China; improved treatment of workers; a 20 per cent wage increase; release of those imprisoned; and strike pay.[106] Shortly, Yu Xiaqing, too, became involved in the negotiations. Yet neither Pan nor Yu could dent the determination of the NWK company to be rid of its militants. On 15 September the strike committee scaled down its conditions for a return to work, insisting only that there be no unjust dismissals; that women receive a $5 maternity bonus; that there be two days' leave a month, and that two days' wages be paid to those who were dismissed or resigned.[107] But even these demands were unacceptable to the company, so on the 16th about three-quarters of the workforce returned to work with nothing. The *North China Herald* was mightily satisfied: 'The workers returned unconditionally and voluntarily. There were no negotiations. The doors of the mills were always open and the workers could have returned at any time.'[108] In fact, as a result of public outcry, two crew members were eventually arrested for the murder of Chen Atang, but they were sent for trial to Japan. Otherwise the achievements of the strike were nil. Two hundred and sixty-seven workers were dismissed at once by the NWK company, and the final number who lost their jobs rose to around 400, according to the cotton workers' federation.[109] On 19 September those who had been fired formed the Association of Ex-Workers of the Japanese Cotton Mills, which asked for $30 severance pay from the company and 30 coppers per day from the GLU. The GLU agreed to the latter, and offered blacklisted workers travel expenses to Hankou.[110]

The CCP was badly affected by the defeat of the strike which they had struggled to prolong. Membership of the Shanghai organization fell from 2,223 in August to 1,380 in the wake the strike.[111] On 5 December 1926 the CEC reported that 300 secretaries of union and party branches in the Japanese mills had been sacked, and that many had left Shanghai in search of work.[112] The setback proved to be temporary, however, and by the end of the year the CCP had recovered completely. The GLU also sustained serious damage. Particularly hard hit was the federation of cotton unions, whose membership – which had been 126,670 in August 1925 – fell from 30,468 in September 1926 to just 25,640 by January 1927. Many mill unions, moreover, ceased to pay dues to the federation.[113] The seamen's union, another previously well-organized union, but one in which the dominant political force was the GMD, also fell on hard times, after its Shanghai headquarters was shut down in October.[114] In the wake of the strike, the GLU decided to concentrate not on rebuilding its base in the cotton industry, but on building its influence among strategically-important sectors of workers, such as those in the power stations, on the trams and in the docks.[115]

Hostile observers claimed that the strikes of the long hot summer were the work of Communist agitators.[116] The vast majority of strikes, however, were spontaneous protests at the rocketing cost of living and management arbitrariness. Moreover, the campaign by the Japanese Millowners' Association to extirpate trade unionism soon itself became a cause of labour unrest. Workers, in other words, did not need Communist agitators to make them stop work: their grievances were plentiful and acute. Indeed the party was accused of "tailism", i.e. of failing to keep abreast of worker militancy, and at various points the GLU appears to have been forced into taking action against its better judgement by angry workers on the ground.[117] Of course, strikers relied on CCP and GLU militants for leadership, and without the organization, finance, strategy and ideological legitimation that they supplied, the strike movement would have been far less effective. To that extent, one could argue that the Communists exacerbated and prolonged industrial unrest and exploited it for their own purposes. At the same time, one should be wary of exaggerating the influence of the Communists over the workers. In addition to the scenario where rank-and-file workers pressured the GLU into taking action it would otherwise have deemed imprudent, we have seen, in the case of the NWK pickets, that the GLU also faced challenges from its own activists. And last but not least, there were ubiquitous challenges to the GLU's efforts to consolidate its grass-roots base from foremen, contractors and secret-society leaders. These local bosses still, undoubtedly, carried more weight among the rank-and-file than the GLU. In the last analysis, therefore, workers' protests had a dynamic which the Communists could influence but not completely control.

Yet it remains the case that the broad policy of the labour movement was determined by the Shanghai regional committee and the GLU, notwithstanding possible tensions between the two. The party made little effort to involve the GMD in the strike, reflecting the disinclination of the local party to practise a united-front strategy in the labour movement. The secret societies were eminently capable of frustrating the carefully-laid plans of the GLU, but while they could impede and subvert, they were far less able to bid for leadership, far less able to match the organizational capacity and strategic vision of the GLU. Similarly, the so-called "reformist" unions and remnants of the SFS were still active, but they, too, were not able to mount a serious challenge to the CCP as they had done prior to the May Thirtieth Movement. Consequently, even though the Communists' control of the strike movement was far from complete, they must bear the largest measure of responsibility for its outcome. The decision to generalise the strike to the entire NWK company, and then to broaden it to all Japanese enterprises, was taken solely by the Communists, and it proved to be a serious miscalculation.

Chapter 8 ─────────────────

The First and Second Armed Uprisings

On 9 July 1926 the National Revolutionary Army (NRA) of the GMD launched the Northern Expedition which aimed to reunify the country through the elimination or neutralization of the warlords and, in the longer term, to roll back the influence of the foreign powers. The NRA fought effectively, and by late November the GMD was in a position to set up a national government in Wuhan in central China. The dramatic success of the expedition, however, greatly strengthened the hand of Chiang Kai-shek, as commander-in-chief of the NRA, increasing the likelihood of a split between him and left-dominated national government. On 16 September the FEB met with the CEC for two days of discussion. Voitinskii feared that Borodin, captivated by the upsurge in the mass movements that had accompanied the Northern Expedition, was now gratuitously antagonizing Chiang Kai-shek. He opined: 'Subjectively, Chiang Kai-shek has not become an enemy of the revolution, he has struck against the right, and needs us, and it is possible to work with him.'[1] The meeting thus resolved 'in no case to give Chiang Kai-shek grounds for a decisive action against the left GMD nor to leave the front.'[2] Since many in the GMD were calling for the return of Wang Jingwei, leader of the GMD Left, to serve as a counterweight to Chiang Kai-shek, the meeting agreed not to back Wang against Chiang, but to call for cooperation between them. It hoped that if Wang took charge of the party, this would reduce the threat posed by Chiang.[3] Chen Duxiu and Peng Shuzhi now adhered to a policy of preserving the united front at all costs, whether for reasons of party discipline or out of newly-acquired conviction. Peng, for instance, criticized the Canton comrades. 'They deny not only the big, but also the small bourgeoisie, taking only workers and peasants into considera-tion ... Borodin considers that Chiang Kai-shek will be a military dictator. But China is going through a long revolution and does not need military dictatorship.'[4] Six days later, the FEB wrote to ECCI calling for Borodin to be withdrawn from China, a request that was turned down by the Politburo on 20–1 October.[5]

Although as recently as the July plenum, Voitinskii and the FEB had compelled the CEC to preserve the united front at all costs, by the time that Wuchang fell to the NRA on 10 October, they seem to have been concerned that the CEC was pursuing too moderate a course and was 'completely unprepared for struggle against the growing danger of victory of the bourgeois tendency in the revolution.'[6] On 22 October Voitinskii sent a telegram to Moscow, proposing that policy towards the labour and peasant movements be radicalized.[7] A week later, the Politburo rejected the suggestion out of hand: 'the sharpening of the struggle against the Chinese bourgeoisie and gentry proposed by Voitinskii is premature and extremely dangerous'; adding that unleashing civil war in the countryside would weaken the fighting capacity of GMD in its struggle against imperialism.[8] In response, Voitinskii once again moderated his position, urging restraint on the CCP, especially in the countryside, in order to preserve maximum unity in the struggle against warlordism and imperialism.[9] Chen Duxiu seems genuinely to have backed a moderate policy, believing that the Northern Expedition would lead to a 'democratic dictatorship of all oppressed classes' under the leadership of a left GMD that could promote 'national democratic capitalism'.[10] In his political report of 4 November he criticised those, 'including certain foreign comrades', who believed that the national revolution was almost over and was moving towards a proletarian revolution.[11] He repeated the standard argument that the CCP should continue to work through the GMD in order to exercise influence over the petty bourgeoisie and the peasantry. At the same time, he still spoke of there being only a right and left wing in the GMD – denying, in effect, that Chiang Kai-shek represented the 'centre'.[12]

By the time the special plenum of the CEC opened in Wuhan on 12 December, the extent to which the growth of the mass movements had exacerbated social tensions within the NRA and the GMD was plain. Chen Duxiu observed that 'most political and military power is now in the hands of the right' and that Chiang Kai-shek was behaving in a very 'right-wing' fashion, and predicted that he might do a deal with the imperialists. At the same time, he tacitly accused Borodin and the Canton comrades of 'infantile leftism', for seeking to monopolize positions of power within the GMD and in the mass movements. To reduce the widening gap between left and right, he proposed, first, to 'unite military power with the mass movement', in order to develop the popular base of the struggles against warlordism and imperialism and to strengthen the left wing of the GMD; second, to fight the right through the GMD left-wing, in the party's base organizations as well as in its central organs. More controversially, he proposed that certain curbs be placed on the mass movements: in particular, agitators in the peasant movement should concentrate on reducing rent and interest rates rather than on land confiscation; and workers' pickets should be prevented from inflicting 'excesses' on traders and small producers.[13] These policies were in line with those which had up to this time been advocated by ECCI (and reaffirmed by the Politburo as late as 29 October) and had the backing of Borodin, as well as of Voitinskii, both of them attending the plenum.[14] Nevertheless it was for these decisions that Chen Duxiu would be branded with the charge of 'right opportunism'. For unbeknown to Chen, just as the plenum was happening in Wuhan, the VII ECCI plenum was coming to a close in Moscow. And the Comintern had decided that it was time to push its policy in China in a much more radical direction.

The first armed uprising

During the summer of 1926 the idea of self-government for Shanghai was revived by certain merchants and industrialists. A Self-Government Guild (*zizhi gongsuo*) was formed by the Zhabei chamber of commerce, which represented some sixty businesses, at the instigation of its chairman, Wang Xiaolai, an ally of Yu Xiaqing and active GMD member. In June Yu was ousted as president of the GCC by the pro-Japanese faction of Fu Xiaoan, who was an avid supporter of Sun Chuanfang, the warlord who controlled the five eastern provinces. This, together with the less than democratic means by which Fu gained control of the GCC, gave rise to bitter political conflict among Shanghai's capitalists.[15] Following Sun Chuanfang's disbandment of the Self-Government Guild and the merchant militia (*baoweituan*) on 28 August, Yu Xiaqing toyed with the idea of an armed uprising against Sun aimed at establishing self-government in Shanghai.[16]

On 3 September the Shanghai regional committee backed the call for popular self-government and agreed to try to involve Yu Xiaqing in a campaign for a national assembly (*guomin huiyi*).[17] Four days later, Wang Shouhua told the committee that he had had talks with Yu and that he was enthusiastic about the possibility of an uprising, once Wuchang, the last stronghold of the warlord Wu Peifu, had fallen. At this stage, the Communists envisaged that a strike should precede any uprising, so Wang and Yu Xiaqing discussed ways in which a dockers' strike – crucial to halting the movement of supplies to Sun's forces – could be financed.[18] Meanwhile Niu Yongjian (1870–1965), a native of Shanghai who had fought with the Alliance Society during the 1911 revolution, was sent by the GMD government in Canton to take charge of operations against Sun Chuanfang. On 4 September he formed the Jiangsu Special Committee of the GMD, which consisted of seven members, including two Communists, Hou Shaoqiu and Zhu Jixuan, and three GMD rightists, Ye Chucang, Zhang Jingjiang and Wu Zhihui, the latter both former anarchists.[19] Niu entered into negotiations with Xia Chao, the civil governor of Zhejiang, about the possibility of his defecting from Sun's alliance. Xia said that he was willing to do so if the NRA were successful in defeating Wu Peifu's troops at Wuchang, and Niu promised to assist him by staging a simultaneous uprising against Sun Chuanfang's garrison in Shanghai.[20]

Wuchang fell to the NRA on 10 October, leaving Sun Chuanfang as its main opponent. Niu Yongjian sent envoys to Wang Shouhua and Lin Jun to discuss how the GMD and CCP might carry out an uprising in Shanghai in synchrony with a declaration of independence by Xia Chao.[21] The Communists were eager to be involved, since they saw an uprising as the way to establish popular self-government in the city.[22] They claimed to have a militia of 350 at their disposal, but only twenty-two revolvers. With difficulty, they persuaded Niu Yongjian to give them $10,000 – out of a sum of $100,000 he had been given by the Canton government – to buy 130 revolvers.[23] From his headquarters in the French Concession, Niu established contact with Huang Jinrong, chief of the detectives of the French Concession, with a view to raising a plain-clothes corps (*bianyi dui*) of 3,600 secret-society members, financed with money from the national government. He also liaised with Yu Xiaqing, who offered him 500 well-armed men, though A.P. Appen (Khmelev), the Soviet adviser training the Communist pickets, cast doubt on the effectiveness of this merchant militia as a fighting force.[24] The insurgents were to take on the 1,000-strong garrison of Sun Chuanfang, commanded by Li Baozhang, and 2,000 members of the Wusong-Shanghai constabulary. In addition, there were two gunboats in the Huangpu River, one of which had gone over secretly to Niu.[25] The military commission of the regional committee planned the uprising carefully, since it believed that only an uprising based on workers' pickets would strengthen the political position of the left. Niu Yongjian, however, was never completely committed to an uprising, preferring to seek the peaceful capitulation of Sun Chuanfang.[26]

At a meeting of the regional committee on 9 October, Luo Yinong declared: 'the merchants must play the main part ... the proletariat must avoid taking a leadership role, for if it is eager to lead the revolution, this will alarm the imperialists and cause them to attack or even massacre us ... Leadership must therefore pass to Yu Xiaqing.'[27] This policy had the broad backing of the FEB, though later it would deny that this was the case. On 15 October Rafes wrote: 'the initiative in the planned Shanghai uprising must belong to the bourgeoisie, it must be carried out under the slogan of independence, peace and agreement with Canton ... I already feel, however, that the bourgeoisie is indecisive and is detaching itself from the uprising.'[28] His concern was shared by the regional committee, since it was clear that there was little unanimity between the parties about the aims of the uprising. On 14 October Yu Xiaqing told the Communists that he would not declare his support for an uprising publicly nor accept offers of military assistance. The regional committee, however, decided to stay fully involved in Yu's plans to establish a committee to uphold peace (*heping weizhihui*).[29] This committee was a bone of contention between Yu and

Niu Yongjian, who insisted that the uprising be carried out in the name of the GMD. Further disagreements arose because the right-wing members of the Special Committee would not back the Communist slogan of 'popular local government'. A compromise was patched up, whereby all sides agreed to recognize Yu Xiaqing's peace committee as the organ of power, so long as workers had representation on it.[30] In the light of disagreements about the aim of the uprising, FEB members pressed the Communist leadership to organize 'an independent action of the proletariat' parallel to the uprising. But at a meeting on 19 October Chen Duxiu and Peng Shuzhi told them that workers were demoralized and that even a one-day strike would expose them to reprisals from management. They did, however, agree to a limited stoppage by dockers, tramworkers, postal workers and workers in the power stations – a limitation opposed by Rafes.[31]

On 13 October the 6th corps of the NRA captured Nanchang. Three days later, Xia Chao declared the independence of Zhejiang and his support for the GMD. The expedition against Sun Chuanfang, however, had been inadequately prepared, and on the 16th the NRA was forced to withdraw from Nanchang.[32] Xia Chao had barely 10,000 men, most of them poorly trained and armed, but he did move one of his regiments in the direction of Shanghai.[33] Sun's forces waited anxiously for reinforcements from the north, tearing up sections of the railway to Hangzhou in order to prevent Xia's forces reaching the city. By the evening of the 17th, Xia's regiment was only 5 kilometres away, and artillery fire could be heard to the south-east of the city. However, at that point reinforcements arrived to fortify Sun's garrison. It is just possible that Xia's forces might have been able to capture Shanghai had an uprising gone ahead immediately, since Sun's forces did not begin to counterattack until 20 October.[34] According to Luo Yinong, the CEC and regional committee pressed Niu Yongjian to proceed with the uprising, but he refused, claiming he had no arms.[35] At a special meeting of activists on 18 October, the local Communists were bullish, claiming that 10,000 could be mobilized for the insurrection, and stressing the importance of winning support from all social groups.[36] They specified the aims of the uprising as being the overthrow of Sun Chuanfang, demonstration of the power of armed mass struggle, and the establishment of a bourgeois-democratic 'citizens' government' to guarantee basic civil rights – above all, the right to form labour unions.[37] Niu Yongjian seems to have spent most of the time between 18 and 21 October trying to persuade Li Baozhang to desert to the NRA.[38] On 20 October, however, Sun Chuanfang's forces began their counter-offensive, regaining control of Jiaxing on the 21st and Hangzhou on the 23rd. The capture of Hangzhou spelt defeat for Xia Chao. Precisely on that day, however, Niu finally gave the order for the uprising to commence the following morning. It has always been a puzzle why he decided to go ahead.[39] According to Luo Yinong, he was sceptical of the news about the capture of Hangzhou and convinced that the garrison in Shanghai would come over to the insurgents.[40] After wavering, the Shanghai regional committee decided to obey Niu's order, issuing an order at 4 pm for pickets to mobilize in the small hours of the 24th.[41]

According to the plan, a flare was to go up from Niu Yongjian's headquarters in the French Concession just before 3am as a signal to a gunboat in the Huangpu river to fire a salvo to indicate the start of the insurrection.[42] On the evening of the 23rd, pickets gathered in groups of five to ten, ready to assemble at the agreed points as soon as the salvo was fired.[43] In the event, the flare went up but was invisible to the gunboat five kilometres away, so a salvo was never fired.[44] In Pudong 136 picketers assembled at the appointed time, with about a dozen rifles between them, but became demoralized waiting, and eventually dispersed.[45] Niu's gangsters attacked a precinct police station in Pudong – where most of them lived – in the course of which a policeman was killed and five gangsters attacked. However, the Pudong police organized a pre-emptive raid on the headquarters of the dockers' picket at Wujiating, arresting Tao Jingxuan and six others.[46] The planned dockers' strike failed to materialize. According to the cryptic minutes of the Shanghai regional committee, 'the masses were afraid, and we ourselves did not understand their psychology, when so many dockers could be bought off for only four mao.'[47] In Nandao a couple of hundred insurgents assembled, including several pickets sent from the Xiaoshadu cotton mills, but an attack on a Chinese police station near St. Catherine's Bridge was easily repulsed, leaving seventeen wounded and one dead. A raid by police on the barracks at Qinxian Street led to the arrest of four picketers.[48] Meanwhile, tipped off in advance about the uprising, Li Baozhang sent two companies to reinforce the arsenal and the Longhua barracks, to the south-east of the city.[49] As soon as they realised that the arsenal was in a state of alert, several hundred gang members fled. Luo Yinong commented: 'we were too gullible, for Niu Yongjian has no real strength at his disposal'.[50]

Thus ended what the CCP came to call the 'first armed uprising'. It was, of course, far too grand an appellation. As the historian Hua Gang observed: 'While it can reasonably be interpreted as an uprising in essence, it cannot be called an uprising in practice, being more the seizure of an opportunity (*yizhong shi touji*).'[51] Twenty-one arrests are documented, but the Communists put the true figure closer to 100.[52] Among the ten or so who were executed were Tao Jingxuan, aged 36 and chair of the dockers' union, and Xi Zuoyao, one of the six members of the Communist general staff in charge of the uprising. Aged 30, he had been a work-study student and, after joining the CCP in Belgium, had gone to Moscow to study military science. In 1926 he returned, getting a job as a designer at the French Concession Tram Company.[53]

Responding to criticism from district party secretaries on 25 October, Luo Yinong accepted that there had been inadequate preparation, too few weapons, and too long a delay in launching the uprising. He also conceded that the party had handled the military side badly, and that the general staff set up by the regional committee had not liaised with other party bodies.[54] Analysing the débâcle in detail the following day, Wang Yanxia supplemented this by saying that the uprising might have succeeded had it taken place on the 16th or 17th, when workers and local GMD activists were heartened by the capture of Nanchang. But delay had proved fatal. Yu Xiaqing had not supported the uprising, slinking back to Ningbo, and there had been no response from small and middle-ranking businessmen.[55] The opportunism of the GMD – especially its willingness to work with any force to hand – had also proved a handicap. Wang, however, reserved his most withering scorn for workers, so few of whom had risen to the summons: 'We shall not reproach other sections of the masses, only the workers, since workers ought to be specialists in insurrection. On this occasion the workers revealed very many deficiencies.'[56]

In the light of this botched attempt to cooperate with the 'bourgeoisie', the regional committee altered its assessment of the class forces involved in the national revolution. At a meeting of district party secretaries on 25 October, Luo Yinong said: 'In the resolution of the enlarged plenum we overestimated the significance of the Shanghai capitalists ... We now know that the capitalists have no real strength, and so we will not again exaggerate this. In the next Shanghai movement we must resolutely affirm that only the working class can be the driving force, there is no one else.'[57] Despite sharp differences of opinion, the committee pledged in future 'to strive ourselves to play the leading role, although formally the bourgeoisie must be counted the leader.'[58] This downgrading of the role of the national bourgeoisie was not well received by the FEB, which construed it, rather oddly, as a form of rightism, as evidence of the CCP's loss of faith in mass action. On 28 October Luo Yinong and Peng Shuzhi infuriated Voitinskii and Rafes by suggesting that a mass uprising was not on the cards in Shanghai, since not even students, still less the small and medium bourgeoisie, had shown an inclination to rise up.[59] Peng Shuzhi said that he was completely sceptical that the bourgeoisie had any role to play.[60] Voitinskii's response was that the CCP had only itself to blame, since it had sidelined the campaign for self-government which could have pushed the bourgeoisie to the fore and drawn in the medium and small bourgeoisie.[61] Chen Duxiu retorted that the outcome would have been the same even if they had relied on Yu Xiaqing instead of Niu Yongjian, since three hours before the uprising, Yu had still been quibbling about the composition of the peace committee.[62] Rafes insisted that this was beside the point: action by the proletariat, such as had been urged by the FEB, could have drawn in the petty bourgeoisie and 'even the big bourgeoisie'.[63] With some justice, he pointed out how much the orientation of the CEC had changed since the October 1925 plenum. 'Now not only is there no talk of (proletarian) hegemony, but the party has completely written off the proletariat even in a city like Shanghai.'[64] Chen Duxiu replied that Rafes only knew the city of Shanghai, and that at present there were neither the subjective nor objective conditions for proletarian hegemony. 'China is a semi-colonial country in which the military factor plays the paramount role. Without military forces there cannot be an uprising either here or in Hunan.'[65] The comment was prescient in the light of the party's subsequent reliance on gun-barrels to carry out its revolution.

The background to the second armed uprising

The unexpected capture of Jiujiang by the NRA in early November, together with defeats in Fujian and Jiangxi, left Sun Chuanfang with little option but to turn for help to his erstwhile foes, the Fengtian and Shandong warlords. During the first couple of weeks of November, the CCP, assuming that an occupation of Shanghai was imminent, energetically prepared and propagandized for a new armed uprising, though neither Yu Xiaqing nor Niu Yongjian was supportive.[66] At the same time, the CCP campaigned vigorously for a national assembly, democratic self-government in the provinces and full civil liberties. The alliance between Sun Chuanfang and Zhang Zongchang, the Shandong militarist, appalled Shanghai's business-men, since Zhang had flooded his domain with unsecured banknotes (*fengpiao*). They were adamant that Shanghai should be spared the military conflict which in the Yangtze delta had led to heavy losses of trade and high prices of staple goods.[67] On 11 November, therefore, the GCC backed the call of the GLU and the Greater Shanghai bureau of the GMD for the formation of a municipal government.[68] In return, the GLU agreed to support the campaign for 'autonomy of the three provinces' (i.e. Zhejiang, Jiangsu and Anhui), a project that had the strong support of the SSU and the good will of the GMD.[69] On 28 November a huge meeting of 50,000 people, representing all public organizations, denounced Sun Chuanfang for selling out to the Fengtian clique, and called for Shanghai to be formed into a special area under an autonomous government, elected by representatives of the workers, merchants and students.[70] On 6 December a citizens' assembly was convened, chaired by Shen Junru of the Three Provinces Association, designed to establish municipal autonomy in Shanghai and uphold the welfare of its citizens. About five of the ten members of the executive of the assembly were Communists.[71] Li Baozhang denounced the body as the work of 'Reds', and on 8 January the French Concession police shut it down.[72] In Zhabei a citizens' assembly continued to exist until the third armed uprising of March 1927.[73]

One of the principal objects of the citizens' assembly, so far as the Communists were concerned, was to entrench civil liberties and, in particular, to legalize the GLU. For the first time since the end of the May

Thirtieth Movement, the political climate was once again conducive to trade unionism. By January 1927 there were 187 unions affiliated to the GLU, with a membership of 76,000.[74] Recovery was strongest among groups of workers who hitherto had had a poor record of unionization, such as shop employees, public utility workers and handicraft workers. Yet efforts by the GLU to place itself on a legal footing came to nothing. On 30 November it tried to reopen unofficially, but its office was shut down on 8 December.[75] Three days later it reopened, after 300 workers broke the seal on the office, but again it was quickly closed.[76]

To Chiang Kai-shek's chagrin, the sweeping victories of the NRA produced a national government dominated by the left (though not by the Communists). By 10 December most GMD leaders, accompanied by Mikhail Borodin, had moved to Wuhan. A few days later they established a joint council of members of the national government and the GMD CEC which claimed to be the "supreme authority" in China. Chiang Kai-shek refused to acknowledge the new body. Yet as the CEC of the CCP recognized, the balance of military and political power was swinging in Chiang's favour. On 7 December he held a conference at Lushan, attended by Borodin, which agreed that the priority was to eliminate Sun Chuanfang. This meant a continuation of the NRA's offensive into the lower Yangtze delta, with the ultimate aim of securing Shanghai. Although Chiang's principal Soviet aide, General V. Bliukher, had misgivings about the plan, the Soviet advisers at Nanchang planned the operation in detail. The NRA was divided into three route armies, and advance units of the eastern army under Bai Chongxi, a Guangxi militarist who had come over to the NRA, were tasked with concentrating in western Zhejiang with the aim of taking Hangzhou.[77] Early in February Bai's units advanced into Zhejiang to penetrate the rear of Sun Chuanfang's forces guarding the approaches to Hangzhou. To their amazement, they had captured that city by 17 February. Sun's forces proved to be demoralised and retreated in the face of their offensive.[78] An emergency meeting of the CEC of the CCP on 16 February decided that if the NRA reached Songjiang, 30 km from Shanghai along the Shanghai-Hangzhou railway, they would call a new uprising. The decision was approved the same day by the regional committee, and intensive preparation of pickets began.[79]

Meanwhile Yu Xiaqing was instrumental in consolidating support for Chiang Kai-shek among Shanghai's businessmen. Many were antipathetic to Sun Chuanfang, but not yet convinced that Chiang Kai-shek would be an improvement.[80] Yu formed the Shanghai Commercial Association (*Shanghai shangye lianhehui*) in January, though it was not formally constituted until 22 March, to rally support for Chiang Kai-shek.[81] It expanded rapidly from an initial nineteen organizations to more than sixty, including the FSA and many guilds and banking associations. Most of these were also members of the GCC, but the Association opposed the dominant faction within the GCC, led by Fu Xiaoan. The Association insisted that only the GMD could bring an end to economic and political instability and curb the excesses of the Communists.[82] At the same time, Yu Xiaqing assured the press that he was a mere merchant who had no political ambitions.[83]

On 5 January a mob burst into the British concession in Hankou and effectively seized control of it, sending a wave of panic through the foreign community in Shanghai. Fear that the arrival of the NRA would lead to the seizure of the International Settlement and rule by militant labour led to clamour for military intervention. The new Minister to China, Miles Lampson, had recently intimated to the GMD that the British Government might be willing to accommodate to the changing political realities in China, and throughout January some Shanghailanders were in high dudgeon at what W. Bruce Lockhart called the 'jelly-fishiness and flapdoodle in England.'[84] Yet the commitment to defend the International Settlement by force of arms was never seriously in doubt. In the end, the British government despatched a full division to China, the largest force ever sent abroad in peacetime.[85] As the spring arrived, Shanghai took on the aspect of an armed camp. The perimeters of the International Settlement and French Concession were fortified, and defences extended into the Chinese areas to all defensible points. Barbed-wire barricades appeared on the streets from the North Station down through Hungjao Road to Xujiawei, thus cutting the foreign settlements off from Chinese territory. By late March there were 22,400 foreign troops in the city, 16,000 of them British, 3,000 American, 2,000 Japanese and 1,000 French. Forty-two warships were anchored offshore, fourteen of them Japanese, thirteen American, eight British and three French. By agreement with Sun Chuanfang, 3,000 British soldiers were stationed in the Chinese areas of the city.[86]

The new Comintern policy

On 21 January Voitinskii informed Moscow that the resolution of the VII ECCI plenum, which set out a perspective of developing the national revolution into an 'anti-imperialist dictatorship of workers, peasants and the petty-bourgeoisie', had just arrived and was being translated into Chinese.[87] At the end of the month, the CEC discussed the resolution, by then almost two months old, and apparently approved the perspective laid down, going so far as to say that in the past the party had 'obstinately clung to a logical error', by drawing too sharp a line between the national and the proletarian revolutions.[88] In fact, the CEC did little to implement the resolution, keeping it 'under a bushel', according to the members of the FEB.[89] One of the members, T. Mandalian, reported that four issues, in particular, provoked opposition on the CEC: the first was the demand that the Communists enter the government in Wuhan; the second that Communist workers join the NRA; the third that the GMD be transformed into a mass party; and the fourth the change in tactics on the agrarian question.[90] According to M.N. Roy, the Indian Communist sent to oversee the implementation of the new perspectives, Chen Duxiu was not entirely convinced by the resolution, but believed that it opened up new perspectives that the CCP should follow, whereas his ally, Peng Shuzhi, opposed the resolution outright, telling the Shanghai regional party conference in February that the perspective differed little from that which the CCP was already following.[91] The principal champion of the Comintern line was Qu Qiubai, supported by Ren Bishi and Xiao Zizhang of the CC of the CYL, whose stance was influenced by the hostility felt towards Voitinskii by the KIM in Moscow.[92]

The at best lukewarm response of the CEC provoked Qu Qiubai into writing an angry polemic against Peng Shuzhi (and by implication Chen Duxiu) that was published in March. Peng Shuzhi may not have been confident as he once was that the proletariat was already hegemonic in the revolution, but he was convinced that the revolution would spill beyond its bourgeois-democratic confines. In an article published in January he argued that 'China's revolution will move directly from a national revolution to a proletarian revolution', referring to this as a 'continuous revolution' (*yongxu geming*).[93] He dismissed the national capitalists as 'impotent devils' (*shi wu de gui*), and argued that a victory for Chiang Kai-shek would represent a temporary triumph for the compradore bourgeoisie.[94] Qu Qiubai vehemently rejected these claims: he insisted that the revolution was still in its bourgeois-democratic phase and that the key to pushing it forward in a socialist direction lay through agrarian revolution. He castigated Peng for failing to appreciate that the national capitalists still had a role to play in the revolution, pointing out that they had an interest in tariff autonomy, the abolition of extraterritoriality and the return of the foreign concessions. He accused him of being thoroughly inconsistent, by claiming, on the one hand, that the national capitalists 'amounted to nothing'; yet seeking, on the other, to involve Yu Xiaqing *et al.* in plans for democratic government in Shanghai. Qu contended that the real danger to the revolution came not from the compradores, but from the vacillations of the national capitalists. Finally, he charged that by assuming proletarian hegemony to be a fact, Peng was dangerously neglecting the tasks of winning over the urban petty-bourgeoisie, the peasants and the soldiers to the side of the proletariat.[95]

The FEB, which had immediate responsibility for ensuring that the CCP carry out the VII ECCI plenum resolution, was still hopelessly split. Two of its members – A.E. Albrecht, responsible for organization and T.G. Mandalian, Profintern representative – together with the Shanghai representative of KIM, N.M. Nasonov, seem broadly to have shared the views of Qu Qiubai. But they were principally united by their detestation of

155

Voitinskii's 'opportunism'.[96] In a letter of 25 February to the secretary of ECCI, Albrecht denounced him in the fiercest terms: 'All his work consists of forming combinations, smoothing corners, and conciliationism. Instead of giving the party a clear directive, he confuses it by the most base diplomacy.'[97] Even so, the three supported Voitinskii against Borodin, who they believed was wilfully antagonizing Chiang Kai-shek.[98]

Borodin later claimed that he foresaw that a split with Chiang Kai-shek was underway as early as 3 January, but that the CEC (and by implication the FEB) refused to recognise it. Borodin opposed the campaign by the eastern route army to take Shanghai and derided the CEC's alleged belief that Chiang 'would drown in the mass movement' of the city.[99] He had the backing of CEC members Zhang Guotao and Zhang Tailei, who were now in Wuhan. When Voitinskii met Chiang in Jiujiang on 22–3 February, the latter insisted that Borodin be removed. He effectively demanded that party and government be subordinated to himself: otherwise 'we are ready to split'. At the same time, he sought to appear reasonable by assuring Voitinskii that he wished to restore regular relations with the CCP and to meet with Chen Duxiu. He proved to be remarkably well-versed about developments inside the CCP, complaining that at the recent Shanghai regional conference (a week previously) he had been called a militarist and a dictator.[100]

Chiang Kai-shek's refusal to recognize the government in Wuhan caused the Soviet Politburo to moderate its rigid insistence on caution at all costs. On 3 March it informed the CEC that 'further victories' were possible only through the 'decisive course of developing mass movements', and instructed it to 'exclude the right' from the GMD and 'systematically demote them from leading positions'. It also resolved to replace the existing FEB with 'new authoritative comrades', though this decision was soon overtaken by events.[101] The new directive did not reach the CEC in Shanghai until 22 March, when it was formally accepted.[102] In spite of its bolder policy, the Politburo continued to insist that a split with Chiang Kai-shek be avoided at all costs and that concessions be made to this end. It was particularly alarmed by Borodin's seemingly reckless provocation of Chiang, for the third plenum of the second CEC of the GMD, which met from 10 to 17 March, curbed his power by abolishing the chairmanship of the standing committee of the CEC and transferring the powers of the commander-in-chief of the NRA to the presidium of the military committee.[103] Borodin evidently persuaded Tan Yankai, head of the Wuhan government, to sign a secret order for Chiang's arrest.[104]

The workers' pickets

Following the failure of the first armed uprising, the CEC got down to making serious military preparations for a new uprising. In December

Zhou Enlai came to Shanghai from the Huangpu Military Academy to join the CEC's military commission, though according to Appen, the Soviet military adviser to the CEC, he and his fellow officers knew little about the city.[105] Most of the energy of the commission went into improving the competence of the pickets, whose numbers had now grown to around 2,000, but who still had only 100 weapons at their disposal. On 30 January 1927 the Shanghai regional committee called for a strict separation of function between a new armed militia and the pickets. Condemning the pickets for tending to become a 'standing armed force' (*jingchang wuzhuang*), it claimed that they had arrogated powers to arrest people, close down workplaces and levy union dues by force.[106] It observed that the pickets contained too many unemployed, artisanal and shop workers. It reminded comrades that pickets were supposed to be temporary bodies for the maintenance of order during strikes, and complained that the proliferation of pickets was undermining the efforts to build the labour unions. It concluded that the functions of the pickets should be whittled back, and that a new armed militia should be set up alongside them.[107] This should recruit only the most disciplined and politically reliable industrial workers, who were to be given thorough military and ideological training.[108] It proved difficult to set up the proposed militia, not least because of lack of weapons. Appen said that the party had no money to buy revolvers, and that its plan to persuade domestic servants to steal weapons from their foreign masters was ludicrous.[109] He also criticized the Communists for moving key people out of military work because of shortage of personnel.[110] It is also likely that the labour unions resisted the attempt to limit the functions of the pickets under their control. Whatever the reason, a militia was not formed: the second armed uprising, like the first, was carried out by ramshackle pickets accountable to the unions.[111]

There is relatively little data on the social composition of the pickets. Skilled male workers, such as printers, iron workers, tram workers and railway workers, were relatively more active in forming pickets than cotton and tobacco workers; though because of their preponderance in the workforce, the latter's pickets outnumbered those of the former. The Commercial Press had the largest and best organized picket in the city. Of seven members of the detachment who lost their lives in the battle for the Commercial Press during the third armed uprising, all were printers, including a 23-year-old woman. Their average age was 21.[112] The most striking feature about the pickets, however, was the high proportion of unemployed workers in their ranks, most being militants who had lost their jobs because of activism in the labour movement. They also included many secret-society members. The *North China Herald* observed that the pickets consisted of 'unemployed labourers, seamen, discharged workers and loafers [i.e., gangsters, SAS].'[113] And this is broadly confirmed by the resolution passed by the Fifth CCP Congress which admitted that there was widespread reluctance among employed workers to join the pickets and too many gang members and unemployed in their ranks.[114] Nevertheless praise for the pickets came from an unlikely quarter in the shape of Eric Teichman, a British diplomat, who in a memorandum of 1 March, wrote: 'despite the monstrous illegalities they practise, (they) compare most favourably in demeanour and appearance with any Chinese soldiers and, though usually armed only with long staves, seem to be the only authority, civilian or military, capable of controlling labour mobs.'[115]

In January Li Baozhang, commander of the Shanghai garrison, launched a White Terror to bolster the faltering administration of Sun Chuanfang. A single judge went about the streets, led by a man bearing a shield on which was written the martial law directive. Behind the judge strode two executioners with broadswords, on whose backs was an arrow symbol. Any hapless worker or student caught leafleting, was seized, forced to bend over and executed on the spot (*gesha wulun*). Their heads were then stuck on bamboo poles or piled on platters.[116] Official figures admit to only six executions in January, but the true figure was certainly higher.[117] When the GLU announced a general strike on 18 February 1927, Li ordered soldiers and police summarily to execute anyone breaching martial law. On the first day of the strike, 19 February, at least twenty people were decapitated, among them two metalworkers from Nanshi, whose heads were placed in cages and hung up at a crossroads.[118] During the next two days the terror intensified. The *North China Herald* reported: 'One man whose head now adorns the West Gate was an employee of the Shanghai Tramway Company. He, in company with two others, was arrested for distributing inflammatory literature. The other two men were employees of Chinese wine shops in the International Settlement.'[119] On 21 February a hawker, shouting 'Buy my cakes' (*mai dabing*), was stabbed by a soldier who thought he was crying 'Defeat the army!' (*dabai bing*).[120] As the general strike turned into an insurrection, the terror intensified. On 22 February there were a dozen executions in Nandao and Zhabei of people caught handing out leaflets or making speeches.[121] The GLU estimated that between 19 and 23 February forty were killed and 300 arrested.[122] By the beginning of March as many as 200 may have been killed, though the estimate of 500 killed and 700 arrested is certainly exaggerated.[123]

Foreigners may have felt queasy at the sight of severed heads, but they generally applauded Li Baozhang's vigour. The *North China Herald* editorialized: 'The political strike is open rebellion which should be dealt with promptly and unsparingly.'[124] The British and French police showed no compunction in handing troublemakers over to Li Baozhang. Anti-Communists within the GMD also backed the White Terror, the Western Hills Faction and its newspaper, the *Jiangnan Evening Post* allegedly receiving funds from Li.[125] Within a few weeks, they had the satisfaction of seeing Li welcomed into the NRA and rewarded with the command of the 18th army.[126]

The general strike

On the evening of 18 February, the day after the capture of Hangzhou by Bai Chongxi's eastern route army, the GLU held a secret meeting, attended by a couple of hundred delegates.[127] In the course of the meeting news arrived that NRA troops had reached Jiaxing, prompting delegates to call for a general strike in order to prepare the city for the entry of the NRA, to create a revolutionary-democratic government in Shanghai and to press for a national assembly.[128] A decision was taken to commence a general strike the next day, though nothing was said about it being the prelude to an armed uprising. The decision was taken without consultation with the CEC, and conflicted with CEC policy, which was to call a general strike only when the NRA reached Songjiang. However, Zhao Shiyan, head of the organization department of the Shanghai regional committee, was present at the meeting and evidently acquiesced in the decision. He was unable to inform the secretary of the Shanghai regional committee, Luo Yinong, until the following morning, since a curfew was in place after 10 pm. The first that members of the CEC knew of the general strike was when they discovered that there were no buses or trams running the following day.[129]

As the strike commenced, the GLU published a programme of seventeen demands. These called for the continuation of the anti-imperialist struggle; the destruction of the 'dark forces' of the warlords; the elimination of all reactionary forces in Shanghai; the creation of a government that would protect popular interests; and a variety of labour reforms, such as improved safety at work and equal pay for women.[130] The GLU took pains to assure the middle classes that the aim was a democratic citizens' government rather than a workers' government, but argued that this could only be achieved through revolutionary mobilization by the working class.[131] It also issued strict guidelines concerning discipline: there was to be no destruction of factories or shops; no violence against foreigners; no extortion of money; absolute obedience to GLU directives; and no action unless authorized by the GLU.[132] Faced with the strike, Li Baozhang determined to step up his terror, issuing a warning that 'every striker is breaking martial law, and must be dealt with as a seditionary.'[133]

On 20 February the Shanghai regional committee issued a proclamation, 'To the revolutionary people of Shanghai', which called for a citizens' assembly to form a democratic municipal government subject to the National Government. This was to be composed of delegates from representative bodies of workers, merchants, students, soldiers and the liberal professions, together with delegates from the political parties and factions (*pai*). It was to guarantee civil liberties, bring about the withdrawal of foreign troops and the restitution of the foreign settlements, and carry out a wide range of municipal and labour reforms.[134] On the same day the regional committee issued a call to the citizenry (*shimin*) to support the general strike, in order to create 'a new Shanghai, free and independent, and to wash away the disgrace suffered by its citizens for eighty years.'[135]

The GLU boasted with justice that the February general strike was the largest ever witnessed in Shanghai, and for this reason it deserves to be examined separately from the armed uprising which flowed out of it. A later calculation, based on press reports, put the number who halted work during the four-day stoppage at 420,970 workers in nearly 6,000 workplaces, including 324,970 men, 90,000 women and 6,000 children.[136] The GLU estimated that 150,000 struck on Saturday, 19 February; 275,000 on the 20th; 350,000 on the 21st; and 360,000 on the 22nd. It ridiculed the figures published in the British press for underestimating the number of strikers by a factor of six.[137] According to Zhou Enlai's postmortem, most joined the strike not to promote a citizens' government, a concept which they understood but dimly, but to welcome the NRA, which had acquired massive popularity during the preceding six months.[138] What distinguished the strike from those of the summers of 1925 and 1926 was the high proportion of workers in Chinese-owned enterprises who took part, such as 100,000 workers in the handicraft sector and the women in the silk filatures, who had been passive during the May Fourth and May Thirtieth general strikes.[139] Another feature of the strike, which distinguished it from both the triple strike of May Thirtieth Movement and the third armed uprising of March 1927, was the relatively poor response that it evoked from small traders and shopkeepers. On 21 February the GLU called on the latter to join the strike, but though the Shanghai Commercial Association and the FSA called a one-day protest on 21 February against the White Terror 'to show our sympathy and support for the workers', no great enthusiasm was evinced.[140] This may have been because Green Gang potentate, Du Yuesheng, who appears to have been supporting Fu Xiaoan of the GCC, specifically ordered merchants in the French Concession to continue business as usual. He also ensured that supplies of water and electricity continued as normal in the French Concession.[141]

Strikers displayed admirable valour. Shen Lianfang, president of the Silk Guild, asked Li Baozhang to order district police officials to warn strikers in eighty-three silk filatures that if they did not return to work immediately, they risked decapitation.[142] To the irritation of the foreign community, 2,900 postal workers went on strike, having been brought out by picketers wearing red arm bands saying 'Welcome to Chiang Kai-shek'.[143] This was in spite of the fact that Du Yuesheng, one of the protectors of the postal workers' union, was opposed to the strike. The union, which had up to now been dominated by those the Communists contemptuously called 'reformists", publicly tore up Li Baozhang's order and said that it would obey only the GLU. Picketers, however, had the sense to remove themselves from the gateway to the main post office.[144] By attaching itself to the cause of national unification, the GLU acquired great moral authority and workers showed no hesitation in responding to its strike call.

The armed uprising

For two crucial days following the start of the general strike, the four members of the CEC resident in Shanghai procrastinated over whether or not to transform the strike into an armed uprising. On 19 February a joint committee of the Jiangsu provincial bureau and Greater Shanghai bureau of the GMD, in which the Communists participated, was formed to direct the uprising at some unspecified time.[145] In fact, Niu Yongjian was anxious to avoid an uprising if possible because he realized it was likely to strengthen the CCP's hand, so he concentrated on trying to induce Li Baozhang to defect to the NRA. However, since he recognized that this outcome was uncertain, he supported an uprising as a fall-back position.[146] The Communists, by contrast, were bent on an uprising as a matter of principle. Their preference was to carry out an uprising under cover of the united front, but this time they placed no confidence in Niu Yongjian's secret-society force or Yu Xiaqing's merchant militia.[147] By 20 February it was clear that the NRA did not intend to advance at once on Shanghai. Nevertheless after a long debate, the CEC decided to go ahead with an insurrection against Li Baozhang. However, it was not until the morning of Monday, 21 February, that a precise time was set for it to start, namely, 6 pm on that day.[148]

The balance of military force had tipped slightly in the CCP's favour since the first armed uprising, for there were now fewer than 500 soldiers in the city, plus 2,000 police. Agitators had been busy in the navy and two out of four gunboats, anchored off Longhua, were on the side of the insurgents. Naval officer Guo Yuheng, who had joined the CCP, was in charge of operations, and was optimistic that the other two gunboats would participate in the uprising once they had neutralized their officers.[149] According to the plan drawn up, the uprising was to begin with Guo Yuheng ordering the two gunboats under his influence to begin a bombardment of Nandao, aimed at facilitating the seizure of the Jiangnan arsenal. Once the bombardment started, 100 unarmed picketers in Pudong were to board a motor launch and sail to the gunboats, where they would receive seventy rifles. They would then proceed to Longhua to capture the arsenal there, while it was being bombarded from the river. It was thought that the officer in charge of the company of engineers at the arsenal was sympathetic to the insurgents and unlikely to resist. By 4 pm on 21 February pickets were in place around the city. However, at 6 pm no signal was forthcoming from the two gunboats, since the person with the keys to the cellar where the shells were kept could not be found. The pickets thus melted away.[150] A somewhat different account is given by the FEB representatives who suggest that the CEC called off the uprising in the course of the afternoon. 'Qu Qiubai and Xiao Zizhang knew nothing about the cancellation. Indeed staff learnt of postponement only at 3 pm. Peng Shuzhi said the postponement was due to the fact that the working class was not ready, since it had no arms, and that the petty bourgeoisie had not yet acted decisively.'[151] On 21 February the joint committee of the Jiangsu provincial bureau and the Greater Shanghai bureau of the GMD held an emergency meeting, at which Niu Yongjian agreed to support an insurrection, but insisted that it should not commence until Thursday, 24 February.[152]

The following morning, 22 February, the CEC of the CCP met again. The strike was at its peak, but some workers were beginning to drift back to work. In addition, reinforcements were being sent by rail from Nanjing to augment Sun Chuanfang's garrison in Shanghai. The CEC was determined to have a second stab at an uprising, and resolved that it should go ahead that day at 6 pm.[153] As that hour struck, local Communists were in discussion with Niu Yongjian about the shape of a democratic municipal government. Cannon fire was heard and Niu sensed immediately what was going on. He turned furiously on Luo Yinong, accusing the Communists of 'bad faith' and 'wild ambition' and of wanting a bloc with the GMD, yet acting behind its back.[154] That meeting proved to be the first and last of a 'council of government' that the Communists and Niu had established, comprising two Communists and five GMD members, including Yu Xiaqing, none of whom was on the left of the party.[155]

Several hours prior to 6 pm, 250 strikers, led by 60 to 70 men armed with pistols, iron bars and sticks, attacked the police station of the second precinct of the No.5 district in Zhabei, beating up a policeman and smashing windows and furniture.[156] This may have been pickets acting off their own bat or some initiative by the secret societies. At 6 pm prompt, however, the gunboats began to bombard Nandao, after Guo Yuheng arrested several naval officers who promised to recognize the national government. As soon as the Jiangnan arsenal came under bombardment, the company of engineers inside hoisted a white flag. In Pudong pickets waited for a motor launch to take them to the gunboats to collect rifles, but it arrived an hour late, with the result that a landing party was not able to cross the Huangpu river to attack the Longhua arsenal. Following the surrender of the Jiangnan arsenal, gunboats turned their fire on the South Station in Nandao, where a special trainload of northern troops was holed up. They also fired on the headquarters of Li Baozhang and the civil governor, but after several shells landed in the French Concession, French warships threatened to shell the mutinous gunboats unless they called off the bombardment. They had little choice but to comply. By that stage, picketers, possibly no more than forty in number, were in occupation of several police stations and government buildings in Nandao. Unfortunately, the police had taken their arms with them as they fled, so the action yielded only a few revolvers and two or three rifles. Since the pickets did not think to join with the sappers who had risen up at the Jiangnan arsenal, the administration there was able to reestablish control. By midnight, having failed to take either the Jiangnan or the Longhua arsenals, and lacking clear guidance, the pickets retired.[157]

On 23 February sporadic shooting, directed mainly at police stations and sentry points, persisted in Zhabei, Nandao and the eastern districts. However, the failure of the merchant militia and Niu Yongjian's corps of secret society members to mobilize meant that the uprising was effectively over.[158] The gunboats now came under fire from Sun Chuanfang's field artillery, and only the energetic ministrations of Admiral Yang Shuzhuang, commander of the Bohai fleet of Zhang Zuolin, prevented bloody reprisals. Although Admiral Yang got off lightly, with a mere reprimand from Sun Chuanfang, he entered secret negotiations with Niu Yongjian, finally coming over to the NRA on 14 March.[159] On 23 February the drift back to work by strikers intensified. That night, the CEC and the regional committee decided to call off the general strike and the uprising, and the next morning the GLU announced that it was halting the strike 'on the advice of the commercial circles'. Given the failure of the FSA and GCC to support the strike, this justification was odd, but presumably reflected the GLU's desire to placate the middle classes.[160] Either because the CCP did not have complete control over the insurgents or because some were responding to Niu's original call to rise up on the 24th, the following morning saw pickets in Zhabei renew the assault on the police station in the third precinct. Some eighty attackers, armed with automatic pistols and iron rods, fought with police who repelled them with rifle fire. Two attackers and one policeman were wounded and two attackers were arrested. They and two thirteen-year-old boys, arrested on the 22nd, were summarily executed.[161] This extinguished the last embers of resistance.

The Red Terror

A Red Terror squad had been established in November to impose tighter control over the 'dog-beating squads'. Zhou Enlai, now head of the regional committee's military commission, lamented the indiscipline of the squad, pointing that it was only capable of attacking 'small running dogs' rather than big shots.[162] On 19 January, for example, a dismissed employee at NWK, suspected of betraying the union, was shot dead when four men burst into his house on Robison Road. Another tenant in the house was killed and a third wounded.[163] On 14 February a Chinese foreman at NWK No.3 mill and his brother were murdered, when three men, armed with pistols, invaded his house.[164] A man charged with the murder of a forewoman said that the GLU had given him a pistol and $10 to carry out the crime.[165] And a certain Wang, a major in the 7th Battalion of the 7th Regiment of the NRA stationed in Zhabei, when charged with murdering Wang A'er on 24 February, confessed that Gu Shunzhang had ordered him to carry out the murder.[166] Such an uncoordinated campaign was clearly powerless in the face of Li Baozhang's White Terror, so on 24 February 1927 the Shanghai regional committee formally launching a Red Terror.[167] It declared that only two forms of terror were permissible: retaliatory attacks on Li Baozhang's henchmen and actions designed to boost popular morale, such as the assassination of foremen and 'running dogs' known to be responsible for the arrest of trade unionists and party members.[168] Two days later, at a meeting of 150 labour union activists only the representative of the shop-employees' association, a body which preserved some distance from the GLU, spoke out against the terror.[169]

The regional committee, however, still proved unable to exercise control over the assassinations that now ensued. This was partly because the GLU believed that it, and not the party leadership, should direct the campaign of terror, and partly because it relied on apolitical mercenaries to carry it out. On 5 March a father and son, employed in a Japanese silk filature on Brenan Road, came under fire, recognizing their assailant as a brass-smith formerly employed at their factory.[170] Around the same time, Zhang Afeng, chief contractor of the Shanghai Dock and Engineering Company in Pudong, was murdered.[171] On 11 March a foreman at the Doko mill in Xiaoshadu and one at the Japanese-owned Shanghai Cotton Manufacturing Company in Yangshupu were killed by 'men who had the appearance of being mill hands'.[172] In his report for March 1927 the International Settlement police commissioner said that there had been eleven terrorist incidents in that month resulting in eight deaths, though the figure refers only to the International Settlement. The CCP claimed that between 24 February and 20 March nineteen 'running dogs' were killed, and that more were kidnapped or received threatening letters.[173] All of these were directed against 'small running dogs', who were far easier to eliminate than soldiers bearing broadswords. Faced with this, and the reluctance of the GLU to seek its authorization, on 19 March the Shanghai regional committee announced:

> From today all attacks on running dogs of whatever stripe must cease. Too many comrades have made too many mistakes. There have even been public acknowledgements that unions have been

killing running dogs. This should only be the secret political work of the party, and cannot be the work of the labour unions. ... If there are any attacks to be made, the decision must be that of the regional committee alone and not of the labour unions.[174]

Acts of terror seem to have elicited sympathy from many workers. In one case, however, they were driven to protest by what they perceived to be a particularly despicable act. According to a memoir of Wang Ruqing (Huang Hao), the 'dog-beating squad' at the NKW No.9 mill, which was led by Shi Congyan, killed three foremen at the mill.[175] The first was Zhu Asan, overseer of the weaving shed; the second Feng Baoru, a foreman from Subei, slain on 13 March while relaxing in the bath-house opposite the No.9 mill; and the third Zeng Fugen.[176] Zeng, the 26-year-old temporary foreman of the weaving shed at NWK No.9 mill, was mowed down on 15 March at 10 pm, when two armed men burst into the union-run canteen. Precisely why he was targeted is unclear, since he was an active member of the union. He may have been singled out because he had accepted promotion or he may have been shot by mistake. What the 'dog beaters' could not have foreseen is the outcry that his death would provoke. The next day 1,520 women, 420 men and 60 children went on a one-day strike in protest, and a longer strike was averted only when the company agreed to pay Zeng's family compensation for its bereavement. The union at the No.9 mill blamed the Japanese imperialists – 'they kill our people, they insult our national rights' – but whether they knew the truth is uncertain. More disingenuous seems to have been the decision of the western district federation of cotton unions to organize a funeral for Zeng, on the grounds that he had died 'on behalf of the masses.' If the murder was indeed carried out by the dog-beating squad, as Wang Ruqing claims, the federation's attitude was deeply cynical.[177]

The aftermath

The secretaries of the district committees of the CCP in Shanghai met twice, on 24 and 26 February, to undertake a post-mortem on the second armed uprising. In Yangshupu district the secretary reported that one communications worker had been arrested, another man killed and several wounded. He said that a rumour had circulated that all labour union leaders had gone underground, so the workers had seen no point in continuing the strike. But although unions at the new Ewo and Hengfeng mills had been raided by military police, they were still functioning.[178] In Yinxianggang district the secretary reported that only nine people had turned up to a party meeting on the 25th, and that there was an atmosphere of panic, since twenty-one party members had been arrested and nine of them shot.[179] In Wusong district the secretary said that the raids on the union and party headquarters had thrown the masses into panic. On the 23rd most had returned to work. Ten women had been arrested after smashing up a factory. Twenty-seven comrades had been fired. There was said to be widespread loss of confidence in the party.[180]

In the west of the city, the secretary of the Xiaoshadu district committee reported that the local organization was in reasonably good shape, despite police raids on the factories. The pickets on the docks remained well organized. In retaliation for the shooting of nine workers, local party activists were carrying out a Red Terror.[181] In Caojiadu the secretary reported that one comrade had been arrested and that many had confessed. Forty workers had been sacked. At Shenxin mill strike leaders dared not go back to work. Five speakers from the people's school had been arrested, and two killed.[182] The secretary of the French Concession branch said that seventeen tramworkers had been arrested, along with three picketers, two members of the district party committee, two students and two members of the union of foreign employees. The repression made communication between branches difficult.[183] In Nanshi the workers were said to be fearful, and there was general dissatisfaction with the leadership's handling of the uprising.[184] From these two meetings it emerges that even the secretaries of the CCP's district committees were none too clear about the aims of the uprising, and felt disgruntled with the central leadership. Nevertheless predictions that it would take a long time for the party to rebuild its organization proved unfounded.[185]

On 26 February a meeting of 150 labour union militants took place. Seamen and postal employees congratulated the GLU and questioned whether the uprising had been a complete failure. Only the association of shop employees expressed dissatisfaction, since dozens had been sacked at the Xinxin, Yongan, and Xianshi department stores. On 24 February two representatives from the union at the Yongan department store had told the CCP district secretaries that 100 workers had been fired and the union raided.[186] It was reported from Yangshupu district that the Nanyang tobacco union was still functioning, despite a raid the previous day, and that the union at the Ruirong iron works was intact. The leaders of the union of makers of southern delicacies were frightened, since one of their number had been executed, and it was said that the unions of pharmacy employees and makers of foreign cloth were defunct. The union of coal hauliers, which had recently changed its allegiance from the SFS to the GLU, was reported to be unhappy, since it had gained nothing from the strike, and the union of silk workers was said to have collapsed.[187]

In a public statement on the uprising the CEC of the CCP was strangely positive. Refusing to concede defeat, it talked of the five-day general strike as having produced no clear result. It claimed that the strike had been an educative experience for workers and the urban masses and a dress rehearsal for the final battle.[188] Qu Qiubai's internal report was far more critical of the party's policy. He argued that the principal reason for failure had been the leadership's lack of clarity about aims. It had not intended the strike to lead to an uprising, and workers were out on the streets for three days before the party gave a clear lead.[189] That the strikers seemed to lack direction was noticed even by the NCH: 'The strikers have shown little inclination to cause trouble. Indeed their general attitude as displayed by crowds around the streets – 'mooning' alone describes their behaviour – is one of apathetic listlessness.'[190] And another journal said that some workers thought that the purpose was to celebrate the capture of Hangzhou by the Nationalist army, while others thought it was to oppose the landing of British troops.[191] In his report Zhou Enlai criticised the inadequate preparation of the pickets, only 600 of whom had been involved, together with the weakness of the military commission of the regional committee.[192]

Subsequently, the CCP blamed the failure of the second uprising on the decision of Bai Chongxi not to advance on Shanghai immediately. This decision has sometimes been represented as a deliberate act of betrayal. Harold Isaacs and others have suggested that Bai's motive for delaying entry was to allow Li Baozhang to behead as many militants as possible.[193] This may have been a 'bonus', so far as Bai and Chiang Kai-shek were concerned, but the prime motive for delay was Bai's belief that it was necessary to await reinforcements from He Yingqin, commander of the eastern route army, before advancing on Shanghai.[194] Niu Yongjian did advise Chiang Kai-shek not to let Bai's units proceed beyond Jiaxing, but he appears to have been concerned about the implications of the massive build-up of military force by the British and Japanese in Shanghai.[195] When on 20 February the Communists resolved to press ahead with the uprising anyway, they knew that the NRA had no immediate plans to occupy Shanghai, but simply did not wish to end up toeing Niu Yongjian's line.[196]

The uprising hardened the resolve of businessmen and GMD rightists to be rid of the CCP. It also paved the way for a deal between Chiang Kai-shek and the foreign powers. At the end of February, Stirling Fessenden, the American chairman of the MC, the French chief of police and an interpreter met with Du Yuesheng. Du said that he was willing to stop the Reds but required at least 5,000 rifles plus ammunition from the French and permission to drive military trucks through the International Settlement. Fessenden consented to his request.[197]

Chapter 9 _____

The Third Armed Uprising

The upsurge of the CCP and the GMD

By the end of 1926 the CCP's membership had passed 20,000, and within the next four months it almost trebled. By the time of the Fifth CCP Congress, which opened on 27 April 1927, membership stood at 57,967.[1] Growth of membership in Shanghai, despite the peculiar difficulties faced in that city, largely replicated the national pattern. On 10 January there were said to be only 3,075 members in Shanghai city (4,500 if one includes adjacent areas under the jurisdiction of the regional committee). By 4 March there were 3,856 and, six days later, 4,400.[2] On 17 March the regional committee called on comrades to loosen restrictions on recruitment, with a view to increasing the party's forces to 10,000 within a month.[3] Following the NRA's occupation of the city, membership surged to 8,374 by 4 April.[4] At the Fifth Congress Chen Duxiu claimed that the entire Shanghai region had a membership of 13,000.[5] Yet most party branches continued to be small. Of 143 on 10 January, fifty-nine had less than ten members; thirty-six had ten to twenty members; seventeen had twenty to thirty members; twenty-two had thirty to fifty members; four had fifty to 100 members; and five had over 100 members.[6]

The effect of the spurt of growth was to increase the number of workers in the CCP, but to reduce their overall share of membership. Whereas in 1926 the proportion of workers was over two-thirds, by the time of the Fifth Congress it had fallen to one-half. According to Zhao Pu's recalculation of figures given in the Congress report, 50.8 per cent of members were workers; 19.1 per cent intellectuals; 18.7 per cent peasants; 3.15 per cent soldiers; 0.5 per cent middle and small merchants; and 7.8 per cent of miscellaneous social origin.[7] We do not have figures for the social composition of the Shanghai party organization, but it is likely that the share of working-class members was higher than the national average. On 25 January, at a time when membership of the regional organization was 4,500, it was reported that there were 500 student members of the CCP, so a large proportion of the 4,000 non-student members would have been workers.[8] The party continued to be strongest in the cotton industry, the western district committee having forty-four branches with 2,200 members, and the eastern district committee having thirty-seven branches and 1,501 members on 1 April.[9] The largest branches in the western district were at NWK Nos. 7 and 9 mills, Doko and Nikko – all Japanese cotton mills.[10]

Ironically, political repression may have made it easier to form a CCP branch in a factory than a labour union. A union required a degree of publicity to establish itself, which meant that the authorities could nip the initiative in the bud, whereas secrecy was of the essence in setting up a workplace party branch. This may explain why at the Commercial Press a CCP branch existed from 1923, whereas a union was not formed until 25 June 1925.[11] At the BAT works there was no union between September 1925 and March 1927 but a significant CCP presence. In June 1926 the Housheng mill had the largest CCP branch in Yangshupu, with a membership of twenty, but no union.[12] Similarly, the union at the Xiangsheng shipyard was suppressed in the autumn of 1925, yet Yang Peisheng was able to form a CCP branch there in November, which by late 1926 had twenty members, organised into three cells.[13] Since the priority of Communists was always to form a union, this may have created a situation in which the distinction between a workplace party branch and an embryonic labour union was blurred.

The proportion of women in the party increased little. In December 1926 there were still only 1,992 women in the party nationally – just over 10 per cent of the membership.[14] In April 1927 Chen Duxiu's report to the Fifth Congress put the proportion of women at 10 per cent, but _Pravda_ gave a percentage of 8.27 per cent.[15] In Shanghai the proportion of female members remained higher than the national average, though there are no statistics for this period. Most district committees in city had a women's committee, but women's work seems to have remained low on the party's list of priorities. District organizers reported on 1 April that the women's movement was poorly organized in Zhabei, the western district, the French Concession and Nanshi.[16] How far Communist neglect was cause or consequence of an apparent decline in the women's movement in general is difficult to say. Various women's organizations were still alive. The Shanghai Association of Women of all Sections of Society, for example, supported the citizens' assembly and there were plans to hold a women's delegate conference to foster the link between the women's and labour movements.[17] On 8 March 200 women met to celebrate International Women's Day – the principal speaker being Yang Zhihua – and agreed to participate in the citizens' assembly and to demand equal pay, maternity provision for women workers, legal equality with men, freedom of marriage and divorce, abolition of the sale of women etc.[18] Yet the meeting also voiced the now perennial complaint that there was still no single organization representing all women in the city. And though many women did mobilize during the third armed uprising – especially by forming welcoming parties for the NRA – the impression is that they did not mobilize as a distinct social constituency as they had in 1911, 1919 and 1925.

The youth movement in Shanghai was more vigorous than the women's movement. At the start of January the CYL had 1,950 members, but 300 student members left the city to go home at the end of the semester. During 'Lenin week' – to mark the third anniversary of Lenin's death on 21 January 1924 – 500 joined the organization, so that in late January membership stood at around 2,100. By February there were 2,184 members in the Shanghai CYL, the biggest branch still being at Shanghai University, with 130 members.[19] Despite this growth, activists were in short supply, and many functional departments of CYL branches consisted of only one person.[20] At the Fifth Congress Chen Duxiu blamed this shortage on the fact that many CYL members worked full-time for the CCP.[21] Nor was the quality of activists high. Zheng Chaolin recalls that many CYL delegates to the Fifth CCP Congress were 'virtually children', who passed around pieces of paper containing the latest conference jokes written in the style of Shanghai tabloid gossip column (e.g. such-and-such a woman delegate 'was staring at the handsome Li Qiushi without blinking').[22] Moreover, in spite of relentless efforts to impose democratic centralism, the CYL still retained some independence from the CCP.[23] Yet the CYL remained the largest and best organized political grouping in the student movement, the Sun Yat-sen Three People's Principles Study Groups having lost some of their momentum and the outrightly nationalist groupings, such as the Young China Party and supporters of the Western Hills faction, being in desuetude.[24]

The pattern of expansion of the GMD was similar to that of the CCP. In October 1926 it still had only 2,266 members in Shanghai.[25] On 11 January Li Baozhang closed down the Greater Shanghai bureau, a bastion of the GMD left, at which time there were said to be 2,700 members in the city.[26] After that, as the NRA approached the city, membership rocketed to reach 16,000 by April.[27] The GMD grew faster than the CCP, although we do not know how many GMD members were also CCP members. At district level, however, the GMD remained more poorly structured than the CCP. Only at the end of March, for example, was a district organization established in Pudong; in Nanshi several precinct organizations were said to be feeble; and even in Zhabei, where there were 3,500 members, the thirty-three branches were reported to be weak. In Zhabei there was also said to be a significant right-wing presence among student members, but not among workers.[28] We have no information about the social make-up of the GMD in Shanghai prior to a survey of the 6,234 members of the Greater Shanghai organization conducted in October 1928. This survey must be used with caution for the earlier period, since the Shanghai GMD was purged of its left wing in February 1928. The first thing that springs to notice is the extremely low proportion of women, at barely 5 per cent; the second is the relative youthfulness of the membership: 27 per cent were aged 24 (*sui*) or less; 26 per cent were 25 to 34; 24 per cent aged 35 to 49; and up to 3 per cent were aged fifty or over.[29] At the same time, the membership of the CCP was almost certainly more youthful. Thirdly, the GMD was a well-educated party: no fewer than 21 per cent had been to university and close to 9 per cent had undergone other forms of higher education (teacher training, education abroad etc.). This high level of educational qualification was reflected in the occupational make-up of the membership: 14.4 per cent were teachers and 10.5 per cent were students, compared with 22.2 per cent who were workers, 16.8 per cent who were in commerce, 5.5 per cent who worked in government, 5.2 per cent who worked for the party, 5 per cent who were members of the liberal professions, 4.2 per cent who were military, 4.2 per cent who were police, 2.7 per cent who worked in the mass movements, 0.58 per cent who were unemployed, and only 0.5 per cent (31 in number) who were peasants. Just how different the GMD was from the CCP is revealed by answers to a question about what work members had done for the party. An astonishing 35.5 per cent admitted that they had done nothing; a further 50.9 per cent said that they had engaged in 'propaganda'; only 6 per cent replied that they had participated in the mass movements. The latter figure, however, was almost certainly diminished by the purge of the left that had taken place prior to the survey being conducted.[30]

From the social profiles of the GMD and CCP one can deduce something of the political character of the two parties. The bulk of members of both were inexperienced. In the case of the GMD, many joined the party as a symbol of their identification with the national revolution, and had little intention of getting involved in its practical work. By contrast, the CCP was a party of activists, so that even though it had 5,000 to 6,000 members fewer than the GMD by April 1927, its members were far more committed. Even so, CCP members were younger than their GMD counterparts and were mainly very recent recruits, so they had little political experience and hardly measured up to the stereotypical leninist cadre, capable of responding to any call from the party leadership. And though the GMD may have appeared structurally weak, when compared with relatively tight-knit, hierarchical CCP, the events of spring 1927 were to prove that it was perfectly capable of playing an independent role by mobilizing its factional networks, whether those were personal or ideological in character. In terms of membership, the CCP was, paradoxically, more representative of the city's population than the GMD, notwithstanding the latter's claim to represent the broad alliance of patriotic forces. This greater representativeness, however, was evident only in relation to social class. Neither the CCP nor the GMD bore much resemblance to the city population in terms of age or gender. Finally, neither party was a mass party. The CCP's membership peaked at about 10,000 – a figure sustained for at most a couple of weeks – in a city of around 2.7 million people. Such a small membership hardly provided a mandate for the CCP to run a municipal administration.[31]

Preparing for the third armed uprising

Sun Chuanfang's survival hinged on the support of the warlord, Zhang Zongchang. From 24 February his Zhili-Shandong forces gathered on the southern bank of the Yangtze, and during the first days of March completely replaced Sun's garrison in Shanghai. This was a boon to the Communists, since the citizens of Shanghai heartily detested these northern interlopers.[32] Zhang had about 60,000 men in the field, fresh and relatively well-trained, many of their instructors being White Russians, and some special units, such as the armoured train, being entirely staffed by Russian soldiers. They held the Jiaxing-Shanghai-Nanjing line with fewer than three corps and Shanghai with no more than one infantry brigade.[33] Against them were ranged some 70,000 troops of the NRA, of which the 1st and 26th corps of Bai Chongxi were targeted on Shanghai.[34] Following the collapse of the second armed uprising, a special committee of the CCP was set up to prepare energetically for a new insurrection. This functioned as the supreme policy-making body in Shanghai up to the 12 April coup. On 19 January ECCI had ordered the CEC to move to Wuhan, and by the time Roy arrived there on 2 April most CEC members had moved to that city, Qu Qiubai being the most recent. Chen Duxiu and Peng Shuzhi, however, were reluctant to leave Shanghai, and the party's secretariat remained there, producing a situation which Roy described as 'organizational chaos'.[35] Meanwhile the Shanghai regional committee had been subject to its first democratic election. Taking advantage of the weakening position of Sun Chuanfang, the committee had called a conference from 11 to 15 February, attended by fifty-two delegates, which elected a committee of thirteen (plus seven candidate members), with Luo Yinong as party secretary (also responsible for work among the peasantry), Zhao Shiyan in charge of organization, Yin Kuan in charge of propaganda and Wang Shouhua in charge of labour movement work.[36] The special committee consisted of three members of the CEC and five members of the Shanghai regional committee, namely, Chen Duxiu, Peng Shuzhi and Zhou Enlai; and Luo Yinong, Zhao Shiyan, Wang Shouhua, Yin Kuan and Xiao Zizhang. The committee was chaired by Chen Duxiu, who attended thirty of its thirty-one sessions, all of which took place within the space of a month. Attached to it were a military commission, headed by Zhou Enlai, and a propaganda commission, headed by Yin Kuan.[37]

The special committee overhauled the structure of the pickets. There were to be eight battalions, making a total of 2,160 men, consisting of workers who were to do a two-month stint of duty before returning to their normal jobs. Each picketer was to be paid four jiao a day.[38] Workers with military experience (such as former soldiers) were to officer groups of twenty to thirty picketers. In each district there were to be general staffs responsible for the pickets in the area. These staffs, in turn, were accountable to a general staff, headed by Chen Duxiu, Gu Shunzhang and Zhao Shiyan.[39] A report by Zhou Enlai, written in the second week of March, said there were about 1,200 in the 'workers' shock brigades' (*gongren tujidui*), only half of whom knew how to handle arms, with only 250 pistols and 200 hand grenades between them. With difficulty, the military commission persuaded the CEC of the GMD in Wuhan to give it 7,000 Mexican dollars to buy 100 Mausers. Some pickets secretly joined the merchant militia to get hold of rifles.[40] The plan for the third armed uprising was much more detailed than its predecessors. The aim was to combine an armed uprising with a triple strike by workers, students and merchants. This time there was to be only the shortest interval between the call for a general strike and the commencement of the uprising. The police were to be disarmed as a matter of urgency, and measures taken to prevent them regrouping. Each district command was informed in detail of its tasks, and apprised of the difficulties of coordinating action across the three Chinese-administered areas of Shanghai.[41] Speaker teams were formed to conduct propaganda: by early March there were 154 teams made up of 1,270 students, and 205 teams, each consisting of three to five people, answerable to the Greater Shanghai bureau of the GMD.[42] The GLU advertised the political aims of the triple strike through leaflets, posters and its illegal newspaper, *The Common People* (*Pingmin*). Once the Zhili-Shandong troops were defeated, a city-wide and district citizens' assemblies were to convene immediately and the GLU was to reopen with all speed.[43]

In planning the uprising the special committee was still concerned to be seen to be operating within the framework of the united front. Although Communist influence was significant in the Greater Shanghai bureau and the Jiangsu provincial bureau of the GMD, the special committee had no option but to work with what was now the most authoritative GMD organ in the city, the Shanghai branch of the GMD Political Council, set up on 27 February by the CEC. Its seven members – Wu Zhihui, Cai Yuanpei, Niu Yongjian, Yang Xingfo, Guo Taiqi, Ye Chucang and Hou Shaoqiu – were supposed to reflect the breadth of views within the GMD, but the body was dominated by supporters of Chiang Kai-shek.[44] Wu Zhihui and Niu Yongjian hailed from Jiangsu and were longstanding friends, having met at the Nanqing academy at Jiangyin. Wu was, in effect, a member of the Zhejiang clique that surrounded Chiang, and it was he who was responsible for bringing Cai Yuanpei back into the political fold, his connections to Cai going back at least to 1913.[45] At the beginning of March, Niu Yongjian informed the CCP that he would not support an insurrection. Instead he put his energies into trying to neutralize the Zhili-Shandong forces by encouraging the defection of key officers. The Communists managed to persuade the Shanghai branch of the Political Council to support a general strike – as a 'way to prevent rioting', pending the arrival of the NRA – but it would have no truck with an insurrection.[46] Moreover, on 18 March, Niu Yongjian informed the regional committee that even a general strike was unacceptable to Chiang Kai-shek, since the NRA had now reached Songjiang and the northern forces were in disarray.[47]

The Communists' effort to cultivate the members of the Political Council did not mean they were gullible in respect of Chiang Kai-shek. Until March Moscow continued to regard him as a 'centrist', the political representative of the Chinese bourgeoisie, who might be kept on side if enough mass pressure were brought to bear on him. But this position was not shared by the Communist leadership in Shanghai, whose doubts about Chiang's 'centrism' were longstanding. On 1 January 1927 Zhou Enlai warned activists of the looming danger from the GMD right; and nine days later Luo Yinong spoke specifically of the threat posed by Chiang. On 16 February the regional conference was informed that Chiang was now the lynchpin of the reactionary forces.[48] Nevertheless, the Communists were anxious to preserve the united front as long as possible, so they did not criticize Chiang openly or in writing: the most they would allow was verbal criticism.[49]

All Power to a Soviet?

As Niu Yongjian well understood, the Communists did not intend the triple-strike-cum-insurrection simply to prepare the city for take-over by the NRA. They were bent on creating a government that would strengthen the power of the left. Yet the precise nature of this government was an issue on which the Communists were at odds. The failures of the first armed uprising and the attempt to establish a citizens' assembly in December, combined with the authorization by Moscow of a 'non-capitalist' perspective for the development of the national revolution, had led the Shanghai Communists to abandon their earlier view that a citizens' government would be 'bourgeois' in character. They now envisaged one in which workers' representatives would form the majority of members. But whether this was tantamount to a 'soviet' or even 'semi-soviet' government was contentious. Peng Shuzhi, Luo Yinong and, possibly, Chen Duxiu favoured a soviet-type government as a means whereby the proletariat could assert hegemony over the petty-bourgeoisie. Qu Qiubai, by contrast, probably with the backing of Borodin, favoured a 'people's government'. The Comintern representatives, Mandalian, Nasonov and Albrecht, claimed also to have opposed Peng Shuzhi: 'Instead of a popular delegate assembly Petrov (i.e. Peng Shuzhi) proposed in February to create soviets of workers' deputies, on the grounds that the petty bourgeoisie was insufficiently prepared for the former. We rejected this since it amounted to a rejection of the union with the petty bourgeoisie and the isolation of the workers.'[50] Written in May, after they had been recalled to Moscow in disfavour, these lines may rewrite history, since evidence from February suggests that the three were keen proponents of a soviet-type government. On 5 February, i.e., before the second armed uprising, Nasonov wrote to the EC of KIM that soviets were the appropriate form for 'organizing the strengthening of the hegemony of the proletariat and its union with artisans and other labouring elements of the city, including the petty bourgeoisie. Soviets should be organized on a broad base, but the system should essentially be taken from our Soviets.'[51] And on 4 March the three, together with Fokin, wrote to Moscow to say that on 18 February, they had raised with the CEC the question of the nature of the government to be established in Shanghai. 'We felt that it was fully possible and necessary to create an organ based on the soviet system under the name "assembly of people's representatives"'.[52] On 22 February, at the start of the second armed uprising, the regional committee set up a Shanghai citizens' provisional revolutionary committee (*shimin linshi geming weiyuanhui*), as a preparatory step to the creation of a citizens' government, which consisted of eleven people, of whom five were Communists.[53] In their postmortem on the uprising of 4 March, however, the FEB agents criticised the committee for being too narrow, and for not giving sufficient scope to the left GMD and the petty bourgeoisie, and accused the special committee of spending too much time trying to win over the likes of Niu Yongjian and Yu Xiaqing.[54] Even so, Wu Zhihui accused the Communists of using the uprising to establish a 'workers' dictatorship'.[55]

At the beginning of March, the Shanghai Communists paid close attention to the role and composition of a citizens' assembly and to the municipal government which was to be answerable to it. A plan was drawn up for an assembly to comprise 1,000 delegates, of whom 50 per cent would be workers, 20 per cent merchants, 10 per cent students, 10 per cent liberal professions and 10 per cent miscellaneous. However, the regional committee decided that the proportion of workers was too low, and recommended that the number of delegates be raised to 1,200, with the proportion of workers increased to two-thirds, to be elected directly from the workplaces.[56] The plan suggests that most of the Shanghai Communists favoured a soviet model (indeed a minority believed that students should not be represented, since they were not an occupational group).[57] However, a soviet model was anathema to the GMD. On 5 March

Niu Yongjian dismissed the plan as 'almost comic', not only because it gave workers the lion's share of delegates, but also because it made the municipal government accountable to the citizens' assembly. In accordance with the Three People's Principles, the GMD argued that it was the task of the party, not the people, to rule during the period of political tutelage, which Sun Yat-sen had prescribed as being necessary following national reunification.[58]

The CCP took some notice of these objections, but not much. A new constitution for a citizens' government was hastily drawn up on 6 March. This envisaged the establishment of a city-wide citizens' assembly, plus eight district ones, answerable to the national government in Wuhan. Assembly members were to be elected on the basis of occupational groupings: 'Every handicraft union, every shop employees' union, every peasant association, every merchants' organization, every barracks, every school, every professional association ... must elect representatives'. By contrast, scholarly societies, charities, the Red Cross, educational bodies, religious associations and native-place associations were barred, since they were not based on the occupational principle of representation. Delegates to the city assembly were to be elected on the basis of one per thousand electors, and delegates to the district assemblies on the basis of one per 500 electors. Each delegate was to hold office for one year and to be recallable at any time. In so far as it envisaged that industrial workers would comprise the majority of representatives, this model was still close to that of the soviets. However, key concessions were made with regard to the executive of the citizens' assembly, which was intended to become the municipal government. This was now to comprise thirty members, including eight workers, eight merchants (including two 'big capitalists'), three students, and one representative each from the associations of teachers, seamen, lawyers, accountants, writers and doctors. In addition, there were to be individual representatives from the CCP, the CYL, the Wuhan government, the Greater Shanghai bureau and the Jiangsu provincial bureau of the GMD. The weight given to business and professional people in the revised constitution was thus increased, as was that of political parties. On 9 March, Niu Yongjian, Yu Xiaqing and Wang Xiaolai, chair of the GMD's Shanghai Merchant Association (*Hushang xiehui*), endorsed the proposed executive, but it is clear that they envisaged a citizens' assembly based on public organizations, rather than popularly elected.[59] The next day GMD left-winger, Yang Xingfo, told Chen Duxiu bluntly that the idea of an elected municipal government was unacceptable and that any government would have to be accountable to the Greater Shanghai and Jiangsu provincial bureaux of the GMD.[60]

On 12 March 300 delegates from over 200 public organizations met in secret to launch the Shanghai provisional citizens' representative assembly (*Shanghai shi linshi shimin daibiao dahui*).[61] The thirty-one-person executive was selected in the way that had been agreed on 9 March, with labour organizations having eight representatives, merchants eight and so forth. The Communists clearly exercised considerable influence, since fourteen members of the executive were open or secret members of the CCP and CYL, including the crypto-Communist chair of the executive, Ding Xiaoxian.[62] Nevertheless they had no choice but to acquiesce in the principle of GMD selection rather than popular election. At its meeting on 19 March the executive submitted a list of thirty-five names to the Shanghai branch of the GMD Political Council and to the city and provincial bureaux of the party. These bodies chose nineteen members to form a provisional municipal government. Moreover, they insisted that the government accept 'leadership and supervision' from local GMD organs.[63]

In spite of these concessions to the GMD, the Communists did not back away from their ambition of eventually creating a soviet-style government. At the regional committee on 17 March a minority expressed grave doubts about the realism of this goal – even in the long term – but a resolution was passed which stated that the democratic municipal government should be as much like a soviet as possible. 'We hope that the Shanghai citizens' representative assembly will become a soviet of the revolutionary people of Shanghai. The working class must form its main body, since without the workers as a backbone it cannot be the soviet of the national revolution.'[64] It went on:

1) Representation must be by direct election on the basis of occupation; those who do not work, or are drifters without jobs, cannot be elected representatives. This aspect will provoke conflict with the bourgeoisie, for they will realize that workers are bound to be victorious in the future since they are in the majority. They will thus advocate representation on the basis of territory, so that jobless drifters, local tyrants and evil gentry participate in government. 2) Representatives must be directly connected to the masses, in contrast to all elected bodies hitherto where there has been no accountability between those elected and those who elected them. 3) There must be no separation between legislature and executive.[65]

Yet if the Communists appeared to be intent on establishing a government based on direct popular democracy, they believed, like their rivals in the GMD, that it was the party, not the masses, which should lead the revolution. As early as 8 March the regional committee agreed that CCP cells were to be the 'backstage boss' (*houtai laoban*) in both city and district assemblies.[66] And although the party denied that its aim was to seize power, it had no doubt that its duty was to exercise political leadership within the citizens' government.[67]

The triple strike

The CCP special committee was determined that the third armed uprising would commence only when the entry of the southern forces was guaranteed. On 12 March Chiang Kai-shek ordered Bai Chongxi to begin the advance on Shanghai, but advised him not to proceed too quickly, in order to allow troops that were moving from Wuhu to reach Nanjing and cut off access to that city for retreating northern forces. On 18 March Bai's forces arrived in Songjiang, about 30 km south of Shanghai along the railway to Hangzhou, where it was decided to wait until the left-flank corps reached Zhenjiang, about 30 km east of Nanjing along the railway towards Shanghai. This operation was to take two days. On the morning of Saturday, 19 March, knowing that Bai's forces had reached Songjiang, the special committee decided to commence the general strike and uprising at noon on Monday, 21 March.[68] The Communists were poorly informed about events at the front. On the morning of 20 March the special committee learnt that northern forces had withdrawn to Longhua, about 15 km south-east of Shanghai, and that the eastern route army was in hot pursuit, so it concluded that the NRA was about to enter Shanghai.[69] On arrival at Longhua, however, Bai Chongxi was informed by Niu Yongjian that Chiang Kai-shek's orders were to delay entry, pending negotiations for the surrender of Bi Shucheng, the new head of the Shanghai garrison and commander of the 8th corps of the Shandong army.[70]

On 16 March the GLU resurrected the seventeen demands raised at the time of the February general strike, and added a further five to them. They were a mix of political and economic demands, including calls to continue the anti-imperialist movement; destroy the warlords; support the Wuhan government and the Shanghai citizens' assembly and implement popular democratic government; protect the rights of assembly, association, free speech, a free press and the right to strike; institute workers' armed defence; implement protective legislation; and improve working conditions. These demands were supplemented by a set of fourteen economic demands to be raised by workers in their workplaces.[71] The GLU also issued strict instructions about the maintenance of discipline.[72]

On the evening of Sunday, 20 March, the GLU held an emergency meeting, attended by 300 delegates, representing 158 labour unions, of whom half were said to be Communists.[73] This meeting approved the plan of action drawn up by the special committee, and agreed that the general strike and insurrection should start the following day.[74] The next morning, the executive of the provisional citizens' representative assembly also approved the triple strike, but made no mention of an armed uprising.[75] The arrival of the NRA in the outskirts of the city greatly alarmed the foreign community, which feared that it presaged an onslaught on the foreign settlements. George Sokolsky wrote: 'The foreigners were nervous, tense, irritable. A fear psychology possessed us. We were all to be murdered by our own servants.'[76] The authorities blocked off all roads into the International Settlement with large spiked gates, and foreigners living in the Chinese areas were advised to come within the gates.

The general strike began promptly at midday on Monday, 21 March. Within hours Shanghai was at a standstill. The labour unions sent teams to all parts of the city to announce the arrival of the NRA, Shanghai newspapers being prohibited from reporting the news. GMD flags and slogans appeared everywhere. Shops closed to honour the arrival of the army. Students in some twenty colleges walked out of classes, and student speaker teams busily urged traders and workers to support the triple strike.[77] The GLU reckoned that 200,000 workers obeyed the strike summons.[78] The Municipal Council responded by declaring a state of emergency, and troops disembarked from the thirty to forty foreign warships that were anchored along the river. By 22 March, according to the low estimates of the International Settlement police, there were more than 150,000 workers on strike from forty-three cotton mills, fifty-four silk filatures, six tobacco factories, six saw mills, four printing houses, the public utilities and the major shipping companies.[79] The next day, in spite of the victory of the pickets, still more joined the strike.[80] The total number who participated in the triple strike is predictably contentious. The International Settlement police reckoned that at its peak there were 161,000 strikers, but admitted that this did not include employees in thousands of small workshops and retail outlets, whereas *Shenbao* reckoned that 800,000 people stopped work, closed their businesses or quit school to demonstrate support for the NRA.[81] A later GMD source calculated that around 300,000 workers went on strike, and around 4,000 enterprises closed down.[82] On 23 March the GLU called for a return to work the following day, though it asked pickets and propaganda teams not to disband.[83]

The third armed uprising

Shortly after the general strike commenced, at 1 pm on 21 March, the pickets took up their positions. Many acted under the authority of labour unions rather than of the district staffs of the pickets. Hongkou was the first district to fall to the rebels, since there were no northern troops there. Pickets, consisting mainly of workers from the power station, silk workers and gold and silver smiths, clashed with several hundred gangsters in league with the police, but their resistance was quickly snuffed out.[84] In Yangshupu the pickets, poorly organized and heavily reliant on the secret societies, also met minimal opposition, the 1,500 US marines who were stationed in the district refusing to intervene. In the attack on Hongzhen police station the workers self-defence corps (*ziweituan*) killed four policemen and wounded several more.[85] In neighbouring Yinxianggang pickets killed one policeman and wounded two others in the process of capturing the No.5 precinct police station.[86] The next day, pickets from Yangshupu and Yinxianggang, together with the handicraft workers' picket, joined the battle for North Station in Zhabei.[87] In Wusong, downriver to the north, pickets disarmed sentry posts within an hour or so and seized more than 1,000 rifles. A citizens' assembly was formed, whose membership was said to be drawn exclusively from the popular classes. Many northern troops fled to the Wusong forts in the hope of escaping by boat or along the railway to Nanjing, but they were disarmed by pickets of railway workers, iron workers and textile workers, backed by the merchant militia.[88]

The Communists paid particular attention to Pudong, where there was a fairly heavy concentration of troops. Zhang Shuping had been responsible for organizing a picket of seventy to eighty dockers, led by Chen Boyun, a subcontractor on the Butterfield and Swire dock and a secret-society boss. He spent much time seeking out rifles, ammunition, axes and staves, some of which were procured in a raid on the headquarters of the local merchant militia and fire brigade.[89] At noon on the 21st, 30,000 strikers assembled on waste ground, carrying red flags and shouting slogans. They toured Pudong, calling on the local populace to support the NRA, singing 'Filled with ardour, our blood boiling, we are fighting for justice. The old world is like fallen flowers, carried away by flowing water. Slaves! Rise Up! Rise Up!'[90] The picket from the Nanyang tobacco plant, led by teenage members of the CYL, terrified police by setting off firecrackers in kerosene cans to imitate machine-gun fire, a trick devised by women at the factory.[91] The pickets in Pudong also helped the merchant militia disperse Fengtian forces who had surrounded the residence of Du Yuesheng, though the head of the militia was later said to have been intriguing against the pickets.[92] Here, as in Hongkou and elsewhere, the police bolstered their small numbers with roving pickets made up of secret-society members, but they were easily disarmed. Despite having only 120 rifles and being poorly led, the various pickets – of dockers, seamen and tobacco workers – captured the third district police station and overcame about 150 police and some 200 patrolmen. Several were killed, including Chen Boyun, who fell into the clutches of northern troops. Victory was consummated by the formation of a Pudong citizens' assembly.[93]

Battle in Nandao was not as fierce as might have been anticipated, given that the district was home to the Jiangnan arsenal and shipyard, to the headquarters of the Wusong-Shanghai constabulary and to about one-third of the city's police force of 2,000. The principal pickets were those at the Compagnie Française de Tramways et d'Eclairage Electrique, which had 139 members; the Chinese Tramways company; the Qiuxin iron works in the French Concession, which was led by Sun Jinchuan of the railworkers' federation; and one of railway workers at the South Station.[94] In theory, the pickets were under the command of Xu Meikun in the district staff, but in practice they answered to their unions, agreeing only on 23 March to accept the district staff's authority.[95] In addition, 180 members of the merchant militia joined the fray.[96] As soon as battle commenced, most policemen fled, so that the first and second district stations, together with six precinct stations, were quickly captured. Bi Shucheng sent a company to strengthen defence of the arsenal, but the garrison fled on seeing the pickets. Two hundred to 300 soldiers also abandoned the South Station and it, together with the Chinese law court and adjacent jail – from which prisoners were liberated – was quickly captured. There was some looting, which the Communists blamed on local hoodlums. By 4.30 pm all of Nandao was under the control of the pickets, who moved their headquarters from the Chinese Tramway company to the Sanshan regional guild, which belonged to construction workers.[97] The seizure of the arsenal solved the pickets' shortage of arms. By evening, they had in their possession 600 rifles, three or four heavy machine-guns and seven light machine-guns.[98]

In Caojiadu, in the far west of the city, workers at the Shenxin No.1 mill toured the district, bringing out workers in local firms such as the Toyoda mill, and stopping periodically to hold impromptu meetings to explain to onlookers the significance of the events that were underway.[99] Pickets quickly disarmed police at the No.6 district station and then joined forces with pickets from Xiaoshadu, led by Bao Xiaoliang, a worker at NWK No.5 mill, Li Yushu and Wang Yanxia, secretary of the western district committee of the CCP, to attack the No.4 police station. In Xiaoshadu, as in Nandao, pickets clashed with irregulars of the NRA. The local Communist organizer reported

> The right wing (*youpai*) took advantage of the fact that we were not wearing insignia and came and demanded our rifles. Not a few were taken in by this ruse. When I heard about it, I rushed to the front line and gathered together the 300 or so who had not handed over their arms. I immediately bought some cloth and handed out arm bands. Then having received a note from Zhabei to transfer men there, I led the 300 into that district where we met up with the party's army at the North Station.[100]

Pickets from the western district, who included a handful of women, took part in bitter fighting in Zhabei on 22 March.[101]

The insurgents met their fiercest challenge in Zhabei, where the bulk of Zhang Zongchang's troops – numbering around 3,000 – were concentrated. The northern forces were well-armed, with machines guns, heavy artillery and armoured cars. The largest contingent was settled on the North Station, where it was backed by the Nechaev brigade of White

Russian mercenaries in an armoured train. On the afternoon of the 21st, pickets cut communications between this main contingent and smaller contingents holed up at the Oriental Library and the Tiantongan station.[102] The insurgents, led by Guo Bohe, secretary of the Zhabei district committee of the CCP, comprised mainly printers, postal workers, electricians and railway workers. Students from Fudan, Shanghai and Jinan universities also took part in the fighting, as did members of the merchant militia.[103] At around 3 pm some eighty men, twenty of whom had arms, attacked the police station of the fifth precinct of the No.3 district – a key target during the second armed uprising. Ten policemen were taken hostage. By early evening pickets had gained control of six of the eleven police stations in Zhabei, as well as of the Huzhou guild of the tailors. The insurgents were reported to be backed by crowds of students and local people, including women.[104] By the late afternoon, fierce fighting had broken out around the Russian church in Tiantongan and around the five-storey building of the Oriental Library on Baoshan Road, which was occupied by northern forces.[105] On the other side of the road, inside the main Commercial Press building was the staff headquarters of the district pickets, with which Zhou Enlai, Zhao Shiyan and others were in contact. The pickets pushed the soldiers back from the area around the Russian church, and as night fell, under a hail of gunfire, they took the area around the Oriental Library, thus tightening the ring around the troops at the North Station.[106] At about 6 pm the armoured train began a steady bombardment, which continued until midnight. Northern soldiers may deliberately have set fire to the area around the third district police station, in an attempt to give themselves some light, the pickets having cut off the electricity supply. The fire raged out of control, burning down a police station and more than 150 adjacent houses, and making 3,000 families were homeless. Pickets stopped fighting in a vain attempt to quench the flames.[107] As day broke on the 22nd, the fire was still burning. The northern resistance was still concentrated on the North Station and, to a lesser extent, the Oriental Library and the Tiantongan railway station. In tough street-by-street fighting, the rebels gradually gained the upper hand. At noon 300 soldiers at the Tiantongan station surrendered, and the rebels then turned their sights on the Oriental Library. Only thirty soldiers occupied the building, but they were well-equipped and in a strong defensive position, since they could shoot from the upper windows of the building. It was not until 4 pm that the building was finally subdued.[108] The rebels rallied for the final assault on the North Station, whose 2,500 occupants had been deprived of water.[109]

It is said that Niu Yongjian persuaded Bai Chongxi three times to postpone his entry into the city. How far this was a cynical manoeuvre, designed to give the northern soldiers the time to crush the pickets, is uncertain. Niu claimed that he needed the time to persuade Bi Shucheng to transfer his allegiance to the NRA; and when the uprising began, Bi did indeed flee to the Astor House hotel, losing all contact with his troops. However, as late as the afternoon of the 22nd, and for a fourth time, Niu sent an emissary to ask Bai Chongxi to postpone his entry into the city. For their part, the insurgents sent emissaries three times to Bai Chongxi to beg him not to delay his advance any longer.[110] Each time Bai prevaricated. However, after the third delegation arrived, Xue Yue, the Cantonese commander of the first division of the first corps, said that he could no longer sit idly by, and at 3 pm Bai finally gave orders for the troops to move.[111]

Xue Yue's first division arrived in Zhabei in the late afternoon, having come up the railway loop via Jessfield Station, which was occupied by British troops. At around 5 pm they and some 800 picketers, many still without arms, finally captured the North Station. Northern soldiers tried to escape along the railway towards Hangzhou and towards the gates of the International Settlement. Seeing the panic-stricken northerners, British soldiers assumed them to be pickets intent on invading the International Settlement, and opened fire. Only when the northerners flung down their weapons did they realise their mistake.[112] As dusk fell, rifle fire was heard from the east. Earlier in the day some 300 northern soldiers had set off by train in the direction of Wusong. Pickets in control of the rather grandiosely-named Wusong 'forts', with only a handful of revolvers and rifles between them, managed to convince the escaping soldiers that they would be crushed if they continued to Wusong, whereupon the train turned round. By the time it arrived back in Zhabei a picket of Daxia university students had lifted the rails. This forced the soldiers to retreat to Tiantongan railway station, where they holed up, surrendering the following day.[113] In all, more than 2,000 northern soldiers were allowed into the International Settlement and handed over to the Japanese, who organized their repatriation to Shandong.[114] By 7 pm the city had been liberated from the warlords. Red flags flew throughout Zhabei, people wore red armbands, some wept openly, speakers addressed impromptu meetings on street corners.

It is often claimed that the pickets defeated the northern forces entirely by their own efforts.[115] Certainly, the pickets played the principal role, one in which they showed great heroism, but others did their bit too. Merchant militias, for example, took part in fighting in Wusong, Pudong, Nandao and Zhabei. More important was the participation of bands of secret-society members. In some districts these fought on the side of the police, as happened in Pudong and Hongkou, where Du Yuesheng prevailed upon local Green Gang boss, Sun Jiefu, to call off his attack on the pickets.[116] More commonly, secret-society bands fought against the northern forces, often in the guise of those the Chinese press called *biedong dui* and the British press 'NRA irregulars'. The origin of these units is obscure, though some originated in the "plain clothes corps" which Niu Yongjian had formed during the first armed uprising. Others may have been brought into being by the Western Hills faction after it decided on 14 March rather ambitiously to organize 2,000 picketers.[117] The different detachments, each with its own insignia and commander, had no unified structure, some commanders claiming loyalty to He Yingqin, others to Bai Chongxi, others to Niu Yongjian. Some, though not all, of these commanders were secret-society bosses. Described as 'black gunmen' in the British press, they wore long black gowns, mandarin jackets and skull caps, their sinister appearance heightened by the fact that they were accompanied by bodyguards toting Mausers. The International Settlement police appear to have taken them more seriously than the pickets, since they evidently had greater experience of combat. One 'NRA plainclothes command', led by Zhao Baocheng, operated out of the Anhui guild in Zhabei, while the 'plainclothes command of the second route army', under Wang Tiezheng, had its headquarters at the Qianjiang guild.[118] The 'special detachment of the 1st eastern route army', commanded by Wang Guilin, pledged to implement the Three People's Principles, uphold order and ensure the prosperity of business.[119] The most significant of the irregular units was led by Xu Langxi, master of the Yuyun mountain lodge in the Red Gang and also bearer of the highest (*da*) generational status in the Green Gang.[120] As the self-styled envoy of Bai Chongxi, his militia of several hundred gangsters established a 'temporary headquarters of the NRA' in the building of the Wusong-Shanghai constabulary in Nanshi.[121] It was probably this detachment – described as a 'roving picket of Red Gang members' – which disarmed the metalworkers' picket at one point during the uprising. When the latter succeeded in recapturing the police headquarters, they arrested twenty-nine irregulars and one gang boss.[122] Despite his professed loyalty to Bai Chongxi, Xu Langxi was arrested on 24 March and taken off to Longhua: but he lived to fight another day. In spite of skirmishes with pickets, these NRA irregulars played a substantial part in overcoming the northern forces.[123]

The CCP and GLU had pulled off a substantial victory, albeit at a not inconsiderable cost, especially in Zhabei, where fatalities numbered at least eighty.[124] Estimates of the numbers who died in the city as a whole vary. It is reckoned that over 200 insurgents were killed and 1,000 wounded, not counting casualties among the northern forces.[125] Another source suggests that on both sides a total of 322 were killed and 2,000 wounded.[126] Taking into account non-combatant casualties, the number of dead and wounded may have run into several thousands.[127] At the same time, with the exception of Zhabei, the Communists had not engaged in any really punishing fighting. Even before the uprising was launched, northern forces were demoralized by the news of the arrival of the NRA, and put up little resistance to the pickets. The main task of the latter – a large number of whom relied on nothing more than axes and stones – had been to put up a sufficiently serious display to scare the warlord soldiers – who were much better armed than they – into flight.[128]

The triumph of the revolution

On the morning of 22 March an exultant citizens' assembly met at the Xinwutai theatre, made up of 4,000 representatives from up to 1,000 organizations, none of them elected in accordance with the constitution drawn up by the CCP. Indeed worker representatives may have been in a minority.[129] Chaired by Lin Jun of the NSU, Wang Shouhua of the GLU and Wang Xiaolai of the Commercial Association, the assembly hailed the victory of the nationalist forces and pledged loyalty to the National Government and the local bureaux of the GMD.[130] The meeting endorsed the list of nineteen members of a provisional municipal government (*linshi shi zhengfu*) that had been ratified by the GMD. Members of the executive told the assembly that they intended to implement the broad programme of demands put forward by the GLU on 16 March.[131] On the afternoon of the 22nd, the GMD, CCP, GLU and SSU[132] presided over a gigantic meeting at the Public Recreation Ground near the West Gate to welcome the NRA and inaugurate the Nanshi citizens' assembly.[133] Merchants were said to outnumber workers on the executive of the latter, reflecting the social composition of the population of the old Chinese City, which was the heart of Shanghai's handicraft and retail trades. Even so, eleven of the twenty-one members of the district executive were Communists.[134] On 23 March in Zhabei more than 50,000 people met on waste ground near the Qingyun road and, having listened to speeches, ratified a citizens' government.[135] In Pudong twenty of the twenty-five members of the executive of the district citizens' assembly were said to be Communists, and no fewer than six of the seven members of the standing committee. Nevertheless on 1 April the Shanghai regional committee was told that real power in the district lay with the Pudong federation of labour unions.[136] In Wusong, too, Communists dominated the executive of the district assembly, but real authority lay with the local NRA commander, who was sympathetic to the labour unions.[137] In Yangshupu the citizens' assembly barely got off ground – the nine members of its executive being pressed into serving on it – presumably because much of the area was under the jurisdiction of the International Settlement. In Yinxianggang, which was outside the International Settlement, the embryonic assembly was said to be dominated by the GMD right.[138]

On 27 March more than 1,000 representatives from 300 labour unions assembled to reopen the GLU in new premises at the Huzhou guild in Zhabei under a red banner proclaiming 'Long Live the Victory of the Proletariat'. There was music, fireworks, three minutes' silence for the 'martyrs of the working class', a gun salute and a speech by the chairman, who said that the workers had met with success because they had maintained unity and were armed. The meeting elected a new executive committee of forty-one people, chaired by Wang Shouhua.[139] The GLU claimed that the number of affiliated labour unions had increased from 187 at the start of the year to 502, and that the number of union members had risen from 76,245 to 821,280.[140] Meanwhile the executive of the municipal government was inundated with expressions of support and requests for help. It created a presidium and sections for finance, police, internal administration and popular education. Meeting each day, it discussed such matters as the ending of the general strike, the attempt by the International Settlement authorities to prevent workers returning to work, recognition of the GLU, a dispute affecting the Nanshi defence corps and education policy. Yet it barely got beyond the stage of talking.[141] Elected members Bai Chongxi, Niu Yongjian, and Chen Guangfu (1881–1976), chairman of the Shanghai Bank of Trade and Savings, refused to take part in its proceedings. On 29 March the government was officially installed in the presence of some 5,000 people. Only thirteen of the nineteen members of the executive attended the ceremony. Yu Xiaqing was there, but had, evidently, already announced his intention to resign.[142] Speeches were made by delegates from labour unions, student unions and women's organizations, and Sun Yat-sen's will was read out and an oath of allegiance to the GMD taken. The executive members swore to 'abide by the testament of the premier, stand by the will of the masses and work hard for revolutionary construction'.[143]

Given the thousands who had lost their jobs and the scores who had lost their lives as a consequence of the activities of spies and traitors, it is not surprising that the revolution brought popular clamour for vengeance. This had been evident at the time of the second armed uprising, when on 22 February a crowd of over 1,000 gathered on waste ground in Yangshupu for the trial of a well-known police spy, nicknamed Xiao Huatou. Zhang Weizhen, secretary of the CCP branch at the old Ewo mill, asked the crowd to raise their hands if they were in favour of a death sentence, which they duly did. To shouts of 'Down with Running Dogs', Zhang got out his revolver and shot him on the spot. The GLU put out a statement saying that revolutionary justice demands an eye for an eye.[144] For a couple of days after the third armed uprising, Shanghai witnessed events which adumbrated those of the Land Reform Campaign (1948–53) and the Cultural Revolution, with class enemies subjected to ritual humiliation, show trials and 'speak bitterness' campaigns. In Yangshupu on 21 March, as pickets were storming the Hongzhen police station, a plainclothes detective, said to be a well-known extortioner, was found hiding on the roof. A trial was improvised and he was summarily shot.[145] Crowds in Pudong were particularly zealous in punishing 'labour scabs and running dogs'. On 21 March a man was arrested at Nikko mill, bound, gagged and paraded around the district. Two days later, he was shot in front of the mill gate.[146] The *Guide Weekly* commented: 'Reactionaries and counter-revolutionaries, of course, oppose this kind of trial, considering that the masses have behaved cruelly, but in fact this is exceedingly revolutionary behaviour ... The enemy have killed dozens of us, now we shall try each of them.'[147]

The heroism, emotionalism, fanaticism, self-sacrifice and ruthlessness that permeated the inner life of the CCP at this time are well captured in Jiang Guangci's novel, *The Party of Sans-culottes*, written at breakneck speed as the events it describes were unfolding. Heroism – defined by Ernest Becker as the 'capacity to persevere in the face of doubt, to choke down what is distasteful'[148] – is conveyed in an incident where the head of the women's bureau leads a group of women workers, bearing bottles of paraffin, to set fire to a police station in a working-class district. Noting the straw huts surrounding the police station, she reflects that poor people will be made homeless 'or worse' by their arson attack, but consoles herself with the thought that their suffering will ultimately benefit the masses. Elsewhere the silk worker, Xing Cuiying, in a frenzied act of annihilation, hacks off the heads of two policemen with a kitchen knife in revenge for the death of her husband during the second armed uprising, only to die in a hail of bullets. And a third incident in the novel captures the merciless utopianism of the Communists when Lin Hesheng (Wang Shouhua?), exulting in the Red Terror, declaims: 'Kill, kill, kill ... if only we could kill all of the evil people of humanity without the least pity...'[149] We should not, of course, confuse Jiang Guangci's revolutionary romantic story with reality, but his novel encapsulates important elements in the structure of feeling of the party at this time which do not emerge from the cryptic stenographic record of its proceedings.[150]

For the ordinary folk of Shanghai the acme of the revolution seems not to have been the defeat of warlord troops or the creation of a democratic municipal government but the arrival of the NRA, some 20,000 of whose troops passed through Shanghai in the ensuing days (mostly in transit).[151] By far the biggest public gathering was that which took place on the afternoon of 22 March, when as many as half a million people poured on the Public Recreation Ground in Nanshi to welcome the NRA. Yet the hero of the hour, Bai Chongxi, made no bones of the fact that his principal aim was to restore order by ending the general strike and disarming the pickets. On 24 March in an interview with foreign journalists at Longhua, he said that his troops would do everything possible to suppress armed civilians. Asked about the Communists, he said ominously that 'China does not want Communism. It needs production.'[152] He made a point of reassuring the foreign powers that the NRA did not intend to storm the International Settlement and French Concession, the British Consul-General describing him as 'moderate and reasonable'.[153] On Saturday afternoon, 26 March, Chiang Kai-shek arrived in Shanghai. The following day, more than 50,000 'labourers, radicals and agitators' met at the Public Recreation Ground to welcome him. Called by the Greater Shanghai bureau of the GMD, the meeting was presided over by Communist student leader Lin Jun. Bai Chongxi was chief speaker and, while paying tribute to the Shanghai people for their help in liberating the city, repeated his call for order. Others, however, called for the defeat of the reactionary forces and the preservation of the alliance of workers, soldiers, merchants and students.[154] According to the *North China Herald*, Chiang Kai-shek was present at the meeting, though his presence is not reported by any other source, its reporter noting that all speakers 'were superlatively laudatory towards Canton and Chiang Kai-shek'.[155]

As early as 23 March the special committee of the CCP discussed how best the pickets could resist being disarmed. They resolved to reorganize the pickets and hide some of the arms captured during the uprising.[156] Communist anxieties intensified on 24 March when news came through that in Nanjing that afternoon British and US warships had bombarded the city after NRA troops rampaged through the foreign concession. Faced by the threat of Bai Chongxi, on the one hand, and the determination of the foreign powers, on the other, the Shanghai Communists discussed calling a general strike with the aim of seizing control of the foreign settlements, on the calculation that this would embroil Chiang Kai-shek in conflict with the imperialists and thus prevent him from disarming the pickets. On 25 March, probably without authorization from the regional committee, the GLU wrote to the International Settlement and French Concession authorities to say that unless workers were allowed back into the still heavily fortified settlements to resume work, it would call a general strike.[157] The FEB representatives claim that on 25 March they were told by Peng Shuzhi and Chen Duxiu that a general strike against all the foreign powers was due to start on Monday 28 March. 'In answer to our question whether this strike could turn into an uprising they replied positively. We said that we considered such a strike inopportune and proposed they limit it to British enterprises and to the domestic servants of the British as a protest against Nanjing, and that the question of returning the concessions be discussed with Wuhan and Moscow.'[158] The CEC apparently heeded this advice, for on 25 March a meeting of 500 Communist activists on 25 March was told to prepare a political strike by British employees, including clerks of trading companies and domestic servants.[159] That evening, at a meeting of the executive of the provisional government, Wang Xiaolai challenged the GLU publicly to deny that it was planning a general strike to take back the foreign settlements by force.[160] The following day, the regional committee discussed the planned strike against the British, stating that its aim was to force the retrocession of the International

Settlement and drive a wedge between Chiang Kai-shek and the imperialists.[161] The CEC, however, decided it had better consult with Wuhan and Moscow. On 27 March it withdrew the plan and decided instead to lobby the national government to begin negotiations with the foreign powers about the return of the concessions.[162] Whether this decision was taken in response to advice from Borodin and Voitinskii in Wuhan is unclear.[163] The Soviet Politburo was alarmed to learn of the planned strike and lost no time in responding to the CEC's telegram on 27 March: 'We consider that at the present stage a prolonged general strike to demand the return of the concessions is harmful, since it may isolate Shanghai workers and lead to new violence against the workers. It will be better to organize a demonstrative strike in protest at the violence in Nanjing.' On 28 March Moscow sent a second telegram: 'We order you to avoid at all costs any clash with the NRA in Shanghai'.[164]

The triumphalist accounts of the third armed uprising which represent it as an action led by the CCP, which delivered power into the hands of the Communists are, obviously, in need of considerable qualification. It is true that the Communists seized the political initiative in a way that they had not done during the previous two uprisings, or even during the May Thirtieth Movement. But the GMD, in the shape of both the Shanghai branch of the GMD Political Council and the national government in Wuhan, remained very much an independent player: one which had the measure of the Communists and one which was determined not to be dragged along on their coat-tails. Indeed in the wrangles about the composition and functions of the provisional municipal government, the GMD effectively got the better of the Communists, who gained influence in, but not control over, the municipal government that was set up on 22 March. Similarly, though the CCP can justly claim to have led the workers' uprising against the northern forces, the pickets were never the sole fighting force in the field, and the role played by secret societies, NRA irregulars and the merchant militias – not to speak of the last-minute intervention of the NRA – robbed the CCP of decisive military victory. In other words, if the CCP emerged from the third armed uprising stronger than it had ever been in Shanghai – and stronger than it would become for another two decades – it was still in a position where it faced political and military competition from redoubtable rivals, including the GMD, the city's businessmen and the secret societies.

Chapter 10

The 12 April 1927 Coup

Rallying to Chiang Kai-shek

The first person to meet Chiang Kai-shek upon his arrival in Shanghai on 26 March was Huang Jinrong, chief of the detectives of the French Concession, and one of the three leaders of the Green Gang. The latter – Huang, Du Yuesheng and Zhang Xiaolin – were bent on stopping the Communists from jeopardizing their recently acquired monopoly of the opium trade and their control over labour recruitment and racketeering in the city. In addition, they were eager to demonstrate their usefulness to the incoming political rulers. For his part, as Brian Martin suggests, Chiang Kai-shek, may have felt militarily vulnerable and keen to strike a deal with the Green Gang in order to liquidate the Communist challenge and to consolidate his political authority.[1] It was probably at the meeting with Huang Jinrong that Chiang sanctioned the arming of a Green Gang unit to smash the GLU. Whether he offered $600,000 to pay for the unit is contentious, since Du Yuesheng claims that the gangs raised the money themselves.[2] However, since February, General Yang Hu, head of the special services bureau of Chiang's military headquarters, had been recruiting gangsters in the clear expectation that they would be needed once the GMD occupied Shanghai.[3] The plan to liquidate the pickets was worked out by the three Green Gang leaders, assisted by Yang Hu, Chen Qun, Zhang Xiaolin's secretary and incoming political director of Bai Chongxi's Political Bureau, and Wang Boling, the deputy commander of the First Army. A Common Progress Society (*Gongjinhui*), named after a revolutionary organization set up in May 1907 to overthrow the Qing dynasty, was formed to recruit gang members. On 1 April the International Settlement police reported that they were using Huang Jinrong's house as a recruiting station. On 5 April an advertisement appeared asking veterans of the Common Progress Society, and anyone who supported its aims, to come forward to 'roll up their sleeves in support of the national flag, strengthening the people's will and submission to the Three People's Principles'.[4]

As ever, it was difficult for the Communists to know how to respond to this threat from the secret societies. In recent months, relations between the CCP and the Green Gang had been rather cordial. As a self-styled friend of labour, Du Yuesheng wished to keep abreast of the CCP's plans and, in return, was willing to intercede with the French Concession authorities on behalf of arrested Communists.[5] Wang Shouhua, president of the GLU, pledged discipleship to Du, and may have been released from arrest more than once after Du wrote the eight diagrams on a piece of paper and sent them to his captors. Wang and Du met no fewer than five times between 28 February and 8 March, Du informing him of plans by the northern warlords to arrest four CCP leaders.[6] On 19 March the Shanghai regional committee was told that Lin Jun had been released from captivity by ten Shandong soldiers after Du Yuesheng prevailed upon the French Concession police to intervene. Du may even have offered to reorganize the Green Gang and put it under CCP control, if the party would agree not interfere in his opium-smuggling operations.[7] Finally, Huang Jinrong was known to supply the GLU with tidbits of intelligence and may have subsidized the GLU financially.[8] Yet the Communists were under no illusions that secret-society bosses would block their efforts to extend the influence of the GLU and the armed pickets at grass roots. And whenever it seemed that the balance of power was shifting in their favour, they did not hesitate to strike at secret-society bosses who stood in their way. Following the third armed uprising, therefore, attacks on 'running dogs' resumed. In Pudong Zhang Wanfeng, chief contractor at the Gongmao warehouse and a local gang boss, was killed by pickets. On 24 March a guard at the Nikko company, Yang Xiaozhao, known as 'Yang the Egg', was lined up against a wall and shot; four days later, a forewoman at the same mill was killed.[9] In the western district a gang leader at the Shenxin No.1 mill, 'Telephone' Asan, was arrested by Shi Liqing, the chair of the union, after complaining when the union took over the factory school; and an overlooker in the fly-frame room was driven out because of his harsh treatment of the workers. A meeting of workers at the mill called for the overthrow of all gangsters.[10]

The Communists were fully aware of the measures that were being taken to form a unit of secret-society members. On 1 April Luo Yinong told the regional committee that 60,000 gangsters – a wild exaggeration – were being recruited to attack the GLU.[11] Both the GLU and the Greater Shanghai bureau of the GMD warned that the Common Progress Society was a conspiracy to wreck the labour movement, and the GLU threatened to organize strikes at newspapers which printed the Society's statements.[12] Meanwhile a prestigious group of GMD veterans, based upon the supervisory commission of the party, pressed Chiang Kai-shek to purge the GMD. Calling their campaign the 'Movement to Protect the Party and Rescue the Country', they drew up a list of 197 Communists holding important positions in the GMD who were to be removed. On 10 April the group formally requested the Shanghai executive bureau to suppress CCP conspirators.[13]

On 29 March a delegation from the Commercial Association and the Shanghai Bankers Association met Chiang Kai-shek and promised financial support if he would guarantee stable conditions for industry and commerce. They pointed to a number of problems, including the militant labour unions, taxation and the disruption of trade. Chiang replied that 'so far as the question of labour and capital is concerned, we already discussed a method in Nanchang [this was when Yu Xiaqing had gone to visit him in November, SAS] and all the conditions for protecting business and benefiting labour can be published within a matter of days, so as to ensure that Shanghai does not become another Wuhan.'[14] On 4 April Yu Xiaqing paid an initial advance of $3 million via the Shanghai Chinese Bankers' Association, followed by a loan of $7 million a few days later.[15] In addition, George Sokolsky may have persuaded BAT to advance $2 million against future tax stamps.[16] It is probably fair to say that most businessmen wished to see the back of Communists and the armed pickets. Yet this was only one consideration, albeit an important one, in their decision to back Chiang Kai-shek. They rallied to him because they believed he alone could create the stable government which would lead to the regeneration of China and provide optimal conditions for business in the long term. They took a calculated risk, since they appreciated that Chiang Kai-shek might milk them mercilessly (which he proceeded to do), but reckoned that he offered the best prospect for overcoming the disorders posed by the warlords, bringing an end to class conflict and establishing a strong state.

On 3 April Wang Shouhua, chair of the GLU, came to speak to the Commercial Association. He began by dismissing rumours that a workers' uprising to take back the foreign concessions by force was imminent. He said that at some point in the future it might be appropriate to call an economic boycott of the foreign concessions or a general strike by employees of foreign companies, but the time was not yet ripe. He agreed that the revival of industry was vital, but insisted that this could only come about by regaining customs autonomy and not by cutting wages or staff. He urged employers to recognize that workers had changed – they were no longer an ignorant rabble liable to explode. Industrial conflict would diminish and efficiency increase if they treated their staff well, raised wages, kept prices down and introduced an eight-hour day. Those present at the meeting expressed their disquiet at the activities of the armed pickets.[17] This disquiet was shared by small business. In the Chinese City, for example, local shopkeepers, on seeing armed pickets on 21 March, had shut their shops in alarm and panicked when the pickets liberated 200 prisoners from the local jail.[18] Wang, however, insisted that the pickets existed purely for workers' self-defence and to maintain order. On 9 April he wrote a leaflet to the citizens of Shanghai, explaining that the pickets existed to defend workers against attacks by ruffians in the pay of foreign companies, to protect factory property, and uphold law and order in the localities. However, Yu Xiaqing turned down Wang's request to circulate the leaflet among the members of the Commercial Association.[19]

The provisional municipal government

Shortly before the uprising, the Shanghai branch of the GMD Political Council had been supplanted by a liaison committee of eight, which proclaimed itself the supreme party and governmental authority in Shanghai and demanded recognition as the new Shanghai branch of the Political Council. It comprised Yang Xingfo, as chair, Niu Yongjian, Wu Zhihui, three representatives of the Greater Shanghai bureau of the GMD – Gao Erbo, Wang Shouqian and Tang Jicang – and two of the Jiangsu provincial bureau, Dai Pengshan and Hou Shaoqiu, the latter a crypto-Communist.[20] Even before the northern forces were defeated, however, the Political Council in Wuhan sent Chen Youren, Song Ziwen (T.V. Soong) and Sun Ke to Shanghai to direct political work, and appointed its own seven people to the Shanghai section of the Political Council, including Wu Zhihui, Niu Yongjian, Yang Xingfo, Bai Chongxi, Zhang Shushi and the two Communists, Hou Shaoqiu and Wang Shouhua.[21] It is not clear whether the Political Council was deliberately overriding the aforementioned liaison committee or whether there was simply a failure of communication.[22] The dominance of right-wingers in its list is puzzling, since no fewer than four of the seven came out against the municipal government, in spite of its having the backing of Wuhan.[23] When the government was formally inaugurated on 29 March, Chiang Kai-shek issued a statement calling for its postponement, declaring through his spokesman, Wu Zhihui, that its form was 'contrary to the party system of government'. Members of the executive on whose participation the Communists were banking in order to give the government a pan-class character – including Niu Yongjian, Bai Chongxi, Yang Xingfo, Wang Hanliang, Yu Xiaqing, Chen Guangfu, Zheng Yuxiu, the female Chief Judge of the Shanghai District Court, and Xie Fusheng of the *China Courier* – all proceeded to resign.[24] The Communists could only accept the resignations, though they sought to replace these 'bourgeois' representatives with representatives of small business. The GMD businessman, Wang Xiaolai, was appointed chair of the executive on 4 April at its second meeting.[25] Despite the withdrawal of support from key GMD figures (including a left-winger like Yang Xingfo), the majority of ordinary GMD members in Shanghai supported the municipal government. On 31 March it received enthusiastic endorsement from a mass meeting of party members, which also denounced the Western Hills faction and called for the return of the foreign settlements.[26]

Soon the Comintern would accuse the Shanghai Communists of having dashed popular hopes in the municipal government by failing to act decisively, a criticism that was repeated by subsequent left-wing critics.[27] Undoubtedly, there was popular enthusiasm for the government – although much less than for the NRA. If Yang Xiaoren's testimony is reliable, agitators going about the districts were constantly asked why the government was doing so little.[28] On 3 April at the fifth meeting of the citizens' assembly, secretary Lin Jun reported that many petitions had been received seeking redress against 'local tyrants and evil gentry'.[29] On 11 April at its seventh and last meeting, the government did finally publish an ambitious programme of reforms, which included the elimination of the reactionary forces, popular government, the return of the concessions, assistance to the NRA, civil rights, expansion of the anti-imperialist movement, the abolition of the unequal treaties, return of the Mixed Court and law enforcement by worker pickets or a merchant militia responsible to the people. Detailed commitments were given regarding popular welfare, reform of municipal finances, popular education and labour conditions.[30] Arguably, the government could have done more to capitalise on these demands, but its critical problem was that it could do no more than make paper commitments, since it had no financial, organizational or military resources at its disposal.

The impotence of the government was evident from the first. Immediately following the NRA's arrival, Niu Yongjian appointed Zou Jing, a stalwart of the GMD right wing, as chief-of-police, an act which Chen Duxiu could only protest.[31] Following Chiang Kai-shek's arrival, the balance of power shifted rapidly away from the government. Chiang immediately set up a committee to take charge of local finances, consisting of businessmen Chen Guangfu, Chen Qicai, Qian Yongning and Yu Xiaqing, and he ordered many of the police ejected by the insurgents to return to their posts.[32] The Communists were disgruntled, but were fobbed off with the excuse that the police would no longer bear arms – something that proved to be true only for a short time. To make matters worse, the municipal government was required publicly to acknowledge that it accepted Chiang Kai-shek's authority to make appointments to such posts.[33] As yet the political situation was not clear-cut: there was no single authority in the city – the Shanghai branch of the Political Council, for example, vied with Bai Chongxi's new power base, the Political Bureau of the eastern route army, based at the Longhua arsenal – but the writing was on the wall for the municipal government. The death knell came on 8 April, when Chiang Kai-shek appointed Wu Zhihui to head yet another branch of the Political Council, to 'deploy all military, political and financial power in the city and to direct party affairs.' The Chinese press was banned from reporting the municipal government's activities and it slid into oblivion.[34]

The balance of armed force

After his recall to Moscow, A. Albrecht, one of the FEB members, claimed on 21 May that 'our military advisers unanimously showed that in the period between 23 March and 3 April it would have been extremely easy to disarm Chiang Kai-shek'.[35] He claimed that he, Mandalian and Nasonov made a number of proposals to the CEC which they then set out in a letter on the 24th.

> These proposals amounted to the following: Chiang had brought the first and second divisions into the city. The commander of the first division and part of the officer staff were leftists and expressed full readiness to go along with us. The second division was right-wing. The first division of Xue Yue had 4,000 bayonets and 5,000 spare rifles. We proposed that we immediately declare a mobilization among party, CYL and trade union activists in order in the first place to recruit 2,000 to 3,000 workers into Xue Yue's division, something on which the divisional commander himself insisted. That way we would have had in Shanghai 8,000 to 10,000 bayonets on the side of the Wuhan government against the 3,000 of the second division, which had already been successfully demoralized. Later, we proposed to draw to Shanghai the (left-wing) 21st division and the second and sixth corps to Nanjing and Suzhou. This would have radically changed the military balance of forces and, to a very large extent, would have disarmed the right, complicating and encumbering their break with Wuhan.[36]

He claimed that the plan collapsed because of temporizing by the CCP leadership.

Certainly, the first division, under the command of Xue Yue, the first unit to enter Shanghai on 22 March, was radical in mood. Upon his arrival on 28 March, General Li Zongren, a Guangxi general who, like Bai Chongxi, had thrown in his lot with the NRA, professed to be appalled by the extent of Communist influence in the division.[37] And from the first, there were rumours that Bai Chongxi intended to move it out of the city. Thus on 23 March, the special committee of the CCP launched a campaign to have the first division stay in Zhabei and to encourage workers to enlist in its ranks. It also resolved to give some of the ammunition confiscated from the northern forces to the division.[38] On 25 March the GLU launched an appeal to Bai Chongxi to keep the first division in the city.[39] The following day Xue gave a belligerent speech to a 1,000-strong meeting of the Zhabei first district branch of the GMD, in which he said that he was not afraid to take on any counter-revolutionary, however prestigious.[40] On 27 March, however, the first division was ordered to move out of Zhabei into Nanshi, to be replaced by the sixth regiment of Liu Qi's second division.[41] The next day, Xue went to the Communists and offered to arrest Chiang Kai-shek, but Chen Duxiu demurred, allegedly advising him to feign illness.[42] Meanwhile the GLU arranged a concert party for the Liu Qi's troops in the hope of encouraging them to support the workers.[43] By 1 April things were beginning to look bleak, for Chiang Kai-shek declared a state of emergency in Shanghai. Three days later, he met 200 officers from the first and second divisions and warned them that there were people actively demoralizing the NRA.[44] The following day both the first and second divisions were ordered to leave for Nanjing, and from 6 April were replaced by Zhou Fengqi's 26th army, which until recently had fought alongside Sun Chuanfang.[45]

It is clear that there was considerable sympathy for the left among the soldiers of the first division, but it does not follow that given a fighting lead from the Communists, they would have rebelled against Chiang Kai-shek, as Comintern and Trotskyist critics later suggested. Even if Xue Yue had been in a position to arrest Chiang, one cannot assume this would have elicited support from the mass of NRA troops. At the end of March, Major-General Sir John Duncan, commander of the Shanghai Defence Force, received intelligence to the effect that three-quarters of the 12,000 NRA soldiers were loyal to their leader.[46] Moreover, even the supposedly revolutionary troops of the first division continued to carry out orders emanating from 'right-wing' commanders. On the very day that Xue Yue was professing undying loyalty to the labour unions, for example, the third unit of his first division, with backing from British soldiers, disarmed NRA irregulars in Zhabei who had fought against the northern forces.[47] Underlying the Comintern critique of the CCP's policy is an inappropriate analogy between the NRA and the Russian army in 1917. In that year the Bolsheviks and Left Socialist Revolutionaries succeeded in winning over soldiers embittered by almost three years of suffering and humiliation. But in the spring of 1927, the NRA was a victorious army in which morale was high. It would not have been easy to persuade rank-and-file soldiers that Chiang Kai-shek was a traitor to the revolution or that they should disobey their commanders.[48]

Comintern critics also charged that the CEC flouted an order from the Seventh ECCI plenum to recruit workers into the NRA.[49] In fact, the plenum resolution merely stated that 'one of the most important tasks of the CPP is to draw the broad working masses and workers' organizations into providing all possible help to the NRA in its daily military work', which was not a call to draft workers into the NRA.[50] Persuading workers to join the NRA, however, was easier said than done. On 1 April the regional committee was told that efforts to persuade workers in Yangshupu to enlist had fallen on deaf ears.[51] It was reckoned that in the whole of the city the Communists managed to induce only 300 unemployed workers to join the NRA. Chen Duxiu and Peng Shuzhi explained to the FEB members that 'it is impossible to bring workers into the army. They simply won't go there since conditions are so bad. You just do not know what the attitude of workers towards the army is. We can try to draft 3,000 unemployed workers into the army, but it is quite likely that even they will not agree.'[52] Again, Comintern criticism was underpinned by an assumption that there was some natural affinity based on class interest between soldiers and revolutionary workers, but again one may dispute this. By this stage of the northern expedition, many units of the NRA differed little from those of the warlords, with the ranks made up of impoverished peasant mercenaries who were bound to their officers by vertical ties of personal loyalty and obligation and among whom horizontal ties of class were largely absent.

If left-wing critics of the CCP's actions have underestimated the problems associated with subverting the NRA, they have overestimated the fighting capacity of the pickets. For the pickets were by no means the disciplined, revolutionary force, answerable to the CCP, that some assume.[53] First, they included many secret-society members, NRA irregulars and even former soldiers of the northern armies. Chiang Kai-shek recorded on 13 April that when the second company of the 26th army raided a group of pickets in Zhabei, more than 40 of the 90 arrested were wearing the insignia of the northern forces.[54] Secondly, the pickets were not liked by the common people. There were complaints of pickets demanding money from shopkeepers with menaces, of bullying the citizens of Zhabei and of their being beyond the control of the district staff in Pudong.[55] On 3 April Wang Shouhua admitted to the Commercial Association that unemployed gang members were passing themselves off as pickets and acting illegally.[56] Thirdly, some 'pickets' – in the shape of units of NRA irregulars – did put up resistance to being disarmed, of precisely the type advocated by critics of the Shanghai leadership. On 24 March 100 Chinese marines stationed at the Jiangnan arsenal tried to disarm a unit holding out at the Guandi temple near the West Gate. A gun battle ensued in which five were killed and many more injured. Among the casualties were three painters, a carpenter, a rice shop employee and an ironsmith.[57] Another shoot-out occurred when Xue Yue's soldiers tried to disarm what was described by the Chinese press as a defence corps (*baoweituan*) and by the British press as a group of '500 armed workers' at the central police station in Zhabei.[58] On 2 April Liu Qi's second division carried out half a dozen raids against groups of irregulars in Zhabei, which entailed heavy casualties. At the Taiyang Temple six members of the so-called 'second regiment' of irregulars were killed, a dozen wounded and over 200 arrested.[59] These irregulars were not loyal to the GLU, but the fact that their resistance was so easily crushed suggests that the Communists were right to think that the pickets would have had little chance in an all-out confrontation with the NRA.

In focusing on the failure of the CCP leadership physically to oppose Chiang Kai-shek, critics massively underestimate the extent to which the wider balance of military forces was tipped against the left. At the beginning of April there may have been as few as 3,000 NRA soldiers stationed in Shanghai, although General Duncan claimed 12,000, which might include the wider region.[60] Meanwhile the number of picketers may have grown to as many as 4,000.[61] Yet in reality there was no real match, especially when one considers that it would not have taken long to move soldiers north from Hangzhou or east along the Nanjing railway in the event of an emergency. On 28 March Zhou Enlai reckoned that there were more than 10,000 'right-wing' troops along the Shanghai-Nanjing railway.[62] What was much more critical was the presence of foreign troops in a city still largely controlled by the foreign powers. By the end of March, there were as many as 37,000 foreign naval and military forces in Shanghai.[63] It is highly likely that in the event of a showdown between the Communists and Chiang Kai-shek, foreign forces would have sided with the latter: indeed they were already helping the NRA to disarm pickets.

Finally, Comintern critics of the CCP leadership conveniently overlooked the fact that the latter did toy with the idea of an offensive policy in the form of a general strike against the British, but that the proposal was overruled by Moscow. When the CEC sent a telegram on 31 March, saying that Chiang Kai-shek 'has already begun a coup in Shanghai', the Soviet Politburo replied on the same day: 'Do not for the moment engage in open battle ... do not give up arms, hide them if necessary.'[64] Chen Duxiu later recalled that the leadership in Shanghai was furious, especially Luo Yinong. But to compound its problems, the leadership apparently received flatly contradictory orders. According to the FEB representatives, around this time another directive was received from Wuhan, signed by Voitinskii, saying that if Chiang Kai-shek tried to disperse the provisional municipal government the Communists should rise up. With bizarre logic, the FEB representatives concluded that 'owing to this second directive and also to the policy of the Shanghai committee, or more precisely that of Luo Yinong, the workers of Shanghai lost their arms and were bled white by the senseless putsch'.[65]

The fact remains that the Communist leadership pursued a contradictory and inconsistent policy, though not a strategy of 'capitulation' and 'appeasement', as claimed by later leftwing critics.[66] The leadership was by no means supine in the face of the rising threat. As early as 25 March, Chen Duxiu urged a meeting of 500 activists to ensure that pickets retaliated if attacked by the GMD Right, and outlined a plan to provide workers with an eight-hour training course as pickets, plus advanced training for 100 leaders.[67] However, when the CYL called on the CEC to arm all workers with staves, it refused on the grounds that this might encourage hooliganism.[68] On 26 March the regional committee advised cadres to tell workers that Chiang was preparing to eliminate the pickets, to undermine the citizens' government and to trample on the people's will, but to only do so orally.[69] Meanwhile, publications such as *Common People's Daily* (*Pingmin ribao*), the organ of the GLU, continued to argue for the united front, so it is not surprising that workers remained confused.[70] On 1 April the regional committee was told that in the eastern district the masses were distrustful of propaganda against Chiang, having been persuaded by 'running dogs' that the CCP was out to overthrow him.[71]

For his part, Chiang cleverly exploited the hesitation of the Communists by emitting conflicting signals. On 28 March he told the GLU that he 'sincerely approved' of the general strike in support of the NRA and denied any intention to disarm the pickets. On 30 March he met Zhou Enlai, to whom he expressed his deep mistrust of Borodin. And on 6 April he personally presented to the pickets a silk banner for their part in liberating the city from the warlord forces.[72] How far this fed illusions within the Communist leadership is impossible to say. More significant in raising false hopes was the return to Shanghai on 1 April of Wang Jingwei, leader of the GMD left wing. The very next day, he took part in a meeting of GMD leaders to discuss the impeachment of the CCP, yet this did not deter Chen Duxiu from reaching an agreement with him whereby the CCP would restrict its activities in return for Chiang Kai-shek's good will.[73] On 5 April the two issued a joint statement, which Chen later described as 'shameful', reaffirming the necessity of the united front and declaring that the GMD 'has demonstrated to the whole world that it does not have the slightest intention to expel the CCP... and suppress labour unions'.[74] The best complexion that can be put on this statement is that it was a vain attempt to play for time and prevent Wang from aligning with the right, but it surely contributed to the confusion of workers and rank-and-file party members.

Thanks largely to Luo Yinong, the party continued to prepare as best it could for Chiang Kai-shek's impending coup. On 1 April Luo called on a meeting of district secretaries to expand party membership to 18,000 within ten days with the aim of overthrowing Chiang.[75] On 6 April he told a meeting of CCP activists: 'Chiang Kai-shek is the focus of all the reactionary forces ... As soon as Nanjing has fallen [Chiang made his triumphal entry into that city on 9 April, SAS], he will settle accounts with the CP'.[76] The activists were told that the pickets must hold on to their weapons, and that if Chiang tried to disarm them, they must call a strike. 'There are many who advocate that the GLU should temporarily hide its arms. This is a suicidal policy. ... Of course we must not use our arms provocatively, but we cannot avoid clashes or bloodshed.'[77] In public, the CCP was more cautious. On 6 April Wang Shouhua urged a mass meeting of pickets to abide by GLU regulations concerning the use of firearms, to improve training and to combat reactionary forces.[78] The next day, 800 delegates, representing 231 labour unions, were told that in the event of an armed attack on the pickets they should mobilize all Shanghai's workers, but also remember that the function of the pickets was to maintain order.[79] Luo Yinong's clear disregard for Moscow's instruction to hide weapons may have been the reason why on 10 April he was removed by the CEC in Wuhan as secretary of the regional committee. Following Chiang Kai-shek's coup two days later, the CEC claimed that this was because he had pursued too 'mild' a policy towards Chiang, but the real reason may have been exactly the opposite.[80] Overall, the policy pursued by the Shanghai leadership during these fateful two weeks does not impress by its consistency or vigour but, on the other hand, it certainly does not amount to 'appeasement'. The CCP leadership wavered, but it did so in the forlorn but entirely understandable hope that a clash with Chiang Kai-shek might be averted.

The 12 April Coup

On the night of Monday, 11 April, the head of the GLU, Wang Shouhua, was invited to dine at the home of Du Yuesheng in rue Wagner in the French Concession. Upon arrival, four of his lieutenants trussed him in a sack and bundled him in a car; and after being severely beaten, he was buried alive in a remote wood.[81] That evening Zhou Fengqi's troops began to post sentries around the city, concentrating on Zhabei. By prearrangement with the foreign authorities, about 500 members of the Common Progress Society passed through the French Concession and the International Settlement into the Chinese areas. Armed with pistols and dressed in blue Chinese-style jackets and trousers, with white armbands displaying the character for 'labour', they were organized into three units, each with a specific target.[82] Drawn predominantly from the Green Gang, it is noteworthy that several of their leaders, such as Yang Qitang, Hou Quangen, Yao Laosheng and Huang Jiafeng, were artisans by trade.[83]

Yang Hu and Chen Qun ordered the gangsters to pick fights with the pickets, and thus create a pretext for the troops of Bai Chongxi and Zhou Fengqi to intervene.[84] At 4.30am on 12 April sixty gangsters started firing on the GLU headquarters at the Huzhou guild in Zhabei. Twenty minutes later, a company of soldiers from the fifth company of the second division of the 26th army made as if to disarm the gangsters. The officer in charge shouted to those in the building that he had come to 'suppress internal strife among the workers', and called on them to stop shooting. He was invited in for tea and cigarettes by Gu Shunzhang, the GLU's commander of the pickets. Gu and six of his men agreed to accompany the officer, but once outside they realised they had been duped, for they were disarmed and taken back into the building. The soldiers then stood aside to let in 300 gangsters. It is said that sixty picketers were disarmed and two killed. In the melée both Gu and Zhou Enlai escaped.[85] The main target of the gangsters was the general headquarters of the pickets in the Oriental Library. Some 300 picketers put up fierce resistance when they came under attack at 5.20am. After several hours of rifle and machine-gun exchange, interspersed by the throwing of hand grenades, soldiers from the fifth regiment of the second division of the 26th army arrived and again demanded that both gangsters and workers put down their arms. When the pickets refused, the soldiers weighed in on the side of the attackers. Gangsters also attacked the Commercial Press union on the same road.[86] In Nandao the pickets, based at the Chinese Tramways Company near the south station and at the Sanshan regional guild, were quickly subdued by some 300 gangsters, with four heavy machine guns. Several truckloads of Du Yuesheng's men emerged from the French Concession and attacked 500 to 600 picketers at the Fuzhou guild, who fought bitterly at the cost of six dead. Soldiers from the first company of the 26th army took part in the attack.[87] In all, some twenty groups of pickets were disarmed by what the International Settlement police estimated to be 15,000 armed men.[88] Some 60 picketers were killed and 220 wounded.[89]

At noon on Tuesday, 12 April, tens of thousands gathered at the Public Recreation Ground near the West Gate for a meeting organized by the Nanshi citizens assembly to celebrate Wang Jingwei's arrival in Wuhan, but the authorities refused to let the meeting take place. At 2.30 pm 6,000 people set off for Longhua to demand that Bai Chongxi respect the 'people's will'. Bai's secretary, Pan Yizhi, told the delegation that the pickets had been disarmed to prevent internal strife among the workers. He said that he did not rule out rearming workers and peasants in the future, but only under the control of the NRA. The crowd outside waited patiently for three hours in the pouring rain until the delegation emerged, by which time their indignation had been dampened.[90] That same afternoon in Zhabei as many as 20,000 gathered for a meeting of the citizens' assembly to hear Wu Yuanli of the China Relief Society declare that the workers had consistently aided the national government and asked for no more than the right to bear arms. The meeting called for a general strike the following day. Workers then marched to the GLU headquarters. Several thousand handbills denouncing Chiang Kai-shek were distributed. On arriving at the Huzhou guild, about 2,000 demanded that the soldiers occupying the premises withdraw. Outnumbered, they agreed to do so, thereby allowing the workers to retake the GLU headquarters. At 8am the next morning 800 workers left the Huzhou guild and marched to the Oriental Library in Baoshan Road where they set up a training headquarters for a new picket, to be armed with iron bars.[91] At 1 pm soldiers and gangsters began to besiege the library and, according to NCH, 'at least six attackers and many more inside' were killed.[92] Soldiers also retook the Huzhou guild. According to Xu Meikun, who was among those allowed to escape, the commander of the forces which took the building was the younger brother of Bai Chongxi. He recognized Zhou Enlai, since he was a graduate of the Huangpu Academy, and allowed him and a few others to flee.[93]

In defiance of an order from General Bai, the GLU called a general strike to begin the next day, 13 April. The seamen's union endorsed the call:

> The workers of Shanghai obtained arms by sacrifice of their own blood. These arms were taken from them by forces of the right-wing of the GMD. In order to do this, they besieged the workers' clubs and shot down our comrades. The treatment meted out to us by the conservatives is in no way different from that to which we had to submit under the Northern warlords ... Acting under urgent orders of the GLU, we the seamen's union now appeal to you to leave your ships. You must be prepared to sacrifice your lives for the cause and renew the war and disarm the forces of the GMD Right.[94]

On 13 April the International Settlement police reckoned that 104,856 strikers stayed away from work.[95] This was well below the number which had struck in February and March, but the International Settlement police figures were invariably underestimates, and one Chinese source puts the number of strikers as high as 240,000 strikers.[96] Given the prevailing repression, it seems that a remarkably large number of workers did respond to the GLU strike call, even though they were confused about the aims of the stoppage.[97]

At noon on 13 April a huge rally gathered on open ground off Qingyun Road, Zhabei. Despite the fact that soldiers prevented delegations from east and west Shanghai getting to the rally, it was attended by more than 60,000 people. Speakers blamed the bloodshed on the 'warlords and imperialists', yet refrained from mentioning Chiang Kai-shek by name, presumably to avoid provoking the troops who were standing by. According to the International Settlement police daily report, revolver shots were fired from the crowd whereupon 500 soldiers from the second company of the 26th army opened fire, wounding over a hundred demonstrators.[98] The meeting drew up a petition which called for the return of arms to the pickets; the return of property to the labour unions and compensation for damage; compensation to the families of those killed or injured; punishment of the military commander who ordered the attack on the workers; retribution for the death of Wang Shouhua; return of the premises of the GLU; the restraint of the secret societies; and the elimination of the reactionary forces. Calls were also made for the overthrow of the 'new warlords' and in support of the Wuhan government, though these do not appear to have been included in the petition.[99]

At 1 pm a parade set off for the headquarters of the second company of the 26th army to present the petition to General Zhou Fengqi. They were led by a military band and union banners, followed by pickets, labour unions and members of the organization of toilers' children and various civic organizations. The only arms the marchers bore were iron bars. At around 4 pm, as they were filing along Baoshan Road in the pouring rain, machine gunners opened fire without warning near the corner of Hongxing Road. Attackers swarmed out of adjacent alleyways, stabbing, shooting and clubbing the panic-stricken crowd. Because the adjacent alleys were so narrow, the crowd could not easily escape the troops with their fixed bayonets. In all, more than 100 were killed, some 200 wounded and about fifty unaccounted for. It took eight trucks and several hours to clear the streets of corpses.[100] The Zhabei citizens' assembly expressed outrage at the massacre in a letter to the authorities, declaring it far worse than the May Thirtieth incident, not least because it was carried out by 'soldiers baptised in the Three People's Principles'.[101]

The next day, 14 April, the strike remained solid – evidence of great courage in the face of continuing arrests and killings. According to the low estimates of the International Settlement police, 111,808 workers stayed on strike.[102] Yet there were reports that workers were disconcerted by calls for the overthrow of Chiang Kai-shek.[103] That afternoon the Shanghai Party Purification Committee (*Shanghai shi qingdang weiyuanhui*), established by Yang Hu and Chen Qun, organized raids on the Shanghai municipal government, the Shanghai party bureau of the GMD, the SSU, the GLU, and the China Relief Society, and more than 1,000 'Communists' were arrested. In the evening the Shanghai regional committee of the CCP agreed that the strike must be called off, but pledged to broaden propaganda, prepare for a new armed uprising, carry out party work in the utmost secrecy, step up the Red Terror, intensify the economic struggle and increase the recruitment and training of comrades.'[104]

On 15 April the GLU called for a return to work. It also finally condemned Chiang Kai-shek by name, accusing him of being in league with the imperialists and their hirelings, of betraying the workers, of stabbing the army in the back, of slaughtering hundreds of workers, of destroying labour unions and of closing down the press.[105] The same day, soldiers of Zhou Fengqi raided a GLU hostel near the railway station and, before sealing the place, seized thirty-two rifles. Over the next few days, the seamen's union and many other unions were closed down, and their leaders arrested.[106] Some groups of workers ignored the GLU's call to return to work. On 16 April, according to the International Settlement police, 63,500 were still on strike.[107] Even by 20 April, according to the

International Settlement police, 13,133 workers were still not working normally, though some may have been locked out.[108]

The fearsome toll of the coup gradually became evident. On 15 April the GLU estimated that more than 300 militants had been killed, more than 500 arrested, and that more than 5,000 had fled or were missing.[109] The NCH reported casualties at approximately 400 for the pickets and twenty-six for the gangsters and soldiers.[110] Of the several hundred taken to the Longhua arsenal according to one report, 145 were executed.[111] Among them was Wang Yanxia, chair of the western district federation of labour unions. Born in Changsha in 1901, he had gone to France as a work-study student and become a founding member of the European branch of the Chinese Communist Youth League. In 1923 he went to the Soviet Union and the following year returned to China, becoming secretary of the national railway workers' union and secretary of the CYL in Zhengzhou. In 1926 he had come to Shanghai. In addition to his trade-union position, he was secretary of the Xiaoshadu district committee of the CCP.[112] Another victim was Chen Boyun, born in Hubei, chief of the Pudong picket and a leader in the secret societies on the docks. Active in the labour movement since 1922, he had formed a fire-fighting unit as a way of bringing workers together, and later joined the merchant militia to get hold of weapons. His younger brother had died in the fighting during the third armed uprising. On 24 April Chen was spotted by gang leader, Jiang Laosan, and handed over to Yang Hu's men.[113] On 3 May Shanghai University, whose students had been active in the battle for Zhabei, was closed down.[114] The repression continued over the next few months, though it became increasingly sporadic. On 19 July 1927 Zhao Shiyan was executed after the head of the secretariat of the regional committee, Han Buxian, betrayed his address to the police. He was just 26.[115] The membership of the Shanghai regional organization of the CCP fell from a peak of over 8,000 members in March to 1,220 by late July.[116] So vicious was the persecution unleashed by Yang Hu and Chen Qun that their names gave rise to a pun, *yanghu chengqun*, roughly meaning 'to rear tigers in packs'.[117] The terror continued at a lesser level until the end of the year. Between 12 April and 31 December 1927, it is reckoned that up to 2,000 Communists and worker militants were killed in Shanghai, and thousands more arrested or fired from their jobs.[118]

On 18 April 3,000 of Chiang Kai-shek's supporters held a meeting at the Xinwutai theatre to celebrate the removal of the Nationalist capital to Nanjing. The meeting passed a resolution: 'Contrary to all expectations, Borodin has for years availed himself of the advisorship in order to stir up dissension among members of the GMD and, in collusion with the conspirators in Wuhan, has recently done all in his power to disturb the rear of the Nationalist forces in the hope of subverting the basis of the revolutionary operations'. They called for his expulsion from China, but expressed support for the continuance of the alliance with the Soviet Union. Fu Xiaoan, soon to be removed as president of the Chamber of Commerce, praised Chiang Kai-shek for the excellent way in which he had subdued the Reds.[119] On 23 April at a dinner held by the Shanghai GMD in honour of Chiang Kai-shek, speakers said that China was 'a civilized country and she never could nor would bear to see such barbarism as was practised by the Bolsheviks'. Leng Xin, chair of the GMD, said the Wuhan government was composed of corrupt and undisciplined persons who had robbed the people of $21 million.[120]

About this time, the three leaders of the Green Gang, Huang Jinrong, Zhang Xiaolin and Du Yuesheng, sent a telegram, which provides interesting insight into their anti-Communism.

By their underhand methods the Bolsheviks have been responsible for tumultuous meetings and processions and disorderly strikes to oppress the 'capitalists' and to force them to comply with their demands for ever-increasing wages. The local gentry and merchants, whom the people have always recognized as honourable and just leaders, are bitterly hated by them. They blame the rich people for 'severity' and yet steal official and personal property. They make arrests at random and murder innocent people at will. If anybody opposes them, he is branded as a counter-revolutionary and is killed immediately. Since the establishment of the so-called labour unions, the leaders have collected membership fees to the amount of $10 million or more. The so-called committees and chairmen of the unions put on foreign dress and ride in motor cars, have concubines and live in large foreign houses, while their ignorant and unfortunate followers live in poverty and are forced to heed their demands for the destruction of the 'imperialists' and 'capitalists'. ... We are merchants and have properties like many others, yet our movement can be as patriotic as that of the Communists, if not more so. We are connected with no political party, nor do we work for any political party. Being patriotic Chinese, therefore, it rests upon us and upon all other patriotic Chinese to do our duty and exert the best of our efforts for the protection and salvation of China. We cannot and must not sit by patiently and let the Communists spoil our country with its civilization several thousand years old.[121]

Soon, the three formed an Anti-Communist League.

The Communists in disarray

When the FEB representatives heard on 12 April that a general strike had been declared, they urged the Shanghai regional committee to call it off and hide their arms. But the committee refused to listen, hoping, according to the representatives, to turn the strike into an armed uprising. Whether Luo Yinong knew that he had been removed as general secretary on 10 April is uncertain, but he remained in his post.[122] According to the representatives, on 13 April they and members of the CC of the CYL managed to persuade the Shanghai leadership to abandon any attempt to turn the general strike into an armed uprising.[123] The following evening, the committee called off the general strike itself. Luo Yinong explained:

> Our work has never gone through such a tough patch in the past, but we must not regard recent events as a defeat, otherwise we shall lose heart ... Chiang Kai-shek has carried through so much that is reactionary that it will force the masses to recognize him for the reactionary he is. These last few days have been truly very painful for us, but this was inevitable. Now we must redouble our efforts, and must coolly analyze the conditions of struggle.[124]

The next day, the 15th, FEB representatives finally got to see Luo Yinong. He told them that the masses were crushed and that in order to raise their spirits, it was necessary to begin mass Red Terror and prepare for a new uprising. The FEB representatives opposed Luo and made a number of proposals which were set forth in a telegram of 15 April, which remains undiscovered.[125]

On 15 April Zhou Enlai presented theses to the Shanghai regional committee, which suggest that the way was already being paved to exonerate the Comintern of responsibility for the débâcle. 'The party's policy appeared to attack the capitalists, but in fact the policy adopted towards the capitalists was one of compromise, for the party believed that the capitalist class could complete the national revolution, that they were the main force, that we were simply assisting them. This was an idealist point of view within the party, since the proletariat, of course, remained the leading force.'[126] In fact, this had not been the view of the regional committee since November; nor did it fairly characterise the view of the majority of the CEC. The next day, Li Lisan, Chen Yannian and Voitinskii arrived from Hankou and met the regional committee. A special committee was revived, consisting of Li Lisan, Chen Yannian, Zhou Enlai, Luo Yinong, Zhao Shiyan, Voitinskii and the three FEB representatives, to take over from the regional committee.[127] The following day, when the regional committee met, it was accused of having been too 'mild' (hehuan) toward Chiang Kai-shek; of having been insufficiently tough towards the capitalists and of having failed to establish proletarian hegemony over the petty-bourgeoisie. Luo Yinong rejected the charges, saying that these had been mistakes of the whole party, and not just the Shanghai organization.[128] On the 18th, the debate continued. One speaker said: 'Previously we believed that Chiang Kai-shek represented a capitalist tendency within the country, but we only perceived this partially. ... So our policy frequently wavered. This undoubtedly led to mistakes in leadership by both ECCI and the CEC. ... We still do not seem to have been able to identify the social nature of Chiang Kai-shek.'[129]

According to ECCI, Chiang's coup shifted the balance of forces away from the left, but not sufficiently to terminate the united front. On the contrary, it claimed the front was now purer and stronger. The four-class bloc had become a three-class alliance of proletariat, peasantry and petty-bourgeoisie, the bourgeoisie having joined the feudal-imperialist alliance. M. N. Roy, ECCI representative in Wuhan, maintained that there were contradictions in the alliance, but argued that they could be overcome if properly handled. Despite recent waverings, the mantle of leadership had now passed to the petty-bourgeoisie, as represented by the left wing of the GMD. The CCP leaders swallowed their reservations and fell into line, though they were painfully aware that in Shanghai, at least, the coup had shown just how weak the GMD left was.[130] Yet in a situation where the mass movements had no military backing there seemed no alternative to persevering with the united front. By July, any lingering illusions in the GMD left were scuppered, when Wang Jingwei also turned against the Communists.

At the emergency plenum of the Central Committee that took place in Hankou in August the CCP under Chen Duxiu was accused of having pursued a policy of 'right opportunism'.[131] The charge was levelled by those eager to absolve ECCI of responsibility for the bloodbath of 12 April 1927, who claimed that the leadership had deliberately ignored or distorted the correct revolutionary line laid down by Moscow. But it was also a charge echoed by Trotskyist critics, who argued that the CCP's 'right opportunism' arose precisely because it had implemented Moscow's line all too faithfully. It is indisputable that the CCP's conduct of the first and second armed uprisings was inept, and that even after the success of the third uprising it displayed indecisiveness and equivocation. Yet the general charge of 'right opportunism' does not hold water. If anything, to use the parlance of the day, the Shanghai leadership had pursued a policy more akin to leftist adventurism, at least since the onset of 1927. Without clear guidance from ECCI and its representatives, it had doggedly pursued a strategy of armed uprising based on the working class, with the aim of shifting political power to the left. To this end, it had toyed with creating soviets and with Red Terror. In particular, there is no evidence to substantiate the charge, made by both Stalinists and Trotskyists, that the CCP undertook measures that actively weakened workers' defences in order to keep Chiang Kai-shek sweet. In an appallingly difficult situation it did its best to strengthen the pickets and to ensure that the most revolutionary divisions of the NRA stayed in Shanghai. Of course the leadership compromised: but never out of myopia or credulousness; only in the vain hope of delaying or preventing the CCP's destruction. If it failed, it was not for want of revolutionary will but because the balance of forces was tipped hopelessly against it.

The perverse and contradictory policies foisted on the CCP by the Comintern aggravated the fundamental predicament of the CCP, but it is doubtful that they created it. As Hans van de Ven demonstrated so trenchantly, the brute reality was that a national revolution based on workers and peasants, capable of proceeding in a socialist direction, could not have succeeded in 1927 because the balance of military and political forces was overwhelmingly against it.[132] If the ECCI policy had been less rigid, especially after the 20 March Incident, perhaps allowing the CCP to establish a 'bloc without' alliance with the GMD, as a majority of the leadership wished to do, the débâcle of April 1927 might have been avoided.[133] Yet the party's lack of an army and its inability to control and defend territory would still have ruled out the kind of revolution favoured by Communists of virtually all stripes. As Mao Zedong recognized in August, in a society where there was no centralized state power and where society was severely fragmented 'power comes from the barrel of a gun'. And only when the party gained its own armed force would it find a way out of the deadlock. This is not to fall into a bleak determinism: different policies could have helped to produce a different outcome. But it is to insist that people do not make history in circumstances of their own choosing. In retrospect, what it striking is not the extent of conflict within and between the Comintern and the CCP, but the failure of all levels of the Communist movement to appreciate just how overwhelmingly the odds were stacked against them.

Conclusion

The Role of the Comintern

Much work by western historians in the past decade has been concerned to locate the roots and dynamics of revolution within Chinese society. This study has followed that lead by seeking to situate the activities of the CCP in Shanghai in their social context and, more broadly, by emphasising the agency of the party itself, in interaction with other players, in making the national revolution. Yet the opening of the Comintern archives has reminded us how critical was the contribution made by Soviet Russia to the national revolution in China in the 1920s. By far and away the most important aspect of the contribution was the reorganization of the GMD along centralized, hierarchical lines and the creation of an effective party-army. Without the vast organizational, military and financial assistance of the Comintern, the GMD would never have been in a position to bring the national revolution to fruition, however compromised that revolution ultimately turned out to be. By comparison with this achievement, the creation of a CCP was a relatively minor element in the Soviet contribution to China's history. Here, too, however, the impetus provided by the Comintern was vital. Without its strategic vision, organizational and military expertise and, above all, its sustained and substantial financial support, the party would have been stillborn. It is true that the May Fourth Movement had encouraged an orientation to the working class and an interest in marxism among certain young radicals in Shanghai, but it is unlikely that they would have left their study groups and made contact with workers had it not been for the arrival of Voitinskii in April 1920 and, more importantly, of Sneevliet in June 1921. It was these Comintern operatives – backed by the organizational, ideological and financial resources of that organization – who gave shape to the political fumblings of these inexperienced young intellectuals by orienting them towards building a leninist party and organizing a labour movement. The hand of the Comintern is particularly visible in the subsequent redirection of the CCP away from proletarian revolution towards the united front policy, a policy which gave a much broader swathe of revolutionaries a practicable strategy for national liberation, geared towards the elimination of warlordism and the rolling back of foreign imperialism. Seen from this perspective, it is hard to exaggerate the Comintern's contribution to the national revolution of the 1920s. That said – and it is to say a great deal – the Comintern was never in a position unilaterally to impose its policies on the GMD, or even on the CCP, still less to subordinate the Chinese revolution to the state interests of the Soviet Union.

In respect of the general strategy of the CCP, Moscow's writ undoubtedly ran. This was most evident in relation to the 'bloc within' strategy, which a reluctant CCP was compelled to uphold, even though its misgivings were shared by high-ranking members of ECCI, such as Voitinskii, and by Stalin's opponents within the Soviet Politburo. Such high-handed imposition of policy was typical of Moscow's relations towards all national Communist parties, but it was particularly blatant in respect of the CCP, which it viewed as weak and inexperienced. On 9 July 1927 Stalin wrote contemptuously to Molotov: 'What is the current CC of the CCP? Nothing but an 'amalgamation' of general phrases gathered here and there, not linked to one another with any line or guiding idea.'[1] Such condescension towards the CCP leadership was evinced by many Comintern operatives, although Voitinskii and Borodin appear largely to have abjured it. In their reports to Moscow in the spring of 1927, for example, the four Comintern representatives in Shanghai were merciless in their criticism of the CCP, yet their own qualifications for directing a revolution in a country of almost half a billion people were hardly impressive. Moreover, when Comintern policy went disastrously wrong, its operatives were quick to absolve themselves of responsibility. Back in Moscow in May 1927, three of the aforementioned declared: 'We regarded the uprising in Shanghai as a dangerous game and several times quarrelled with Chinese comrades who stubbornly prepared for an uprising, beginning in September 1926.'[2] This was breathtaking in its mendacity, yet an utterly predictable response, given that even to hint that Comintern policy might be at fault would be to question the claim to infallibility on which its legitimacy rested.

At the deepest level, the Comintern's misguided strategy sprang from the mechanical application to China of perspectives rooted in European experience. Much has been made of the conflict between the Stalin majority and the United Opposition over policy in China. And certainly by spring 1927, such matters as the 'bloc within', the social nature of the GMD, the strategy to be pursued towards the peasantry and the feasibility of soviets, had become acutely contentious within the Russian Communist Party. Yet the doubts of the Left Opposition were remarkably late in surfacing. Moreover, both sides in the inner-party struggle subscribed to certain premises with regard to Chinese policy which, in hindsight, may be seen as questionable. Both exaggerated the role of the proletariat in the national revolution; both assumed that the national revolution had reached a more 'advanced' social stage than it actually had; both steadily upped the ante with regard to the goals deemed appropriate to the current stage of the revolution. Moreover, both sides in the inner-party struggle analysed Chinese politics with categories derived from European, or even more narrowly Russian experience. This is not to imply that class was irrelevant to Chinese reality: indeed the emphasis placed by the Comintern on class struggle attuned the CCP to the ways in which national unity was likely to buckle under the weight of social contradictions. Nevertheless the manifold sources of solidarity and schism within Chinese society could not be reduced to the single one of class. There were forces of social cohesion around lineage, native place and secret society that cut across horizontal class divisions, and which had substantial bearing on political behaviour, yet which entirely escaped Moscow's purview. Similarly, in the reports of Comintern operatives (though least of all in Borodin's) there is a tendency to see Chinese realities through Russian spectacles, especially on matters such as rural social relations or the nature of the NRA. In this respect, the Left Opposition was even more schematic than the Stalin majority, imposing its universal calculus of 'class forces' regardless of national and historical specificities.[3] So far as the CCP itself was concerned, there was necessarily a degree of ideological adaptation of Marxism-Leninism to Chinese conditions, but few real signs of that "independent and relatively unique system of thought" that Michael Luk sees emerging in this period.[4] Throughout the 1920s Marxism-Leninism in China is more accurately characterized as a 'derivative discourse'.[5]

The materials that have become available since the opening of the Comintern archives demonstrate that political division within the Comintern was far greater than was once supposed.[6] In determining policy for national liberation in an economically backward, semi-colonial country such as China, ECCI was largely working in the dark. One consequence of the wrangling that took place at the highest level was that Comintern policy was invariably the outcome of compromise and marked by a calculated ambiguity that Harold Isaacs likened to 'double-entry book-keeping'. This allowed ECCI to claim credit for or repudiate the CCP's implementation of policy, according to the outcome.[7] Yet for all that the CCP suffered from the misunderstandings and miscalculations of the Comintern leadership, we should not confuse the latter's determination to control the CCP with its capacity to do so. For many reasons, both objective and subjective, the CCP proved able to carve out a limited degree of political autonomy. In particular, the policy of armed uprisings which the Shanghai Communists pursued from November 1926 was largely initiated by them themselves, and by the spring of 1927 they were committed to a policy at considerable variance from that laid down by

Moscow, although hardly to the 'right-opportunist' deviation which Comintern apologists subsequently claimed.

Moscow was ill-informed and far away and events moved fast, so the CCP was forced to rely on its own judgment far more than Moscow would have liked. Telegrams were regularly intercepted by foreign intelligence services, sometimes failing to arrive at their destination, sometimes arriving late or incomplete. According to Borodin, 'weeks would go by and we would receive nothing, especially after the attacks on the embassy in Beijing and the consulate in Shanghai [in March 1927, SAS].'[8] As events rushed towards their dénouement, directives from Moscow were often out of date by the time they reached the CEC. The Soviet Politburo's directive of 3 March, for instance, which ordered the CCP to 'exclude the right' from the GMD and radicalize its policies in the mass movement did not reach Shanghai until 22 March, by which time the Communists were in power in the city.[9] But the CCP leaders also took more active steps to maximise their autonomy. The CEC may have complained about the 'abstract' (*chouxiang*) character of the ECCI directives, but it turned this to advantage, exploiting their ambivalence by interpreting them as it suited.[10] Its ability to do this was facilitated by the fact that Comintern operatives on the ground were bitterly at odds with one another. When the resolution of the Seventh ECCI plenum of December 1926 – a masterpiece of 'double-entry book-keeping' – finally reached the CEC, it accepted it formally, but shelved it to all intents and purposes, possibly with the connivance of Voitinskii (at least that was the charge made by his colleagues in the FEB). Moreover, CCP leaders had other tactics for keeping the Comintern at bay. On 24 April 1926 Voitinskii wrote to Chen Duxiu from Moscow complaining that he had heard nothing from him for three months (though, to be fair, Chen had been ill).[11] And the FEB representatives regularly complained that the CEC and Shanghai regional committee failed to keep them abreast of developments. Unable to speak Chinese, they relied on regular briefings from local leaders, and after Qu Qiubai left for Wuhan, they lost their most garrulous informant.[12] They also complained that party leaders went through the motions of appearing to accept their advice, but then followed their own inclinations.[13] Roy was furious when, in spite of fierce disagreements between Qu Qiubai and Peng Shuzhi, the CEC closed ranks at the Fifth CCP Congress in April-May 1927 and resisted Comintern pressure to repudiate past policies. He was particularly incensed because he thought that he had extracted a promise from Chen Duxiu to make a grovelling self-criticism, which Chen then failed to make.[14] In general, the CEC and Shanghai regional committee refrained from opposing Comintern policy outright, preferring to avoid conflict rather than meet it head on. Yet they did stand up to Moscow on occasion. Voitinskii was unable to persuade the CEC to come out against the Northern Expedition, for example, though Chen Duxiu was induced to pen an article against it. And, according to Roy, the party leadership openly rejected the resolutions of the Eighth ECCI plenum of June 1927. 'They were rejected by the CC, which declared that people in Moscow did not understand the real situation here and sent instructions that could not be carried out.'[15]

The United Front in Practice

For most of this early period, the activities of the CCP were determined by the exigencies of the united front with the GMD: by the formidable task of 'building the left of the GMD, unifying with the centre and attacking the right'. The rationale for the 'bloc within', so far as Moscow was concerned, was that the CCP should work to build the GMD, to do 'coolie service' for the nationalists, as Borodin put it, by drawing the popular classes into that party and involving them in the national revolution. There were assumed to be benefits for the CCP, in so far as working inside the GMD would allow the party to make contact with wider layers of the populace than it could do in isolation. This was not a strategy of 'entryism' – short-term utilization of the GMD as a recruiting ground – but a strategy based on the assumption that the CCP could best expand its influence in the long term by working with the party which was destined to lead the national revolution. In the south the benefits of the 'bloc within' were fairly obvious: the CCP had access to a large and politically influential party, and once the GMD consolidated power in Guangdong province, the mass movements were able to flourish under its aegis. In Shanghai the benefits of the 'bloc within' were less clear-cut, since the GMD was never in a position to oust the warlord authorities nor to become a mass party through which the Communists could make contact with the petty-bourgeoisie and proletariat. The government of the city was split between the International Settlement, the French Concession and the Zhejiang or northern militarists, all of whom were hostile to the mass-mobilizing campaigns of the GMD/CCP. There was thus no possibility of the CCP's benefiting from the military and political protection of the GMD as it did in Guangdong. In spite of this, the CCP in Shanghai did reap some benefit from the united front. A coterie of inexperienced intellectuals prior to the alliance with the GMD, the party became transformed in the course of the May Thirtieth Movement into a workers' party on the radical wing of the national revolution. Much of the success of the CCP in the labour movement derived not from its exploitation of class issues in a pure sense, but from its popularization of a radical, class-inflected anti-imperialism. Particularly with the onset of the Northern Expedition, the CCP's rapid metamorphosis into a mass party was due, in large part, to its identification with the NRA and the struggle against warlordism and the foreign powers. It would not be unfair to say that by March 1927 the CCP in Shanghai basked in the reflected glory of the NRA. Finally, the CCP in Shanghai gained a wealth of experience from working through the GMD, gaining insight into and practice in negotiating the social, political and military forces that determined politics in China.

If, as Patrick Cavendish suggested, a 'true united front' embraces 'business leaders, communist trades union organizers and Kuomintang veterans', then such a united front never existed in Shanghai.[16] There was for one thing persisting suspicion of a united front with the Communists among many GMD members in Shanghai, not to speak of businessmen. For the Communists, work inside the mass movements always took precedence over work inside the GMD, with the exception of the period of inception of the united front, since in contrast to Canton, there was no role for the party in military and government affairs. Moreover, its most important work in the mass movement – agitation and organization of workers – was executed entirely outside the framework of the united front. More importantly, the nationalist movement in Shanghai did not really assume the form of a united front. The May Thirtieth Movement of 1925 was remarkably similar to the May Fourth Movement of 1919, in that it was conducted as a triple strike, coordinated by the representative organizations of workers, students and small merchants. Both the CCP and the GMD exerted influence within these representative organizations but they were not in unqualified control of them. The nationalist movement thus took the form of a loose coalition of social movements rather than of a movement clearly led by political parties. To an extent, this was still true in March 1927 when the triple stoppage accompanied the third armed uprising.

The labels 'right', 'left' and 'centre' that were used by the Comintern and the CCP leadership to make sense of the politics of the GMD were of limited value, since internal alignments within the GMD, though increasingly determined by ideology, still had a strongly personalistic character. In reality, the GMD consisted less of a set of formal institutions than of a series of personal networks which overlapped the structures of party, army and government. Behind the bureaucratic facade of committees and conferences, power was brokered in ways that Moscow largely failed to comprehend. The Chinese, of course, understood things better: on 5 May 1925, for example, the CEC and CC of the CYL complained of what they called the 'clan-patriarchal' (*jiaren-fuzi*) understanding of politics endemic in the GMD, saying that it harmed party discipline and the political consciousness of party activists.[17] But Soviet advisers – with the exception of Borodin, who as an arch political manipulator seems to have had the measure of the GMD – displayed little interest in the party's internal networks and factions, assuming that such groupings were a reflection of class fractions. Secondly, Moscow assumed that the success of the Communists in gaining positions of influence within the GMD reflected the extent of their support among the rank-and-file. It was partly this assumption that led Stalin and others to assume that the

GMD was mutating into a 'popular' or even a 'worker-peasant' party. Yet in practice it proved relatively easy for the CCP – with its hardworking activists, effective apparatus and energetic propaganda organs – to gain positions in the higher echelons of the GMD without having commensurate political influence in the party as a whole. Ironically, Borodin's success in reorganizing the GMD may have complicated the CCP's task of building the party's left wing through the mass movements, since extreme centralism left the base organizations of the GMD weak, and meant that there was little room for grass-roots initiative. In consequence, the development of an independent left rooted in the mass movements was inhibited and the CCP was kept in the position of being its life-support machine. The same phenomenon can be observed in the mass organizations – in the labour unions, the NSU, the women's movement – where Communists were able to acquire leading positions with relative ease, without necessarily commanding the solid support of the rank-and-file. In this instance, this was due not so much to the centralist structures of the mass associations as to the weakness of a culture of formal and democratic organization in general. The Communists discovered to their cost that *in extremis* they were not able to count on the support of the rank-and-file and that rivals whom they were in the habit of underestimating – such as the Shanghai branch of the GMD Political Council in March 1927 – could thwart them by rallying informal networks of supporters, based on personal, native-place or secret-society ties.

The united-front policy never enjoyed the unconditional support of the leadership of the CCP. On at least three occasions following the inception of the alliance with the GMD – in October 1924, December 1925 and June 1926 – Chen Duxiu called on ECCI to permit the CCP to withdraw from the 'bloc within', and each time it refused. It is hard to resist the conclusion that had the CCP been allowed to withdraw after the 20 March Incident, when Chiang Kai-shek's political inclinations became evident to all but the most self-deceiving, the party might have been spared the bloodshed of 1927. In Shanghai, where the CCP's activities in the mass movements never benefited from the military protection of the NRA, emancipation from the constraints of the 'bloc within' would have simplified the party's tasks, although it would have done nothing to shift the fundamental balance of military and political power in its favour. At the same time, such emancipation would have left the CCP very exposed to some backlash from militarists or anti-Communist elements in the GMD. This might have forced the party to create its own armed force sooner than it did, although it would certainly have been a provocative action to take. On the other hand, if the CCP had eschewed the attempt to create its own army, to avoid provoking its opponents, it would have become something akin to the 'third parties' of subsequent decades, whose record of achievement was hardly impressive.[18]

Finally, we should note that the 'bloc within' fostered practices in the CCP that would have long-term corrupting consequences. For within the GMD, the CCP and CYL operated as secret organizations, subject to their own discipline, yet at no time prepared publicly to admit this. This reticence was due not to considerations of security – the danger that such information might fall into the hands of the foreign or Chinese police – but to the Communists' belief that secrecy was an indispensable weapon in the struggle against opponents within the GMD. Borodin was expert at putting the best gloss on such behaviour; yet it was guaranteed to create mistrust among even the most well-disposed members of the GMD. Of course, GMD leaders were as adept as the Communists in the arts of dissembling – possibly more so – but there is no gainsaying that habits of dishonesty and manipulation developed during this period became an ineradicable feature of the culture of the CCP.

The CCP and Mass Mobilization

The CCP was committed to a project of organizing the Chinese people in pursuit of their own liberation. It scored some impressive successes in leading the nationalist movement particularly during the May Thirtieth Movement and in campaigns for a national assembly and a Shanghai citizens' assembly. In all such campaigns the party's aim was to foster a spirit of militancy, especially vis-a-vis the foreign powers, and to ensure that the project of reunifying the state was wedded to a radical programme of social and economic reform. But the CCP never sought to unify the 'nation' as some nebulous unity: rather it sought to give political articulation to the nation by rooting it firmly in the common people through the organization of its constituent interest groups (*jie*) – workers, youth, peasants, women, merchants. For each of these groups, it drew up a set of demands as a focus for militant struggle, in the belief that only the self-activity of the masses could ensure that the nation was politically constituted in terms of its oppressed masses and that liberation from the shackles of warlordism and imperialism was thoroughgoing and complete. The GMD had its own programmes for the mass movements – shaped largely but not completely by Borodin – but the extent to which they were acted upon depended heavily on the Communists. Towards the end of his life Sun Yat-sen came to see mass mobilization as necessary to the national revolution; but to the last he cleaved to what John Fitzgerald has called a 'pedagogical politics', believing that a tutelary party-state should relate to the masses as teacher to pupil.[19] Ultimately, the Communists would prove no less 'pedagogical' in their relation to the masses; but at this stage they acted as though the masses would become architects of their own destiny through struggle and education. At the same time, the CCP never pretended to be merely a facilitator of mass action or a 'representative' of the masses: it always claimed to be their leader. So while it could inspire different sections of the populace to fight on their own behalf, it was principally concerned to control and channel the energies unleashed by such struggles. So from the first, the tendency for the party's relationship to the masses to turn from one of empowerment to one of domination was evident.

With respect to its programmes of mass mobilization, the priorities of the CCP in Shanghai were, first, the labour movement, then the youth movement, then the women's movement and, finally, the merchants' movement. The party achieved some notable successes in virtually all of these spheres. The SYL and its successor, the CYL, enjoyed an influence among the city's students out of all proportion to its numbers, as can be seen in respect of the anti-Christian movement. The CCP leadership, however, was always more committed to the SYL's extending its base among working-class youth than it was to work in the student movement: the result was that by 1926 anti-Communist tendencies had gain some ground among the student population. Work in the largely middle-class women's movement also suffered as a consequence of the leadership's preoccupation with the labour movement. As heirs to the May Fourth belief that women's liberation was vital to national salvation, the Communists showed a determination to combat the oppression of women that was impressive by the standards of communist parties elsewhere. But the rise of a dynamic labour movement during the May Thirtieth Movement caused the party to allow the women's programme to dwindle. The city's tens of thousands of small traders and businessmen were never of serious concern to the CCP and, in so far as political work was done inside the Federation of Street Associations and the Commercial Association, it was done through the GMD. This neglect was a reflection of the party's ideology rather than of social reality, since the CCP was rudely reminded on more than occasion of the political clout wielded by organized commerce and industry, most notably when the ULCE was marginalized by Yu Xiaqing during the May Thirtieth Movement and again following the third armed uprising, when Yu and Du Yuesheng mobilized business sentiment against organized labour.

Jean Chesneaux observed of the GLU labour unions that 'even if their internal organization was not very strong, the(y) ... were nevertheless able to influence the masses and organize them for action'.[20] This was no mean achievement, given the particularistic solidarities that structured the world of Shanghai workers. Collective action – whether at the level of the economic strike or the political general strike – was always prone to fracture under the stress of internecine divisions based on native place, occupational specialism, clientelist ties with foremen and labour contrac-tors or informal brotherhoods and sisterhoods. The principal way in which the GLU constituted this heterogeneous mass as a political unity was through a discourse of class-marked anti-imperialism which legitimated workers' efforts to fight on their own behalf and on behalf of the nation. Yet as Chesneaux suggests, the Communists had greater success in mobilizing workers in short-term movements of protest than they did in organizing them on a solid, durable basis. The GLU established some fairly secure bases among more skilled groups of workers, such as printers, tram employees and ironworkers; crucially, it implanted itself among the city's largest sector of industrial workers, the cotton workers. But as the July 1926 plenum of the CEC pointed out: 'Although the Shanghai GLU is supported by all Shanghai workers, its foundation is built only on a portion of the printers and textile workers. Henceforward our most important task is the organization of seamen, railway workers, postal workers, electrical workers, longshoremen and street transportation workers.'[21] Such groups were of considerable strategic importance yet some, such as seamen or postal workers, were more drawn to the reformist unionism of the GMD, with its rejection of the rhetoric of class struggle. Moreover, with the exception of gold- and silver-smiths and pharmacy employees, the GLU had little influence among the large numbers of handicraft workers and retail employees in the city – at least until early1927. Even then, the Fifth Congress was scathing about the recent inroads made into these sectors by the GLU, noting that many such unions 'are little more than guilds under a new name. We must make every effort to combat such traditional forms of organization and, in particular, to restrict the number of workshop owners, shopkeepers and labour contractors who have entered the unions.'[22] All of which reminds us that we should not assume that because huge numbers of workers joined the GLU unions in the spring of 1927 – more as a sign of identification with the national revolution than as a consequence of an upsurge in class consciousness – that the Communists had a firm and reliable base among the city's workers. It is true that the challenge from anti-Communist unions, principally in the shape of the SFS, weakened with the May Thirtieth Movement, though it was never decisively seen off. Yet the GLU unions failed to displace the foremen, contractors and secret-society bosses who were such a force to be reckoned with in the workplace and in working-class neighbourhoods. In particular, the CCP failed to find a means of neutralizing the secret societies, oscillating between seeking to placate Green Gang bosses by pledging discipleship to them, and violently opposing them – as in the campaign to kill 'running dogs' and the Red Terror. Neither strategy worked. By pledging discipleship, Communists such as Li Qihan, Li Lisan or Wang Shouhua ran the risk of becoming absorbed by the very organizations they set out to oppose: indeed certain worker members of the party, such as Tao Jingxuan or Jiang Weixin, became virtually indistinguishable from secret-society brothers. Conversely, impulsive and arbitrary attacks on 'running dogs' helped convince the 'Big Three' leaders of the Green Gang – who would probably have preferred a policy of suborning rather than subduing the Communists – that the GLU was a menace that must be eliminated.

If the CCP deserves credit for helping workers organize to remedy their manifold grievances, we should not forget that its involvement was never disinterested. The party believed that it was called by history to lead the proletariat to victory and it never wavered in its belief that it alone knew what was good for workers. Consequently, it had no qualms about interfering in the operations of the GLU or in wider labour struggles as a matter of right. On 9 August 1926, for example, the Shanghai regional committee of the CCP appointed new heads to the general labour unions in each branch of industry. Such interference could in part be justified by the fact that it was impossible, given extant political conditions, for unions to operate democratically. Nevertheless on 28 March 1927 – when the GLU was operating openly once more – the same committee arrogated to itself the task of appointing the GLU's standing committee.[23] In fact the party never concealed the fact that, in the words of the Fifth CCP Congress resolution on the labour movement, 'workers' struggles must be completely under the leadership of the party'.[24] Nevertheless in practice, this remained something of a pious wish – not only because the progress of the labour unions was blocked by foremen and gang bosses, but also because the GLU's own cadres proved to be very much a law unto themselves. At the end of the May Thirtieth Movement, the Shanghai regional committee complained that comrades in the labour movement in Xiaoshadu showed no faith in the party, ignored party discipline and used the unions as a way of feathering their nests.[25] And in early 1927 when the party was preparing for insurrection, the same committee deplored the fact that members in the GLU were acting off their own bat, failing to carry out orders and failing to keep the party centre informed of the situation on the ground.[26] If the hold of the GLU over its own activists – not to speak of its rank-and-file – was so tenuous, then it is doubtful that one can, with Jean Chesneaux, blame the defeat of the labour movement in 1927 on the supposed policy of 'appeasement' practised by its leaders.[27] The foregoing account has argued that policy of the GLU during the second and third armed uprisings can scarcely be described as 'moderate', given the crackpot campaign of assassinations and the destruction of factories. Yet any explanation of failure in terms of errors of policy misses the point, since it was rooted, ultimately, in the realities of a divided workforce, of labour unions obstructed by foremen and secret-society bosses and, above all, of a balance of military and political power overwhelming unfavourable to any attempt to establish an 'anti-imperialist dictatorship of workers, peasants and the petty-bourgeoisie'.

The Culture of the CCP

Between 1920 and 1927 the CCP was transformed from a congeries of study groups into a bureaucratic, hierarchical and centralized party. This process entailed a corresponding transformation in the social composition of the party from a loose network of intellectuals, bound by ties of native place, friendship and education, into a mainly working-class party staffed predominantly, though not exclusively, by intellectuals who had undergone formal organizational, ideological or military training in the Soviet Union. This process of what was known in Comintern parlance as 'Bolshevization' was very much one in which Moscow imposed its own models and norms, even though the Chinese Communists themselves strove to become a genuine Bolshevik party.[28] If 'Bolshevization' – in van de Ven's sense of 'deep changes in the norms of behaviour and styles of action of CCP members' – was not achieved much before 1927, Michael Luk is correct to stress the speed with which the standard Bolshevik concepts and the rudiments of leninist organization were assimilated.[29] Central to 'Bolshevization' was a rejection of the May Fourth style.[30] Intellectuals threw in their lot with the CCP because they were dissatisfied with the individualistic, 'romantic' style of politics associated with that era. Instead they aspired to transform themselves into a 'party intelligentsia', as defined by the Second CCP Congress in July 1922. 'Every comrade should sacrifice his own opinions, feelings and advancement to protect the unity of the party ... He should not possess any individual interest apart from that of the party.'[31] A 'party intelligentsia' was indeed forged during this period, yet we should not overlook the extent to which the May Fourth search for individual liberation continued to be the deepest wellspring of commitment among many intellectuals. Moreover, as new intellectuals joined the party – and particularly the CYL – elements of the May Fourth style reproduced themselves, as witnessed by Ren Bishi's despairing complaints about those who treated the CYL as no different from a 'study group'.[32]

The manual on party training produced by the Moscow branch of the SYL in April 1923 declared that 'within the organization (there should be) no class distinction or division between workers and students.'[33] Yet the deepest social cleavage within the CCP was that between intellectuals and workers. In this period it was more salient than it would later become, when the party official (*ganbu*) became a more distinct social type, capable of absorbing recruits from different social backgrounds and remoulding them in the party's image. This first generation of party intellectuals, in contrast to its successors in the 1930s and 1940s, was a deeply cosmopolitan one, many of whose members had studied in France or Russia. And in its urban phase, the CCP relied heavily on skills that were the exclusive possession of those who had had a relatively high level of education. Party membership made heavy demands on intellectuals, requiring them to forego the possibility of lucrative careers and to subordinate their personal and family life to that of the party. For some it demanded the ultimate sacrifice. At the same time, party membership provided intellectuals with the chance to achieve personal fulfilment through service to the nation – a nation construed as the common people – and provided a milieu in which they could seek emancipation from the trammels of the traditional family and experiment with freer and more open relationships. In this formative period, in spite of exhortations to eschew a 'petty bourgeois' life-style, intellectuals continued to embody a style of individuality, expressed in dress, gesture and deportment, that sprang from the New Culture Movement. It should be noted, however, that although all who had secondary education and were not workers were sometimes classified as 'intellectuals', in practice this category was by no means homogeneous. There were huge differences with respect to level of education or degree of cultural westernization between figures like Chen Duxiu or Qu Qiubai and the part-work, part-study types, such as Xu Meikun, Liu Hua or Gu Shunzhang, many of whom came from very poor families and whose educational qualifications were limited. It was out of this stratum that many party officials would later emerge; and their resentment at the prestige enjoyed by intellectuals from wealthy families and elite educational establishments would later become palpable.

Following the May Thirtieth Movement, hundreds of workers joined the CCP, especially young men with a few years' work experience in the cotton mills. For them, too, party membership exacted a high price. Mao Qihua, a mechanic at the China Book Company, joined the CCP in 1925 after becoming secretary of his union branch. Soon, he was secretary of the CCP branch at the Book Company, deputy chair of the business department of the Shanghai printers' federation and secretary of its party fraction. In addition, he was a member of the West Shanghai district committee of the CYL. In autumn 1925 he was asked by the party to quit his job and work full-time for the underground press.[34] In addition to the heavy demands on time and the ever-present risk of arrest, such worker militants faced the likelihood of losing their jobs as a result of their activism. Intellectuals could sometimes rely on subventions from relatively well-off families or else survive by doing bits of writing, translation, editing and teaching, whereas workers who lost their jobs faced the real prospect of starvation.[35] Yet if the costs of party membership were arguably higher for workers than intellectuals, the rewards were also correspondingly greater, the party offering its worker members a basic education, the opportunity to develop skills as orators, agitators, organizers and leaders, contact with a wider circle of society and a wider world of culture than they would otherwise have had access to. Party membership offered some the prospect of upward social mobility through a full-time career in the organization. Among the workers who joined the party in Shanghai during this period, Chen Yun most dramatically illustrates this career trajectory. Born in 1905 in Qingpu -now part of Shanghai municipality – he became an apprentice and shop assistant at the Commercial Press at the age of 15. Joining the

CCP during the May Thirtieth Movement, he became a member of the executive of the shop employees' federation in late 1926 and took part in the third armed uprising.[36] After 1947 he became China's leading economic planner and, by the time of his death in 1995, one of its most powerful and conservative gerontocrats.

Given differences in education, social status and degree of cultural westernization, the distinction between workers and intellectuals within the party remained marked, however much it may have been blurred by the existence of the part-work, part-study stratum.[37] Mao Dun was sensitive to the tensions that existed between intellectual and worker members of the CCP. In his novel *Midnight* he shows how intellectuals, frequently, if unwittingly, misunderstood or slighted the workers they aimed to serve. The young Communist woman Ma Chin gives a speech to striking silk women: 'Although Ma Chin had done her best to purge her speech of formulas and jargon, it was still an intellectual's speech and so it had not made an immediate appeal to the girls' hearts'. Later in the book, the one worker who attends a crucial party meeting to decide whether a strike should continue finds herself ignored: 'It had cost Chen Yueh-ngo a great deal of effort to find words to express what she wanted to say, but neither Ke Tso-fu nor Tsai Chen paid the slightest attention to her.'[38] Such condescension must have rankled with many workers, but it is clear that there was also an ingrained tendency for workers to defer to those with education. As George Sokolsky noted: 'Chinese labour has a profound respect for the student because he is the direct heir to the scholar who was the recipient of all honour and glory in the traditions of the Chinese people.'[39] This is borne out by a recollection of the postal sorter, Shen Mengxian, whose first mission for the party was to distribute leaflets at the memorial meeting for Gu Zhenghong in 1925, where workers mistook him and his comrades for students. 'They saw that we wearing long gowns and looked rather refined, and took us for students. They said to one another in low, excited voices, 'the students have come'. Their warmth and hopefulness moved us a great deal.'[40]

When intellectuals went to talk to working-class audiences they donned workers' clothes, in an attempt to mask the cultural difference between them.[41] Wu Xianqing, a school teacher from Hangzhou sent to organize women mill workers in Yangshupu in late 1924, deemed it prudent to wear a false pigtail and cotton jacket and trousers, since bobbed hair was unthinkable for most mill girls.[42] It is perhaps not too far-fetched to see in such impersonation a metaphor of the party's relationship to workers in general – an organization claiming to be something it could never be, as leader of a non-existent proletariat – although whether workers were taken in by, or tacitly connived in the deception can never be known. It also suggests that the very identity of being a Communist may, for some at least, have been a kind of 'impersonation'. There is something faintly unsettling, for example, about the facility with which Kang Sheng, soon to acquire an unsavoury reputation as the CCP's security chief, could operate in Shanghai as, successively, a rickshaw puller, a conductor for the British Tramways Company and, most bizarrely, as personal secretary of Yu Xiaqing during the years of the 'white terror'.[43] To think of identity in terms of impersonation is to challenge a western way of thinking of political identity in terms of personal ontological authenticity. Of course, in part, such impersonation was a pragmatic response to the dangers that faced being exposed as a Communist. But personal identity in traditional China had, arguably, always been rather mutable – at least among the educated – to judge by the penchant for assuming a variety of personal names, given that names were deemed to carry a certain transformative power. This was in spite of the fact that identity was otherwise tightly bound up with the performance of strictly-defined social roles. With the onset of modernity, as these social roles came under strain, identity for radical intellectuals may have come to seem unusually contingent, a matter of performance and impersonation.

Within the party the tendency for intellectuals to prevail over workers was paralleled by a tendency for men to prevail over women. Although a few women, notably Xiang Jingyu and Yang Zhihua, did rise to positions of influence, that influence was confined mainly to carrying out the party's women's programme. Moreover, to some extent, such influence was enjoyed, in part at least, as a function of these women's relations to powerful men.[44] Moreover, as the party became bureaucratized, leadership became increasingly associated with models of authority and decision-making that were implicitly masculine, with the result that the chances of women achieving decision-making and executive positions were further reduced.[45] Later, women were placed at a still greater disadvantage, as the culture of the party became thoroughly militarized. Divisions between men and women and between intellectuals and workers may, however, have been partially softened by shared youthfulness. Even in comparison with the GMD, the CCP in this period was an extremely youthful party and common generational experience may have done something to override profound social and gender divisions.

As the party developed a more ramified division of labour, its power structure became more hierarchical and less susceptible to control by the membership. To some extent, this was an inevitable process, characteristic of all large, complex and enduring organizations (the 'iron law of oligarchy'), but it was also facilitated by the particular conditions in which the party operated. Subject to surveillance by police and infiltration by spies, party members had few opportunities to meet to elect leaders or discuss policy. Only once in February 1927 was the Shanghai regional committee elected in accordance with its constitution. Otherwise, its members were appointed by the CEC or by its own presidium. Similarly, it proved impossible to organize city-district conferences to elect district committees, the latter simply being appointed by the regional committee. Such reliance on appointment rather than election inevitably encouraged habits of top-down command and did little to foster involvement of the rank-and-file in party affairs. Yet lack of participation and accountability were by no means due solely to inhospitable political circumstances. Just as important was the democratic centralist model of party organization imposed on all Communist parties by Moscow. Those trained at the KUTV soon acquired habits of directing rather than of involving, of automatic obedience to higher authority, of expecting compliance from those beneath them in the hierarchy.[46] Some of those who returned from Moscow to take up positions of leadership also brought back habits of muzzling dissent and discouraging debate. At the first three party congresses, factions did crystallize and disagreement with the line proposed by Moscow was tolerated; by the time of the Fifth Congress, however, a culture of conformism had taken hold. According to Zheng Chaolin (whose point is echoed by Roy), 'The real decisions were made outside the congress, which was simply a convenient place to proclaim and record them. The speakers spoke without passion, the debaters debated without fervour.'[47]

Yet if the absence of democracy in the CCP was due, in part, to the transplantation of an authoritarian model of party organization onto Chinese soil, it was also due to the influence of norms and practices rooted in that soil. Qu Qiubai eloquently pointed to the influence of Confucian culture in respect of the 'unhealthy fear of splits', 'the belief that there is only one correct way to do something', the habit of taking control of things from above, of refusing to allow initiative from below. 'Responsible comrades cannot admit mistakes for reasons of preserving face; there is no open or direct criticism, in accordance with the traditional precept that "domestic shame should not be made public"'.[48] Chen Duxiu, known as the 'old man' (*lao touzi*) just as Lenin had been in the Bolshevik party, tended to exercise authority in a 'patriarchal' fashion.[49] When Zhang Guotao disagreed with him, for example, he 'flew into a temper, banged his fist on the table and cursed Zhang. Since Zhang was Chen's student, he dare not respond in kind. His voice gradually dropped to a whisper and finally he fell silent.'[50] Even so, Chen tolerated a level of dissent in the party leadership that would not be acceptable to his successors.

The later CCP is sometimes seen as a blend of confucianism and leninism. However, what is most striking about the CCP in its formative phase is the extent to which it adopted an intransigent stance of rejection towards traditional culture, much in the spirit of the New Culture Movement. Nevertheless, as Qu Qiubai's criticisms suggest, even in these early years the influence on internal party life of deep-rooted cultural norms and dispositions is detectable, particularly where these could be reinflected in terms of Bolshevik norms. The Comintern celebration of monolithic party unity, for example, reinforced a characteristically Chinese valorization of social harmony and disavowal of open conflict. Moreover, since the stalinist party provided few institutionalized methods of handling internal dissent – factions had been banned in the Russian Communist Party in 1921 – this reinforced a pre-existing cultural tendency for conflict, once let out of the bag, to assume virulent forms.[51] Another way in which 'tradition' asserted itself was in the taken-for-granted assumption that individual personality and behaviour were a matter of concern for the group. Here, too, it is difficult to distinguish the relative contributions of confucianism and stalinism. In Chinese culture the harmony of the group depended on suppressing individual quirks, not so much through coercion as through the inculcation of shared moral norms. As early as June 1920, when Cai Hesen convened a five-day meeting at Montargis in France to form a marxist party, the proto-Communists devoted an entire day to a session in which individuals were rebuked for their failings, Cai being hailed as strong but needing to guard against aloofness, Xiao Zizhang as logical but needing to avoid narrow-mindedness etc.[52] Such practices were further encouraged in the Soviet Union: indeed Chinese students were said to find the self-criticism sessions at KUTV extremely upsetting, although they were probably mild by the CCP's own later standards.[53] Certain other cultural practices persisted in spite of Moscow's efforts to discourage them. The manual on party training produced in Moscow exhorted comrades to disavow loyalties based on kinship and territoriality, yet networks of schoolmates and fellow-provincials – such as that based upon the First Normal School in Hangzhou – remained influential in brokering power within the party. Moreover, because native-place ties were used to recruit members, there were a few party branches which consisted entirely of people from one area, such as that at the Xinshi department store, which in 1927 consisted exclusively of Ningbonese.[54] Impulses to clientelism were further encouraged by the practice of 'apprenticeship' among new recruits. In 1924 the postal sorter, Shen Mengxian, became the 'apprentice' of Shen Zitian, a party member and primary school teacher, and worked for several months under his instruction.[55] In this way, though not necessarily in this case, personal bonds of dependency could develop. Zhou Enlai was accused, perhaps scurrilously, of promoting his clients after he was chosen to head the CEC's military commission in 1927. Those officer cadets with whom he had been associated at the Huangpu Academy were said to have been elevated 'like the dogs and geese of one who has become a buddha.'[56] Thus in spite of Moscow's exhortations to overcome primordial loyalties, the CCP remained criss-crossed by networks of influence, by no means all of which were ideological in character.[57]

To conclude a history of the CCP in 1927 is to end on a note of failure. Yet we should not overlook the accomplishments of the party in the first

225

phase of its existence. From being a tiny and marginal group, it had grown into a significant force in national politics, whose influence derived from its success in organizing and propagandizing among the masses for the purposes of national liberation and social reform. Together with the GMD, it had established key institutions and practices that were to characterise Chinese politics for the next two decades: the centralized, bureaucratic, but mass-incorporating party; an orientation towards mass mobilization; the party-army; the institution of a political language which, though abstruse in many respects, served to harness themes of class and anti-imperialist nationalism.[58] The CCP could take credit for popularizing a rendition of nationalism that defined the nation in terms of the common people and construed national liberation in terms not only of emancipation from warlordism and foreign control, but also of emancipation of the popular masses from poverty, exploitation and ignorance. This was to shape Chinese national identity in lasting ways. In addition, the CCP had gained considerable practical experience in linking its agenda of social revolution to that of national liberation, especially with regard to the labour movement. Moreover, if the 'bloc within' strategy had proved suicidal, the 1930s would show that some form of united front was inescapable in the face of foreign aggression.[59] With some justice, therefore, the CCP could claim to have shown the Chinese people a way forward after the disillusionment that had set in after 1912. As Lu Xun had said in 1921, hope is made, just like a road. 'It appears through trampling on a place where there was no road, where only brambles grew.'[60] By 1927 the Communists in Shanghai had made a rough-and-ready road, even though it would ultimately prove to be a cul-de-sac.

Abbreviations

NCH	North China Herald.
SGRSCWZQY	*Shanghai gongren sanci wuzhuang qiyi*, Zhou Qisheng (ed.), Shanghai, 1983.
SGRSCWZQYYJ	*Shanghai gongren sanci wuzhuang qiyi yanjiu*, Xu Baofang and Bian Xingying (eds.), Shanghai 1987.
SMPF	Shanghai Municipal Police Files
VKP(b)	*VKP(b), Komintern i natsional'no-revoliutsionnoe dvizhenie v Kitae. Dokumenty* vol.1, 1920–1925; vol.2, 1926–27. Moscow, 1994, 1996. The reference is to volume 1 unless specified.
WSYD	*Wusa yundong*, 3 volumes, Shanghai, 1991.
WSYDSL	*Wusa yundong shiliao*, vol.1, Shanghai, 1981; vol.2, Shanghai, 1986.
ZGDSRWZ	*Zhonggongdang shi renwu zhuan*, (55 vols. at time of writing), Xi'an, 1980–1994.
ZGGCDSH	*Zhongguo gongchandang Shanghai shi zuzhishi ziliao, 1920.8–1987. 10*, Shanghai 1991.
ZGZYWJXJ	*Zhonggong zhongyang wenjian xuanji*, vol.1, 1921–1925; vol.2, 1926; vol.3, 1927, Hebei, 1989.

Notes

Introduction

1 B.R. Mitchell, *International Historical Statistics: Africa and Asia*, London, 1982, p. 70. In 1930 54% of the population lived under Chinese jurisdiction, compared with 32% in the International Settlement and 14% in the French Concession. Zou Yiren, *Jiu Shanghai renkou bianqian de yanjiu*, Shanghai, 1980, p. 92.

2 J.K. Fairbank, 'The Creation of the Treaty System', *Cambridge History of China*, vol. 10, part 1, Cambridge, 1978, p. 242.

3 The war is the subject of A. Waldron, *From war to nationalism: China's turning point, 1924–25*, Cambridge, 1995.

4 Tsai Kyung-we, 'Shanghai's Foreign Trade: An Analytical Study', *Chinese Economic Journal*, vol. 9, no. 3, 1931, pp. 967–78.

5 R. Murphey, *Shanghai: Key to Modern China*, Cambridge, Mass., 1953.

6 Sun Yutang (ed.) *Zhongguo jindai jingji shi cankao ziliao congkan: Zhongguo jindai gongye shi ziliao*, vol. 1, Beijing, 1957, pp. 34–6.

7 *Wusa yundong shiliao*, vol. 1, Shanghai, 1981, p. 198. (Hence: WSYDSL).

8 *Shanghai shi zhinan*, ed. Shen Bojing, Shanghai, 1933, pp. 140–1.

9 P. Anderson, 'Modernity and Revolution', *New Left Review*, 144, 1984, p. 97.

10 Zou Yiren, *Jiu Shanghai*, p. 112.

11 *Shanghai shi zhinan*, p. 143. On Subei immigrants see the fascinating study by E. Honig, *Creating Chinese Ethnicity: Subei People in Shanghai, 1850–1980*, New Haven, 1992.

12 See the following pioneering studies of, respectively, native-place networks and secret societies. B. Goodman, *Native Place, City and Nation: Regional Networks and Identities in Shanghai, 1853–1937*, Berkeley, 1995; B.G. Martin, *The Shanghai Green Gang: Politics and Organized Crime, 1919–1937*, Berkeley, 1996. On clientelism, see S.A. Smith, 'Workers and Supervisors: St Petersburg, 1905–1917, and Shanghai, 1895–1927', *Past and Present*, 139, May 1993, 131–177.

13 F. Wakeman and Wen-Hsin Yeh, 'Introduction', *Shanghai Sojourners*, Berkeley, 1992, p. 5.

14 Li Dazhao, 'Xinde, Jiude', *Li Dazhao Wenji*, vol. 1, Beijing, 1984, p. 537.

15 This would be most true for R.C. North, *Moscow and the Chinese Communists*, (2nd ed.), Stanford, 1963.

16 C. Brandt, *Stalin's Failure in China, 1924–1927*, Cambridge, Mass., 1958; A.S. Whiting, *Soviet Policies in China, 1917–1924*, New York, 1954; B.I. Schwartz,

Chinese Communism and the Rise of Mao, Cambridge, Mass., 1951; M. Meisner, *Li Ta-chao and the Origins of Chinese Communism*, Cambridge, Mass., 1967.

17 H.J. van de Ven, *From Friend to Comrade: The Founding of the Chinese Communist Party, 1920–1927*, Berkeley, 1991.

18 Wen-hsin Yeh, *Provincial Passages: Culture, Space and the Origins of Chinese Communism*, Berkeley, 1996.

19 P. Stranahan, *Underground: The Shanghai Communist Party and the Politics of Survival, 1927–1937*, Lanham, MD, 1998.

20 Daniel Kwan's estimable study of Deng Zhongxia is only the most recent work to underestimate the impact of the Comintern, stressing Deng's capacity to initiate policy independently of Mikhail Borodin. D.Y.K. Kwan, *Marxist Intellectuals and the Chinese Labor Movement: a Study of Deng Zhongxia, 1894–1933*, Seattle, 1997, pp. 116–17.

21 F. Schurmann, *Ideology and Organization in Communist China*, Berkeley, 1968, p. 1.

22 A. Dirlik, *The Origins of Chinese Communism*, New York, 1989.

23 M.Y.L. Luk, *The Origins of Chinese Bolshevism*, Hong Kong, 1990.

24 Van de Ven, *Friend*, p. 4.

25 For some of this period the correct title of the Shanghai regional committee was the Jiangsu and Zhejiang regional executive committee (*Jiang-Zhe qu zhixing weiyuanhui*), but I refer to it throughout as the Shanghai regional committee.

26 T. Saich, *The Origins of the First United Front in China: the role of Sneevliet (alias Maring)*, (2 vols.), Leiden, 1991.

27 The city's merchants are examined in J. Fewsmith, *Party, State and Local Elites in Republican China: Merchant Organizations and Politics in Shanghai, 1890–1939*, Honolulu, 1985, and in M-C Bergère, *The Golden Age of the Chinese Bourgeoisie, 1911–1937*, Cambridge, 1989. The city's students are examined in Wen-shin Yeh's *The Alienated Academy: Culture and Politics in Republican China, 1919–1937*, Cambridge, Mass., 1990, and J.N. Wasserstrom, *Student Protest in Twentieth-Century China: The View from Shanghai*, Stanford, California, 1991.

28 There is a rich literature on labour in Shanghai. See J. Chesneaux, *The Chinese Labor Movement, 1919–1927*, Stanford, 1968; E. Honig, *Sisters and Strangers, Women in the Shanghai Cotton Mill, 1919–49*, Stanford, 1986; E.J. Perry, *Shanghai on Strike: The Politics of Chinese Labor*, Stanford, 1993; A. Roux, *Le Shanghai ouvrier des années trente: coolies, gangsters et syndicalistes*, Paris, 1993.

29 Martin, *Shanghai Green Gang*, pp. 9–18; Zhou Yumin and Shao Yong, *Zhongguo banghui shi*, Shanghai, 1993, pp. 257–64; Li Shiyu, 'Qingbang zaoqi zuzhi kaolü', in *Jiu Shanghai de banghui*, Shanghai, 1986, pp. 29–50.

30 J.N. Wasserstrom, 'Toward a social history of the Chinese Revolution: a review', part 2, *Social History*, vol. 17, no. 2, 1992, p. 312.

31 C.K. Gilmartin, *Engendering the Chinese Revolution: Radical Women, Communist Politics and Mass Movements in the 1920s*, Berkeley, 1995.

32 *Zhonggongdang shi renwu zhuan*, 55 volumes available at time of writing, Xi'an, 1980–1994 (Hence: ZGDSRWZ); *Zhongguo gongchandang renming da cidian*, Beijing, 1991.

33 J.W. Esherick, 'Ten Theses on the Chinese Revolution', *Modern China*, vol. 21, no. 1, Jan. 1995, 45–76. The most recent example is the detailed history of the CCP published in the PRC, the first two volumes of which cover our period. This relocates the history of the party in a narrative of the nation – wherein class is marginalized – emphasising how, by offering organization and leadership to the patriotic people, the CCP saved China. See Sha Jiansun ed., *Zhongguo gongchandang tongshi*, vols. 1 and 2, Changsha, 1996.

34 Journals such as *Dangshi ziliao congkan, Zhonggong dangshi ziliao, Dangshi yanjiu, Dangshi yanjiu ziliao* and *Dang'an yu lishi* have published much interesting material. Some of the new material on the foundation of the CCP was discussed by Tony Saich, 'Through the Past Darkly: Some New Sources on the Founding of the Chinese Communist Party', *International Review of Social History*, vol. 30, part 2, 1985, 167–80. Important materials on the Shanghai 'small group' are in *Gongchanzhuyi xiaozu*, vol. 1, Beijing, 1987.

35 *Zhonggong zhongyang wenjian xuanji* [Selected Materials of the Central Committee of the CCP], vol. 1, 1921–1925; vol. 2, 1926; vol. 3, 1927, Hebei, 1989. (Hence: ZGZYWJXJ).

36 'Wusa yundong qijian Zhonggong Shanghai diwei huiyi jilu (xuanzai) (Yijiuerwu nian wuyue)', *Zhonggong dangshi ziliao*, 22, 1985, 3–12; *Shanghai gongren sanci wuzhuang qiyi*, Shanghai, 1983. (Hence: SGRSCWZQY); *Zhongguo gongchandang Shanghai shi zuzhishi ziliao, 1920.8 – 1987.10*, Shanghai 1991. (Hence: ZGGCDSH).

37 *VKP(b), Komintern i natsional'no-revoliutsionnoe dvizhenie v Kitae. Dokumenty.* vol. 1, 1920–1925; vol. 2 (in two parts), 1926–27, Moscow, 1994, 1996. (Hence: VKP(b)).

38 These thoughts were stimulated by Lydia Liu's provocative study, *Translingual Practice*, Stanford, 1995. One small example may suffice. A reader unaware of the original title of Lenin's seminal work, *State and Revolution*, might legitimately translate its Chinese title – *Guojia yu geming* – into English as *Nation-State and Revolution*, or even *Nation and Revolution*, something which the Russian title, *Gosudarstvo i revoliutsiia*, would quite preclude. Both terms in the Chinese title are fraught with cultural and historical resonances. Leaving aside the etymology of the term for revolution, *geming*, which originally referred to the withdrawal of the mandate of Heaven from the emperor, the term *guojia* was a neologism, introduced at the end of the nineteenth century from Japanese to denote the modern concept of the nation-state. It linked the 'kingdom' (*guo*) to the 'family' (*jia*) so, while it denoted a territorially-bounded state representing the Chinese nation, it carried resonances of the polity as the direct, vertical extension of the family, of authority as hierarchically organized and of subjects, rather than active citizens, as the constituents of the state. The term 'state' (*gosudarstvo*) in the original Russian title carried an equally heavy, though quite different freight of meaning. Originally understood as an attribute – the dignity – of the divinely-appointed sovereign (*gosudar'*), it came to denote the sovereign's personal domain. Later, like its English counterpart, it came primarily to denote the institutions of government, yet never lost the sense that these institutions were the personal property of the sovereign. The point is that marxist-leninist concepts could not pass in an unadulterated form across barriers of language: their meaning was necessarily shaped by the cultural context in which they were implanted. J. Levenson, *Confucian China and Its Modern Fate*, Berkeley, 1958, pp. 105–08; M.V. Il'in, *Slova i smysly*, Moscow, 1997, pp. 192–3; R. Pipes, *Russia Under the Old Regime*, London, 1974, p. 78.

Chapter I

1 Xin Qingnian, vol. 7, no. 1, Dec. 1919.

2 *Ibid*. See the translation in Chow Tse-tsung, T*he May Fourth Movement: Intellectual Revolution in Modern China*, Cambridge, Mass., 1960, p. 175.

3 A. Dirlik, *The Origins of Chinese Communism*, New York, 1989, p. 259.

4 Wang Jiagui and Cai Xiayu, *Shanghai daxue*, Shanghai, 1986 pp. 68–9.
5 ZGDSRWZ, vol. 25, Xi'an, 1985, pp. 4–5.
6 *Shanghai xuesheng yundong shi*, Shanghai, 1995, pp. 67–8.
7 'Yu Xiusong gei Luo Zhixiang de xin' in *Gongchanzhuyi xiaozu*, vol. 1, Beijing, 1987, pp. 63–4; ZGDSRWZ, vol. 25, pp. 8–9.
8 *Shanghai xuesheng*, p. 68. Despite broad backing the corps was never established.
9 Xingqi pinglun 45, 1 Apr. 1920, p. 2. Cited in Wen-hsin Yeh, *Provincial Passages*, Berkeley, 1996, p. 329.
10 *Wusi yundong zai Shanghai shiliao xuanji*, Shanghai, 1960, pp. 532 –3. The Communist Manifesto was not published in its entirety until August 1920. Sha Jiansun ed., *Zhongguo gongchandang tongshi*, vol. 1, Changsha, 1996, p. 268.
11 M.Y.L. Luk, *Origins of Chinese Bolshevism*, Hong Kong, 1990, p. 33.
12 S.A. Dalin, *Kitaiskie memuary, 1921–1927*, Moscow, 1975, p. 30.
13 Xiang Ying, Shi Zhifu and Sun Yan, 'Gongchan guoji daibiao deng renwu jieshao', *Dangshi ziliao congkan*, 2, 1980, p. 182. One of the earliest sources, a report from the Siberian Bureau of the Bolshevik party (1918–24) to the Executive Committee of the Comintern (ECCI) of December 1920, states that the delegates were Voitinskii, Titov (a graduate of the Oriental Institute) and V.I. Serebriakov, an alias of Kim, a Korean Communist who worked in Shanghai between 1920 and 1926. See *VKP(b), Komintern i natsional'no-revoliutsionnoe dvizhenie v Kitae. Dokumenty.* vol. 1, 1920–1925, Moscow, 1994, pp. 48–9. (Hence VKP(b)).
14 Tang Zhengchang, *Shanghai shi*, Shanghai, 1989, pp. 570–1; T. Saich, *The Origins of the First United Front in China*, vol. 1, Leiden, 1991, p. 43.
15 Chow Tse-tsung, *May Fourth*, pp. 42–3, p. 52.
16 Chester C. Tan, *Chinese Political Thought in the Twentieth Century*, Garden City, N.Y., 1971, pp. 95–6; Dirlik, *Origins*, p. 198, p. 200.
17 See the memoirs of Li Da, Bao Huiseng and Luo Zhanglong in *Gongchan guoji, liangong (Bu) yu Zhongguo geming wenxian ziliao xuanji, 1917–1925* Beijing, 1997.
18 *Gongchanzhuyi xiaozu*, vol. 1, pp. 24–5.
19 Memoirs, which are the principal source of information for the foundation of the Communist party in Shanghai, give differing figures on the number of participants, which reflects disagreement between those who distinguish between the Marxist Research Society and the so-called 'small group' and those who do not. See *Gongchanzhuyi xiaozu*, vol. 1, pp. 180–96.
20 Ren Wuxiong, 'Shanghai gongchanzhuyi xiaozu de youguan jige wenti', *Dangshi ziliao congkan*, 1 (2), 1980, 49–59; Yeh, *Provincial Passages*, p. 155, p. 133.
21 H.J. van de Ven, *From Friend to Comrade*, Berkeley, 1991, p. 55. See more generally V. Schwarcz, *The Chinese Enlightenment*, Berkeley, 1986, pp. 69–71.
22 Wang Fan-Hsi, *Chinese Revolutionary. Memoirs, 1919–1949*, Gregor Benton (trans.and ed.), Oxford, 1980, p. 2.
23 Yeh, *Provincial Passages*, ch.8.
24 Christina K. Gilmartin, *Engendering the Chinese Revolution*, Berkeley, 1995, p. 221.
25 ZGDSRWZ, vol. 25, pp. 6–7; Yeh, *Provincial Passages*, pp. 199–200.
26 K Shevelyov, 'On the History of the Formation of the Communist Party of China', *Far Eastern Affairs*, 1, 1981, pp. 129–30; *Dangshi yanjiu ziliao*, vol. 3, Sichuan, 1982, pp. 129–30.
27 VKP(b), p. 28, p. 27.
28 *Voprosy kitaiskoi revoliutsii*, vol. 1, Moscow, 1927, p. 228.

29 VKP(b), p. 39.
30 VKP(b), p. 49.
31 VKP(b), p. 32.
32 *Xin qingnian*, vol. 8, no. 1, 1920, p. 125.
33 Zheng Chaolin. *An Oppositionist for Life. Memoirs of the Chinese Revolutionary, Zheng Chaolin*, Gregor Benton (ed. and trans.), Atlantic Highlands, N.J., 1997, p. 60.
34 See ZGDSRWZ, vol. 1, Xi'an, 1982, pp. 62–108. See the obituary by Qu Qiubai in *Qu Qiubai xuanji*, Beijing, 1985, pp. 388–92.
35 ZGDSRWZ, vol. 9, Xi'an, 1983, p. 164, p. 171; Wang Jiagui, *Shanghai daxue*, p. 59.
36 Zheng Chaolin, *Oppositionist*, p. 49, p. 85.
37 Gilmartin, *Engendering*, p. 231; 'Yang Zhihua huiyi', '*Yida*' qianhou, vol. 2, Beijing, 1980, p. 26.
38 Tang Zhengchang, *Shanghai shi*, p. 572.
39 'Cao Jinghua de huiyi', *Gongchanzhuyi xiaozu*, vol. 1, p. 202.
40 ZGDSRWZ, vol. 21, Xi'an, 1985, p. 4.
41 ZGDSRWZ, vol. 21, pp. 1–16. I have modified some of the details in this source in the light of advice from Alexander Pantsov, who has seen Yang's personal file in the Comintern archive.
42 Claude Cadart and Cheng Yingxiang, *Mémoires de Peng Shuzhi. L'envol du communisme en Chine*, Paris, 1983, p. 184.
43 The transition from study society to political organization was not as clearcut as this formulation suggests. Historians in the PRC see this as the first of several 'small groups' which merged to form the CCP in July 1921. For clarity's sake, I too shall refer to it as the Shanghai 'small group'. However, it is clear that Voitinskii intended the Shanghai group to be the nucleus of the CCP, and members of the Shanghai group saw themselves as members of a party, even if their understanding of the leninist party was still confused. *Zhongguo gongchandang tong zhi*, vol. 1, Beijing, 1997, p. 620. Similarly, I follow PRC historians in distinguishing between the Shanghai 'small group' and the SYL, though at least one memoirist denies that there was any firm distinction between the two. See 'Yuan Zhenying de huiyi', *Gongchanzhuyi xiaozu*, vol. 1, p. 195.
44 *Gongchanzhuyi xiaozu*, vol. 1, pp. 27–8.
45 VKP(b), p. 30.
46 '*Yida*' qianhou, vol. 1, Beijing, 1980, p. 2.
47 VKP(b), p. 31; Li Da, 'Huiyi dang de zaoqi huodong', *Dangshi ziliao congkan*, 1, 1980, p. 50. Yuan Zhenying recalls that *Gongchandang* was known as *Kangmin zhuyi zhoubao*, to fool the authorities. 'Kangmin zhuyi', literally, 'Health and Agility-ism', was a punning homophone on the English sounds 'Com-mun', plus the Chinese equivalent of 'ism'. See 'Yuan Zhenying de huiyi', p. 195.
48 Tang Zhengchang, *Shanghai shi*, p. 572; *Wusi shiqi qikan jieshao*, vol. 1, Beijing, 1958, p. 26.
49 VKP(b), p. 30; Li Da, 'Huiyi', p. 50.
50 Shao Weizheng, 'Jiandang qianhou de Shanghai gongren yundong', *Dangshi ziliao congkan*, 1982, 3, pp. 80–1.
51 VKP(b), p. 35, p. 37.
52 *Dal'nevostochnaia politika sovetskoi Rossii, 1920–22gg*, Novosibirsk, 1995, pp. 106–7; VKP(b), p. 34, p. 50.
53 *Dal'nevostochnaia politika*, p. 142, p. 176. Liu was not himself a worker. Born in Guangzhou in 1892, his father, a tea-planter, had been invited to work on the tea plantations in Georgia. Liu graduated from a gymnasium in Batum in 1909

and entered the faculty of physics and mathematics at St Petersburg University. *Kitaiskie dobrovol'tsy v boiakh za sovetskuiu vlast'*, Moscow, 1961, p. 40.

54 VKP(b), p. 39.
55 *Dal'nevostochnaia politika*, p. 175, p. 180.
56 G.M. Adibekov, E.N. Shakhnazarova, K.K. Shirinia, *Organizatsionnaia struktura Kominterna, 1919–1943*, Moscow, 1997, p. 26; *Gongchan guoji, liangong (Bu)*, pp. 98–9.
57 Li Yuning and M. Gasster, 'Chü Ch'iu-pai's Journey to Russia, 1920–22', *Monumenta Serica*, 29, 1970–71, p. 543.
58 Li and Gasster, 'Chü Ch'iu pai's Journey', p. 543.
59 J.D. Spence, *The Gate of Heavenly Peace. The Chinese and Their Revolution, 1895–1980*, London, 1982, p. 176.
60 T.N. Akatova, 'Tsiui Tsiu-bo [Qu Qiubai] v rabochem dvizhenii Kitaia', *Gosudarstvo i obshchestvo v Kitae*, Moscow, 1978, p. 254.
61 *Zhongguo gongchandang tong zhi*, vol. 1, p. 621; vol. 3, p. 2544; 'Xiao Jingguang huiyi lü E zhibu qianhou de qingkuang', *Gongchanzhuyi xiaozu*, vol. 1, pp. 200–01; 'Cao Jinghua de huiyi', *Ibid*, pp. 202–3. There is much confusion regarding the timing of departure of the different cohorts. For various dates, see Li Da, 'Guanyu Zhongguo gongchandang', '*Yida' qianhou*, vol. 2, p. 4; 'Cao Jingyu de huiyi', p. 203; Xu Zhizhen, 'Guanyu Xin Yuyangli liuhao de huodong qingkuang', *Gongchanzhuyi xiaozu*, vol. 1, pp. 197–99. Bao Huiseng suggests that Liu Shaoqi et al. did not go to Russia until the spring of 1921, and this seems the most likely timing, being confirmed by the greatest number of memoirists. Bao Huiseng. 'Huiyi Yuyangli liuhao he Zhongguo laodong zuhe shujibu', '*Yida' qianhou*, vol. 2, p. 352. It is not, however, certain that Liu Shaoqi was in the first cohort to leave, at least according to the testimony of Hua Lin. Hua, who was in the first group, reckons that they did not leave until April, though this must have been the latest possible date. See Hua Lin, 'Yuyangli liuhao he fu E xuexi de qingkuang', *Gongchanzhuyi xiaozu*, vol. 1, pp. 204–206.
62 J.L. Price, *Cadres, Commanders and Commissars: the Training of the Chinese Communist Leadership, 1920–45*, Colorado, 1976, p. 33.
63 C.M. Wilbur, and J. Lien-ying How, *Missionaries of Revolution: Soviet Advisers and Nationalist China, 1920–1927*, Cambridge, Mass., 1989, p. 33.
64 *Gongchanzhuyi xiaozu*, vol. 1, p. 23.
65 VKP(b), p. 30.
66 VKP(b), p. 31.
67 Shanghai huoyou, 2, 17 Oct. 1920, p. 15.
68 Shen Yixing, Jiang Peinan and Zheng Qingsheng, *Shanghai gongren yundong shi*, vol. 1, Liaoning, 1991, pp. 81–2; Li Hong, 'Dang de chuangli shiqi zhongyao de gongren baokan jieshao', *Zhongguo gongren yundong shiliao*, 1958, 2, p. 83.
69 Shanghai huoyou, 2, 17 Oct. 1920, p. 15; ZGDSRWZ, vol. 6, Xi'an, 1982, p. 166.
70 *Shanghai jiqi ye gongren yundong shi*, Beijing, 1991, p. 333.
71 *Shanghai jiqi ye*, pp. 332–5. Another source says that he remained in Shanghai only until November 1922. See Shao Weizheng, 'Jiandang qianhou', p. 74.
72 Laodongjie, 9, 10 Oct. 1920.
73 Laodongjie, 9, 10 Oct. 1920. The constitution of the union is reprinted in *Gongchanzhuyi xiaozu*, vol. 1, pp. 111–15.
74 Laodongjie, 19, 19 Dec. 1920.
75 Laodongjie, 19, 19 Dec. 1920; Shao Weizheng, 'Jiandang qianhou', pp. 78–9.
76 *Shanghai jiqi ye*, p. 310.
77 Ma Chaojun, *Zhongguo laogong yundong shi*, Taibei, 1958, p. 52, p. 136.

78 'Zhang Tailei xiang Gongchan guoji yuandong shujichu de baogao' [Spring 1921], *Gongchan guoji, liangong (Bu)*, p. 97.
79 Laodongjie, 18, 12 Dec. 1920; Liu Mingkui, '1912–1921 nian Zhongguo gongren jieji de zhuangkuang', *Zhongguo gongren yundong shiliao*, 1, 1958, p. 84.
80 Laodong zhoukan, 18, 17 Dec. 1921; Laodongjie, 4, 5 Sept. 1920.
81 Laodongjie, 8, 3 Oct. 1920.
82 *Zhongguo gongchandang diyici daibiao dahui dang'an ziliao*, Beijing, 1982, p. 9.
83 Lin Jianbai, Li Zhining, *Li Qihan*, Guangdong, 1984; Si Binghan, 'Li Qihan', *Zhongguo gongren yundong de xianfeng*, vol. 2, Beijing, 1983, 149–87.
84 Laodongjie, 20, 26 Dec. 1920; Chen Weimin, 'Zhongguo gongchangdang chuangli qi de Shanghai gongren yundong pinggu', *Shilin*, 4 (11), 1988, p. 73.
85 Shen Yixing et al., *Shanghai gongren*, p. 63.
86 Shanghai huoyou, 6, 14 Nov. 1920. Cheng Yaojin is a character who appears in a series of vernacular novels and plays about Li Mi (581–618), an unsuccessful contender for the throne at the end of the Sui dynasty. Cheng is his general and has a reputation for turning up in unlikely places.
87 Municipal Gazette, 23 Apr. 1921, p. 164.
88 Municipal Gazette, 12 May 1921, p. 190; Municipal Gazette, 18 June 1921, p. 216; Shao Weizheng, 'Jiandang qianhou', p. 83.
89 Wilbur, *Missionaries*, p. 474.
90 Xu Meikun, 'Jiang-Zhe quwei chengli qianhou de pianduan huiyi', *Dangshi ziliao congkan*, 2 (7), 1981, p. 27.
91 The quotations are from a manual on party training produced by the SYL branch in Moscow. See Wilbur, *Missionaries*, pp. 527–8, where the document is undated. It appears to have been drafted in late April 1923. See Zhang Wenxin (ed.), *Ren Bishi zhuan*, Beijing, 1994, pp. 41–2.
92 P.G. Pickowicz, *Marxist Literary Thought in China: the Influence of Chü Ch'iu-pai*, Berkeley, 1981, p. 46.
93 Wilbur, *Missionaries*, p. 527.
94 See the articles from *The Awakening* and *New Youth* reprinted in *Gongchanzhuyi xiaozu*, vol. 1, pp. 124–32;145–60. See the discussion of Zhang Dongsun's polemic with the Communists in Dirlik, *Origins*, pp. 134–8.
95 Gongchandang, 4, 7 May 1921; p. 24; A. Dirlik, *Anarchism in the Chinese Revolution*, Berkeley, 1991, ch.6.
96 T. Saich, 'Through the Past Darkly: Some New Sources on the Founding of the Chinese Communist Party', *International Review of Social History*, vol. 30, part 2, 1985, p. 177.
97 Xianqu, 8, 15 May 1922, p. 1; Wilbur, *Missionaries*, p. 473.
98 ZGZYWJXJ vol. 1, Beijing, 1989, pp. 90–1.
99 ZGZYWJXJ, vol. 1, p. 91.
100 ZGZYWJXJ, vol. 1, pp. 96–7.
101 Xiang Ying, 'Gongchan guoji', p. 183.
102 Xiang Ying, 'Gongchan guoji', p. 225; VKP(b), p. 57.
103 Chang Kuo-t'ao, *The Rise of the Communist Party, 1921–27*, Lawrence, 1971, p. 137.
104 'Yida' qianhou, vol. 2, p. 68. See Bao Huiseng, 'Gongchandang diyici quanguo daibiao huiyi qianhou de huiyi', *Dangshi ziliao congkan*, 1980, 1, p. 136. He never abandoned marxism, although after the 7 February 1923 massacre he took refuge in Beijing, where his brother, a relatively affluent GMD veteran, helped him find a job in the Ministry of Education, which was then controlled by the Zhili clique. For this he was much criticised. At the end of 1926 he taught briefly at Shanghai University, before becoming a

member of the EC of the Hubei provisional government in 1926 and director of education in Wuhan government. He was arrested in that city in 1927 and shot. For a sympathetic treatment see Chen Shaokang and Tian Ziyu, 'Li Hanjun yu "Xingqi pinglun"', *Shehui kexue*, 3, 1984, 56–7. Li Da was elected to the three-person central bureau at the First Congress, and was responsible for propaganda. After failing to be re-elected to the CC at the Second Congress, Li Da returned to his native province to teach at the University of Hunan. From 1923 he dropped out of party activity, allegedly because he did not get on with Mao Zedong. From 1953 he was rector of the University of Hunan, and died in 1966 from injuries sustained at the hands of Red Guards. See Cadart, *Mémoires*, p. 186.

105 Li Da, 'Huiyi', p. 13. Li Da claimed in 1957 that as late as the First Congress in July there were only seven communists in Shanghai. *Ibid.*, p. 23.

106 Saich, *Origins*, vol. 1, p. 53.

107 VKP(b), p. 57.

108 Saich, 'Through the Past', pp. 167–80.

109 VKP(b), p. 39.

110 Tang Zhengchang, *Shanghai shi*, p. 574.

111 M. Fromberg had been in China promoting trade unionism since January and was in Shanghai for several months prior to Nikol'skii. Saich, *Origins*, vol. 1, p. 306; Huang Xiurong, *Gongchan guoji yu Zhongguo geming guanxi shi*, vol. 1, Beijing, 1989, pp. pp. 90–1; Sha Jiansun ed., *Zhongguo gongchandang*, vol. 1, pp. 383–4.

112 Du Weihua, 'Diyici Guo-Gong hezuo shiqi Sineifulitu (Malin) zai Hua jishi', *Zhonggong dangshi ziliao*, 36, 1990, p. 228.

113 The thirteenth delegate, Bao Huiseng, was Chen Duxiu's personal envoy rather than one of the official delegates from Canton. See *Zhongguo gongchandang diyici daibiao dahui*, p. 95; Zhang Zurong and Dong Tingzhi, 'Guanyu Zhonggong 'Yida' daibiaoren shu de jige shuofa', *Dangshi ziliao congkan*, 1, 1979, 139–143.

114 *Dangshi yanjiu*, 5, 1983, pp. 64-6.

115 Zhang Zurong and Dong Tingzhi, 'Guanyu Zhonggong "Yida"', p. 143.

116 I have followed the dates given by Sha Jiansun ed., *Zhongguo gongchandang*, vol. 1, p. 394. Shao Weizheng says the congress finished in early August. Shao Weizheng, 'Guanyu Zhongguo gongchandang diyici quanguo daibiao dahui zhaokai riqi de chubu kaozheng', *Dangshi ziliao congkan*, 1, 1979, p. 138.

117 ZGZYWJXJ, vol. 1, p. 3.

118 Chang Kuo-t'ao, *Rise*, pp. 144–49.

119 ZGZYWJXJ, vol. 1, p. 8.

120 'Zhang Guotao huiyi Zhongguo gongchandang 'Yida' qianhou, *'Yida' qianhou*, vol. 2, 122–183; J.P. Harrison, *The Long March to Power: A History of the Chinese Communist Party, 1921–72*, London, 1972, p. 34.

121 Cai Hesen, 'Makesi xueshuo yu Zhongguo wuchanjieji', *Cai Hesen wenji*, Beijing, 1980, p. 79.

122 Compare Van de Ven: 'While it is probable that without Comintern agents a unified party would eventually have emerged in China, it would have taken longer'. Van de Ven, *Friend*, p. 81.

123 The most recent history of the CCP published in the PRC still claims that marxist organization predated Voitinskii's arrival. Sha Jiansun ed., *Zhongguo gongchandang*, vol. 1, p. 301.

124 Van de Ven, *Friend*, p. 55.

125 Dirlik, *Origins*, p. 13.

Chapter 2

1 VKP(b), p. 55.
2 Du Weihua, 'Diyi ci Guo-Gong hezuo shiqi Sineifulitu (Malin) zai Hua jishi', *Zhonggong dangshi ziliao*, 36, 1990, p. 228.
3 T. Saich, *The Origins of the First United Front in China*, vol. 1, Leiden, 1991, p. 307.
4 VKP(b), pp. 78–9.
5 Du Weihua, 'Diyi ci Guo-Gong hezuo', p. 235.
6 Saich, *Origins*, vol. 1, p. 307.
7 VKP(b), p. 80. Vil'de was known to be in touch with local Communists. See Shanghai Municipal Police, 'History of the Communist Movement in Shanghai', 1933. SMPF (Shanghai Municipal Police Files), D files, 4825. Soviet officials had their own cell of the Russian Communist Party in Shanghai. Jay Calvin Houston archive, Hoover Institution Archives, Box no. 1.
8 H. van de Ven, *From Friend to Comrade*, Berkeley, 1991, pp. 99–102; VKP(b), p. 91, p. 79.
9 Bao Huiseng, 'Gongchangdang di yici quanguo daibiao huiyi qianhou de huiyi', *'Yida' qianhou*, vol. 2, Beijing, 1980, p. 307.
10 A. Dirlik, *The Origins of Chinese Communism*, Oxford, 1989, p. 249.
11 Li Da, 'Zhongguo gongchandang chengli shiqide sixiang douzheng qingkuang', *'Yida' qianhou*, vol. 2, Beijing, 1980, p. 54. One should bear in mind that this was written in 1959, when Chen was a target of universal revilement.
12 Xu Meikun, 'Jiang-Zhe quwei chengli qianhou de pianduan huiyi', *Dangshi ziliao congkan*, 2 (7), 1981, p. 25; Xu Meikun, 'Huiyi "Xiangdao"' de chuban faxing', *Dangshi ziliao congkan*, 3, 1980, p. 63. Some sources suggest that Chen continued in his post until April 1923, when he allegedly resigned from the party after the ECCI representatives refused to let him go to the Soviet Union. See Wang Jianying (ed.), *Zhongguo gongchandang zuzhishi ziliao huibian*, Beijing, 1982, p. 3. In 1925 he was professor of Chinese at Shanghai University and, subsequently, acquired fame as a scholar, editing the first systematic study of rhetoric in Chinese and founding the China Linguistic Society. After 1949 he served briefly as minister of culture and then as president of Fudan University in Shanghai. He was also vice-director of the Chinese Democratic League. See Xu Meikun, 'Jiang-Zhe quwei', p. 25; Christina K. Gilmartin, *Engendering the Chinese Revolution*, Berkeley, 1995, p. 221.
13 *Dangshi ziliao congkan*, 3, 1981, p. 104. The Third CCP Congress in 1923 laid down that cells (*xiaozu*) were the basic unit of organization, to be formed wherever there were five to ten party members. The Fourth Congress revised this decision, and decided that the branch (*zhibu*) was the standard unit of party organization.
14 Xu Meikun, 'Jiang-Zhe quwei', p. 25.
15 'Yijiueryi nian zhi yijiuerqi nian Shanghai, Jiangsu, Zhejiang dang zuzhi fazhan gaikuang', *Zhonggongdang shi ziliao*, 10, 1984, p. 182.
16 'Yijiueryi nian', p. 183.
17 ZGZYWJXJ, vol. 1, p. 47.
18 ZGZYWJXJ, vol. 1, p. 47.
19 VKP(b), p. 81.
20 VKP(b), p. 123, p. 165; *Zhongguo gongchandang tong zhi*, vol. 1, Beijing, 1997, p. 1034.
21 Saich, *Origins*, vol. 2, p. 539; *Zhongguo gongchandang tong zhi*, vol. 1, p. 1016.
22 Jiang Peinan, Chen Weimin, 'Zhongguo laodong zuhe shujibu shimo kao', *Dangshi ziliao congkan*, 3(4), 1980, p. 108.

23 *Gongchandang*, 6, 7 July 1921.
24 Saich, *Origins*, vol. 1, p. 70.
25 Saich, *Origins*, vol. 1, p. 71; '*Yida*' *qianhou*, vol. 1, Beijing, 1980, pp. 18–19.
26 ZGDSRWZ, vol. 9, Xi'an, 1983, p. 166.
27 Chang Kuo-t'ao, *The Rise of the Communist Party, 1921–27*, Lawrence, 1971, p. 155; A.I. Kartunova, *Politika kompartii Kitaia v rabochem voprose nakanune revoliutsii, 1925–27gg.*, Moscow, 1983, p. 56.
28 Saich, *Origins*, vol. 1, pp. 210–11; Kartunova, *Politika kompartii*, p. 48.
29 Chang Kuo-t'ao, *Rise*, p. 169.
30 Laodong Zhoukan, 14, 19 Nov. 1921.
31 Si Binghan, 'Li Qihan', *Zhongguo gongren yundong de xianfeng*, vol. 2, Beijing, 1983, p. 158. Li Zhenying left the party after Chiang Kai-shek's coup in 1927, and spent the last ten years of his life working as an assistant in a silk shop in Tianjin.
32 Laodong zhoukan, 13, 12 Nov. 1921. The term *gongjie* originally meant the 'industrial section of society' and could in principle include employers, managers, technical personnel and workers. In the wake of the May Fourth Movement, however, it was used increasingly to denote workers alone.
33 Laodong zhoukan, 14, 19 Nov. 1921.
34 Minguo ribao, 19 Nov. 1921.
35 Laodong zhoukan, 14, 19 Nov. 1921.
36 Laodong zhoukan, 28, 5 Feb. 1922.
37 Ma Chaojun, *Zhongguo laogong yundong shi*, Chongqing, 1942, p. 98.
38 Laodong zhoukan, 15, 26 Nov. 1921; 14, 19 Nov. 1921.
39 Deng Zhongxia, *Zhongguo zhigong yundong jianshi*, Beijing, 1957, p. 40.
40 Shen Yixing, Jiang Peinan and Zheng Qingsheng, *Shanghai gongren yundong shi*, vol. 1, Liaoning, 1991, p. 153; *Strikes and Lockouts in Shanghai since 1918*, Shanghai, 1933, appendix, pp. 7–11, gives lower figures of 33 strikes in 1920; 19 in 1921 and 29 in 1922.
41 For subtle accounts of workers in Shanghai in this period which illuminate the narrow solidarities that structured their world, see E.J. Perry, *Shanghai on Strike: The Politics of Chinese Labor*, Stanford, 1993; E. Honig, *Sisters and Strangers, Women in the Shanghai Cotton Mill, 1919–49*, Stanford, 1986.
42 Chang Kuo-t'ao, *Rise*, p. 172; *Bao Huiseng huiyilu*, Beijing, 1983, pp. 66–7. Kong Fanjun, 'Dang zai chuangli shiqi dui bangkou he huidang de zhengce yu celüe' *Zhonggong dang shi yanjiu*, 4, 1990, pp. 93–4.
43 Shen Yixing, *Shanghai gongren*, p. 32.
44 Gongchandang, 6, 7 July 1921, pp. 60–1; *Zhongguo gongren yundong shiliao*, 1, 1958, p. 58.
45 Laodong zhoukan, 12, 5 Nov. 1921.
46 *Shanghai juanyanchang gongren yundong shi*, Beijing, 1991, p. 58; Lin Jianbai, Li Zhining, *Li Qihan*, Guangdong, 1984, pp. 51–2.
47 Lin Jianbai, *Li Qihan*, pp. 60–1; Zhou Yumin, Shao Yong, *Zhongguo banghui shi*, Shanghai, 1993, p. 497.
48 *Chinese Economic Journal*, vol. 3, no. 5, 1928, p. 922.
49 *Zhongguo gonghui lishi wenxian, 1921–27*, Beijing, 1958, p. 2.
50 Jean Chesneaux, *The Chinese Labor Movement, 1919–1927*, Stanford, 1968, pp. 180–4.
51 Chen Da, 'Guonei zhongyao gonghui de gaikuang', *Shehui xuejia*, vol. 1, June 1927, p. 123.
52 NCH, 18 Mar. 1922, p. 787. In the end only 300 out of the 1040 Shanghai seamen who initially expressed readiness to break the strike went south to Canton. Shen Yixing, *Gongyun shi ming-bian lu*, Shanghai, 1987, p. 19.

53 Saich, *Origins*, vol. 1, p. 83.
54 Saich, *Origins*, vol. 1, p. 81.
55 *Shanghai haiyuan gongren yundong lishi*, Beijing, 1991, pp. 311–12; Shen Yixing et al, *Shanghai gongren*, p. 103.
56 *Diyici guonei geming zhanzheng shiqi de gongren yundong*, Beijing, 1954, p. 177; ZGDSRWZ, vol. 6, Xi'an 1982, p. 102.
57 Shen Yixing, *Shanghai gongren*, p. 138; SMPF, IO 4652.
58 Born in Xiangshan county, Guangdong, in 1887, the son of a poor peasant, Lin Weimin started work at the age of 19 in a restaurant and had then had a series of jobs as a ship's cook. ZGDSRWZ, vol. 6, pp. 91–2.
59 NCH, 12 Aug. 1922, p. 457; 26 Aug. 1922, pp. 602–3; Public Record Office, London (hence PRO), Foreign Office (FO), 228/3527, 'S. Barton, Acting-Consul, to HM Minister, 29 Aug. 1922'; Ma Chaojun, *Zhongguo laogong yundong shi*, Taibei, 1958 pp. 218–9.
60 Minguo ribao, 17 Sep. 1922; PRO, FO 228/3140, 'S. Barton, Consul-General, to HM Minister, 16 Aug. 1924'. Yuan Dashi was from a poor peasant family and had been a cowherd in his youth. He was one of the main protagonists in the factional strife at the University of the Toilers of the East. After his return to China, he was active in the lower levels of the labour movement, where he worked loyally and hard. At the end of 1927 he became head of the organization department of the Jiangsu provincial committee of the CCP. Zheng Chaolin, *An Oppositionist for Life. Memoirs of the Chinese Revolutionary*, Atlantic Highlands, N.J., 1997, p. 212.
61 Minguo ribao, 8 Sep. 1920; 9 Sep. 1920.
62 PRO, FO 228/3291, 'Shanghai Intelligence Report, Quarter Ended Sep. 1922'; Minguo ribao, 21 Oct. 1922; 22 Oct. 1922.
63 PRO FO 228/3291, 'Shanghai Intelligence Report, Sep. 1922'; Shen Yixing, *Shanghai gongren*, p. 147.
64 *Zhongguo gongren yundong shiliao*, 1, 1958, p. 63; NCH, 22 Apr. 1922, p. 275.
65 Tang Hai, *Zhongguo laodong wenti*, Shanghai, 1926, p. 387; Ma Chaojun, *Zhongguo laogong* (1958), p. 221.
66 Minguo ribao, 24 May 1922.
67 *Zhongguo gongchandang diyici daibiao dahui dang'an ziliao*, Beijing, 1982, pp. 39–40.
68 Tang Chunliang, *Li Lisan zhuan*, Heilongjiang, 1984, p. 42, p. 52.
69 Minguo ribao, 4 June 1922; Tang Hai, *Zhongguo laodong*, p. 390.
70 Ma Chaojun, *Zhongguo laogong* (1942), p. 98; 1958, p. 223; Chesneaux, *Chinese Labor Movement*, p. 487, footnote 208.
71 Minguo ribao, 31 Oct. 1922; 4 Nov. 1922.
72 PRO FO 228/3291, 'Shanghai Intelligence Report, Sep. 1922'.
73 *Zhongguo gongren yundong shiliao*, 1, 1958, p. 58; Minguo ribao, 21 Oct. 1922.
74 Shen Yixing, et al., *Shanghai gongren*, p. 150; S. Cochran, *Big Business in China: Sino-Foreign Rivalry in the Cigarette Industry, 1890–1930*, Cambridge, Mass., 1980, p. 139.
75 Dong Chuping, 'Huiyi Zhongguo laodong zuhe shujibu', *Zhonggong dangshi ziliao*, 1, 1982, p. 83.
76 NCH, 25 Nov. 1922, p. 529; PRO FO 228/3291, 'Shanghai Intelligence Report, Sep. 1922'.
77 Shen Yixing, *Shanghai gongren*, p. 151; PRO FO 228/3291, 'Shanghai Intelligence Report, Sep. 1922'; Tang Hai, *Zhongguo laodong*, p. 392.
78 PRO FO 228/3291, 'Shanghai Intelligence Report, Sep. 1922'; Tang Hai, *Zhongguo laodong*, p. 392; Chesneaux, *Chinese Labor Movement*, p. 199.

Notes

79 It is not certain that Xu was a worker by social origin. Shao Lizi hints that he had been a student at the Zhejiang First Normal School. See Shao Lizi, 'Dang chengli qianhou de yixie qingkuang', *Gongchanzhuyi xiaozu*, vol. 1, Beijing, 1987, pp. 189.

80 Xu Meikun, 'Jiang-Zhe quwei', p. 25; Xu Meikun, 'Huiyi Shanghai gongren sanci wuzhuang qiyi de yixie qingkuang', *Dangshi ziliao congkan*, 3 (8), 1981, 91–4; *Shanghai shangwu yinshuguan zhigong yundong shi*, Beijing, 1991, pp. 153–4.

81 *Shanghai lieshi xiaozhuan*, Shanghai, 1983, pp. 79–80; Shen Yixing, *Shanghai gongren*, p. 178. Zheng did not join the CCP until 1924, when he launched a union of Zhejiang workers in Shanghai with the party's blessing. During the May Thirtieth Movement of 1925 he led the printers' general labour union (*yinshua zonggonghui*), and in the summer of 1927 became chair of the Shanghai General Labour Union. He was arrested in February 1928 and executed in June.

82 Wang Jiagui, Cai Xiyao, *Shanghai daxue*, Shanghai, 1986, p. 62.

83 *Shanghai shangwu yinshuguan*, p. 143.

84 Zhu Bangxing, Hu Linge and Xu Sheng, *Shanghai chanye yu Shanghai zhigong*, Shanghai, 1984, p. 2.

85 Chinese Economic Journal, vol. 11, no. 6, 1932, p. 425.

86 *Nanyang xiongdi yancao gongsi shiliao* Shanghai, 1958, p. 291; A. Roux, *Le Shanghai ouvrier des années trente: coolies, gangsters et syndicalistes*, 1993, pp. 177–8.

87 Roux, *Le Shanghai ouvrier*, pp. 177–8.

88 PRO FO 228/3291, 'Shanghai Intelligence Report, Sep. 1922'.

89 SMPF, IO 4831.

90 NCH, 11 Nov. 1922, p. 377.

91 *Nanyang xiongdi yancao*, pp. 323–5; PRO FO 228/3291, 'Shanghai Intelligence Report, Sep. 1922'.

92 Zhongguo gongren, no. 2, Nov. 1924, p. 55; *Diyici Zhongguo laodong nianjian*, part 2, Beijing, 1928, p. 52; *Nanyang xiongdi yancao*, pp. 538–9.

93 Laodong Zhoukan, 11, 29 Nov. 1921.

94 Minguo Ribao, 9 Mar. 1922; 27 Mar. 1922; 19 June 1922; Shen Yixing et al., *Shanghai gongren*, pp. 106–7.

95 C.M. Wilbur and J. Lien-ying How, *Missionaries of Revolution*, Cambridge, Mass., 1989, p. 55.

96 Chesneaux, *Chinese Labor Movement*, p. 199; Jiang Peinan, Chen Weimin, 'Shanghai zhaopai gonghui de xingwang', *Jindai shi yanjiu*, 6, 1984, pp. 63–4.

97 Chesneaux, *Chinese Labor Movement*, pp. 223–7.

98 Deng Zhongxian, *Zhongguo zhigong yundong*, pp. 38–9.

99 Jiang Peinan, Chen Weimin, 'Zhongguo laodong zuhe shujibu', p. 111; Deng Zhongxia, *Zhongguo zhigong yundong*, p. 40; L.N. Shaffer, *Mao and the Workers: the Hunan Labor Movement, 1920–23*, Armonk, N.Y., 1982, pp. 50–61.

100 For an account of the Congress, see Chesneaux, *Chinese Labor Movement*, pp. 185–7.

101 PRO FO 228/3527, 'S. Barton, Acting Consul-General, to HM Minister, 14 Aug. 1922'.

102 PRO FO 228/3291, 'Shanghai Intelligence Report for Quarter Ended Mar. 1922'; *Zhongguo gongren yundong shiliao*, 1, 1958, pp. 66–7.

103 *Zhongguo gongren yundong shiliao*, 1, 1958, pp. 66–7; Jiang Peinan, Chen Weimin, 'Zhongguo laodong zuhe shujibu', p. 111. According to the International Settlement police, Dong Chuping was acting secretary after Li's arrest, but vanished. SMPF, IO 4639.

239

104   Deng Zhongxia, *Zhongguo zhigong yundong*, pp. 182–3.
105   See the discussion of the summoning of the Second National Congress in *Zhongguo lici laodong dahui wenxian*, Beijing, 1957, p. 8.
106   Jiang Peinan, Chen Weimin, 'Zhongguo laodong zuhe shujibu', p. 115; Wang Jianying (ed.), *Zhongguo gongchandang zuzhishi*, p. 31.
107   Deng Zhongxia, *Zhongguo zhigong yundong* pp. 182–3; Chang Kuo-t'ao, *Rise*, p. 409; Jiang Peinan, Chen Weimin, 'Zhongguo laodong zuhe shujibu', p. 113.
108   *Zhongguo gongchandang Shanghai shi zuzhishi ziliao, 1920.8 – 1987.10*, Shanghai 1991, p. 18 (Hence: ZGGCDSH); *Shanghai xuesheng yundong dashi, 1919.5 – 1949.9*, Wang Min (ed.), Shanghai, 1985, p. 45.
109   Xianqu, 1, 15 Jan. 1922, p. 1.
110   Xin Qingnian, 9, no. 6, 1922, p. 117.
111   'Yida' qianhou, vol. 1 p. 422; VKP(b), p. 89.
112   Xianqu, 8, 15 May 1922, p. 2.; *Shanghai xuesheng yundong dashi*, p. 50.
113   ZGGCDSH, pp. 18–19.
114   ZGGCDSH, p. 20.
115   Wilbur, *Missionaries*, p. 37.
116   Xianqu, 4, 15 Mar. 1922.
117   Ka-Che Yip, *Religion, Nationalism and Chinese Students: the Anti-Christian Movement of 1922–27*, Bellingham, 1980, p. 26. Jiang Zhichan, 'Dageming shiqi de Shanghai xuelian', in *Diyici guogong hezuo shiqi de Gongqingtuan zhuanti lun wenji*, Beijing, 1985, 108–9.
118   VKP(b), p. 87.
119   Dong Chuping, 'Huiyi', p. 85.
120   VKP(b), p. 86.
121   *Zhongguo gongren yundong shiliao*, 1, 1979, pp. 219–21.
122   Gilmartin, *Engendering*, p. 40.
123   Gilmartin, *Engendering*, p. 34, p. 54, p. 56.
124   Gilmartin, *Engendering*, p. 59.
125   'Yang Zhihua de huiyi', 'Yida' qianhou, vol. 2, Beijing, 1980, p. 28.
126   Sha Jiansong ed., *Zhongguo gongchandang tongshi*, vol. 1, Changsha, 1996, p. 464; Gilmartin, *Engendering*, pp. 62–3.
127   Gilmartin, *Engendering*, p. 66.
128   Gilmartin, *Engendering*, pp. 81–2; PRO FO 228/3291, 'Shanghai Intelligence Report, Sep. 1922'.
129   Xiangdao, 8, 2 Nov. 1922.
130   ZGDSRWZ, vol. 6, Shaanxi, 1982, pp. 62–3.
131   Dai Xugong, *Xiang Jingyu zhuan*, Beijing, 1981, p. 33, p. 39.
132   Marilyn A. Levine, *The Found Generation*, Seattle, 1993, p. 49.
133   Gilmartin, *Engendering*, pp. 78–9; Levine, *Found Generation*, pp. 53–4.
134   Zheng, *Oppositionist*, p. 142. Yang Zilie, who generally got on with Xiang, thought her proud and self-satisfied, and was mortified when she insinuated that her husband, Zhang Guotao, had written a successful speech she gave to a women's conference in 1925. Yang Zilie, *Zhang Guotao furen huiyi lu*, Hong Kong, 1970, p. 134.
135   Qianfeng, 1 July 1923.
136   ZGZYWJXJ, vol. 1, p. 53. This refers to the initiative of Shen Xuanlu who in September 1921 formed the Yaqian Farmers' Association in his native Xiaoshan county. See R. Keith Schoppa, *Blood Road: The Mystery of Shen Dingyi in Revolutionary China*, Berkeley, 1995, pp. 106–114; *Gongchanzhuyi xiaozu*, vol. 1, pp. 42–3. This was the first instance of CCP peasant

organizing, and predated Peng Pai's more famous initiative in Haifeng county in Guangdong of 1922. Fernando Galbiati, *P'eng P'ai and the Hai-lu-feng Soviet*, Stanford, 1985, p. 90, p. 95, p. 152.

137 *'Yida' qianhou*, vol. 1, p. 424.

138 *Kommunisticheskii Internatsional i kitaiskaia revoliutsiia: dokumenty i materialy*, Moscow, 1986, pp. 24–5.

139 Du Weihua, 'Diyici Guo-Gong hezuo shiqi', p. 228, pp. 230–1.

140 VKP(b), p. 82.

141 VKP(b), p. 86.

142 VKP(b), p. 83.

Chapter 3

1 *Zhongguo gongchandang tong zhi*, vol. 1, Beijing, 1997, p. 505; ZGZYWJXJ, vol. 1, Hebei, 1989, pp. 31–2.

2 T. Saich, *The Origins of the First United Front in China*, vol. 1, Leiden, 1991 p. 111.

3 Saich, *Origins*, vol. 1, p. 333; *'Erda' he 'Sanda': Zhongguo gongchandang dier-san daibiao dahui ziliao xuanbian*, Beijing, 1985, p. 66–8.

4 Saich, *Origins*, vol. 1, p. 115; vol. 2, p. 612.

5 *'Yida' qianhou*, Beijing, 1980, vol. 1, p. 422; Saich, Origins, vol. 1, pp. 317–23.

6 Saich, *Origins*, vol. 1, p. 97, p. 100.

7 *Kommunisticheskii Internatsional i kitaiskaia revoliutsiia*, Moscow, 1986, p. 26; Saich, *Origins*, vol. 1, pp. 328–9.

8 VKP(b), p. 113.

9 VKP(b), p. 164.

10 Saich, *Origins*, vol. 1, pp. 117–18.

11 Saich, *Origins*, vol. 1, pp. 361–67.

12 *Kommunisticheskii Internatsional*, pp. 37–41. Note that the four social groups said to comprise the GMD do not correspond to the later 'four-class bloc' formula. According to that, the GMD was a revolutionary bloc of the national bourgeoisie, the urban petty-bourgeoisie, the peasantry and the proletariat. Yet there was never absolute consistency with regard to this formula, the 'intelligentsia' frequently being substituted for the 'urban petty-bourgeoisie', an indication of the vagueness of Comintern understanding.

13 VKP(b), pp. 188–99.

14 VKP(b), p. 159.

15 VKP(b), pp. 207–9, 212–14, 219–25.

16 Huang Xiurong, *Gongchan guoji yu Zhongguo geming guanxi shi*, vol. 1, Beijing, 1989, pp. 175–6.

17 Saich, *Origins*, vol. 2, p. 496.

18 VKP(b), pp. 227–8.

19 VKP(b), pp. 230–1; *Kommunisticheskii Internatsional*, pp. 39–40.

20 VKP(b), pp. 161–2. It is also worth noting that the practical measures of 'agrarian revolution' which Bukharin advocated showed scant appreciation of Chinese conditions, being little more than a mechanical application of the Russian experience to China, conveniently defined by Bukharin as a 'feudal regime'. VKP(b), p. 230.

21 Saich, *Origins*, vol. 1 pp. 594–6. Chen Duxiu's doubts about the political potentiality of the proletariat at this stage are well-known. See L. Feigon, *Chen Duxiu: Founder of the Chinese Communist Party*, Princeton, 1983, p. 173, and

footnote 52. The party programme passed by the Third Congress affirmed the capitalist character of the national revolution but declared: 'In this revolution the proletariat is a vital and powerful element, the most thorough-going element, since other classes are all fettered by economic strength of the big powers.' Qu Qiubai, who drafted the programme, said that this was an amendment by Chen to his original, which read: 'In this revolution the proletariat alone is the most vital, the most progressive, the most thorough-going force, since other classes. . .' ZGZYWJXJ, vol. 1, p. 139; *Qu Qiubai xuanji*, Beijing, 1985, p. 342.

22 Saich, *Origins*, vol. 1, p. 185.

23 Chang Kuo-t'ao, *The Rise of the Communist Party, 1921–27*, Lawrence, 1971, ch.6.

24 VKP(b), p. 399. Sneevliet left China in August.

25 VKP(b), p. 240.

26 *Zhongguo gongchandang tong zhi*, vol. 1, p. 21; ZGZYWJXJ, vol. 1, pp. 200–01.

27 VKP(b), pp. 309–11.

28 VKP(b), p. 400.

29 VKP(b), p. 374–76.

30 VKP(b), p. 394.

31 ZGZYWJXJ, vol. 1, p. 222–25.

32 VKP(b), p. 362.

33 VKP(b), p. 448; ZGZYWJXJ, vol. 1, pp. 230–1; H.J. van de Ven, *From Friend to Comrade*, Berkeley, 1991, p. 134.

34 J.P. Harrison, *The Long March to Power*, London, 1972, p. 57.

35 V.I Glunin and A.M. Grigor'ev, 'Komintern i Kitaiskaia revoliutsiia', *Voprosy Istorii KPSS*, 1989, p. 106. The order of 21 July, as published in ZGZYWJXJ, I, pp. 282–3, does not actually call for this.

36 VKP(b), pp. 468–9.

37 VKP(b), pp. 472–3.

38 *Zhongguo gongchandang tong zhi*, vol. 1, p. 506.

39 VKP(b), pp. 472–3.

40 VKP(b), p. 481.

41 VKP(b), p. 482.

42 VKP(b), p. 504; Yang Yunruo and Yang Kuisong, *Gongchan guoji he Zhongguo geming*, Shanghai, 1988, p. 107.

43 As we have seen, as early as 24 May 1923 the ECCI directive to the Third CCP Congress had prescribed that 'leadership must belong to the party of the working class'. *Kommunisticheskii Internatsional*, p. 40.

44 V.I. Glunin, 'Grigorii Voitinskii, 1893–1953', *Vidnye Sovetskie Kommunisty – uchastniki kitaiskoi revoliutsii*, Moscow, 1970, p. 82. The concept of proletarian hegemony illustrates the difficulties of translating concepts from one cultural context to another. The concept (*gegemoniia*) was invented by Russian Social Democrats at the turn of the century to denote the capacity of the proletariat – a minority in an overwhelmingly rural society – to win to its side the majority of the oppressed and exploited in the struggle against tsarism. [See, for example, V.I. Lenin, *Collected Works* (fourth edition), Moscow, 1963, vol. 17, pp. 231–2.] During the 1920s, its meaning was extended by Bukharin to denote the capacity of the proletariat to extend its influence over the peasantry during the struggle for socialism. See R.B. Day, *N.I. Bukharin: Selected Writings on the State and the Transition to Socialism*, M.E. Sharpe, Armonk, NY, 1982, p. 175, p. 223. The concept was not synonymous with that of 'leadership' (*rukovodstvo*), and it lost vital connotations when translated into Chinese as *lingxiuquan*, literally, 'leadership power'. Qu Qiubai, who probably had the deepest knowledge of

the Russian language of any of the Communist leaders, was careful when using the term *lingxiuquan* to gloss it by writing the word 'hegemony' in brackets in English. But most Communists were not sensitized to the political and cultural connotations of the Russian term. Qu Qiubai, 'Zhongguo geming zhong zhi zhenglun wenti', in *Liu Da yiqian: dang de lishi cailiao*, Beijing, 1980, p. 671. In October 1926, for example, the Shanghai Communists spoke of the business-man, Yu Xiaqing, exercising 'hegemony' during the first armed uprising. For a trenchant account of the peregrinations of the concept of hegemony, see P. Anderson, 'The Antinomies of Antonio Gramsci', *New Left Review*, 100, 1976–77, 5–80.

45 However, Alexander Pantsov shows that it was not until the spring of 1925 that Stalin embraced the view that the left could seize power in the GMD and transform it into a 'workers' and peasants' party'. A. Pantsov, 'Stalin's Policy in China, 1925–27: New Light from the Russian Archives', *Issues and Studies*, 34, no. 1, Jan. 1998, p. 135.

46 Peng Shuzhi, 'Shui shi Zhongguo guomin geming zhi lingdaozhe?', Xin Qingnian, 4, 2 Dec. 1924; Zheng Chaolin, 'Chen Duxiu and the Trotskyists' in G. Benton, *China's Urban Revolutionaries: Explorations in the History of Chinese Trotskyism, 1921–1952*, Atlantic Highlands, N.J., 1996, p. 128. In his polemic with Peng in spring 1927, Qu Qiubai made much of this claim, though there is evidence that by this time Peng was less confident than he had been in 1924 that proletarian hegemony would be an inevitable feature of the national revolution. Qu Qiubai, 'Zhongguo geming'.

47 In 1925, for example, Deng Zhongxia asserted that the working class had acquired hegemony in the united front; yet after Chiang Kai-shek's coup of 20 March 1926, he conceded that the working class had retreated to a supporting role in the national revolution. D.Y.K. Kwan, *Marxist Intellectuals and the Chinese Labor Movement*, Seattle, 1997, p. 170.

48 Sha Jiansun (ed.), *Zhongguo gongchandang tongshi*, vol. 2, Beijing, 1996 pp. 235–45; VKP(b), p. 509.

49 ZGZYWJXJ, vol. 1, pp. 338–41.

50 ZGZYWJXJ, vol. 1, pp. 345–6.

51 VKP(b), p. 520.

52 In two articles written in 1923, Chen Duxiu had discussed the relative strength and potential of the bourgeoisie and working class in China. In the first he argued that 'in colonial and semi-colonial countries the force of the bourgeoisie is more concentrated than that of the peasantry and more powerful than that of the proletariat.' In the second he concluded: 'No doubt the working class is an important element in the national revolution, but it is only an important element, and not an independent revolutionary force'. Chen Duxiu, 'Zichanjieji de geming yu geming de zichanjieji', Xiangdao, 22, 25 Apr. 1923; idem, 'Zhongguo guomin geming yu shehui ge jieji', Qianfeng, 2, 2 Dec. 1923. This was broadly in line with the Comintern position at that time. By late 1924, however, Chen had come to the view that the proletariat was the 'main force' (*zhuli jun*) and the 'supervisor of operations' (*duzhanzhe*) in the national revolution. Chen Duxiu, 'Ershi qi nian yilai guomin yundong zhong suode jiaoxun', Xin qingnian, 4, 2 Dec. 1924.

53 VKP(b), p. 492. The notion of the GMD as a 'worker-peasant party' never became official Comintern policy, which continued to characterise it as a 'four-class bloc'.

54 Saich, *Origins*, vol. 2, p. 538, p. 573. Another source says that membership stood at 432. See Wang Jianying, (ed.), *Zhongguo gongchandang zuzhishi ziliao*

huibian, Beijing, 1982, p. 17; 'Chen Duxiu zai Zhongguo gongchandang disanci quanguo daibiao dahui de baogao', *Dangshi yanjiu*, 2, 1980, p. 42.

55 Wang Jiangying (ed.), *Zhongguo gongchandang*, p. 30.

56 Huang Zhirong, 'Guanyu yijiuersan nian zhi yijiuerqi nian Shanghai daxue dangzuzhi de fazhan qingkuang', *Zhonggong dangshi ziliao*, 2 (11), 1982, p. 98.

57 ZGZYWJXJ, I, p. 256.

58 ZGGCDSH, p. 2.

59 Wang Jianying, *Zhongguo gongchandang*, p. 8. Chen Duxiu said that national membership at this time was 123, of whom workers comprised 19 per cent. 'Chen Duxiu zai Zhongguo', p. 42.

60 'Chen Duxiu zai Zhongguo', p. 42.

61 ZGZYWJXJ, vol. 1, p. 256.

62 ZGZYWJXJ, vol. 1, p. 190.

63 P. Mif, *Heroic China: Fifteen Years of the Communist Party of China*, New York, 1937, p. 24, p. 49; R.C. North, *Moscow and the Chinese Communists*, Stanford, 1963, p. 131.

64 'Yijiueryi nian zhi yijiuerqi nian Shanghai, Jiangsu, Zhejiang dang zuzhi fazhan gaikuang', *Zhonggongdang shi ziliao*, 10, 1984, p. 196.

65 *Zhongguo gongchandang tong zhi*, vol. 1, p. 626.

66 ZGZYWJXJ, vol. 1, p. 167; *Zhongguo gongchandang tong zhi*, vol. 1, p. 626.

67 Van de Ven, *Friend*, p. 137.

68 Van de Ven, *Friend*, p. 136.

69 S. Dalin, 'Na dalekom Kitae', *Molodaia gvardiia*, 2, Mar. 1923, pp. 307–8.

70 Ding Shouhe, 'Lun Qu Qiubai de sixiang fazhan ji qi dui Zhongguo geming de gongxian' *Zhongguo geming shi conglun*, Guangdong, 1985, pp. 270–87.

71 Zheng Chaolin, *An Oppositionist for Life. Memoirs of the Chinese Revolutionary*, Atlantic Highlands, N.J., 1997, p. 94.

72 Zheng Chaolin, *Huai jiu ji*, Beijing, 1995, p. 96.

73 J.D. Spence, *The Gate of Heavenly Peace. The Chinese and Their Revolution, 1895–1980*, London, 1982, p. 210.

74 Zheng Chaolin, *Oppositionist*, p. 55. For an account of the formation of the CCP branch at KUTV see Zhang Xuexin (ed.), *Ren Bishi zhuan*, Beijing, 1994, ch.5.

75 C. Cadart and Cheng Yingxiang, *Mémoires de Peng Shuzhi*, Paris, 1983.

76 Zheng Chaolin, *Oppositionist*, p. 49. See Jiang Guangci's thinly disguised portrayal of Peng in his novel, 'The Party of Sans-culottes'. Jiang Guangci, 'Duanku dang', *Shiwen xuanji*, Beijing, 1957, p. 300.

77 'Yijiueryi nian', p. 195.

78 Zheng Chaolin, *Oppositionist*, p. 85.

79 M.A. Levine, *The Found Generation*, Seattle, 1993, p. 50, p. 143.

80 Zheng Chaolin, *Oppositionist*, p. 69, p. 19, p. 71. A *xiucai* was the holder of a county-level degree in the imperial order.

81 *Zhongguo gonchandang tong zhi*, vol. 1, p. 627.

82 *Zhongguo gongren yundong shiliao*, 3, 1980, p. 142.

83 Zheng Chaolin, *Oppositionist*, p. 76. This was considerably less than Soviet officials in China were paid, although their salaries were determined according to the scale pertaining in the Soviet Union. In 1926 Hassis, Soviet Vice-Consul in Canton, was paid US$ 178.75 per month. Jay Calvin Houston archive, Box No.1.

84 In 1924 workers earned $15 a month on average, although groups such as rickshaw pullers might earn as little as $8. *China Year Book, 1924–25*, (ed.) H.G.W. Woodhead, Tientsin, 1925, p. 546.

85 Saich, *Origins*, vol. 2, pp. 572–77. Chinese original in ZGZYWJXJ, vol. 1, pp. 167–173.

86 VKP(b), pp. 169–70.

87 VKP(b), p. 159. The projected budget for the Russian Communist Party and Komsomol for the period January to September 1922 was 17.4 million gold rubles. R. Pipes (ed.), *The Unknown Lenin: From the Secret Archive*, New Haven, 1996, p. 142.

88 Saich, *Origins*, vol. 1, p. 191.

89 VKP(b), p. 239 p. 285, p. 478.

90 Saich, *Origins*, vol. 2, p. 611.

91 ZGZYWJXJ, vol. 1, p. 190.

92 ZGZYWJXJ, vol. 1, p. 257.

93 Wen-hsin Yeh, *Provincial Passages*, Berkeley, 1996, p. 245.

94 Wang Kewen. 'The Kuomintang in Transition: Ideology and Factionalism in the 'National Revolution', 1924–32, Ph.D., Stanford University, 1985, p. 13.

95 VKP(b), pp. 339–40; p. 358.

96 C.M. Wilbur and J. Lien-ying How, *Missionaries of Revolution*, Cambridge, Mass., 1989, p. 94. The source used by Wilbur claimed that after recent intensive recruitment, there were 23,360 registered GMD members in China as a whole and 4600 abroad. But the report of the provisional central executive committee gives a national membership of only 11,000. See 'Guomindang yida dangwu baogao xuanze', *Geming shi ziliao*, 2, 1986, p. 28.

97 VKP(b), p. 347; R.K. Schoppa, *Blood Road*, Berkeley, 1995, p. 151; Shao Lizi, 'Dang chengli qianhou de yixie qingkuang', *Gongchanzhuyi xiaozu*, vol. 1, Beijing, 1987, pp. 189.

98 *Xiandai shiliao*, vol. 1, Shanghai, 1934, p. 91. Stuart Schram takes a less sensational view, suggesting that Mao was recuperating from exhaustion at the time of the Fourth Congress. S.R. Schram (ed.), *Mao's Road to Power: Revolutionary Writings, 1912–1949*, vol. 2, Armonk, NY, 1994, p. xxxix.

99 Tang Chunliang, *Li Lisan zhuan*, Heilongjiang, 1984, p. 40; Xiandai shiliao, vol. 1, p. 91; Wang Jianying, *Zhongguo gongchandang*, p. 29. Wang Yizhi was born in 1901 in Zhijiang, Hunan province, into a scholar-official family. She attended the Second Provincial Girls' Normal School in Taoyuan and, upon graduation, taught briefly at the school founded by Xiang Jingyu in Xupu. Moving to Shanghai at the same time as Ding Ling, she enrolled at the Common People's Women's School. She had recently married Shi Cuntong, and become the first woman to be formally admitted into the Shanghai party organization. C.K. Gilmartin, *Engendering the Chinese Revolution*, Berkeley, 1995, p. 230.

100 VKP(b), p. 483.

101 *Zhongguo guomindang dierci quanguo daibiao dahui geshengqu dangwu baogao mulu*, Shanghai, 1926, p. 136; Chen Gongbo, *Guomin geming de weiji he women de cuowu*, 1928, pp. 56–75.

102 Yeh, *Provincial Passages*, p. 246, p. 250.

103 Yeh, *Provincial Passages*, pp. 249–50; ZGZYWJXJ, vol. 1, p. 257.

104 Yeh, *Provincial Passages*, p. 246; *Geming shi ziliao*, 2, 1986, p. 29; *Zhongguo gongren yundong shiliao*, 3, 1980, p. 59.

105 Yeh, *Provincial Passages*, p. 248–9; ZGZYWJXJ, vol. 1, p. 257.

106 *Zhongguo gongren yundong shiliao*, 3, 1980, p. 60; Wang Jianying, *Zhongguo gongchandang*, p. 29.

107 Shen Yixing, Jiang Peinan and Zheng Qingsheng, *Shanghai gongren yundong shi*, vol. 1, Liaoning, 1991, p. 175.

108 C.M. Wilbur, *The Nationalist Revolution in China, 1923–1928*, Cambridge, 1984, p. 18; J. Kong-cheong Leung, 'The Chinese Work-Study Movement: the Social and Political Experience of Chinese Students and Student-Workers in France, 1913–25', Ph.D., Brown University, 1982, p. 565.

109 Sha Jiansun (ed.), *Zhongguo gongchandang tongshi*, vol. 2, p. 229.
110 VKP(b), p. 483.
111 In his illuminating study of Shen Xuanlu, for example, Keith Schoppa has revealed how Shen's personal connections shaped factions at national as well as provincial level. Schoppa, *Blood Road*.
112 A. Dirlik, 'Mass Movements and the Left Kuomintang', *Modern China*, vol. 1, no. 1, January 1975, p. 48, p. 56; N.L. Mamaeva, *Gomin'dan v natsional'no-revoliutsionnom dvizhenii Kitaia, 1923–27*, Moscow, Nauka, 1991, p. 60.
113 J. Domes, *Vertagte Revolution: Die Politik der Kuomintang in China, 1923–7*, Berlin, 1969, pp. 250–9.
114 Xianqu, 23, 15 July 1923, p. 1.
115 Wilbur, *Missionaries*, p. 138.
116 *Zhongguo gongchandang Shanghai shi*, p. 28.
117 Xianqu, 23, 15 July 1923, p. 1.
118 *Shanghai xuesheng yundong shi*, Shanghai, 1995, p. 78.
119 VKP(b), pp. 231–5.
120 *Zhongguo gongchandang tong zhi*, vol. 3, p. 2524, p. 2546, p. 2660.
121 Zheng Chaolin, *Oppositionist*, p. 49. See the second photograph in Zhang Xuexin (ed.), *Ren Bishi*.
122 Zheng Chaolin, 'Chen Duxiu and the Trotskyists', p. 125, p. 132; *Zhongguo gongchandang renming da cidian*, Beijing, 1991, p. 164; Zhang Xuexin (ed.), *Ren Bishi*, p. 60.
123 Jiang Zhichan, 'Dageming shiqi de Shanghai xuelian', *Diyici guogong hezuo shiqi de Gongqingtuan zhuanti lun wenji*, Beijing, 1985, pp. 96–7.
124 *Shanghai xuesheng yundong shi*, p. 79; 'Yang Zhihua de huiyi', *'Yida' qianhou*, vol. 2, Beijing, 1980, p. 29.
125 *Shanghai xuesheng yundong shi*, p. 83; Wang Jiagui, Cai Xiyao, *Shanghai daxue, Yijiuerer – yijiuerqi nian*, Shanghai, 1986, p. 25.
126 *Shanghai xuesheng yundong shi*, pp. 83–4.
127 Wilbur, *Missionaries*, p. 475; VKP(b), p. 510.
128 Wang Jiagui, *Shanghai daxue*, pp. 22–24. Ka-Che Yip, *Religion, Nationalism and Chinese Students: the Anti-Christian Movement of 1922–27*, Bellingham, 1980, p. 40.
129 NCH, 17 Jan. 1925, p. 102; Jiang Zhichan, 'Dageming shiqi', pp. 109–10; *Shanghai xuesheng yundong shi*, pp. 86–7.
130 Jeffrey Wasserstrom shows how Shanghai University students supplanted Fudan as the 'core group' of protesters by 1924. J.N. Wasserstrom, *Student Protests in Twentieth-Century China*, Stanford, 1991, pp. 46–50.
131 Wang Jiagui, *Shanghai daxue*, pp. 1–4; Yeh, *Provincial Passages*, p. 238.
132 *Wusa yundong shiliao*, vol. 1, Shanghai, 1981, p. 260. (WSYDSL).
133 Huang Meizhen, Zhang Yun, Shi Yuanhua, 'Shanghai daxue – suo xinying de geming xuexiao', *Dangshi ziliao congkan*, 2, 1980, p. 154, p. 159.
134 Chen Wangdao, 'Dang chengli shiqi de yixie qingkuang', *Dangshi ziliao congkan*, 1, 1980, p. 27.
135 Cheng Yongyan, 'Huiyi Shanghai daxue', *Dangshi ziliao congkan*, 2, 1980, p. 80; Zheng Chaolin, *Huai jiu ji*, pp. 13–14.
136 Wang Jiagui, *Shanghai daxue*, p. 17. Among the students in the middle school that was attached to the university were 12 females and 86 males in October 1925. Huang Meizhen, Shi Yuanhua, Zhang Yun, *Shanghai daxue shiliao*, Shanghai, 1984, p. 85.
137 Chen Wangdao, 'Dang shengli shiqi', p. 27; Zheng, *Oppositionist*, pp. 92–3.
138 WSYDSL, vol. 1, p. 261, pp. 266–9.

139 Yao Tianyu, 'Peiyang geming ganbu de honglu – Shanghai daxue', *Dangshi ziliao congkan*, 2, 1980, pp. 72–9.
140 Shanghai Municipal Police, 'History of the Communist Movement in Shanghai', 1933. SMPF, D files, 4825.
141 ZGZYWJXJ, vol. 1, pp. 154–5. Although the Communists paid special attention to working-class women, Xiang Jingyu was less adept than Yang Zhihua at relating to working-class women, not least because of her Hunanese accent.
142 'Yijiueryi nian', p. 193.
143 Yang Zilie *Zhang Guotao furen huiyilu*, Hong Kong, 1970, p. 127.
144 Gilmartin, *Engendering*, pp. 87–8.
145 Minguo ribao, 22 Dec. 1924.
146 *Zhongguo funü yundong lishi ziliao, 1921–1927*, Beijing, 1986, p. 423.
147 Shenbao, 1 Mar. 1925; 2 Mar. 1925; Dai Xugong. *Xiang Jingyu zhuan*, Beijing, 1981, p. 108.
148 *Zhongguo funü yundong*, pp. 440–1.
149 *Zhongguo funü yundong*, p. 449.
150 Saich, *Origins*, vol. 2, p. 575.
151 ZGZYWJXJ, vol. 1, p. 258. Part of this report is translated in T. Saich (ed.) *The Rise to Power of the Chinese Communist Party: Documents and Analysis*, Armonk, NY, 1996, pp. 126–9.
152 *Diyici guonei geming zhanzheng shiqi de gongren yundong*, Beijing, 1954, p. 11.
153 *Papers Respecting Labour Conditions in China* No.1, London, 1925, p. 105.
154 *Shanghai gongren yundong shi*, Shanghai, 1935, p. 44; Ma Chaojun, *Zhongguo laogong yundong shi*, Chongqing, 1942, pp. 98–9.
155 *Wusa yundong*, vol. 2, Shanghai, 1991, p. 471 (Hence: WSYD); WSYD, vol. 1, Shanghai, 1991, p. 86.
156 ZGZYWJXJ, vol. 1, p. 260.
157 Deng Zhongxia, *Zhongguo zhigong yundong jianshi*, Beijing, 1957 (orig. 1930), p. 120.
158 Ma Chaojun, *Zhongguo laogong yundong shi*, Taibei, 1958, p. 356.
159 Shi Bing, 'Deng Zhongxia', *Zhongguo gongren yundong de xianfeng*, vol. 2, Beijing 1983, pp. 1–52. Kwan, *Marxist Intellectuals*, pp. 9–28.
160 Yao Tianyu, 'Peiyang geming', pp. 72–79.
161 WSYDSL, vol. 1, pp. 270–1.
162 WSYDSL, vol. 1, pp. 272–3; ZGZYWX, I, p. 260; Wang Jiagui, Shanghai daxue, pp. 20–21.
163 A.I. Kartunova, *Politika kompartii Kitaia v rabochem voprose nakanune revoliutsii, 1925–27gg.*, Moscow, 1983, p. 110. p. 123.
164 WSYDSL, vol. 1, p. 274.
165 WSYDSL, vol. 1, p. 276.
166 *Xiandai shiliao*, vol. 1, p. 298.
167 See the resolution passed by the Second National Labour Congress in May 1925. *Zhongguo lici laodong dahui wenxian*, Beijing, 1957, pp. 24–5.
168 Dai Xugong, *Xiang Jingyu*, pp. 98–9.
169 Tang Chunliang, *Li Lisan*, p. 25.
170 Kartunova, *Politika kompartii*, pp. 122–3; VKP(b), vol. 1, p. 508. Later the *Guide Weekly* claimed a print-run of 9000.
171 This is Wilbur's phrase and is not used in any of the Third Congress resolutions, although it may not be an illegitimate inference to draw. See Wilbur, *Missionaries*, pp. 83–4; ZGZYWJXJ, vol. 1, pp. 146–48.
172 ZGZYWJXJ, vol. 1, p. 232.

Chapter 4

1 ZGZYWJXJ, vol. 1, p. 342.
2 ZGZYWJXJ, vol. 1, p. 346.
3 ZGZYWJXJ, vol. 1, p. 347.
4 ZGZYWJXJ, vol. 1, p. 347.
5 ZGZYWJXJ, vol. 1, p. 235.
6 ZGZYWJXJ, vol. 1, pp. 350–51.
7 ZGZYWJXJ, vol. 1, p. 352.
8 WSYDSL, vol. 1, Shanghai, 1981, pp. 281–6, p. 290. As Perry Link points in respect of comic 'face and voice' routines (*xiangsheng*), as popular and entertaining oral forms, these were ideal vehicles for communicating new ideas. P. Link, 'The Genie and the Lamp: Revolutionary Xiangsheng' in B.S. McDougall, (ed.), *Popular Chinese Literature and Performing Arts in the People's Republic of China, 1949–1979*, Berkeley, pp. 83–111.
9 WSYDSL, vol. 1, pp. 294–5.
10 WSYDSL, vol. 1, p. 276.
11 WSYDSL, vol. 1, pp. 276–80.
12 WSYDSL, vol. 1, 277–8.
13 *Shanghai gongyun zhi*, Shanghai, 1997, p. 771.
14 Xu Haojiong, 'Liu Hua', *Zhongguo gongren yundong de xianqu*, vol. 1, Beijing, 1983, pp. 71–100.
15 WSYDSL, vol. 1, p. 289.
16 Shen Yixing, Jiang Peinan and Zheng Qingsheng, *Shanghai gongren yundong shi*, vol. 1, Liaoning, 1991, p. 183.
17 WSYDSL, vol. 1, p. 374.
18 WSYD, vol. 1, p. 7; VKP(b), p. 537; SMPF, IO 6023.
19 *Shanghai fangzhi gongren yundong shi*, Beijing, 1991, p. 91.
20 Shen Yixing, *Shanghai gongren*, p. 182; WSYDSL, vol. 1, pp. 277–8, p. 291; Zhang Quan, 'Guangyu Huxi gongyou julebu', *Dangshi ziliao congkan*, 3 (4), 1980, p. 121.
21 Wang Jianying, (ed.), *Zhongguo gongchandang zuzhishi ziliao huibian*, Beijing, 1982, p. 30.
22 WSYDSL, vol. 1, p. 298; *Shanghai fangzhi gongren*, p. 93.
23 WSYDSL, vol. 1, p. 298.
24 SMPF, IO 6023. E. Honig, 'The Politics of Prejudice: Subei People in Republican-Era Shanghai', *Modern China*, vol. 15, no. 3, 1989, p. 252.
25 Shen Yixing, *Shanghai gongren*, p. 184.
26 Jacobs collection, Hoover Institution Archives, box 2; NCH, 21 Mar. 1925, p. 496; Deng Zhongxia, *Zhongguo zhigong yundong jianshi*, Beijing, 1957, pp. 136–7.
27 WSYDSL, vol. 1, p. 298.
28 Ke Lao, *Yijiuerwu nian Shanghai rishang shachang gongren bagong zhi neimu ji shi-mo ji*, Shanghai, 1926, p. 11.
29 WSYDSL, vol. 1, pp. 306–8.
30 WSYD, vol. 2, p. 25.
31 NCH, 21 Feb. 1925, p. 302. Ono Kazuko, *Chinese Women in a Century of Revolution, 1850–1950*, Stanford, 1989, p. 131.
32 NCH, 21 Mar. 1925, p. 496.
33 SMPF, IO 6023.
34 WSYD vol. 2, pp. 16–17; Deng Zhongxia, *Zhongguo zhigong yundong*, p. 134.

35 Chang Kuo-t'ao, *The Rise of the Communist Party, 1921–27*, Lawrence, 1971, p. 408.
36 Zheng Chaolin. *An Oppositionist for Life. Memoirs of the Chinese Revolutionary, Zheng Chaolin*, Atlantic Highlands, N.J., 1997, pp. 84–5.
37 Tang Chunliang, *Li Lisan zhuan*, Heilongjiang, 1984; Zheng Chaolin, *Oppositionist*, p. 70. Sailing back to China after his expulsion from France, Li lost a game of chess, whereupon he hurled the chess set overboard in a fit of rage. M.A. Levine, *The Found Generation*, Seattle, 1993, p. 129.
38 Chen Yutang (ed.), *Zhonggong dang shi renwu bieming lu*, Beijing, 1985, p. 118; *Zhongguo gongchandang renming dacidian*, Beijing, 1991, p. 568.
39 E.J. Perry, *Shanghai on Strike*, Stanford, 1993, p. 149; Jiang Guangci, 'Duanku dang', *Shiwen xuanji*, Beijing, 1957, p. 60; Wang Jiagui, Cai Xiyao, *Shanghai daxue*, Shanghai, 1986, p. 96; Liu Guanzhi, 'Guanyu 1924–1925 nian Shanghai gongren yundong de huiyu', *Zhongguo gongren yundong shiliao*, 1, 1960, p. 37.
40 WSYD, vol. 1, p. 6.
41 NCH, 21 Feb. 1925, p. 291.
42 WSYD, vol. 2, p. 47, p. 83. Dai seems to have joined the CCP during the May Thirtieth Movement. He was also known as Dai Qiji, and in secondary sources is described as a worker at NWK No.5. See *Shanghai fangzhi gongren*, p. 87.
43 SMPF, IO 6023.
44 SMPF, IO 6023.
45 SMPF, IO 6023.
46 WSYDSL, vol. 1, pp. 321–2.
47 WSYDSL, vol. 1, pp. 321–2.
48 NCH, 21 Mar. 1925, p. 496.
49 *Wusa yundong, shiliao*, vol. 1, p. 308–9; SMPF, IO 6023.
50 WSYDSL, vol. 1, p. 322.
51 WSYD, vol. 2, p. 17.
52 Ke Lao, *Yijiuerwu nian*, pp. 55–6; WSYD, vol. 1, p. 5.
53 Deng Zhongxia, *Zhongguo zhigong yundong*, p. 137. Having become embroiled in the war between Zhejiang and Jiangsu militarists in September 1924, Shanghai was taken by Sun Chuanfang's Jiangsu army in October. However, the overthrow of president Cao Kun on 2 November by Fengtian forces and the installation of Duan Qirui had destabilizing consequences for Shanghai. At the time of the February mill strikes the city was under the control of Fengtian troops. See A. Waldron, *From War to Nationalism: China's Turning Point, 1924–1925*, Cambridge, 1995.
54 NCH, 21 Feb. 1925, p. 293.
55 WSYDSL, p. 320; NCH 21 Mar. 1925, p. 496.
56 WSYD, vol. 2, p. 31.
57 J. Chesneaux, *The Chinese Labor Movement, 1919–1927*, Stanford, 1968, p. 255; SMPF, IO 6023.
58 SMPF, IO 6023.
59 WSYD, vol. 1, p. 4.
60 WSYD, vol. 2, p. 7.
61 WSYD, vol. 2, p. 12, p. 17. p. 19.
62 SMPF, IO 6023; WSYD, vol. 2, p. 17.
63 Chang Kuo-t'ao, *Rise*, p. 414.
64 WSYDSL, vol. 1, pp. 305–6.
65 Deng Zhongxia, *Zhongguo zhigong yundong*, p. 138; WSYDSL, vol. 1, p. 301.
66 Shenbao, 20 Feb. 1925.
67 Zhongguo gongren, 4, Apr. 1925, p. 56; WSYDSL, vol. 1, pp. 392–6; NCH, 21 Feb. 1925, p. 302.

68 Deng Zhongxia, *Zhongguo zhigong yundong*, p. 139; WSYDSL, vol. 1, pp. 326–7, 374–5.
69 Shenbao, 24 Feb. 1925, p. 14; VKP(b), p. 537.
70 SMPF, IO 6023.
71 WSYDSL, vol. 1, p. 328, p. 375; NCH, 21 Feb. 1925, p. 303; Ke Lao, *Yijiuerwu nian*, pp. 123–30.
72 Shenbao, 25 Feb. 1925.
73 Shenbao, 27 Feb. 1925.
74 Xu Dingxin and Qian Xiaoming, *Shanghai zongshanghui, 1902–1929*, Shanghai, 1991, pp. 327–8; WSYSL, vol. 1, pp. 439–44.
75 WSYDSL, vol. 1, p. 341, p. 343; Ma Chaojun, *Zhongguo laogong yundong shi*, Taibei, 1958, pp. 342–43.
76 Minguo ribao, 27 Feb. 1925; *Diyici Zhongguo laodong nianjian*, part 1, Beijing, 1928, p. 284.
77 NCH, 21 Mar. 1925, p. 496.
78 A 1997 publication states 'On 1 March the strike ended in victory'. See *Zhongguo gongchandang tong zhi*, vol. 3, Beijing, 1997, p. 2347.
79 *Shanghai gongren yundong shi*, Shanghai, 1935, p. 49.
80 Zhongguo gongren, 4, Apr. 1925, p. 53.
81 NCH, 21 Mar. 1925, p. 496.
82 Shen Yixing, *Shanghai gongren*, p. 193.
83 Zhongguo gongren, 4, Apr. 1925, p. 52.
84 WSYD, vol. 2, p. 35.
85 WSYDSL, vol. 1, p. 335; Shi Bing, 'Deng Zhongxia', p. 59.
86 WSYDSL, vol. 1, p. 567; ZGGCDSH, p. 25.
87 NCH, 5 Dec. 1925, p. 435; Liu Guanzhi, 'Guanyu 1924–1925 nian', p. 37.
88 Liu Guanzhi, 'Guanyu 1924–1925 nian', p. 55; NCH, 14 Mar. 1925, p. 437.
89 *Shanghai lieshi xiaozhuan*, Shanghai, 1983, pp. 15–16; Perry, *Shanghai on Strike*, p. 78; C. Cadart and Cheng Yingxiang, *Mémoires de Peng Shuzhi*, Paris, 1983, pp. 418–19.
90 Deng Zhongxia, *Zhongguo zhigong yundong*, p. 141.
91 VKP(b), pp. 536–7.
92 WSYD, vol. 1, p. 7.
93 WSYD, vol. 2, p. 47.
94 Jacobs coll. box 2; *Shanghai fangzhi gongren*, p. 103.
95 WSYDSL, vol. 1, p. 452; SMPF, IO 6023. I was unable to find confirmation of this in Shenbao, 2 Mar. 1925.
96 Deng Zhongxia, *Zhongguo zhigong yundong*, p. 142; WSYDSL, vol. 1, p. 542.
97 WSYD, vol. 2, pp. 74–5.
98 WSYDSL, vol. 1, pp. 553–5.
99 WSYDSL, vol. 1, p. 560. Shenbao reported that twelve workers were wounded. Shenbao, 16 May 1925.
100 ZGDSRWZ, vol. 9, Xi'an, 1983, p. 115; Ma Chaojun, *Zhongguo laogong yundong*, p. 376; Ke Lao, *Yijiuerwu nian*, p. 18.
101 ZGZYWJXJ, vol. 1, pp. 415–8.
102 WSYDSL, vol. 1, pp. 572–3; Minguo ribao, 26 May 1925; NCH, 30 May 1925, p. 374.
103 *Zhongguo gongchandang Shanghai shi*, pp. 23–25. Note that the Fourth Congress replaced party cells with branches (*zhibu*), specifying that any group of three or more Communists should form a branch.
104 'Yijiueryi nian zhi yijiuerqi nian Shanghai, Jiangsu, Zhejiang dang zuzhi fazhan gaikuang', *Zhonggongdang shi ziliao*, 10, 1984, pp. 198–200.

105 Zhao Pu, 'Zhongguo gongchandang zuzhi shi ziliao', *Dangshi yanjiu*, 4, 1982, pp. 30–31.

106 VKP(b), p. 538.

107 VKP(b), p. 538.

108 C.M. Wilbur and J. Lien-ying How, *Missionaries of Revolution*, Cambridge, 1989, p. 140.

109 ZGZYWJXJ, vol. 1, pp. 412–4.

110 'Yijiueryi nian', p. 197.

111 WSYDSL, vol. 1, p. 613.

112 NCH, 23 May 1925, p. 327; 30 May 1925, p. 374; *Xiandai shiliao*, vol. 1, Shanghai, 1934, p. 308; Xiangdao, 117, 6 Jun 1925, p. 1082.

113 WSYDSL, vol. 1, p. 614.

114 WSYDSL, vol. 1, p. 633; *China Year Book, 1926–27* (ed.) H.G.W. Woodhead, Tientsin, 1927, p. 920.

115 WSYDSL, vol. 1, 1991, p. 9; R.W. Rigby, *The May 30 Movement*, Canberra, 1980, p. 31.

116 WSYDSL, vol. 1, p. 93; H.J. van de Ven, *From Friend to Comrade*, Berkeley, 1991, p. 152.

117 *Shanghai xuesheng yundong shi*, Shanghai, 1995, pp. 75–6; Shanghai Municipal Police, 'History of the Communist Movement in Shanghai', 1933. SMPF, D files, 4825.

118 WSYDSL, vol. 1, p. 9, p. 11; *Xiandai shiliao*, vol. 1, p. 308.

119 *Xiandai shiliao*, vol. 1, p. 308.

Chapter 5

1 R.W. Rigby *The May 30 Movement*, Canberra, 1980, pp. 35–6. For a stimulating account of student protest in 1925 as political theatre see J.N. Wasserstrom, *Student Protests in Twentieth-Century China: the View from Shanghai*, Stanford, 1991, ch.4.

2 *China Year Book, 1926–27* (ed.) H.G.W. Woodhead, Tientsin, 1927, pp. 950–1.

3 Ma Chaojun, *Zhongguo laogong yundong shi*, Taibei, 1958, p. 377–8; Zhang Jungu, *Du Yuesheng zhuan*, vol. 1, Taibei, 1980, vol. 1, p. 256.

4 Rigby, *May 30*, p. 37.

5 N.R. Clifford, *Shanghai 1925: Urban Nationalism and the Defense of Foreign Privilege*, Michigan Papers in Chinese Studies, no. 37, 1979, p. 19.

6 Chang Kuo-t'ao, *The Rise of the Communist Party, 1921–27*, Lawrence, 1971, p. 427.

7 H.J. Van de Ven, *From Friend to Comrade*, Berkeley, 1991, p. 153.

8 On 2 May the Communists had called together representatives from 24 labour unions, including the seamen's union, the tramworkers' union, the printers union and more than a dozen mill unions, to discuss the formation of a federation of labour unions in Shanghai. On 18 May over 100 delegates met in Zhabei to found a GLU, electing Li Lisan chair and Chen Xinglin, president of the Shanghai seamen's union, vice-chair. It was agreed that the GLU should remain secret for the time being. Shen Yixing, Jiang Peinan and Zheng Qingsheng, *Shanghai gongren yundong shi*, vol. 1, Liaoning, 1991, p. 225.

9 Minguo ribao, 16 Jun 1925. Liu Shaoqi, who had been elected vice-chair of the National General Labour Union at the Second National Labour Congress in May, rushed to Shanghai from Qingdao on hearing of the May Thirtieth Incident. See Huang Zulin, *Liu Shaoqi qingshao nian shidai*, Beijing, 1991, p. 14.

10 Rigby, *May 30*, p. 39.

11 Rexue ribao, 1, 4 Jun 1925.
12 NCH, 6 Jun 1925, p. 414; Rigby, *May 30*, p. 38.
13 NCH, 6 Jun 1925, p. 414; Rigby, *May 30*, p. 39 says that the last demand was soon dropped.
14 J. Domes, *Vertagte Revolution: Die Politik der Kuomintang in China, 1923–7*, Berlin, 1969, p. 125.
15 WSYDSL, vol. 2, Shanghai, 1986, p. 274.
16 WSYDSL, vol. 2, p. 275.
17 WSYDSL, vol. 2, p. 929. Yu Xiaqing was the most politically influential businessman in Shanghai. Born in poverty in 1867 in Zhenhai in Zhejiang, he came to Shanghai when he was 15. Starting out as an apprentice in a dye shop, he rose to become a compradore for various foreign companies and banks before founding the Sanbei shipping company in 1914. Wang Renze, 'Shanghai zhuming qiyejia – Yu Xiaqing', Xiong Shanghou (ed.), *Minguo zhuming renwu zhuan*, vol. 3, Beijing, 1997, 516–37.
18 WSYD, vol. 2, p. 148.
19 WSYDSL, vol. 2, p. 923.
20 WSYDSL, vol. 2, pp. 278–80.
21 Clifford, 'Shanghai 1925', p. 27.
22 Domes, *Vertagte Revolution*, p. 126.
23 WSYDSL, vol. 2, pp. 923–5; Rigby, *May 30*, p. 43.
24 WSYD, vol. 2, pp. 175–77.
25 WSYDSL, vol. 2, pp. 290–7.
26 'Yijiueryi nian zhi yijiuerqi nian Shanghai, Jiangsu, Zhejiang dang zuzhi fazhan gaikuang', *Zhonggongdang shi ziliao*, 10, 1984, p. 215.
27 Wang Jiagui, Cai Xiyao, *Shanghai daxue, Yijiuerer – yijiuerqi nian*, Shanghai, 1986, p. 61.
28 WSYDSL, vol. 2, p. 928.
29 WSYDSL, vol. 2, p. 935; *Shanghai xuesheng yundong dashi, 1919.5 – 1949*, Shanghai, 1985, p. 79.
30 WSYDSL, vol. 2, p. 936.
31 WSYDSL, vol. 2, p. 968.
32 WSYDSL, vol. 2, pp. 70–83.
33 WSYDSL, vol. 2, pp. 65–7.
34 WSYD, vol. 2, p. 164.
35 WSYD, vol. 2, p. 269.
36 WSYD, vol. 2, p. 287. The police said that 93 workers were kidnapped in the course of the strike in the International Settlement. 'These self-appointed tribunals imposed fines in some cases and in others forced the victims to sign bonds.' *China Press*, 20 Aug. 1925.
37 WSYD, vol. 2, p. 302, p. 308.
38 VKP(b), p. 498.
39 VKP(b), p. 499.
40 NCH, 22 Aug. 1925, p. 218.
41 WSYDSL, vol. 2, p. 578. Since the fractional denominations of the dollar contained a smaller proportion of pure silver, they tended to lose value and were known as 'small money' (*xiaoyang*). Full dollar denominations were known as 'big money' (*dayang*).
42 WSYD, vol. 2, p. 365.
43 NCH, 22 Aug. 1925, p. 218; WSYDSL, vol. 2, p. 555; N.R. Clifford, *Spoilt Children of Empire: Westerners in Shanghai and the Chinese Revolution of the 1920s*, Vermont, 1991, p. 134.

44 WSYDSL, vol. 2, p. 970.
45 WSYDSL, vol. 2, p. 578, pp. 410–11.
46 Gongren zhi lu, 45, 8 Aug. 1925.
47 WSYDSL, vol. 2, p. 973.
48 VKP(b), p. 573, p. 575, p. 587. The Russian title of this organization is more accurately translated as International Organization for Assistance to Revolutionaries; but I have used its English appellation. It was set up by the Fourth Congress of the Comintern in 1923. See E.H. Carr, *The Bolshevik Revolution*, vol. 3, London, 1953, p. 402.
49 Houston archive, Hoover Institution Archives, Box No.1, 28.
50 VKP(b), p. 591.
51 PRO FO 228/3291 'Shanghai Intelligence Report for Quarter Ended Sep. 1925'; WSYDSL, vol. 2, p. 424; Gongren zhi lu, 18, 12 Jul 1925, p. 3.
52 NCH, 25 Jul 1925, p. 52; Rigby, *May 30*, pp. 54–5.
53 WSYDSL, vol. 2, pp. 431–2.
54 NCH, 1 Aug. 1925, p. 81; 15 Aug. 1925, p. 166.
55 Clifford, 'Shanghai 1925', p. 48.
56 VKP(b), p. 582.
57 Xiangdao, 125, 18 Aug. 1925.
58 WSYDSL, vol. 2, p. 971.
59 Minguo ribao, 12 Aug. 1925.
60 *Zhongguo gongren yundong shiliao*, 3, 1981, p. 3, p. 10.
61 Cited in V.I. Glunin, 'Grigorii Voitinskii, 1893–1953', *Vidnye Sovetskie Kommunisty*, Moscow, 1970, pp. 83–4.
62 WSYDSL, vol. 2, pp. 640–1.
63 WSYDSL, vol. 2, pp. 641–3; NCH, 15 Aug. 1925, p. 167.
64 NCH, 22 Aug. 1925, p. 207; Ma Chaojun, *Zhongguo laogong yundong*, p. 426.
65 Minguo ribao, 22 Aug. 1925.
66 Shenbao, 6 Aug. 1925, p. 13. This figure is probably too high, since the figures for membership in individual factories are sometimes higher than the number of workers employed there.
67 Shen Yixing, *Shanghai gongren*, p. 225.
68 WSYDSL, vol. 2, pp. 94–5.
69 WSYDSL, vol. 2, p. 336.
70 *Jiangnan zaochuanchang changshi, 1865–1949.5*, Shanghai, 1983, p. 171.
71 *Shanghai fangzhi gongren yundong shi*, Beijing, 1991, p. 115. 'Zhang Weizhen tan Hunan zaoqi gongyun', *Danshi yanjiu ziliao*, 1, 1980, 236–41.
72 Gongren zhi lu, 88, 20 Sep. 1925, p. 4.
73 Gongren zhi lu, 88, 20 Sep. 1925, p. 4.
74 WSYDSL, vol. 2, pp. 8–9; Ibid, 9–11.
75 *Zhongguo gongchandang renming da cidian*, Beijing, 1991, pp. 760–1; ZGGCDSH, p. 38.
76 Huang Meizhen, 'Wang Shouhua zhuanlüe', *Jindai shi yanjiu*, 1, 1983, 62 4; Chen Qiyin, 'Wusa yundong pianduan', *Dangshi ziliao congkan*, 2, 1980, pp. 89–90.
77 Zheng Chaolin. *An Oppositionist for Life*, Atlantic Highlands, N.J., 1997, p. 90.
78 Liu Guanzhi, 'Guanyu 1924–1925 nian Shanghai gongren yundong de huiyu', *Zhongguo gongren yundong shiliao*, 1, 1960, p. 66; WSYDSL, vol. 2, p. 975.
79 Tang Hai, *Zhongguo laodong wenti*, Shanghai, 1926, pp. 511–20.
80 Chang Chufang, 'Chinese Cotton Mills in Shanghai', *Chinese Economic Journal*, vol. 3, no. 5, 1928, p. 907.
81 Chang Chufang, 'Chinese Cotton', p. 922.

82 *Diyici guonei geming zhanzheng shiqi de gongren yundong*, Beijing, 1954, p. 52.
83 WSYDSL, vol. 2 p. 112.
84 WSYD, vol. 2, p. 144.
85 WSYDSL, vol. 2, p. 113.
86 Jacobs collection, Hoover Institution Archives, box 2.
87 WSYD, vol. 2, p. 174.
88 WSYDSL, vol. 2, pp. 435–6, p. 697.
89 WSYDSL, vol. 2, pp. 438–9.
90 Elizabeth Perry first pointed to the role of gangsters in the May Thirtieth Movement. E.J. Perry, *Shanghai on Strike*, Stanford, 1993, pp. 81–84.
91 Shen Yixing, *Shanghai gongren*, p. 232.
92 Minguo ribao, 6 Sep. 1925.
93 WSYDSL, vol. 2, pp. 437–8.
94 WSYDSL, vol. 2, pp. 437–8.
95 WSYDSL, vol. 2, pp. 441.
96 WSYD, vol. 2, p. 433.
97 Shenbao, 27 Aug. 1925; Gongren zhi lu, 71, 3 Sep. 25, p. 4; NCH, 29 Aug. 1925, p. 249. The International Settlement police daily report states that Wang Agen, a gang leader among the dockers, led the attack. WSYD, vol. 2, p. 427.
98 Xiangdao, 131, 25 Sep. 25, p. 1199.
99 Shenbao, 27 Aug. 1925.
100 NCH, 29 Aug. 1925, p. 249.
101 NCH, 29 Aug. 1925, p. 244.
102 WSYDSL, vol. 1, p. 440; Deng Zhongxia, *Zhongguo zhigong yundong jianshi*, Beijing, 1957, p. 137.
103 WSYDSL, vol. 1, p. 365.
104 WSYDSL 1991, vol. 2, p. 155.
105 'Zhang Weizhen tongzhi tan Shanghai "Wusa yundong"' in *Dangshi yanjiu ziliao*, 1, 1980, p. 307; Van de Ven, *Friend*, p. 154.
106 Tang Chunliang, *Li Lisan zhuan*, Heilongjiang, 1984, p. 52.
107 WSYD, vol. 2, p. 369.
108 WSYD, vol. 2, p. 155.
109 WSYDSL, vol. 2, p. 438.
110 WSYD, vol. 1, p. 215. In a scathing report of May 1926, the labour department of the CEC of the CCP criticised the GLU for failing to appreciate the consequences of the fact that many union leaders were not only members, but 'staff' (*zhiyuan*) of the secret societies. *Zhongguo gongren yundong shiliao*, 3, 1981, pp. 4–5.
111 WSYD, vol. 2, p. 283.
112 'Zhang Weizhen tongzhi tan Shanghai', p. 308.
113 WSYD, vol. 2, p. 431.
114 WSYD, vol. 1, p. 227.
115 WSYDSL, vol. 1, p. 365.
116 Deng Zhongxia, *Zhongguo zhigong yundong*, p. 137.
117 Van de Ven, *Friend*, p. 154. One should note, however, that the Communists did assassinate at least one key figure in the Green Gang, Ni Tiansheng, the chief foreman at the Shanghai Electric Construction Company, who was responsible for breaking a strike at the company. For an account by one of the three assassins, a young mechanic at the company, see *Lao gongren hua dangnian* vol. 1, Beijing, 1962. pp. 31–4.
118 *Wusa yundong he Xianggang bagong*, Jiangsu, 1985, p. 174.
119 *Wusa yundong he Xianggang bagong*, pp. 175–6.

120 WSYD, vol. 2, p. 486.
121 WSYDSL, vol. 2, p. 700.
122 Ma Chaojun, *Zhongguo laogong yundong*, 1958, p. 493; NCH, 26 Sep. 1925, p. 421.
123 Minguo ribao, 11 Dec. 1925.
124 Shen Yixing, *Shanghai gongren*, p. 261.
125 NCH, 26 Sep. 1925, pp. 430–1.
126 NCH, 10 Oct. 1925, p. 55; WSYD, vol. 2, p. 387.
127 *Wusa yundong he Xianggang bagong*, p. 215.
128 *Zhongguo gonghui lishi wenxian, 1921–27*, Beijing, 1958, p. 122.
129 *Shanghai di sanshiyi mianfangzhi chang gongren yundong shi*, Beijing, 1991, p. 48.
130 WSYDSL, vol. 2, p. 665.
131 *Strikes and Lockouts in Shanghai since 1918*, Shanghai, 1933, p. 29; NCH, 12 Dec. 1925, p. 480.
132 NCH, 26 Dec. 1925, p. 564; *Zhongguo gongren yundong shiliao*, 2, 1958, p. 108.
133 Shishi xinbao, 4 Nov. 1925, quoted in WSYDSL, vol. 2, p. 685; Gongren zhi lu, 211, 20 Jan. 1926, p. 3.
134 WSYD, vol. 2, p. 486.
135 WSYD, vol. 2, p. 495.
136 *Zhongguo gonghui lishi wenxian, 1921–7*, p. 143.
137 NCH, 24 Oct. 1925, p. 166; 28 Nov. 1925, p. 388.
138 WSYDSL, vol. 2, pp. 719–20; NCH, 7 Nov. 1925, p. 244.
139 PRO FO 228/3291 'Shanghai Intelligence Report for Quarter Ended Dec. 1925'.
140 Shen Yixing, *Shanghai gongren*, pp. 263–4.
141 Xu Haojiong, 'Liu Hua', *Zhongguo gongren yundong de xianqu*, vol. 1, Beijing, 1983, p. 79, p. 89; Shen Yixing, *Shanghai gongren*, p. 262.
142 NCH, 12 Dec. 1925, p. 480; 26 Dec. 1925, p. 575; *Zhongguo gongren yundong shiliao*, 2, 1958, p. 110.
143 NCH, 2 Jan. 1926, p. 15; WSYD, vol. 1, p. 123.
144 NCH, 12 Dec. 1925, p. 480; 19 Dec. 1925, p. 519.
145 *Diyici Zhongguo laodong nianjian*, part 2, Beijing, 1928, p. 20.
146 Shen Yixing, *Shanghai gongren*, p. 273. Although the CCP was, as one would expect, infiltrated by police spies, the Communists in turn had their own spies in all police stations of the International Settlement, so they were often tipped off about police raids. Incidentally, this infiltration was extremely costly – payments to police insiders amounting to 350 dollars a month. One of the agents of the police in the French Concession, uncovered by Alain Roux, was Yu Fei (Yu Maohuai), who was a leader of the union at the Compagnie Française de Tramways et d'Eclairage Electrique. See *Shanghai gongren sanci wuzhuang qiyi*, Shanghai, 1983, p. 149 (Hence: SGRSCWZQY); A. Roux, *Grèves et politique à Shanghai: les désillusions (1927–1932)*, Paris, 1995, pp. 54–5.
147 *Zhongguo lici laodong dahui wenxian*, Beijing, 1957, p. 58.
148 ZGZYWJXJ, vol. 1, p. 460.
149 C.M. Wilbur and J. Lien-ying How, *Missionaries of Revolution*, Cambridge, Mass., 1989, p. 724.
150 A.I. Kartunova, 'Kitaiskaia Revoliutsiia: Diskussii v Kominterne', *Voprosy Istorii KPSS*, 6, 1989, 58–72, p. 69.
151 Gongli ribao, 20 June 1925, reprinted *Zhongguo gongren shiliao*, 4, 1980, pp. 80–1.

Chapter 6

1 WSYD, vol. 1, p. 180.

2 WSYD, vol. 1, pp. 96–101; SMPF, IO 6932.

3 C. Henriot, 'Municipal Power and Local Elites', *Republican China*, vol. 11, no. 2, 1986, p. 17; Liu Ding, 'Xuesheng yundong yu sanci wuzhuang qiyi', *Shanghai gongyun shiliao*, 2, 1987, p. 40.

4 WSYD, vol. 1, p. 180.

5 C.M. Wilbur and J. Lien-ying How, *Missionaries of Revolution*, Cambridge, Mass., 1989, p. 210. At the Second Congress no membership figure was given for Shanghai, since the city's executive was not recognized by the CEC at that time.

6 Wang Kewen. 'The Kuomintang in Transition: Ideology and Factionalism in the "National Revolution"', 1924–32, Ph.D., Stanford University, 1985, p. 56; ZGZYWJXJ, vol. 1, p. 487.

7 *Zhongguo guomindang dierci quanguo daibiao dahui geshengqu dangwu baogao mulu*, Shanghai, 1926, p. 137; *Xiandai shiliao*, vol. 1, Shanghai, 1934, p. 93.

8 H. Mast and W.G. Saywell, 'Revolution Out of Tradition: The Political Ideology of Tai Chi-t'ao', *Journal of Asian Studies*, vol. 34, no. 1, 1974, 73–98; Sha Jiansun (ed.), *Zhongguo gongchandang tongshi*, vol. 2, Beijing 1996, pp. 320–3.

9 C.C. Tan, *Chinese Political Thought in the Twentieth Century*, Garden City, N.Y., 1971, pp. 176–181.

10 Qu Qiubai, 'Zhongguo guomin geming yu Dai Jitao zhuyi', in *Zhongguo gongren yundong shiliao*, 2, 1981, pp. 12–26; Wilbur, *Missionaries*, p. 166.

11 Xiangdao, 129, 11 Sept. 1925, pp. 1186–90; 130, 18 Sept. 1925, pp. 1196–97.

12 Wilbur, *Missionaries*, pp. 188–89.

13 Wang Kewen, 'Kuomintang in Transition', p. 63.

14 Zhengzhi zhoubao, 10, 3 May 1926, p. 2.

15 VKP(b), vol. 2, p. 232.

16 'Yijiueryi nian zhi yijiuerqi nian Shanghai, Jiangsu, Zhejiang dang zuzhi fazhan gaikuang', *Zhonggongdang shi ziliao*, 10, 1984, p. 217.

17 ZGZYWJXJ, vol. 2, p. 176; VKP(b), vol. 2, p. 274.

18 ZGZYWJXJ, vol. 2, pp. 259–60.

19 ZGZYWJXJ, vol. 2, p. 422.

20 J.P. Harrison, *The Long March to Power*, London, 1972, p. 64; Wang Jianying (ed.), *Zhongguo gongchandang zuzhishi ziliao huibian*, Beijing, 1982, p. 33.

21 Wang Jianying (ed.), *Zhongguo gongchandang*, p. 33. Since the latter figure excludes some local organisations, it is likely that total national membership by the end of 1926 was in the region of 20,000. See Zhao Pu, 'Zhongguo gongchandang zuzhi shi ziliao' *Dangshi yanjiu*, 4, 1982, p. 34.

22 Zhao Pu, 'Zhongguo gongchandang', pp. 30–31. The September figure may be inflated by the fact that in August the area for which the regional committee had responsibility was enlarged.

23 WSYD, vol. 1, p. 178. There are conflicting figures for April: one source says that there were 2241 members, of whom 1809 were in Shanghai; another that there 2269, of whom 1964 were Shanghai. 'Yijiueryi nian', p. 210.

24 Zhao Pu, 'Zhongguo gongchandang', p. 34.

25 In Guangdong province by August 1926 there were 4200 Communists, not counting the 500 at the Huangpu Academy or those in army units, of whom 2000 were in the city of Canton. VKP(b), vol. 2, p. 388.

26 NCH, 16 Apr. 1927, p. 122.

27 Jiang Weixin, 'Huiyi Shanghai gongren sanci wuzhuang qiyi yi qita', *Dangshi ziliao congkan*, 2, 1980, p. 99.
28 Zhao Pu, 'Zhongguo gongchandang', p. 34.
29 Zhao Pu, 'Zhongguo gongchandang', pp. 30–31.
30 ZGZYWJXJ, vol. 1, p. 474.
31 ZGZYWJXJ, vol. 2, p. 504.
32 'Zhonggong Shanghai quwei youguan Shanghai gongren sanci wuzhuang qiyi de wenxian qi pian', *Dang'an yu lishi*, 1, 1987, p. 2.
33 Harrison, *Long March*, p. 92.
34 *Shanghai fangzhi gongren yundong shi*, Beijing, 1991, pp. 474–7.
35 *Shanghai shangwu yinshuguan zhigong yundong shi*, Beijing, 1991, p. 155.
36 *Zhongguo gongren yundong shiliao*, 2, 1958, p. 22; *Shanghai zilaishui gongren yundong shi*, Beijing, 1991, p. 127.
37 'Yijiueryi nian', p. 210.
38 ZGGCDSH, p. 30.
39 ZGGCDSH, p. 62. It is not clear whether the contraction of membership of the CYL in Shanghai, relative to that of the CCP, was due, as it was in other regions, to the transfer of CYL members over the age of 23 *sui* into the party. Zhang Xuexin (ed.), *Ren Bishi zhuan*, Beijing, 1994, p. 80.
40 ZGGCDSH, pp. 68–73.
41 ZGGCDSH, p. 65.
42 VKP(b), vol. 1, pp. 626–7.
43 Ren Jianshu, *Chen Duxiu zhuan*, Shanghai, 1989, pp. 304–5.
44 ZGZYWJXJ, I, 487–491. There is a translation in Wilbur, *Missionaries*, pp. 533–35. VKP(b), vol. 1, p. 623.
45 VKP(b), vol. 1, p. 611; VKP(b), vol. 2, p. 494.
46 Huang Xiurong, *Gongchan guoji yu Zhongguo geming guanxi shi*, Beijing, 1989, p. 283; Chang Kuo-t'ao, *The Rise of the Communist Party, 1921–27*, Lawrence, 1971, pp. 464–5.
47 Yang Yunruo and Yang Kuisong, *Gongchan guoji he Zhongguo geming*, Shanghai, 1988, p. 126.
48 VKP(b), vol. 2, p. 42, p. 44.
49 VKP(b), vol. 2, p. 147, p. 160.
50 VKP(b), vol. 2, p. 191, p. 180, p. 200.
51 Huang Xiurong, *Gongchan guoji*, p. 285. For security reasons, no one knew exactly where Chen lived, so there was serious alarm at his disappearance. At the time, Chen was living with Shi Zhiying about whom he wished to keep the party in the dark. Since he believed he would soon be better, he ignored a missing-person notice posted by the party leadership in *Republican Daily*. Zheng Chaolin, 'Chen Duxiu and the Trotskyists', in G. Benton, *China's Urban Revolutionaries*, Atlantic Highlands, N.J., 1996, pp. 161–2.
52 Yang Yunruo and Yang Kuisong, *Gongchan guoji*, p. 131; Xiangdao, 148, 3 Apr. 1926.
53 Huang Xiurong, *Gongchan guoji*, p. 358; VKP(b), vol. 2, p. 267.
54 VKP(b), vol. 2, p. 265. To judge by an article in *Pravda*, however, Radek, was very critical of the Chinese Communists whom he accused of understanding the role of the proletariat in the national revolution in simplistic terms: 'the proletariat has still to win the confidence of the urban and rural poor, with which it is not yet linked'. K. Radek, 'God kitaiskoi revoliutsii', Pravda, 30 May 1926, p. 2.
55 VKP(b), vol. 2, p. 202; L.T. Lih, O.V. Naumov and O.V. Khlevniuk (eds.), *Stalin's Letters to Molotov, 1925–1936*, New Haven, 1995, p. 111; A. Pantsov,

257

'Stalin's Policy in China, 1925–27: New Light from the Russian Archives', *Issues and Studies*, 34, no. 1, Jan. 1998, p. 142.

56 A.M. Grigor'ev, 'Bor'ba v VKP(b) i Kominterne po voprosam politiki v Kitae (1926–27gg.), *Problemy Dal'nego Vostoka*, part 1, no. 2, 1993, p. 117. It is not clear how committed the United Opposition was to the "bloc without", since Zinoviev told the plenum that "withdrawal from the GMD does not presently seem desirable to us"'. *Ibid.*, pp. 112–13.

57 VKP(b), vol. 2, p. 377.

58 Wilbur, *Missionaries*, p. 268.

59 VKP(b), vol. 2, p. 239.

60 ZGZYWJXJ, vol. 2, pp. 140–44.

61 ZGZYWJXJ, vol. 2, pp. 619–26; Gui Xinqiu, 'Chen Duxiu he Gongchan Guoji zai Guo-Gong hezuo wenti shang de fenqi', *Shehui kexue zhanxian*, 3, 1991, p. 19.

62 Chiang Kai-shek became chair of the military commission of the GMD CEC on 14 April; head of the organization bureau of the CEC on 1 June; supreme commander of the NRA on 5 June; chief of the military personnel department, which appointed party representatives to the NRA, on 5 July; and chair of the standing committee on party affairs of the CEC on the following day. Huang Xiurong, *Gongchan guoji*, p. 291.

63 VKP(b), vol. 2, pp. 268–270.

64 ZGZYWJXJ, vol. 2, p. 176; Wilbur, *Missionaries*, pp. 728.

65 Gui Xinqiu, 'Chen Duxiu', p. 19; Yang Yunruo and Yang Kuisong, *Gongchan guoji*, p. 138.

66 VKP(b), vol. 2, p. 273–4, p. 284.

67 VKP(b), vol. 2, p. 324. The Soviet Politburo did not come out in support of the Northern Expedition until the beginning of September. VKP(b), vol. 2, p. 419.

68 Xiangdao, 161, 7 Jul 1926, pp. 1584–5; VKP(b), vol. 2, p. 325.

69 VKP(b), vol. 2, pp. 553–4. In fact the Far Eastern Bureau itself recognised that there was no alternative to supporting the Northern Expedition on 23 July. VKP(b), vol. 2, p. 299.

70 Zheng Chaolin. *An Oppositionist for Life*, Atlantic Highlands, N.J., 1997, p. 49.

71 ZGGCDSH, p. 30. Another source says the secretary was Liu Bozhuang. *Shanghai xuesheng yundong dashi, 1919.5 – 1949.9*, Shanghai, 1985, p. 72.

72 *Zhongguo gongchandang renming da cidian*, Beijing, 1991, p. 589.

73 *Zhongguo gongchandang renming da cidian*, p. 320; Chen Qiyin, 'Wusa yundong pianduan', *Dangshi ziliao congkan*, 2, 1980, p. 97.

74 *Shanghai xuesheng yundong dashi*, p. 82.

75 Guowen zhoubao, vol. 3, no. 16, 2 May 1926, p. 14.

76 *Shanghai xuesheng yundong shi*, Shanghai, 1995, p. 109; Ka-Che Yip, *Religion, Nationalism and Chinese Students*, Bellingham, 1980, p. 49.

77 *Shanghai xuesheng yundong shi*, pp. 108–9.

78 Wang Jiagui, Cai Xiyao, *Shanghai daxue*, Shanghai, 1986, p. 132, p. 44.

79 *Zhonggong zhongyang qingnian yundong wenjian xuanbian*, Beijing, 1988, pp. 82–4.

80 WSYD, vol. 1, pp. 96–101.

81 *Shanghai xuesheng yundong shi*, p. 125.

82 Zhongguo qingnian, 125, 3 Jul 1926, pp. 688–9; ZGZYWJXJ, vol. 2, p. 261.

83 ZGZYWJXJ, vol. 2, pp. 4–5.

84 Wilbur, *Missionaries*, p. 758.

85 Wilbur, *Missionaries*, pp. 758–9.

86 Jiang Zhichan, 'Dageming shiqi de Shanghai xuelian', *Diyici guogong hezuo shiqi de Gongqingtuan zhuanti lun wenji*, Beijing, 1985, p. 113.

87 *Shanghai xuesheng yundong shi*, pp. 121–5.
88 NCH, 5 Jun 1926, p. 432.
89 VKP(b), vol. 1, p. 539, p. 558.
90 *Daily Worker,* 6 Feb. 1926; VKP(b), vol. 1, p. 609, p. 668.
91 VKP(b), vol. 1, p. 654; Yang Yunruo and Yang Kuisong, *Gongchan guoji he Zhongguo geming,* Shanghai, 1988, p. 99–100; Yang Zilie, *Zhang Guotao furen huiyilu,* Hong Kong, 1970, p. 148.
92 Zhengzhi zhoubao, 2, 13 Dec. 1925.
93 VKP(b), vol. 2, p. 266.
94 VKP(b), vol. 2, p. 470.
95 VKP(b), vol. 2, p. 572.
96 *Zhongguo funü yundong lishi ziliao, 1921–1927,* Beijing, 1986, pp. 390–1.
97 WSYDSL, vol. 2, Shanghai, 1986, p. 336.
98 WSYDSL, vol. 2, pp. 313–14.
99 C.K Gilmartin, *Engendering the Chinese Revolution,* Berkeley, 1995, p. 134.
100 Gilmartin, *Engendering,* p. 143.
101 Zheng Chaolin, *Oppositionist,* p. 207.
102 'Yijiueryi nian', pp. 211–13.
103 VKP(b), vol. 2, p. 437.
104 'Yijiueryi nian', p. 219.
105 Zheng Chaolin, *Oppositionist,* pp. 146–7.
106 Gilmartin, *Engendering,* p. 144.
107 ZGZYWJXJ, vol. 2, pp. 230–33.
108 VKP(b), vol. 2, p. 437.
109 VKP(b), vol. 2, p. 437.
110 Zheng Chaolin, *Oppositionist,* p. 91.
111 Zheng Chaolin, *Oppositionist,* p. 17, p. 151; 'Yijiueryi nian', pp. 201–25.
112 Zheng Chaolin, *Oppositionist,* p. 48; *Shanghai lieshi xiaochuan,* Shanghai, 1983, 71–2.
113 Zheng Chaolin, *Oppositionist,* p. 92. Zheng incorrectly states that Zhao arrived in Shanghai in June.
114 ZGDSRWZ, vol. 7, Xi'an, 1983, pp. 1–48; M.A. Levine, *The Found Generation,* Seattle, 1993, pp. 54–6.
115 Zheng Chaolin, *Oppositionist,* p. 97.
116 Zheng Chaolin, *Oppositionist,* p. 129.
117 Zheng Chaolin, *Oppositionist,* p. 98.
118 Zheng Chaolin, *Oppositionist,* p. 93.
119 *Zhongguo gongchandang faqi ren fenlie shiliao,* Hong Kong, 1968, p. 158.
120 Yang Zilie *Zhang Guotao,* p. 107.
121 Yang Zilie *Zhang Guotao,* p. 107.
122 Zhang Xuexin, *Ren Bishi,* p. 84.
123 Yang Zilie, *Zhang Guotao,* p. 126.
124 Zheng Chaolin, *Oppositionist,* p. 139.
125 Leo Ou-fan Lee, 'Literary Trends I: The Quest for Modernity, 1895–1927', in *Cambridge History of China,* vol. 12, part 1, Cambridge, 1986, pp. 477–8.
126 Zhang Guotao's wife recalls Yang telling her. 'My former husband led a life of complete debauchery . . . My father-in-law Shen Xuanlu, a modern-minded person, asked me to stick closely to his son. I even used to traipse around the brothels after him. There was no way I could reform him. Father-in-law wanted me to go to Shanghai University to study and to divorce his son. He approved my marriage to Qu'. Yang Zilie *Zhang Guotao,* p. 136. (My thanks to Greg Benton for this reference). In 1923 Shen Xuanlu dispensed with his

own (second) wife, by whom he had three children, taking Wang Huafen, a woman twenty years his junior, as a 'revolutionary helper'. When he brought her home to Xiaoshan county, one of welcoming signs declared: 'Welcome to the revolutionary leader, Shen Xuanlu; down with the shameless whore, Wang Huafen'. After her marriage to Shen, Wang was alleged to have had an affair with Xu Meikun. R.K. Schoppa, *Blood Road*, Berkeley, 1995, pp. 73–4.

127 Jiang Guangci, 'Duanku dang', *Shiwen xuanji*, Beijing, 1957, pp. 267–8. Jiang, born in 1901 to a small shopkeeper's family in Liuan county Anhui, studied at the KUTV from 1921 and taught at Shanghai University from spring 1925. As a writer, he was associated with the Creation Society and edited a number of leftist literary journals. In 1930 he was expelled from the CCP for inactivity and died the following year of cancer. Leo Ou-fan Lee, *The Romantic Generation of Chinese Writers*, Cambridge, Mass., 1973, pp. 201–21.

128 Li Da, 'Zhongguo gongchandang chengli shiji de sixiang douzheng qingkuang', *'Yida' qianhou*, vol. 2, Beijing, 1980, p. 54; Gilmartin, *Engendering*, p. 111.

129 L. Feigon, *Chen Duxiu: Founder of the Chinese Communist Party*, Princeton, 1983, p. 53.

130 Ren Jianshu, *Chen Duxiu zhuan*, pp. 309–10.

131 Yang Zilie, *Zhang Guotao*, p. 128.

132 Zheng Chaolin, *Huai jiu ji*, Beijing, 1995, pp. 13–14; *Xiandai shiliao*, vol. 1, pp. 226–7.

133 Zheng Chaolin, *Oppositionist*, pp. 143–44.

134 For a fuller discussion of the privileged position of intellectuals within the CCP see my 'Workers, the Intelligentsia and Marxist Parties: St Petersburg, 1895–1917 and Shanghai, 1921–27', *International Review of Social History*, 41, 1996, pp. 44–50.

135 *Zhonggongdang shi renwu zhuan*, vol. 23, Xi'an, 1985, p. 97.

136 Lee, 'Literary Trends', p. 477. In fact it was realism, rather than romanticism, that dominated Chinese fiction during the first half of the 1920s, progressive writers believing that the realist mode was best suited to inspire readers to involve themselves in the political and social struggles to save the nation. Even in this period, however, Mao Dun, as the chief advocate of realism, came under attack from the proponents of romanticism, principally, Guo Moruo of the Creation Society. As Marston Anderson pointed out, however, the realists' commitment to objective social description did not preclude their fiction serving as a 'field of self-expression and for the exploration of the constraining influences on the self.' M. Anderson, *The Limits of Realism: Chinese Fiction in the Revolutionary Period*, Berkeley, 1990, p. 44.

137 Zheng Chaolin, *Huai jiu ji*, p. 4; M. Dolezelova-Velingerova (ed.), *A Selective Guide to Chinese Literature, 1900–1949*, vol. 1, The Novel, Leiden, 1988, pp. 96–7.

138 Jiang Guangci, 'Duanku dang', *Shiwen xuanji*, Beijing, 1957, pp. 227–316.

139 Dolezelova-Velingerova, *Selective Guide*, pp. 132–3.

140 T. Kataoka, *Resistance and Revolution in China. The Communists and the Second United Front*, University of California, Berkeley, 1974; Chen Yung-fa, *Making Revolution: the Communist Movement in Eastern and Central China, 1937–45*, University of California, Berkeley, 1986; J. Esherick, 'Revolution in a Feudal Fortress: Yangjiagou, Mizhi county, Shaanxi, 1937–48', *Modern China*, vol. 24, no. 4, 1998, 339–77.

141 P. Selznick, *The Organizational Weapon: A Study of Bolshevik Strategy and Tactics*, New York, 1952.
142 Wilbur, *Missionaries*, p. 733.
143 VKP(b), vol. 2, p. 202, p. 247. Rafes (1883–1942) was probably the most experienced of these revolutionaries, having been on the Central Committee of the Jewish Bund from 1912 to 1919 and active in the Ukraine during the civil war, where he brought a section of the Bund into the Bolshevik party.
144 VKP(b), vol. 2, p. 257, p. 293.
145 VKP(b), vol. 2, p. 551.
146 VKP(b), vol. 2, p. 558.
147 ZGZYWJXJ, vol. 2, p. 182.
148 ZGZYWJXJ, vol. 2, pp. 261–2.
149 ZGZYWJXJ, vol. 2, p. 263.
150 H. van de Ven, 'The Emergence of the Text-Centered Party', in T. Saich and H.van de Ven, *New Perspectives on the Chinese Communist Revolution*, Armonk, 1995, pp. 5–32.
151 'Yijiueryi nian' p. 209.
152 Li Yu-ning, *The Introduction of Socialism into China*, New York, 1971, p. 124.
153 Zheng Chaolin, *Oppositionist*, pp. 94–5. In 1928 the author of *Stories of Sex Lives*, a professor of philosophy at Beijing University, was arrested by the Nationalist authorities for 'disseminating sex education and inciting youth'. Gilmartin, *Engendering*, p. 213.
154 Jiang Guangci, 'Duanku dang', pp. 277–8.
155 Qu Qiubai, 'Zhongguo geming zhong zhi zhenglun wenti', in *Liuda yiqian dang de lishi ziliao*, Beijing, 1980, pp. 723–4.
156 VKP(b), vol. 2, p. 592.
157 VKP(b), vol. 2, p. 589.
158 VKP(b), vol. 2, pp. 589–90.
159 VKP(b), vol. 2, p. 592.
160 VKP(b), vol. 2, p. 591.
161 VKP(b), vol. 1, p. 668.
162 VKP(b), vol. 2, p. 253.
163 VKP(b), vol. 2, p. 449.
164 *Sulian yinmou wenzheng huibian*, Peking Metropolitan Police Headquarters, Beijing, 1928, vol. 1, n.p.
165 VKP(b), vol. 1, p. 494.

Chapter 7

1 Jiang Peinan, Chen Weimin, 'Shanghai zhaopai gonghui de xingwang', *Jindai shi yanjiu*, 6, 1984, p. 77. The SFS still existed at the time of Chiang Kai-shek's coup of April 1912, but it was too moribund for the new regime to use as a base on which to reorganize the labour movement. Moreover, its political connections were unacceptable, since it was reputed to have received funds from Li Baozhang and the Japanese millowners. *Zhongguo gongren yundong shiliao*, 4, 1981, p. 33.
2 SMPF, IO 7317; Zhengzhi zhoubao, 10, 3 May 1926, p. 2; Gongren zhi lu, 367, 4 July 1926, p. 1.
3 Xiangdao, 159, 23 June 1926, p. 1562; WSYD, vol. 2, p. 46; NCH, 22 Aug. 1925, p. 206.
4 *Zhongguo lici laodong dahui wenxian*, Beijing, 1957, p. 90.

5 *Zhongguo lici laodong dahui*, p. 90.

6 *Zhongguo lici laodong dahui*, p. 195; SGRSCWZQY, p. 260.

7 WSYD, vol. 1, pp. 224–5; vol. 2, p. 436, p. 445.

8 WSYD, vol. 2, p. 119, p. 449, p. 476.

9 WSYDSL, vol. 2, Shanghai, 1986, p. 677; Gongren zhi lu, 152, 25 Nov. 1925.

10 Tang Hai, *Zhongguo laodong wenti*, Shanghai, 1926, p. 502; WSYD, vol. 1, p. 89; NCH, 3 Oct. 1925, p. 14.

11 NCH, 28 Nov. 1925, p. 388.

12 NCH, 14 Nov. 1925, p. 295.

13 *Shanghai shi tongji*, Shanghai, 1933, part 11, p. 20; Chen Da, 'Guonei zhongyao gonghui de gaikuang', *Shehui xuejia*, vol. 2, June 1927, p. 121; SMPF, IO 7317; Xiangdao, 155, 30 May 1926, p. 1501; *Zhongguo gongren yundong shiliao*, 3, 1981, p. 15.

14 SGRSCWZQY, p. 454.

15 NCH, 24 July 1927, p. 160.

16 In 1928 the Bureau of Social Affairs reckoned that of 52,463 silk spinners in the city, 75.3% were women, 20.1% children and 4.1% men; among 6,262 silk weavers, men comprised 58%, women 35% and children 7%. *Shanghai zhi gongye*, 1929, appendix.

17 Minguo ribao (Canton), 3 July 1926, p. 9; 5 July 1926, p. 12; 6 July 1926, p. 12; E.J. Perry, *Shanghai on Strike*, Stanford, 1993. p. 175.

18 Minguo ribao (Canton), 3 July 1926, p. 9; 6 July 1926, p. 12; Shenbao, 28 June 1926, p. 3; 30 June 1926, p. 13.

19 *Diyici Zhongguo laodong nianjian*, part 2, Beijing, 1928, p. 290. Zhu Yingru (1899–1964) was born in Yangzhou in Subei and from 1913 worked at the Sanxin cotton mill and in the weaving shed at the Ewo mill. In August 1924 she became an overlooker at the Japanese Shanghai Cotton Manufacturing Company, from which she was fired in February 1926. She joined the CCP in summer 1925. *Shanghai gongyun zhi*, Shanghai, 1997, p. 788.

20 Minguo ribao (Canton) 5 July 1926, p. 12; 6 July 1926, p. 10; *Chinese Economic Journal*, vol. 1, no. 3, Mar. 1927, p. 281.

21 Shenbao, 29 July 1926, p. 13; 30 July 1926, p. 13; 6 July 1926, p. 13; R.Y. Eng, 'Luddism and labor protest among silk artisans and workers in Jiangnan and Guangdong, 1860–1930', *Late Imperial China*, vol. 11, no. 2, 1990, p. 90.

22 Shenbao, 27 Mar. 1927, p. 11; *Shanghai gongren sanci wuzhuang qiyi yanjiu*, Shanghai 1987 p. 223. (Hence: SGRSCWZQYYJ).

23 NCH, 17 Apr. 1926, p. 117.

24 NCH, 10 Apr. 1926, p. 63; NCH, 5 June 1926, p. 443; *Shanghai shangwu yinshuguan zhigong yundongshi*, Beijing, 1991, pp. 177–8; Ren Qingxian, Xie Qingzhai et al, 'Zhuiji "Shangwu" jiuchadui de douzheng ji shimin zhengfu de jianli', *Shanghai gongyun shiliao*, 2, 1987, p. 11.

25 Shenbao, 17 June 1926, p. 13.

26 Shenbao, 24 June 1926, p. 14; Shen Yixing, Jiang Peinan and Zheng Qingsheng, *Shanghai gongren yundong shi*, vol. 1, Liaoning, 1991, p. 280.

27 C.M. Wilbur and J. Lien-ying How, *Missionaries of Revolution*, Cambridge, Mass., 1989, p. 743.

28 WSYD, vol. 1, p. 217. The source miscalculates the total at 104,137.

29 *Zhongguo lici laodong dahui*, p. 58.

30 *Diyici laodong nianjian*, part 2, pp. 70–1.

31 VKP(b), vol. 2, p. 476. By contrast, in the summer of 1926 the Communist-backed Delegate Council in Canton claimed to have 130 affiliated unions with 150,000 members. VKP(b), vol. 2, p. 389. Ming Kou Chan says that by the end

of 1926 there were 250 labour organizations in greater Canton with 300,000 members. Ming Kou Chan, 'Labor and Empire: the Chinese Labor Movement in the Canton Delta, 1895–1927', Ph.D. Stanford University, 1975, p. 69.

32 WSYD, vol. 1, p. 217.
33 WSYD, vol. 1, p. 179, 181.
34 ZGZYWJXJ, vol. 2, pp. 262–3.
35 *Zhongguo lici laodong dahui*, p. 191; Xiangdao 159, 23 June 1926.
36 *Zhongguo gongren yundong shiliao*, 3, 1981, p. 52, p. 13.
37 *Zhongguo gongchandang renming dacidian*, pp. 575–6.
38 J-P. Drège, *La Commercial Press de Shanghai 1897–1949*, Paris, 1978, p. 78.
39 Ma Chaojun, *Zhongguo laogong yundong shi*, Taibei, p. 622; Shenbao, 27 Mar. 1927, p. 10.
40 Xiangdao, 160, 30 June 1926, p. 1569; 'Yijiueryi nian', p. 214.
41 Shenbao, 4 July 1926, p. 14.
42 Minguo ribao (Canton), 7 July 1926, p. 7; 9 July 1926; 21 July 1926.
43 Xiangdao, 161, 7 July 1926.
44 Gongren zhi lu, 384, 21 July 1926, p. 3.
45 Gongren zhi lu, 21 July 1926, p. 3; Minguo ribao (Canton), 23 July 1926, p. 12; Shenbao, 14 July 1926, p. 14.
46 NCH 17 July 1926, p. 124.
47 Zhao Shiyan wrote under the pseudonyum Shi Ying. Xiangdao, 159, 23 June 1926, pp. 1559–60; 160, 30 June 1926. The average of four different estimates of the number of strikers in June comes to over 57,000.
48 NCH, 21 Aug. 1926, p. 366; Xiangdao, 167, 15 Aug. 1926.
49 NCH, 18 Sep. 1926, p. 558.
50 PRO FO 228/3291 'Shanghai Intelligence Report, Apr.-Sep. 1926'.
51 *China Year Book 1938*, (ed.) H.G.W. Woodhead, Shanghai, 1938, 216–7; A. Kotenev, *Shanghai: Its Municipality and the Chinese*, Shanghai, 1927, p. 13.
52 NCH, 23 Apr. 1927, p. 170; 25 June 1927, p. 554.
53 Xiangdao, 167, 15 Aug. 1926.
54 Xiangdao, 161, 7 July 1926.
55 NCH, 3 July 1926, p. 14. The phrase 'labour brigands' is a translation of *gongzei*, which I have generally translated as 'scabs'.
56 *Shanghai fangzhi gongren yundong shi*, Beijing, 1991, p. 126.
57 NCH, 3 July 1926, p. 14; Xiangdao, 164, 21 July 1926; NCH, 17 July 1926, p. 111; *Zhongguo lici laodong dahui*, p. 175. There is clear evidence from the minutes of the meetings of the Shanghai regional committee of the CCP that Yu was the preferred mediator of the Communists. SGRSCWZQYYJ, p. 145, p. 156.
58 NCH, 17 July 1926, p. 111.
59 *Zhongguo gongren yundong shiliao*, 2, 1958, p. 117.
60 NCH, 31 July 1926, p. 212.
61 NCH, 24 July 1926, p. 160; NCH 18 Sep. 1926, p. 557.
62 *Zhongguo gonghui lishi wenxian, 1921–1927*, Beijing, 1958, p. 285.
63 NCH, 28 Aug. 1926, p. 403.
64 NCH, 28 Aug. 1926, p. 403.
65 SGRSCWZQYYJ, pp. 142–3.
66 Shen Yixing *Shanghai gongren*, p. 293.
67 *Zhongguo gonghui lishi wenxian*, pp. 285–86.
68 Xiangdao, 169, 29 Aug. 1926.
69 Shenbao, 13 Sep. 1926, p. 14.
70 NCH, 28 Aug. 1926, p. 402; Shenbao, 1 Sep. 1926, p. 12.
71 SGRSCWZQYYJ, p. 148.

72   Xiangdao, 169, 29 Aug. 1926.
73   NCH, 4 Sep. 1926, p. 448.
74   NCH, 28 Aug. 1926, p. 402; 11 Sep. 1926, p. 494; 25 Sep. 1926, p. 602.
75   Shenbao, 5 Sep. 1926, p. 14; 7 Sep. 1926, p. 12.
76   NCH 4 Sep. 1926, p. 448; 18 Sep. 1926, p. 558.
77   NCH, 23 Sep. 1926, p. 182.
78   NCH, 11 Sep. 1926, p. 494.
79   SGRSCWZQYYJ, p. 144.
80   VKP(b), vol. 2, p. 444.
81   *Zhongguo lici laodong dahui*, p. 174.
82   SGRSCWZQY, p. 311.
83   VKP(b), vol. 2, p. 187.
84   *Zhongguo gongren yundong shiliao*, 3, 1981, p. 33.
85   *Rongjia qiye shiliao*, vol. 1, 1896–1937, Shanghai, 1980, p. 320. Shi Liqing (1896–1927), born in Wuxi, studied for a two years in a private academy, but was forced to give up his education. He worked as a farm labourer before going in 1916, at the age of twenty, along with his wife and mother, to work in his uncle's beancurd shop in Suzhou. In 1918, after his father's death, he moved to Shanghai, and was introduced to a job at Shenxin No.1 mill as an oiler. He joined the part-time workers' schools, lost his job as a result of the May Thirtieth general strike and went to Guangzhou, where he joined the CCP. In the autumn of 1926 he resumed work at the Shenxin No.1 mill, where he became leader of the union and chair of the party branch. He was killed during Chiang Kai-shek's coup. *Shanghai fangzhi gongren*, pp. 572–3.
86   WSYD, vol. 1, p. 185.
87   NCH, 4 Sep. 1926, p. 449; ZGGCDSH, *p.* 78.
88   SGRSCWZQYYJ, p. 163.
89   *Shanghai haiyuan gongren yundong shi*, Beijing, 1991, p. 65, p. 314.
90   *China Year Book, 1928*, (ed.) H.G.W. Woodhead, Tientsin, 1928, pp. 968–9; WSYD, vol. 2, p. 266.
91   NCH, 29 Aug. 1925, p. 268.
92   SGRSCWZQYYJ, pp. 142–3.
93   Jiang Weixin, 'Huiyi Shanghai gongren sanci wuzhuang qiyi ji qita', *Dangshi ziliao congkan*, 1980, 2 (3), p. 99.
94   Huang Hao, 'Huiyi da geming shiqi de Shanghai gongren yundong ji qilun', *Dangshi ziliao congkan*, 1980, 2 (3), p. 108; Xu Meikun, 'Yi qiyi qianhou', *Shanghai gongyun shiliao*, 2, 1987, p. 1.
95   SGRSCWZQYYJ, pp. 142–3.
96   NCH, 28 Aug. 1926, p. 402.
97   NCH, 28 Aug. 1926, p. 402; Shenbao, 2 Oct. 1926, p. 13.
98   NCH, 23 Oct. 1926, p. 163.
99   WSYDSL, vol. 1, Shanghai, 1981, p. 365.
100 Xu Meikun, 'Yi qiyi qianhou' p. 1; Gu Shuping, 'Wo liyong Gu Zhuxuan de yanhu jinxing geming huodong', in *Jiu Shanghai de banghui*, Shanghai, 1986, p. 360.
101 Jiang Weixin, 'Huiyi Shanghai', p. 99. Gu Shunzhang, born in 1904 in Hubei, worked at Nanyang tobacco company from a very young age. He went to Germany as a work-study student and, on returning home, joined the CCP. He was commander of the workers' pickets in the armed insurrections which the CCP organized. Later, he rose to become a member of the CC, chief of the CCP's secret police and a candidate member of the Politburo. In April 1931 he fell into the hands of the GMD Special Services Bureau in

Wuhan and turned traitor. His family was murdered by the Communists in revenge. In 1936 Gu secretly re-established contact with the CCP, but his plan to assassinate the chief of the GMD secret policy, Chen Lifu, was uncovered and he was executed. F. Wakeman, *Policing Shanghai, 1927–1937*, Berkeley, 1995, pp. 153–55, p. 253. For his Green Gang membership, see Guo Xuyin, *Jiu Shanghai heishehui*, Shanghai, 1997, p. 63.

102 *Shanghai xuesheng yundong shi*, Shanghai, 1995, p. 95.
103 SGRSCWZQYYJ, pp. 144–5.
104 SGRSCWZQYYJ, p. 154.
105 SGRSCWZQYYJ, pp. 161–2.
106 NCH, 4 Sep. 1926, p. 449.
107 Shenbao, 15 Sep. 1926, p. 13; 16 Sep. 1926, p. 11.
108 NCH, 25 Sep. 1926, p. 587.
109 NCH, 18 Sep. 1926, p. 557; *Zhongguo lici laodong dahui*, p. 194.
110 NCH, 18 Sep. 1926, p. 557; *Zhongguo lici laodong dahui*, p. 174.
111 Zhao Pu, 'Zhongguo gongchandang zuzhi shi ziliao' (part 5), Dangshi yanjiu, 4, 1982, p. 34.
112 ZGZYWJXJ, vol. 2, p. 508.
113 Calculated from *Diyici laodong nianjian*, part 2, pp. 63–5, 70–1, p. 46.
114 NCH 16 Oct. 1926, p. 117; Minguo ribao (Canton), 23 Oct. 1926, p. 9; 30 Oct. 1926, p. 11.
115 VKP(b), vol. 2, p. 476.
116 NCH, 25 Sep. 1926, p. 587.
117 The charge of 'tailism' was made by Zhao Shiyan, See ZGDSRWZ, vol. 7, Xi'an, 1983, p. 36. For a general discussion of this point see A. Roux, *Grèves et politique à Shanghai: les désillusions (1927–1932)*, Paris, 1995, p. 49.

Chapter 8

1 VKP(b), vol. 2, p. 188, vol. 2, p. 415.
2 VKP(b), vol. 2, p. 418.
3 ZGZYWJXJ, vol. 2, p. 320; Yang Yunruo and Yang Kuisong, *Gongchan guoji he Zhongguo geming*, Shanghai, 1988, p. 145.
4 VKP(b), vol. 2, pp. 416–7.
5 VKP(b), vol. 2, p. 439, p. 484. It not only turned down the request, it increased Borodin's status, making him official diplomatic representative of the USSR to the Guangdong government and thus the senior Russian representative in China. See VKP(b), vol. 2, p. 512.
6 VKP(b), vol. 2, p. 564.
7 VKP(b), vol. 2, pp. 485–86.
8 VKP(b), vol. 2, p. 498. Later Stalin conceded that this directive was 'unquestionably a mistake'. J.V. Stalin, *Works*, Moscow, 1954, p. 18.
9 VKP(b), vol. 2, p. 508.
10 Ren Jianshu, *Chen Duxiu zhuan*, vol. 1, Shanghai, 1989, p. 335.
11 ZGZYWJXJ, vol. 2, p. 422.
12 ZGZYWJXJ, vol. 2, p. 425, p. 428.
13 ZGZYWJXJ, vol. 2, pp. 561–68.
14 ZGZYWJXJ, vol. 2, pp. 587–9.
15 There was no regionalist (or generational) dimension to this conflict, since Yu and Fu both hailed from Zhenhai county, Zhejiang, and Yu, at 60, was only five years older than Fu. WSYDSL, vol. 2, Shanghai, 1986, p. 270.

16 M-C Bergère, 'The Chinese bourgeoisie, 1911–37' *Cambridge History of China*, vol. 12, Cambridge, 1983, p. 806; J. Fewsmith, *Party, State and Local Elites in Republican China*, Honolulu, 1985, pp. 81–2; Zhou Shangwen, He Shiyou, *Shanghai gongren sanci wuzhuang qiyi shi*, Shanghai, 1987, p. 33.

17 SGRSCWZQYYJ, p. 151.

18 SGRSCWZQYYJ, pp. 156–7.

19 SGRSCWZQYYJ, p. 18. Hou Shaoqiu, born in Songjiang, Jiangsu, in 1896, had been a student leader in Shanghai in 1919 and head of a girls school in his native town from 1922. After 1924 he headed the middle school attached to Shanghai University and joined the CCP. He was an expert on secondary education. Wang Jiagui, Cai Xiyao, *Shanghai daxue*, Shanghai, 1986, pp. 63–4.

20 SGRSCWZQYYJ, pp. 13–14, pp. 224–5.

21 Ren Jianshu, 'Shanghai gongren wuzhuang qiyi yu shimin zizhi yundong', *Dang'an yu lishi*, 3, 1987, p. 57.

22 SGRSCWZQYYJ, p. 117. On 17 August 1926 the regional committee and the GLU had formed a military commission to train pickets in the use of weapons and tactics of insurrection. It had six members, including two graduates of the Huangpu military academy. Xu Meikun, 'Yi qiyi qianhou', *Shanghai gongyun shiliao*, 2, 1987, p. 3; Jiang Weixin, 'Huiyi Shanghai gongren sanci wuzhuang qiyi ji qita', *Dangshi ziliao congkan*, 2, 1980, p. 99.

23 Zhou Shangwen, *Shanghai gongren* p. 37.

24 Guo Xuyin, *Jiu Shanghai heishehui*, Shanghai, 1997, p. 62; A.A. (A.P. Appen) 'Tri shankhaiskikh vosstaniia', *Problemy Kitaia*, 2, 1930, p. 65. Yu Xiaqing had bankrolled Niu during the 1911 Revolution. H.L. Boorman and R.C. Howard, *Biographical Dictionary of Republican China*, vol. 3, New York, 1970, p. 45.

25 SGRSCWZQYYJ, p. 18; A.A., 'Tri shankhaiskikh vosstaniia', p. 66.

26 A.A., 'Tri shankhaiskikh vosstaniia', p. 65.

27 SGRSCWZQY, p. 6.

28 VKP(b), vol. 2, p. 477.

29 VKP(b), vol. 2, p. 488.

30 SGRSCWZQY, p. 117.

31 VKP(b), vol. 2, p. 480, p. 482.

32 D.A. Jordan, *The Northern Expedition: China's National Revolution of 1926–28*, Honolulu, 1976, p. 82; A.A., 'Tri shankhaiskikh vosstaniia', p. 63.

33 A.A., 'Tri shankhaiskikh vosstaniia', p. 66.

34 A.A., 'Tri shankhaiskikh vosstaniia', p. 67; Zhou Shangwen, *Shanghai gongren*, p. 45.

35 VKP(b), vol. 2, p. 488.

36 SGRSCWZQY, pp. 21–2.

37 SGRSCWZQY, p. 64.

38 Zhou Shangwen, *Shanghai gongren*, p. 43.

39 M.F. Iur'ev, *Revoliutsiia 1925–1927gg. v Kitae*, M.1968, p. 426. Iur'ev suggests that Niu Yongjian received false intelligence about a victory by Xia Chao; Harold Isaacs that he knew of Xia's defeat but deliberately chose not to inform the CCP and the GLU. Donald Jordan denies that there was any trickery, but states that the GMD leader called off the uprising, whereas the CCP pressed ahead with it. See Iur'ev, *Revoliutsiia*, p. 426; H.R. Isaacs, *The Tragedy of the Chinese Revolution*, Stanford, 1961 (orig. 1938), p. 131; Jordan, *Northern Expedition*, p. 209.

40 VKP(b), vol. 2, p. 488.

41 SGRSCWZQY, p. 118.

42 All three uprisings began with such a salvo – an act reminiscent of the salvo fired by battleship Aurora which signalled the start of the storming of the Winter Palace in Petrograd in 1917.

43 A.A., 'Tri shankhaiskikh vosstaniia', p. 67.
44 SGRSCWZQYYJ, p. 241.
45 SGRSCWZQY, pp. 42.
46 Jiang Weixin, 'Huiyi Shanghai', p. 100.
47 SGRSCWZQY p. 34.
48 NCH, 30 Oct. 1926, p. 194; SGRSCWZQY, p. 44.
49 NCH, 30 Oct. 1926, p. 194.
50 SGRSCWZQY, p. 34.
51 Hua Gang, *Yijiuerwu nian zhi yijiuerqi nian de Zhongguo da geming shi*, Shanghai, 1931, p. 316.
52 SGRSCWZQY, p. 62.
53 'Tao Jingxuan lieshi jieshao', *Shanghai gongren yundong shiliao*, 3, 1987, 36–9; Shenbao, 27 Oct. 1926; SGRSCWZQYYJ, pp. 26–7.
54 SGRSCWZQY, p. 40, p. 47.
55 SGRSCWZQYYJ, p. 25.
56 SGRSCWZQY, p. 55.
57 SGRSCWZQY, p. 48.
58 VKP(b), vol. 2, p. 489. Such statements are still interpreted by some historians in the PRC to mean that the Communist leadership continued to believe that the bourgeoisie should lead the national revolution. Shen Yixing, *Gongyun shi ming-bian lu*, Shanghai, 1987, p. 129.
59 VKP(b), vol. 2, p. 490.
60 VKP(b), vol. 2, p. 491.
61 VKP(b), vol. 2, p. 492, p. 493.
62 VKP(b), vol. 2, p. 493.
63 VKP(b), vol. 2, p. 494. In accordance with the norms of democratic centralism, Voitinskii and Rafes purported to be putting the same point of view, but Voitinskii clearly did not share Rafes's enthusiasm for a general strike. Their insistence that they were both saying the same thing can only have confused the Chinese.
64 VKP(b), vol. 2, p. 494.
65 VKP(b), vol. 2, p. 495.
66 SGRSCWZQYYJ, pp. 120–1.
67 VKP(b), vol. 2, p. 537; R. Bush, *The Politics of the Cotton Textile Industry in Kuomintang China*, New York, 1982, p. 87.
68 SGRSCWZQYYJ, p. 33.
69 Xiangdao, 180, 5 Dec. 1926. Jiang Zhichan, 'Dameming shiqi de Shanghai xuelian', *Diyici guogong hezuo shiqi de Gongqingtuan zhuanti lun wenji*, Beijing, 1985, p. 106.
70 SGRSCWZQYYJ, p. 34; NCH, 4 Dec. 1926, p. 435.
71 Shenbao, 7 Dec. 1926; NCH, 18 Dec. 1926, p. 556; SGRSCWZQYYJ, p. 34.
72 Zhou Shangwen, *Shanghai gongren*, p. 116.
73 Shenbao, 11 Feb. 1927.
74 *Diyici Zhongguo laodong nianjian*, part 2, Beijing, 1928, p. 70.
75 Shenbao, 1 Dec. 1926.
76 Minguo ribao (Canton), 15 Dec. 1926, p. 12; NCH, 22 Jan. 1927, p. 107.
77 C.M. Wilbur and J. Lien-ying How, *Missionaries of Revolution*, Cambridge, Mass., 1989, pp. 374–5.
78 A.A., 'Tri shankhaiskikh vosstaniia', pp. 69–70.
79 SGRSCWZQYYJ, p. 3.
80 Doubt has been cast on the oft-repeated claim that in late 1926 Yu Xiaqing went to Nanchang to see Chiang Kai-shek, and promised him a $60 million loan.

See Shen Yu, 'Si yi er fangeming zhengbian de yunniang he fadong', *Dang'an yu lishi*, 2, 1987, p. 82.

81 *Yijiuerqi nian de Shanghai shangye lianhehui*, (ed.) Liu Pinggang, Shanghai, 1983, p. 214.

82 *Yijiuerqi nian*, p. 14–15.

83 Zhou Shangwen, *Shanghai gongren*, p. 98.

84 NCH, 29 Jan. 1927, p. 158; Clifford provides a fine account of the reactions of the foreign community in Shanghai to developments in the spring. N.R. Clifford, *Spoilt Children of Empire*, Vermont, 1991, 11–13.

85 Clifford, *Spoilt Children*, p. 188.

86 J. Chesneaux, *The Chinese Labor Movement, 1919–1927*, Stanford, 1968, p. 349.

87 *VKP(b), Komintern*, vol.2, p. 606. For a more detailed discussion of this plenum, see S.A. Smith, 'The Comintern, the Chinese Communist Party and the Three Armed Uprisings in Shanghai, 1926–27' in T. Rees and A. Thorpe (eds.), *International Communism and the Communist International*, Manchester University Press, 1998, 257–61.

88 ZGZYWJXJ, vol. 3, pp. 19–23; Huang Xiurong, *Gongchan guoji yu Zhongguo geming guanxi shi*, vol. 1, Beijing, 1989, p. 314. A barb may have been concealed in this apparent self-criticism, since Peng Shuzhi attacked Qu Qiubai and the defenders of the Comintern line precisely for continuing to insist that the national revolution was fundamentally bourgeois-democratic in character.

89 VKP(b), vol. 2, p. 740.

90 T. Mandalian, 'Pourquoi la direction du PC de China n'a-t-elle pas rempli sa tâche?' in P. Broué, (ed.), *La question chinoise dans l'Internationale communiste (1926–27)*, Paris, 1965, p. 281.

91 VKP(b), vol. 2, p. 878, p. 629; Cai Hesen, 'Istoriia opportunizma v Kommunisticheskoi Partii Kitaia', *Problemy Kitaia*, I, 1929, p. 16. The Chinese original is in *Gongchan guoji yu Zhongguo geming ziliao xuanji, yijiuerwu nian -yijiuerqi nian*, Beijing, 1985, pp. 541–83.

92 Xiao Zizhang (1897–1983), also known as Xiao San, was born in Xiangxiang, Hunan. He was a work-study student in France and because of his good French liaised on behalf of the European branch of the CCP with the French Communist Party (via Ho Chi Minh). He went to the Soviet Union before returning to China. M.A. Levine, *The Found Generation*, Seattle, 1993, p. 159, p. 238; Zheng Chaolin, 'Chen Duxiu and the Trotskyists', in G. Benton, *China's Urban Revolutionaries*, Atlantic Highlands, N.J., 1996, p. 132.

93 Xiangdao, 184, 21 Jan. 1927, p. 1951;.

94 Xiangdao, 190, Mar. 1927, p. 2042.

95 Qu Qiubai, *Zhongguo geming zhong zhi zhenglun wenti* (Wuhan, 1927), in *Liuda yiqian dang de lishi ziliao*, Beijing, 1980. The limited analytical value of terms such as 'right' and 'left' to capture the positions of the protagonists should be evident. In one sense, Peng Shuzhi was to the 'left' of Qu Qiubai, since he doubted that the national revolution would take place under bourgeois-democratic auspices.

96 VKP(b), vol. 2, p. 614, p. 624.

97 VKP(b), vol. 2, p. 626.

98 VKP(b), vol. 2, p. 629.

99 VKP(b), vol. 2, p. 924–25.

100 VKP(b), vol. 2, p. 631.

101 VKP(b), vol. 2, p. 633.

102 VKP(b), vol. 2, p. 732.
103 Tien-wei Wu, 'Chiang Kai-shek's April 12th Coup of 1927' in F.G. Chan and T.H. Etzold eds, *China in the 1920s*, New York, 1976, p. 148. On the attempts to claw back party and governmental authority from Chiang Kai-shek, see Yang Tianshi, 'Beifa shiqi zuopai liliang tong Jiang Jieshi douzheng de jige zhongyao huihe', *Dangshi yanjiu*, 1, 1990, 31–43.
104 Chang Kuo-t'ao, *The Rise of the Chinese Communist Party, 1921–27*, Lawrence, 1971, pp. 581–2. The claim has been confirmed by A.I. Kartunova, 'Novyi vzgliad na vopros o razryve s Chan Kaishi: ianvar'-aprel' 1927', *Vostok/Oriens*, 1, 1997, p. 42.
105 *Zhou Enlai nianpu*, Beijing, 1989, p. 98; A.A., 'Tri shankhaiskikh vosstaniia', p. 71.
106 SGRSCWZQY, p. 111.
107 SGRSCWZQY, p. 111.
108 SGRSCWZQY, p. 110.
109 A.A., 'Tri shankhaiskikh vosstaniia', p. 71.
110 VKP(b), vol. 2, pp. 715–7.
111 Notwithstanding the desire to differentiate the two organizations, the Communists' own nomenclature subsequently failed to distinguish them, since they continued to use the word *jiuchadui* to refer both to bodies maintaining order and to those with a more combative function. At the Fifth Congress of the CCP a resolution about armed militias used the word *jiuchadui* throughout. *Zhongguo gongren yundong shiliao*, 1, 1982, p. 80.
112 *Shanghai gongren yundong shi*, Shanghai, 1935, p. 171; E.J. Perry, *Shanghai on Strike*, Stanford, 1993, p. 85. The woman was Chen Anfen, a middle-school graduate and the mother of a six-month-old baby, who was killed while tending the wounded on the street. Most women seem to have served in a nursing rather than fighting capacity. Zhou Shangwen, *Shanghai gongren*, p. 179.
113 NCH, 16 Apr. 1927, p. 125.
114 *Zhongguo gongren yundong shiliao*, 1, 1982, p. 80.
115 E. Teichman, 'Analysis of the Chinese Nationalist Complex', PRO FO 228/3021.
116 NCH, 29 Jan. 1927, p. 164; *Krasnyi Internatsional Profsoiuzov*, 4, 1927, p. 460.
117 NCH, 19 Feb. 1927, p. 288.
118 SGRSCWZQY, p. 199; NCH, 26 Feb. 1927, p. 317.
119 NCH, 26 Feb. 1927, p. 317; Shenbao, 28 Feb. 1927, p. 9.
120 SGRSCWZQY, p. 199.
121 NCH, 26 Feb. 1927, p. 317, p. 320.
122 *Zhongguo gongren yundong shiliao*, 4, 1981, p. 32, p. 71. Shenbao said that from 20 to 25 or 26 February 31 were killed and 54 arrested. Shenbao, 27 Feb. 1927.
123 Jordan, *Northern Expedition*, p. 210.
124 NCH, 26 Feb. 1927, p. 315.
125 Xiangdao, 189, 28 Feb. 1927, p. 2031.
126 SGRSCWZQYYJ, p. 56.
127 A.A., 'Tri shankhaiskikh vosstaniia', p. 72 says 200 were in attendance; *Diyici laodong nianjian*, part 2, p. 457 says 500; Minguo ribao (Canton), 12 Feb. 1927, p. 2 says 700.
128 SGRSCWZQYYJ, p. 39; Xiangdao, 189, 28 Feb. 1927.
129 A.A., 'Tri shankhaiskikh vosstaniia', p. 72.
130 *Zhongguo gongren yundong shiliao*, 4, 1981, pp. 28–9.

131 *Diyici laodong nianjian,* part 2, p. 459.
132 *Diyici laodong nianjian,* part 2, p. 458.
133 A.A., 'Tri Shankhaiskikh vosstaniia', p. 72.
134 *Diyici guonei geming zhanzheng shiqi de gongren yundong,* Beijing, 1954, pp. 467–9. It is not clear whether this proclamation was actually disseminated while the strike was in progress, since Qu Qiubai later accused the party of not raising the call for a citizens' provisional representative conference. SGRSCWZQY, p. 154.
135 SGRSCWZQY, p. 127.
136 *Strikes and Lockouts in Shanghai since 1918,* Shanghai, 1933, p. 52. This would represent about 70% of workers in regular employment, which Alain Roux calculates at 600,000 in 1928, about half of whom were in the 'modern' sector. A. Roux, 'Le mouvement ouvrier à Shanghai de 1928 à 1930' (thèse à troisième cycle), Sorbonne, Paris, 1970 p. 11, p. 45.
137 *Zhongguo gongren yundongshiliao,* 4, 1981, p. 30; NCH, 19 Mar. 1927, p. 472.
138 Zhou Enlai, 'Guanyu Shanghai de wuzhuang qiyi', *Dang de wenxian,* 1, 1994, p. 77.
139 Shenbao, 27 Feb. 1927, p. 13; NCH, 19 Feb. 1927, p. 280; *Diyici laodong nianjian,* part 2, p. 459.
140 Zhou Shangwen, *Shanghai gongren,* p. 98.
141 NCH, 26 Feb. 1927, p. 320; Roux, *Grèves,* p. 50. Brian Martin suggests plausibly that Du played a crucial role in the failure of the February general strike. However, it is less clear that this marked the end of all cooperation between Du and the CCP. B.G. Martin, *The Shanghai Green Gang,* Berkeley, 1996, p. 93.
142 NCH, 26 Feb. 1927, p. 118.
143 NCH, 26 Feb. 1927, p. 317.
144 NCH, 26 Feb. 1927, p. 317; *Diyici laodong nianjian,* part 2, p. 460; Minguo ribao (Canton), 28 Feb. 1927, p. 7, 4 Mar. 1927, p. 7.
145 SGRSCWZQYYJ, p. 42.
146 Zhou Shangwen, *Shanghai gongren,* p. 80.
147 A.A., 'Tri Shankhaiskikh vosstaniia', p. 71.
148 SGRSCWZQYYJ, p. 42; *Zhongguo lici laodong dahui,* p. 178.
149 A.A., 'Tri Shankhaiskikh vosstaniia', p. 73.
150 A.A., 'Tri Shankhaiskikh vosstaniia', p. 74; Zhou Shangwen, *Shanghai gongren,* pp. 104–5.
151 VKP(b), vol. 2, p. 636.
152 Huang Songyi, *Zhonggong zhigong yundong zhi yanjiu,* Master's Thesis, Guoli zhengzhi daxue, Taiwan, 1975, p. 67.
153 A.A., 'Tri Shankhaiskikh vosstaniia', p. 74.
154 A.A., 'Tri Shankhaiskikh vosstaniia', p. 74; Zhou Shangwen, *Shanghai gongren,* p. 105.
155 Yang Xiaoren, 'Shankhaiskie sobytiia vesnoi 1927g.', *Materialy po kitaiskomu voprosu,* 13, 1928, p. 10.
156 Shenbao, 27 Feb. 1927.
157 SGRSCWZQYYJ, p. 250; A.A., 'Tri Shankhaiskikh vosstaniia', pp. 75–6.
158 SGRSCWZQY, p. 201; Shen Yixing, *Shanghai gongren,* p. 328; NCH, 26 Feb. 1927, p. 322, p. 320.
159 SGRSCWZQYYJ, p. 249; Iur'ev, *Revoliutsiia,* p. 433.
160 *Diyici guonei geming zhanzheng,* pp. 464–5.
161 NCH, 26 Feb. 1927, p. 321.
162 Jiang Weixin, 'Huiyi Shanghai', p. 100.

163 NCH, 22 Jan. 1927, p. 114.
164 NCH, 19 Feb. 1927, p. 280.
165 NCH, 5 Mar. 1927, p. 372.
166 NCH, 30 Apr. 1927, p. 210.
167 SGRSCWZQY p. 201.
168 SGRSCWZQY, p. 151.
169 SGRSCWZQY, p. 188.
170 NCH, 12 Mar. 1927, p. 418.
171 *Shanghai gangshi hua*, Shanghai, 1979, p. 316.
172 NCH, 5 Mar. 1927, p. 418.
173 'Shanghai gonggong zujie gongbuju jingwu ribao zhaize', *Dang'an yu lishi*, 1, 1987, p. 21; SMPF, IO 7587; SGRSCWZQYYJ, p. 280; NCH, 23 Apr. 1927, p. 177.
174 SGRSCWZQY, 1983, p. 342.
175 Huang Hao, 'Huiyi da geming shiqi de Shanghai gongren yundong ji qilun' *Dangshi ziliao congkan*, 1980, 2 (3), p. 108.
176 Shenbao, 14 Mar. 1927, p. 10; NCH, 19 Mar. 1927, p. 464. In fact, a fourth foreman at the mill, Cheng Caicheng, was killed by Mu Junbo, an official in the GLU office in Baoshan road, which means that we should treat Wang's testimony with some caution. See 'Shanghai gonggong zujie gongbuju', p. 47.
177 Shenbao, 12 Mar. 1927; 17 Mar. 1927, p. 9; 19 Mar. 1927, p. 13; 20 Mar. 1927, p. 9; *Strikes and Lockouts*, p. 54.
178 SGRSCWZQY, p. 138.
179 SGRSCWZQY, p. 180.
180 SGRSCWZQY, p. 138.
181 SGRSCWZQY, p. 180.
182 SGRSCWZQY, p. 139.
183 SGRSCWZQY, p. 138.
184 SGRSCWZQY, p. 186.
185 SGRSCWZQYYJ, p. 192.
186 SGRSCWZQY, p. 188, p. 138.
187 SGRSCWZQY, p. 188.
188 *Diyici guonei geming zhanzheng*, p. 470.
189 SGRSCWZQY, p. 154.
190 NCH, 26 Feb. 1927, p. 319.
191 *China Weekly Review*, 26 Feb. 1927, p. 352.
192 Zhou Enlai, 'Guanyu Shanghai de wuzhuang qiyi', *Dang de wenxian*, 1, 1994, p. 75.
193 Isaacs, *Tragedy*, p. 135.
194 A.A., 'Tri Shankhaiskikh vosstaniia', p. 77.
195 Zhou Shangwen, *Shanghai gongren*, p. 108; Huang Songyi, *Zhonggong zhigong yundong*, p. 67; Jordan, *Northern Expedition*, p. 106.
196 SGRSCWZQYYJ, p. 42.
197 Clifford, *Spoilt Children*, p. 251.

Chapter 9

1 Wang Jianmin, *Zhongguo gongchandang shigao*, vol. 1, Taibei, 1965, p. 360; vol. 2, Taibei, 1965, p. 263. The exactitude of the figure is misleading, and the membership of several regional organizations was clearly rounded up. Zhao Pu, 'Zhongguo gongchandang zuzhi shi ziliao' (part 6), *Dangshi yanjiu*, 2, 1983, p. 40.

2 Ren Jianshu, 'Chen Duxiu yu Shanghai gongren sanci wuzhuang qiyi', *Zhonggong dangshi ziliao*, 4 (13), 1982, p. 76; SGRSCWZQYYJ, p. 53.

3 SGRSCWZQY, p. 331; SGRSCWZQYYJ, p. 53.

4 SGRSCWZQY, p. 451.

5 'Yijiueryi nian zhi yijiuerqi nian Shanghai, Jiangsu, Zhejiang dang zuzhi fazhan gaikuang' *Zhonggongdang shi ziliao*, 10, 1984, 181–244, p. 235; Yang Xiaoren says that by beginning of April there were 12,000 CCP members and 10,000 CYL members in the city. Yang Xiaoren, 'Shankhaiskie sobytiia vesnoi 1927g.', *Materialy po kitaiskomu voprosu*, 13, 1928, p. 15.

6 'Yijiueryi nian', p. 228.

7 Zhao Pu, 'Zhongguo gongchandang' (part 6), p. 40. These percentages are broadly in line with those given by Mif, except that he puts the percentage of workers at 53.8 and those of miscellaneous social origin at 4.2. P. Mif, *Heroic China: Fifteen Years of the Communist Party of China*, New York, 1937, p. 116.

8 SGRSCWZQYYJ, pp. 188–9.

9 SGRSCWZQYYJ, pp. 221–5.

10 Huang Hao, 'Huiyi da geming shiqi de Shanghai gongren yundong ji qilun', *Dangshi ziliao congkan*, 1980, 2 (3), p. 111.

11 *Shanghai shangwu yinshuguan zhigong yundong shi*, Beijing, 1991, p. 155.

12 *Shanghai disanshiyi mianfangzhi chang gongren yundong shi*, Beijing 1991, p. 200.

13 *Shanghai jiqiye gongren yundong shi*, Beijing, 1991, pp. 289–90. On Yang Peisheng, see E.J. Perry, *Shanghai on Strike*, Stanford, 1993, pp. 85–6.

14 Zhao Pu, 'Zhongguo gongchandang zuzhi shi ziliao' (part 2), *Dangshi yanjiu*, 2, 1981, p. 66; Wang Jianying gives a figure of 1892 women among a membership of 18,526, i.e.10.2 per cent. Wang Jianying (ed.). *Zhongguo gongchandang zuzhishi ziliao huibian*, Beijing, 1982, p. 33. The figure of 1992 is repeated in Zhao Pu, 'Zhongguo gongchandang' (part 4), *Dangshi yanjiu*, 3, 1982, p. 37.

15 Zhao Pu, 'Zhongguo gongchandang' (part 6), p. 40; Pravda, 8 May 1927, cited in C.M. Wilbur, *The Nationalist Revolution in China, 1923–1928*, Cambridge, 1984, p. 38. Mif, *Heroic China*, p. 116, however, gives a figure of 10 per cent.

16 SGRSCWZQYYJ, pp. 223–26.

17 Minguo ribao, 5 Jan. 1927.

18 *Zhongguo funü yundong lishi ziliao, 1921–1927*, Beijing, 1986, pp. 734–5.

19 ZGGCDSH, p. 65.

20 SGRSCWZQYYJ, p. 188.

21 Chen Duxiu, 'Chen Duxiu zai Zhongguo gongchandang di wuci quanguo daibiao dahui shang de baogao', *Zhonggong dangshi ziliao*, 3, 1982, p. 57.

22 Zheng Chaolin. *An Oppositionist for Life*, Atlantic Highlands, N.J., 1997, p. 119.

23 Zheng Chaolin, *Oppositionist*, p. 96.

24 SGRSCWZQYYJ, p. 189.

25 C. Henriot, 'Municipal Power and Local Elites', *Republican China*, vol. 11, no. 2, 1986, p. 17.

26 Minguo ribao (Canton), 12 Jan. 1927, p. 4.

27 Henriot, 'Municipal Power', p. 17.

28 SGRSCWZQYYJ, pp. 223–6.

29 *Zhongguo guomindang geshengshi zongdengji he gedangyuan tongji*, Nanjing, 1929, n.p.

30 *Zhongguo guomindang geshengshi zongdengji*, n.p.

31 In October 1917 the Bolsheviks in Petrograd had a membership of over 43,000 in a city of 2.4 million people, but their principal rivals were in disarray at the time of their seizure of power – in contrast to the GMD in Shanghai. S.A. Smith, *Red Petrograd: Revolution in the Factories, 1917–18*, Cambridge, 1983, p. 244.

32 A.A., 'Tri shankhaiskikh vosstaniia', *Problemy Kitaia*, 2, 1930, p. 77; N.R. Clifford, *Spoilt Children of Empire*, Hanover, 1991, p. 200.

33 A.A., 'Tri shankhaiskikh vosstaniia', pp. 77–8.

34 A.A. 'Tri shankhaiskikh vosstaniia', p. 78.

35 VKP(b), vol. 2, p. 594, p. 878; Chang Kuo-t'ao, *The Rise of the Communist Party, 1921–27*, Lawrence, 1971, p. 568.

36 ZGGCDSH, pp. 40–1.

37 SGRSCWZQYYJ, p. 49; ZGGCDSH, p. 41. The CEC military commission does not appear to have been directly involved in the preparation of the uprising, but at a meeting on 13 March Zhou Enlai reported on developments in Shanghai. Unfortunately, the minutes use pseudonyms, so it is not clear who the six people present were. It is clear that at least two of them were Russians (Albrecht and Mandalian). Appen seems to have been the Russian most closely involved in the planning of the uprising. N. Mitarevsky, *World Wide Soviet Plots*, Tientsin, n.d. (1927), p. 171.

38 SGRSCWZQY, p. 401.

39 A.A., 'Tri shankhaiskikh vosstaniia', pp. 78–9.

40 A.A., 'Tri shankhaiskikh vosstaniia', p. 79; SGRSCWZQYYJ, p. 56; Feng Shaoting, 'Qian pu hou ji: duoqu wuzhuang qiyi de shengli', *Shanghai gongyun shiliao*, 2, 1987, p. 22.

41 A.A., 'Tri shankhaiskikh vosstaniia', p. 79.

42 Liu Ding, 'Xuesheng yundong yu sanci wuzhuang qiyi', *Shanghai gongyun shiliao*, 2, 1987, p. 44; Zhou Shangwen and He Shiyou, *Shanghai gongren sanci wuzhuang qiyi shi*, Shanghai, 1987, p. 140.

43 *Zhongguo gongren yundong shiliao*, 4, 1981, pp. 42–3.

44 SGRSCWZQYYJ, p. 126.

45 H.L. Boorman and R.C. Howard, eds., *Biographical Dictionary of Republican China*, vol. 3, New York, 1970, p. 44, pp. 417–8; Wang Ke-wen. 'The Kuomintang in Transition: Ideology and Factionalism in the 'National Revolution', 1924–32', Ph.D., Stanford University, 1985, p. 134.

46 H.J. van de Ven, *From Friend to Comrade*, Berkeley, 1991, pp. 191–2; SGRSCWZQYYJ, p. 57.

47 SGRSCWZQY, p. 245.

48 Zhou Shangwen, *Shanghai gongren*, pp. 121–22.

49 Zhou Shangwen, *Shanghai gongren*, p. 123.

50 VKP(b), vol. 2, p. 733.

51 VKP(b), vol. 2, p. 614.

52 VKP(b), vol. 2, p. 635.

53 Zhou Shangwen, *Shanghai gongren*, p. 98. The four Comintern functionaries in Shanghai claimed erroneously in a report of 4 March that the committee consisted of nine members, of whom two were Communists, which suggests they were not well-informed. The underestimation of Communist strength, however, may be due to the fact that only two of the five – Wang Shouhua and Luo Yinong – were publicly members of the CCP. See VKP(b), vol. 2, p. 637.

54 VKP(b), vol. 2, p. 638.

55 Zhou Shangwen, *Shanghai gongren*, p. 98.

56 Zhou Shangwen, *Shanghai gongren*, p. 193.

57 SGRSCWZQYYJ, p. 331.

58 SGRSCWZQYYJ, pp. 58–9, p. 202;.

59 SGRSCWZQY, p. 305.

60 Zhou Shangwen, *Shanghai gongren*, p. 195; SGRSCWZQYYJ, p. 128. Yang Xingfo (1893–1933) was born in Baoshan in Jiangxi. He joined the Alliance

Society in 1911, but after the failure of the revolution went to study engineering in the USA. He returned to China in 1918 and was Sun Yat-sen's secretary from 1924. He was a founder of the Scientific Society of China and secretary-general of the Academia Sinica. Active in the League for the Protection of Human Rights, he was assassinated in 1933. *Ershi shiji Zhongguo mingren cidian,* Shenyang, 1991, p. 534; H.L. Boorman, and R.C. Howard, *Biographical Dictionary of Republican China,* vol. 4, New York, 1971, pp. 5–6.

61 Shenbao, 13 Mar. 1927, p. 9.

62 Zhou Shangwen, *Shanghai gongren,* p. 198. Zhou says that there were fifteen Communists elected, but his list includes Wang Shouhua, whose name is not on the list of 31 published in Shenbao. Wang, however, was selected to head the organization department at the meeting of the executive on 15 March. Of the remaining 14, 13 can be confirmed as Communists. Zhou claims that Wang Hanliang, a merchant active in the GMD merchants' association (*Hu shang xiehui*), was a Communist, but this seems doubtful. Wang, for example, resigned from the citizens' government in early April, as did other non-Communists.

63 Shenbao, 23 Mar. 1927, p. 9. Zhou Shangwen says that 10 of the 19 were Communists, but includes the doubtful case of Wang Hanliang. Ren Jianshu states – probably correctly – that there were nine. One should remember, however, that Hou Shaoqiu, Ding Xiaoxian, Lin Jun and He Luo acted publicly as GMD rather than CCP members. Ren Jianshu, 'Chen Duxiu', p. 78. Christian Henriot was the first to point out that the selection of the provisional municipal government was made by the GMD rather than the citizens' assembly on 22 March. See C. Henriot, 'La rupture entre PCC-GMD en 1927: suicide ou assassinat?', *Cahiers d'études chinoises,* 5, 1986, p. 60.

64 SGRSCWZQY, p. 326.

65 SGRSCWZQY, p. 327.

66 Zhou Shangwen, *Shanghai gongren,* p. 196.

67 SGRSCWZQYYJ, p. 196.

68 SGRSCWZQY, p. 347; Zhou Shangwen, *Shanghai gongren,* p. 147.

69 A.A. 'Tri shankhaiskikh vosstaniia', p. 81.

70 Shenbao, 21 Mar. 1927, p. 9; Zhou Shangwen, *Shanghai gongren,* p. 146.

71 *Zhongguo gonghui lishi wenxian, 1921–27,* Beijing, 1958, pp. 378–89; *Zhongguo gongren yundong shiliao,* 4, 1981, pp. 42–3.

72 *Zhongguo gongren yundong shiliao,* 4, 1981, p. 45.

73 SGRSCWZQYYJ, p. 211.

74 *Diyici Zhongguo laodong nianjian,* part 2, Beijing, 1928, pp. 460–61.

75 Zhou Shangwen, *Shanghai gongren,* p. 198.

76 G.E. Sokolsky, 'The Kuomintang', *China Year Book,* 1928, (ed.) H.G.W. Woodhead, Tientsin, 1928, p. 1360.

77 SGRSCWZQYYJ, p. 66. Merchants' organizations backed a suspension of trade (*xiuye*) to mark the arrival of the NRA, but were unwilling to back a strike (*bashi*). Ren Jianshu, *Chen Duxiu zhuan,* Shanghai, 1989, p. 354.

78 Shenbao, 22 Mar. 1927, p. 9.

79 NCH, 26 Mar. 1927, p. 484; *Diyici laodong nianjian,* part 2, p. 461.

80 NCH, 26 Mar. 1927, p. 486.

81 NCH, 23 Apr. 1927, p. 174; Shenbao, 22 Mar. 1927, p. 11.

82 *Strikes and Lockouts in Shanghai since 1918,* Shanghai, 1933 p. 29. Note that this compares with 6000 enterprises and 420,970 workers said by the same source to have taken part in the February general strike.

83 SGRSCWZQY, p. 374.

84 SGRSCWZQYYJ, p. 67; SGRSCWZQY, p. 419.
85 SGRSCWZQYYJ, pp. 221–2; Zhao Yinong et al., 'Hudong gongren fenqi bodou', *Shanghai gongyun shiliao*, 2, 1987, p. 34.
86 'Shanghai gonggong zujie gongbuju jingwu ribao zhaize', *Dang'an yu lishi*, 1, 1987, p. 35.
87 SGRSCWZQY, p. 383.
88 A.A. 'Tri shankhaiskikh vosstaniia', p. 82; Xiangdao, 193, 6 Apr. 1927; SGRSCWZQYYJ, p. 68.
89 *Shanghai gangshi hua*, Shanghai, 1979, pp. 312–13.
90 Zhou Shangwen, *Shanghai gongren*, pp. 174–5.
91 *Nanyang xiongdi yancao gongsi shiliao*, Shanghai, 1958, pp. 350–1; Perry, *Shanghai on Strike*, p. 152.
92 Zhou Shangwen, *Shanghai gongren*, p. 175; SGRSCWZQYYJ, pp. 224–5.
93 SGRSCWZQYYJ, p. 67; Shenbao, 23 Mar. 1927, p. 11.
94 Yang Yue et al, 'Nanshi qiangsheng', *Shanghai gongyun shiliao*, 2, 1987, p. 26.
95 SGRSCWZQY, p. 402; *Jiangnan zaochuanchang changshi, 1865–1949.5*, Shanghai, 1983, p. 175.
96 Zhou Shangwen, *Shanghai gongren*, p. 173.
97 SGRSCWZQYYJ, pp. 66–7; Xiangdao, 193, 6 Apr. 1927.
98 A.A., 'Tri shankhaiskikh vosstaniia', p. 82.
99 *Rongjia qiye shiliao*, Shanghai, 1962. p. 322.
100 SGRSCWZQY, p. 367. The 'right wing' here refers to the NRA irregulars, discussed below. The insurgents were supposed to wear a blue armband marked by a white star.
101 Huang Hao, 'Huiyi da geming shiqi', p. 110; Shenbao, 22 Mar. 1927, p. 9; SGRSCWZQYYJ, p. 68.
102 SGRSCWZQYYJ, p. 69.
103 Zhou Shangwen, *Shanghai gongren*, p. 156, p. 183.
104 NCH, 26 Mar. 1927, p. 481; Shenbao, 26 Mar. 1927, p. 21; A.A., 'Tri shankhaiskikh vosstaniia', p. 82.
105 The Oriental Library, which had only opened the previous year, belonged to the Commercial Press and housed a club for its employees. It was the largest library in Asia and was situated opposite the huge Commercial Press complex. See *Shanghai shangwu yinshuguan*, pp. 5–6.
106 Wei Fang'ai, *Shanghai gongren sanci wuzhuang qiyi*, Beijing, 1951, pp. 9–10; NCH, 26 Mar. 1927, pp. 481–2; Zhou Shangwen, *Shanghai gongren*, pp. 184–6.
107 Shenbao, 23 Mar. 1927, pp. 11–12; 26 Mar. 1927, p. 21; A.A., 'Tri shankhaiskikh vosstaniia', p. 83.
108 The chronology of events is by no means easy to reconstruct. I have tended to follow the account by Shi Ying (Zhao Shiyan), which is the earliest. Shi Ying, 'Shanghai gongren di sanci qiyi', Xiangdao, 193, 6 Apr. 1927, p. 2090; SGRSCWZQY, p. 422.
109 A.A., 'Tri shankhaiskikh vosstaniia', p. 83.
110 'Tri shankhaiskikh vosstaniia', p. 84. For an account of Bi's subornation see B.G. Martin, *The Shanghai Green Gang*, Berkeley, 1996, p. 96.
111 SGRSCWZQYYJ, pp. 71–2.
112 Shenbao, 24 Mar. 1927, pp. 9–10; A.A., 'Tri shankhaiskikh vosstaniia', p. 85.
113 A.A., 'Tri shankhaiskikh vosstaniia', pp. 83–4.
114 Shenbao, 24 Mar. 1927, pp. 9–10.
115 L.A. Bereznyi, 'Geroicheskoe vosstanie shankhaiskogo proletariata v marte 1927g.', *Sovetskoe kitaevedenie*, 3, 1958, pp. 97–107, p. 102; Wei Fang'ai, *Sanci wuzhuang qiyi*, pp. 11–12.

116 SGRSCWZQY, p. 368, p. 419; Mar.tin, *Shanghai Green Gang*, p. 97.
117 SGRSCWZQYYJ, p. 129.
118 Zhou Shangwen, *Shanghai gongren*, p. 176, pp. 180–1.
119 'Shanghai gonggong zujie gongbuju jingwu ribao', p. 37.
120 As a student in Japan, Xu had joined the Alliance Society and subsequently become a member of the GMD. In October 1914 Sun Yat-sen appointed him head of the fifth branch of his new Chinese Revolutionary Party. Jiang Hao, 'Hongmen lishi chu tan', *Jiu Shanghai de banghui*, Shanghai, 1986, p. 61, p. 82;. Zhou Yumin, Shao Yong, *Zhongguo banghui shi*, Shanghai, 1993, p. 462.
121 Shenbao, 22 Mar. 1927; Zhou Shangwen, *Shanghai gongren*, p. 174.
122 SGRSCWZQY, pp. 367–8.
123 NCH, 25 Mar. 1927, p. 488.
124 SGRSCWZQYYJ, p. 261.
125 This is the figure given by the GLU in a report to the CEC of the GMD in Wuhan on 15 April 1927. Minguo ribao, 21 Apr. 1927.
126 D.A. Jordan. *The Northern Expedition*, Honolulu, 1976, p. 116.
127 Clifford, *Spoilt Children*, p. 220.
128 It is noteworthy that in his novel, finished within days of the Communist victory, Jiang Guangci said little about the uprising, suggesting that the pickets were fighting 'routed troops' (*kui bing*). Jiang Guangci, 'Duanku dang', *Shiwen xuanji*, Beijing, 1957, p. 307.
129 Shenbao, 23 Mar. 1927, p. 9; Zhou Shangwen, *Shanghai gongren*, p. 198.
130 SGRSCWZQYYJ, p. 75.
131 Shenbao, 23 Mar. 1927, p. 9; SGRSCWZQYYJ, p. 75.
132 Although students were very active in the third armed uprising, the formal role of the SSU was slight. The success of the uprising briefly increased CYL influence in the executive. Jiang Zhichan, 'Dageming shiqi de Shanghai xuelian', *Diyici guogong hezuo shiqi de Gongqingtuan zhuanti lun wenji*, Beijing, 1985, pp. 90–100; Wang Guichang, 'Shanghai gongren sanci wuzhuang qiyi zhongde xuesheng', *Diyici guogong*, pp. 274–82.
133 Shenbao, 22 Mar. 1927, p. 12. The executives of both the Zhabei and Nanshi citizen assemblies appear to have already been determined by the local GMD.
134 SGRSCWZQYYJ, p. 226.
135 Shenbao, 26 Mar. 1927, p. 9; Minguo ribao (Shanghai), 24 Mar. 1927.
136 SGRSCWZQYYJ, pp. 224–5.
137 SGRSCWZQYYJ, p. 214.
138 SGRSCWZQYYJ, pp. 221–2.
139 Shenbao, 28 Mar. 1927, p. 11; NCH, 2 Apr. 1927, p. 19.
140 *Shanghai zonggonghui baogao*, Shanghai, 1927. p. 13, p. 12. The latter figure stretches credibility, but there is no doubt that there had been an extraordinary rush to unionize.
141 Shenbao, 24 Mar. 1927, p. 11; 25 Mar. 1927, p. 11; 26 Mar. 1927, p. 9; 27 Mar. 1927, p. 10.
142 Shenbao, 27 Mar. 1927, p. 10.
143 Shenbao, 30 Mar. 1927, p. 9; NCH, 2 Apr. 1927, p. 16.
144 Zhao Yinong et al., 'Hudong gongren', p. 33.
145 Zhao Yinong et al., 'Hudong gongren', p. 34.
146 'Shanghai gonggong zujie gongbuju jingwu ribao', p. 43.
147 Xiangdao, 189, 28 Feb. 1927.
148 Cited in J.A. Aho, *This Thing of Darkness: A Sociology of the Enemy*, Seattle, 1994, p. 14.

149 Jiang Guangci, *Duanku dang*, pp. 268, 283–4, 305. I deduce that Lin Hesheng is Wang Shouhua because he is described as representing organized labour on the presidium of the citizens' assembly of 22 March.

150 Jiang proclaimed: 'The more violent is the revolution, the more boundless is its scope, the more it can grasp a poet's soul.' Leo Ou-fan Lee, *The Romantic Generation of Modern Chinese Writers*, Cambridge, Mass., 1973, p. 209.

151 C.M. Wilbur and J. Lien-ying How, *Missionaries of Revolution*, Cambridge, Mass., 1989, p. 399.

152 *China Weekly Review*, 2 Apr. 1927.

153 PRO FO 228/3021 'S. Barton, Consul-General, to HM Minister, 23 Mar. 1927'.

154 Shenbao, 28 Mar. 1927, p. 9; NCH, 2 Apr. 1927, p. 3.

155 NCH, 2 Apr. 1927, p. 3.

156 SGRSCWZQYYJ, p. 132.

157 Shen Yixing, Jiang Peinan and Zheng Qingsheng, *Shanghai gongren yundong shi*, vol. 1, Liaoning, 1991, p. 350.

158 VKP(b), vol. 2, p. 735.

159 Zhou Shangwen, *Shanghai gongren*, p. 263.

160 Shenbao, 26 Mar. 1927, p. 9. The International Settlement police believed this was the aim of the GLU. See 'Shanghai gonggong zujie gongbuju jingwu ribao', p. 45.

161 SGRSCWZQY, p. 408; SGRSCWZQYYJ, p. 91.

162 VKP(b), vol. 2, p. 735; Yang Xiaoren, 'Shankhaiskie sobytiia', p. 18. The message from Lin Jun at the mass meeting to welcome Chiang Kai-shek on the same day, 27 March, was mixed. He threatened a general strike unless the foreign concessions were immediately surrendered, but called on the Wuhan government to begin negotiations to this end. NCH, 2 Apr. 1927, p. 3.

163 Communications between the few members of the CEC still in Shanghai and Wuhan were difficult. And it was decided to send Peng Shuzhi to Wuhan to consult with CEC members. He arrived in Nanjing on 1 April but for some reason did not get to Wuhan until the 10th.

164 VKP(b), vol. 2, p. 659.

Chapter 10

1 Brian G. Martin, *The Shanghai Green Gang*, Berkeley, 1996, pp. 99–100.

2 Compare C.M. Wilbur, *The Nationalist Revolution in China, 1923–1928*, Cambridge, 1984, p. 104; Su Zhiliang, 'Shanghai liumang shili yu 'Si yi er' zhengbian', *Jindai shi yanjiu*, 2, 1988, p. 221.

3 Yang Hu was a master in the Green Gang with the second-highest (*tong*) generational status, as well as a member of the Xingzhong mountain lodge of the Red Gang. *Jiu Shanghai de banghui*, Shanghai, 1986, p. 63, p. 80. Brian Martin suggests that only at this point did Yang Hu and Chen Qun become inducted into the Green Gang, as disciples of Zhang Renkui, in order to ensure that the gang operated in accordance with GMD interests. Martin, *Shanghai Green Gang*, p. 100. Guo Xuoyin says that the two had a longstanding connection to the Gang, going back to early years of the Republic when the Big Eight Mob controlled the city's opium trade. Guo Xuyin, *Jiu Shanghai heishehui*, Shanghai, 1997, p. 67.

4 Shenbao, 5 Apr. 1927; Shenbao, 8 Apr. 1927; Xiangdao, 194, 1 May 1927, p. 2111; Zhang Jungu, *Du Yuesheng zhuan*, p. 317; Huang Zhenshi, 'Wo suo zhidao de Huang Jinrong', *Jiu Shanghai de banghui*, pp. 174–6; F. Wakeman, *Policing Shanghai, 1927–1937*, Berkeley, 1995, p. 123.

5 Su Zhiliang, 'Shanghai liumang', p. 215.

6 Zhang Jungu, *Du Yuesheng zhuan*, Taibei, 1980 (orig. 1967), vol. 1, p. 271; Guo Xuyin, *Jiu Shanghai*, pp. 63–4. The eight diagrams were part of secret-society symbolism and would have been recognized by police as indicating that Wang was a member of the underworld.

7 SGRSCWZQYYJ, p. 209.

8 Su Zhiliang, 'Shanghai liumang', p. 215; E.J. Perry, *Shanghai on Strike*, Stanford, 1993, p. 86.

9 *Shanghai gangshi hua*, Shanghai, 1979, p. 316; Shenbao, 28 Mar. 1927, p. 12; NCH 2 Apr. 1927, p. 7.

10 *Rongjia qiye shiliao*, vol. 1, Shanghai, 1980, p. 325.

11 'Zhonggong Shanghai quwei youguan Shanghai gongren sanci wuzhuang qiyi de wenxian qi pian', *Dang'an yu lishi*, 1, 1987, p. 12.

12 SGRSCWZQYYJ, p. 295; 'Shanghai gonggong zujie gongbuju jingwu ribao zhaize', *Dang'an yu lishi*, 1, 1987, p. 52.

13 C.M. Wilbur and J. Lien-ying How, *Missionaries of Revolution*, Cambridge, Mass., 1989, p. 402; D.A. Jordan, *The Northern Expedition*, Honolulu, 1976, p. 124.

14 *Yijiuerqi nian de Shanghai shangye lianhehui*, (ed.) Liu Pinggang, Shanghai, 1983, p. 48.

15 Shen Yu, 'Si yi er fangeming zhengbian de yunniang he fadong', *Dang'an yu lishi*, 2, 1987, p. 79; *China Weekly Review*, 9 Apr. 1927.

16 Wilbur, *Nationalist Revolution*, pp. 84–5.

17 *Yijiuerqi nian*, p. 222, p. 231.

18 Shenbao, 22 Mar. 1927, p. 11.

19 *Yijiuerqi nian*, p. 225.

20 Shenbao 22 Mar. 1927, p. 9; C. Henriot, 'La rupture entre PCC-GMD en 1927: suicide ou assassinat?', *Cahiers d'études chinoises*, 5, 1986, p. 66.

21 SGRSCWZQYYJ, p. 131.

22 Henriot inclines to the view that it was poor communication. Henriot, 'La rupture', p. 67.

23 SGRSCWZQYYJ, p. 75.

24 SGRSCWZQYYJ, p. 77; NCH, 2 Apr. 1927, p. 16.

25 SGRSCWZQYYJ, p. 215, p. 134.

26 Shenbao, 1 Apr. 1927, p. 13.

27 H.R. Isaacs, *The Tragedy of the Chinese Revolution*, Stanford, 1961. p. 166.

28 Yang Xiaoren, 'Shankhaiskie sobytiia vesnoi 1927g.', *Materialy po kitaiskomu voprosu*, 13, 1928, p. 15.

29 Shenbao, 4 Apr. 1927, p. 15.

30 SGRSCWZQYYJ, pp. 261–6.

31 Zhou Shangwen and He Shiyou, *Shanghai gongren sanci wuzhuang qiyi shi*, Shanghai, 1987 p. 245.

32 Henriot, 'La rupture', p. 89.

33 Zhou Shangwen, *Shanghai gongren*, p. 246.

34 Shenbao, 9 Apr. 1927. The 15 members of the Shanghai branch of the Political Council were all GMD members, most on the right of the party.

35 VKP(b), vol. 2, p. 738.

36 VKP(b), vol. 2, p. 734.

37 N.R. Clifford, *Spoilt Children of Empire*, Hanover, 1991, p. 246.
38 SGRSCWZQYYJ, p. 89.
39 Shenbao, 26 Mar. 1927, p. 9.
40 Shenbao, 27 Mar. 1927, p. 9.
41 Shenbao, 28 Mar. 1927, p. 10.
42 P. Mif, *Kitaiskaia revoliutsiia*, Moscow, 1932, p. 99.
43 SGRSCWZQYYJ, p. 224.
44 Shenbao, 5 Apr. 1927.
45 SGRSCWZQYYJ, p. 296.
46 Clifford, *Spoilt Children*, p. 246.
47 Shenbao, 27 Mar. 1927, p. 11.
48 C. Brandt, *Stalin's Failure in China, 1924–27*, Cambridge, Mass., 1958, p. 159.
49 T. Mandalian, 'Pourquoi la direction du PC de Chine n'a-t-elle pas rempli sa tâche?' P. Broué, (ed.) *La question chinoise dans l'Internationale communiste (1926–27)*, Paris, 1965. pp. 288–89.
50 *Kommunisticheskii Internatsional i kitaiskaia revoliutsiia*, Moscow, 1986, p. 104.
51 SGRSCWZQYYJ, p. 222.
52 Yang Xiaoren, 'Shankhaiskie sobytiia', p. 17. Even militant workers refused to join the NRA. *Shanghai fangzhi gongren yundong shi*, Beijing, 1991, pp. 572–3.
53 Isaacs, *Tragedy*, p. 146.
54 See Jiang Jieshi, *Jiang zongtong milu*, vol. 6, p. 154, quoted in Su Zhiliang, 'Shanghai liumang', p. 223.
55 'Shanghai gonggong zujie gongbuju jingwu ribao', p. 42; SGRSCWZQYYJ, pp. 224–25.
56 *Yijiuerqi nian*, p. 225.
57 Shenbao, 25 Mar. 1927, p. 10.
58 Shenbao, 27 Mar. 1927, p. 11; NCH, 2 Apr. 1927, p. 16.
59 NCH, 9 Apr. 1927, p. 51; 'Shanghai gongong zujie jingwu ribao', p. 47.
60 At the beginning of April the *North China Herald* observed: 'There are not more than 3,000 Nationalist troops in Shanghai ... The military forces of General Chiang Kai-shek are now so scattered over so vast an area as not to be very valuable either for offensive purposes or for the suppression of the labourers'. NCH, 2 Apr. 1927, p. 7. For General Duncan see Clifford, *Spoilt Children*, p. 246.
61 According to the GLU, in late March there were 2700 picketers in the city, armed with 1700 rifles, a few dozen automatic weapons, and a large stock of ammunition captured from northern troops, but this seems to have been an underestimate, both of manpower and weaponry. *Zhongguo gongren yundong shiliao*, 4, 1981, p. 73; Xiangdao, 194, 1 May 1927, p. 2107.
62 SGRSCWZQYYJ, p. 213.
63 NCH, 23 Apr. 1927, p. 170. Clifford, who has carefully studied the diplomatic records, suggests a somewhat lower total. See Clifford, *Spoilt Children*, p. 260.
64 VKP(b), vol. 2, p. 659.
65 VKP(b), vol. 2, p. 736.
66 Chesneaux, *Chinese Labor Movement*, p. 368; Isaacs, *Tragedy*, p. 168.
67 Zhou Shangwen, *Shanghai gongren*, p. 263.
68 Yang Xiaoren, 'Shankhaiskie sobytiia', p. 15.
69 'Zhonggong Shanghai quwei youguan Shanghai gongren sanci qiyi', p. 14.
70 Shen Yixing, *Shanghai gongren*, p. 364.
71 SGRSCWZQYYJ, p. 222.
72 Zhou Shangwen, *Shanghai gongren*, p. 250.
73 SGRSCWZQYYJ, p. 95, p. 96.

74 For the full text of the speech, see W. Kuo, *Analytical History of the Chinese Communist Party*, vol. 1, Taibei, 1966, pp. 424–46.

75 SGRSCWZQYYJ, p. 228.

76 SGRSCWZQY, pp. 445–46.

77 SGRSCWZQY, p. 449.

78 NCH, 9 Apr. 1927, p. 80; SGRSCWZQYYJ, p. 100.

79 Shenbao, 8 Apr. 1927, p. 14.

80 VKP(b), vol. 2, p. 737.

81 Shen Yixing, *Shanghai gongren*, p. 368.

82 Fan Shaozeng, 'Guanyu Du Yuesheng', *Jiu Shanghai de banghui*, 210–6; Tien-wei Wu, 'Chiang Kai-shek's April 12 Coup of 1927', in G.F. Chan and T.H. Etzold eds., *China in the 1920s*, New York, 1976, pp. 155–6.

83 Su Zhiliang and Chen Lifei, *Jindai Shanghai hei shehui yanjiu*, Hangzhou, 1991, p. 18.

84 Su Zhiliang, 'Shanghai liumang', p. 221.

85 Shenbao, 13 Apr. 1927, p. 13; NCH, 16 Apr. 1927, p. 102; Xiangdao, 194, 1 May 1927, pp. 2108–2112.

86 Shenbao, 13 Apr. 1927, pp. 13–14; NCH, 21 May 1927, p. 342.

87 Shanghai gonggong jingwu ribao', p. 53; SGRSCWZQY, p. 452.

88 *Zhongguo gongren yundong shiliao*, 2, 1958, p. 125; SGRSCWZQYYJ, p. 107. Even if the figure of 15,000 includes NRA soldiers and other ancillaries such as French Concession detectives, it seems high.

89 Shen Yixing, *Shanghai gongren*, p. 370.

90 SGRSCWZQYYJ, p. 286, p. 340–1; 'Shanghai gonggong jingwu ribao', p. 55.

91 Shenbao, 14 Apr. 1927, p. 13; NCH, 16 Apr. 1927, p. 104; *Zhongguo gongren yundong shiliao*, 4, 1981, p. 82. Some press reports claimed that there were 50,000 at the Zhabei citizens' assembly meeting.

92 NCH, 16 Apr. 1927, p. 103.

93 Xu Meikun, 'Yi qiyi qianhou', *Shanghai gongyun shiliao*, 2, 1987, p. 3.

94 NCH, 16 Apr. 1927, p. 104.

95 NCH, 21 May 1927, p. 342. Roux cites a lower figure of 90,000 from the International Settlement daily police report for 14 April. A. Roux, *Grèves et politique à Shanghai: les désillusions (1927–1932)*, Paris, 1995, p. 68.

96 *Zhongguo gongren yundong shiliao*, 2, 1958, p. 126.

97 Zhou Shangwen, *Shanghai gongren*, p. 297.

98 'Shanghai gonggong jingwu ribao', p. 55; Shen Yixing, *Shanghai gongren*, p. 374.

99 *Zhongguo gongren yundong shiliao*, 4, 1981, p. 92.

100 Shenbao, 14 Apr. 1927, p. 13; SGRSCWZQYYJ, pp. 343–4.

101 *Zhongguo gongren yundong shiliao*, 4, 1981, pp. 92–3, p. 95; Isaacs, *Tragedy*, pp. 179–80.

102 NCH, 21 May 1927, p. 342.

103 Zhou Shangwen, *Shanghai gongren*, p. 297.

104 SGRSCWZQY p. 454.

105 *Zhongguo gongren yundong shiliao*, 4, 1981, p. 105.

106 NCH, 23 Apr. 1927, p. 166.

107 NCH, 21 May 1927, p. 342.

108 'Shanghai gonggong jingwu ribao', p. 59.

109 *Zhongguo gongren yundong shiliao*, 4, 1981, p. 104.

110 NCH, 21 May 1927, p. 342. Roux confirms a figure of 400 deaths in a detailed breakdown, based on the International Settlement police daily report of 21 May. Roux, *Grèves*, pp. 66–67.

111 NCH, 16 Apr. 1927, p. 102; Wilbur, *National Revolution*, p. 109.

112 Shen Yixing, *Shanghai gongren*, p. 382; Huang Hao, 'Huiyi da geming shiqi de Shanghai gongren yundong ji qilun', *Dangshi ziliao congkan*, 1980, 2 (3), p. 110.

113 Shen Yixing, *Shanghai gongren*, pp. 383–4; *Shanghai gangshi hua*, Shanghai, 1979, pp. 312–13.

114 Wang Jiagui, Cai Xiyao, *Shanghai daxue*, Shanghai, 1986, p. 49.

115 ZGDSRWZ, vol. 7, Xi'an, 1983, p. 46.

116 ZGGCDSH, p. 37.

117 Buersaiweike, 8, 12 Dec. 1927. Other sources cite a variant of the pun – *langhu chengqun* – which translates as 'wolves and tigers stalk in packs'. See Isaacs, *Tragedy*, p. 177.

118 Buersaiweike, 8, 12 Dec. 1927. Others, basing themselves on a report in NCH, 10 Sept. 1927, put the number of victims as high as 5,000.

119 NCH, 23 Apr. 1927, p. 165.

120 NCH, 30 Apr. 1927, p. 186.

121 NCH, 29 Apr. 1927, p. 166, p. 187.

122 VKP(b), vol. 2, pp. 736–7.

123 VKP(b), vol. 2, p. 736.

124 SGRSCWZQY p. 454.

125 VKP(b), vol. 2, p. 737.

126 SGRSCWZQY, pp. 474–5; H. J. van de Ven, *From Friend to Comrade*, Berkeley, 1991, p. 220.

127 Zhou Shangwen, *Shanghai gongren*, pp. 301–2.

128 SGRSCWZQY, p. 458, p. 463.

129 SGRSCWZQY, p. 464.

130 As late as 17 March the Communists complained that without their constant efforts the GMD left fell apart. See SGRSCWZQYYJ, p. 206.

131 Van de Ven, *Friend* pp. 229–39.

132 Van de Ven, *Friend*, p. 182.

133 One needs analytically to separate the issue of whether Chiang Kai-shek could have been resisted from the issue of whether a revolution of the type envisaged by the Comintern was on the cards. General Bliukher, whose judgements tended to be sober, reckoned that in late February 1927 some action to remove Chiang could have been successful, since at that time he faced setbacks in Zhejiang and a rising by the third corps of the NRA in Nanchang. A.I. Kartunova, 'Novyi vzgliad na vopros o razryve s Chan Kaishi: ianvar'-aprel'1927', *Vostok/Oriens*, 1, 1997, p. 44. More generally, the precariousness of Chiang Kai-shek's political position right up to 1931 suggests that factions in the NRA and the party might have been successfully mobilized to block Chiang, as Borodin envisaged. This does not, however, alter the fact that the balance of power lay with the NRA, not with the mass movements.

Conclusion

1 L.T. Lih, O.V. Naumov and O.V. Khlevniuk (eds.), *Stalin's Letters to Molotov, 1925–1936*, New Haven, Conn., 1995, pp. 140.

2 VKP(b), vol. 2, p. 734.

3 Karl Radek's 'Theses' of 22 June 1926, for example, though acute in their criticisms of the united-front policy, likened the GMD to Russia's Left SRs, a wholly inappropriate historical analogy. VKP(b), vol. 2, pp. 262–5.

4 M.Y.L. Luk, *The Origins of Chinese Bolshevism*, Hong Kong, 1990, p. 4.
5 The term is Partha Chatterjee's, used to denote how colonial nationalisms produced a discourse which, even as it challenged the colonial claim to political domination, accepted the intellectual premises of 'modernity' on which colonial domination was based. In so far as the Soviet Union assisted China's struggle for national liberation yet nevertheless set the benchmarks against which its progress was to be measured, the CCP may be said to have subscribed to an ideology that was determined heteronomously. P. Chatterjee, *Nationalist Thought and the Colonial World*, Zed Books, London, 1986, p. 30.
6 This is broadly affirmed for Comintern policy in relation to many different national Communist parties in T. Rees and A. Thorpe (eds.) *International Communism and the Communist International, 1919–43*, Manchester, 1998.
7 H.R. Isaacs, *The Tragedy of the Chinese Revolution*, Stanford, 1961, p. 117.
8 VKP(b), vol. 2, p. 928.
9 VKP(b), vol. 2, p. 732.
10 ZGZYWJXJ, vol. 3, p. 19.
11 VKP(b), vol. 2, p. 185.
12 VKP(b), vol. 2, p. 550.
13 VKP(b), vol. 2, p. 735.
14 VKP(b), vol. 2, pp. 880–1.
15 VKP(b), vol. 2, p. 884.
16 P. Cavendish, 'The "New China" of the Kuomintang', *Modern China's Search For a Political Form*, Oxford, 1969, p. 145.
17 ZGZYWJXJ, vol. 1, pp. 413–4.
18 A.M. Grigor'ev, 'Bor'ba v VKP(b) i Kominterne po voprosam politiki v Kitae (1926–27gg.), *Problemy Dal'nego Vostoka*, part 1, no. 2 1993, p. 113.
19 J. Fitzgerald, *Awakening China: Politics, Culture and Class in the Nationalist Revolution*, Stanford, 1996, p. 20.
20 J. Chesneaux, *The Chinese Labor Movement, 1919–1927*, Stanford, p. 399.
21 C.M. Wilbur and J. Lien-ying How, *Missionaries of Revolution*, Cambridge, Mass., 1989, p. 743.
22 *Zhongguo gongren yundong shiliao*, 1982, no. 18, p. 77.
23 *Shanghai haiyuan gongren yundong shi*, Beijing, 1991, p. 266; *Shanghai jiqiye gongren yundong shi*, Beijing, 1991, p. 324; 'Yijiueryi nian zhi yijiuerqi nian Shanghai, Jiangsu, Zhejiang dang zuzhi fazhan gaikuang', *Zhonggongdang shi ziliao*, 10, 1984, p. 235.
24 *Zhongguo gongren yundong shiliao*, 1982, no. 1, p. 81.
25 WSYD, vol. 1, p. 73, pp. 113–14.
26 SGRSCWZQY, Shanghai, 1983, p. 333.
27 Chesneaux, *Chinese Labor Movement*, p. 409.
28 Here I would take issue with Luk, who denies the importance of Moscow's influence. Luk, *Origins*, p. 6.
29 Van de Ven, *Friend*, p. 1; Luk, *Origins*, p. 225.
30 Van de Ven points out that in the 1920s Chinese Communists sought to distance themselves from the May Fourth Movement rather than cast themselves as its inheritors, as they would do in the 1930s. H. van de Ven, 'The Emergence of the Text-Centered Party', in T. Saich and H. van de Ven (eds.) *New Perspectives on the Chinese Communist Revolution*, Armonk, NY, 1995, p. 25.
31 ZGZYWJXJ, vol. 1, p. 91.
32 Zhang Xuexin ed., *Ren Bishi zhuan*, Beijing, 1994, pp. 60–1, 76–7.
33 Wilbur, *Missionaries*, p. 527.

34 Mao Qihua, 'Da geming shiqi dang de dixia yinshua chang', *Dangshi ziliao congkan*, 3 (4), 1980, p. 57; Mao Qihua, 'Da geming chuqi Shanghai Zhonghua shuju zongchang de dang, tuan zuzhi yu gongren yundong' *Shanghai gongyunshi yanjiu ziliao*, 4, 1984, pp. 2–3.

35 Wang Fan-hsi notes that some intellectuals, too, toed the party line because if they had lost their party positions they would have been bereft of alternative employment. Wang Fan-hsi, *Chinese Revolutionary. Memoirs, 1919–1949*, Oxford, 1980, p. 125.

36 *Zhongguo gongchandang renming da cidian*, Beijing, 1991, pp. 441–2.

37 I examine this issue in more detail and from a comparative perspective in S.A. Smith, 'Workers, the Intelligentsia and Marxist Parties: St Petersburg, 1895–1917 and Shanghai, 1921–27', *International Review of Social History*, 41, 1996, 1–56.

38 Mao Tun, *Midnight*, Peking, 1957, p. 381, p. 425.

39 Luk, *Origins*, p. 225; NCH, 20 Mar. 1926, p. 552.

40 WSYDSL, vol. 1, p. 577.

41 Zheng Chaolin, *An Oppositionist for Life*, Atlantic Highlands, N.J., 1997, p. 154.

42 *Shanghai fangzhi gongren yundong shi*, Beijing, 1991, p. 90.

43 P. Stranahan, *Underground*, Lanham, MD., 1998, p. 35, p. 121.

44 C.K. Gilmartin, *Engendering the Chinese Revolution*, Berkeley, 1995, p. 68.

45 R.W. Connell, *Gender and Power*, Oxford, 1987, p. 129.

46 Zheng Chaolin, *Oppositionist*, p. 55.

47 Zheng Chaolin, *Oppositionist*, p. 119.

48 Qu Qiubai, 'Zhongguo geming zhuyi zhi zhenglun wenti', in *Liuda yiqian dang de lishi ziliao*, Beijing, 1980, pp. 723–5.

49 L. Feigon, *Chen Duxiu; Founder of the Chinese Communist Party*, Princeton, 1983, p. 196.

50 Zheng Chaolin, *Oppositionist*, p. 113.

51 D. Yau-Fai Ho and Che-Yue Chiu, 'Component Ideas of Individualism, Collectivism, and Social Organization: An Application in the Study of Chinese Culture', 137–156 in Uichol Kim et al. eds., *Individualism and Collectivism: Theory, Method and Applications*, Thousand Oaks, CA, 1994, p. 155.

52 M. Levine *Found Generation*, Seattle, 1993, pp. 141–2.

53 Yang Zilie, *Zhang Guotao furen huiyi lu*, Hong Kong, 1970, p. 154.

54 *Zhongguo gongren yundong shiliao*, 1960, no. 1, p. 120. Since the staff of this store was largely Cantonese, these workers probably constituted a distinct minority.

55 WSYDSL, vol. 1, p. 575.

56 *Dangdai shichuan*, Shanghai, 1933, p. 272.

57 Van de Ven, *Friend*, p. 241.

58 J.W. Esherick, 'Ten Theses on the Chinese Revolution', *Modern China*, vol. 21, no. 1, Jan. 1995, 45–76.

59 This is the theme of Stranahan's work on the Shanghai CCP during the 1930s. Stranahan, *Underground*.

60 Although Lu Xun appears to endorse a view that involvement in social change will create hope, his representation of 'hope' in the story – as a necessity, a fantasy and a narcotic – is highly ambiguous. See the absorbing reading by T. Huters, 'Ideologies of Realism in Modern China: the Hard Imperatives of Imported Theory', in Liu Kang and Xiaobing Tang, *Politics, Ideology and Literary Discourse in Modern China: Theoretical Interventions and Cultural Critique*, Durham, NC, 1993, pp. 163–5.

Bibliography

Archival Sources

Hoover Institution Archives, Stanford
  Jacobs collection
  Jay Calvin Houston archive
Shanghai Municipal Police Files
Public Record Office, London.
  Foreign Office Correspondence, Series I:
  FO 228/3021
  FO 228/3140
  FO 228/3291
  FO 228/3527

Contemporary Periodicals in Chinese

Buersaiweike (1927–8)
Gongchandang (1920–1)
Guowen zhoubao (1926)
Laodongjie (1920–1)
Laodong zhoukan (1921–2)
Minguo ribao (Canton) (1926–7)
Minguo ribao (Shanghai) (1920–27)
Qianfeng (1923)
Rexue ribao (1925)
Shanghai huoyou (1920–1)
Shenbao (1920–27)
Xianqu (1922–3)
Xiangdao (1922–7)
Xin qingnian (1919–26)
Xingqi pinglun (1919–20)
Zhengzhi zhoubao (1926)
Zhongguo gongren (1924–5)
Zhongguo qingnian (1923–7)

Contemporary Periodicals in Western Languages

China Press (1925)
China Weekly Review (1927)
Krasnyi Internatsional Profsoiuzov (1927)
Municipal Gazette (1919–27)
North China Herald (1919–27)
Voprosy kitaiskoi revoliutsii (1927)

Books and Articles in Oriental Languages

Bao Huiseng. 'Gongchandang diyici quanguo daibiao huiyi qianhou de huiyi' [Recollections of the time around the first congress of the CCP], *'Yida' qianhou*, vol. 2, Beijing, 1980, 303–21.
Bao Huiseng. *Bao Huiseng huiyilu* [Memoirs of Bao Huiseng], Beijing, 1983.
Bao Huiseng. 'Huiyi lao Yuyangli erhao' [Recollections of Old No. 2 Yuyang Lane], *Dangshi ziliao congkan*, 1, 1980, 31–33.
Bao Huiseng. 'Huiyi Yuyangli liuhao he Zhongguo laodong zuhe shujibu' [Memories of No. 6 Yuyang Lane and the Labour Organization Secretariat] *'Yida' qianhou*, vol. 2, Beijing, 1980, 352–5.
Cai Hesen. *Cai Hesen wenji* [Collected essays of Cai Hesen], Beijing, 1980.
'Cao Jinghua de huiyi' [Memoirs of Cao Jinghua], *Gongchanzhuyi xiaozu*, vol. 1, Beijing, 1987, 202–3.
Chen Da. 'Guonei zhongyao gonghui de gaikuang' [Conditions of the most important domestic labour unions], *Shehui xuejia*, 2, 1927, 101–126.
Chen Duxiu. 'Chen Duxiu zai Zhongguo gongchandang disanci quanguo daibiao dahui de baogao' [Chen Duxiu's report to the Third Congress of the CCP], *Dangshi yanjiu*, 2, 1980, 42–3.
Chen Duxiu. 'Chen Duxiu zai Zhongguo gongchandang diwuci quanguo daibiao dahui shang de baogao' [Chen Duxiu's report to the Fifth Congress of the CCP], *Zhonggong dangshi ziliao*, 3, 1982, 26–59.
Chen Qiyin. 'Wusa yundong pianduan' [A fragment on the May Thirtieth Movement], *Dangshi ziliao congkan*, 2, 1980, 89–98.
Chen Shaokang, Tian Ziyu. 'Li Hanjun yu "Xingqi pinglun"' [Li Hanjun and the *Weekly Critic*], *Shehui kexue*, 3, 1984, 56–57.
Chen Wangdao. 'Dang chengli shiqi de yixie qingkuang' [Certain circumstances at the time of the formation of the party] *Dangshi ziliao congkan*, 1, 1980, 25–28.
Chen Wangdao. 'Dang de jianli' [The foundation of the party], *Dangshi ziliao congkan*, 1, 1980, 29–30.
Chen Weimin. 'Zhongguo gongchangdang chuangli qi de Shanghai gongren yundong pinggu' [Evaluation of the Shanghai labour movement at the time of the foundation of the CCP], *Shilin*, 4 (11), 1988, 72–79.
Chen Yutang (ed.). *Zhonggong dang shi renwu bieming lu* [Record of alternative names of members of the CCP], Beijing, 1985.
Dai Xugong. *Xiang Jingyu zhuan* [Autobiography of Xiang Jingyu], Beijing, 1981.
Dangdai shichuan [An abbreviated history of the contemporary era] Shanghai, 1933.
Deng Zhongxia. *Zhongguo zhigong yundong jianshi* [A Brief history of the Chinese labour movement], Beijing, 1957 (orig. 1930).
Ding Shouhe. 'Lun Qu Qiubai de sixiang fazhan ji qi dui Zhongguo geming de gongxian' [On the development of Qu Qiubai's thought and his contribution to the Chinese revolution], *Zhongguo geming shi conglun*, Guangdong, 1985, 270–87.

Diyici guogong hezuo shiqi de Gongqingtuan zhuanti lun wenji, [Essays on topics concerning the CYL in the first United Front period], Beijing, 1985.

Diyici guonei geming zhanzheng shiqi de gongren yundong [The Labour Movement during the First Revolutionary Civil War Period], Beijing, 1954.

Diyici Zhongguo laodong nianjian [The first Chinese labour yearbook], (3 parts), Beijing, 1928.

Dong Chuping. 'Huiyi Zhongguo laodong zuhe shujibu' [Memories of the Chinese Labour Organization Secretariat], *Zhonggong dangshi ziliao*, 1, 1982, 82–7.

Du Weihua. 'Diyici Guo-Gong hezuo shiqi Sineifulitu (Malin) zai Hua jishi' [Chronicle of Sneevliet's (Maring's) Activities in China during the first phase of cooperation between the GMD and the CCP), *Zhonggong dangshi ziliao*, 36, 1990, 223–253.

'Erda' he 'Sanda': Zhongguo gongchandang dier-san daibiao dahui ziliao xuanbian [Selected Materials from the Second and Third Congresses of the CCP], Beijing, 1985.

Ershi shiji Zhongguo mingren cidian, [Dictionary of famous twentieth-century Chinese], Shenyang, 1991.

Fan Shaozeng. 'Guanyu Du Yuesheng' [Regarding Du Yuesheng], *Jiu Shanghai de banghui*, Shanghai, 1986, 195–247.

Feng Shaoting. 'Qian pu hou ji: duoqu wuzhuang qiyi de shengli' [No sooner had one fallen than another stepped into his place: seizing victory in the armed uprisings], *Shanghai gongyun shiliao*, 2, 1987, 16–24.

Gongchan guoji, liangong (Bu) yu Zhongguo geming wenxian ziliao xuanji, 1917–1925 [Selection of documentary materials on the Comintern, the Russian Communist Party and the Chinese Revolution], Zhonggong zhongyang dangshi yanjiu shi diyi yanjiubu (ed.), Beijing, 1997.

Gongchan guoji yu Zhongguo geming ziliao xuanji: yijiuerwu – yijiuerqi nian [Selected materials on the Comintern and the Chinese Revolution, 1925–27], Beijing, 1985.

Gongchanzhuyi xiaozu [Communist small groups], vol. 1, Zhonggong zhongyang dangshi ziliao zhengji weiyuanhui (ed.), Beijing, 1987.

Gu Shuping. 'Wo liyong Gu Zhuxian de yanhu jinxing geming huodong' [I sheltered behind Gu Zhuxuan to carry out revolutionary activity], in *Jiu Shanghai de banghui*, Shanghai, 1986, 360–66.

Gui Xinqiu. 'Chen Duxiu he Gongchan Guoji zai Guo-Gong hezuo wentishang de fenqi' [Differences between Chen Duxiu and the Comintern on the question of cooperation between the CCP and the GMD], *Shehui kexue zhanxian*, 3, 1991, 16–22.

'Guomindang yida dangwu baogao xuanze' [Selections from the report on party affairs to the GMD First Congress], *Geming shi ziliao* (Shanghai), 2, 1986.

Guo Xuyin. *Jiu Shanghai heishehui* [The old Shanghai underworld], Shanghai, 1997.

Hua Gang. *Yijiuerwu nian zhi yijiuerqi nian de Zhongguo da geming shi* [History of the Chinese Revolution, 1925–27], Shanghai, 1931.

Hua Lin. 'Yuyangli liuhao he fu E xuexi de qingkuang' [No. 6 Yuyang lane and the circumstances of going to Russia to study] *Gongchanzhuyi xiaozu*, vol. 1, Beijing, 1987, 204–206.

Huang Hao. 'Huiyi da geming shiqi de Shanghai gongren yundong ji qilun' [Recollections of the revolutionary period of the Shanghai labour movement and other matters], *Dangshi ziliao congkan*, 2 (3), 1980, 108–115.

Huang Meizhen. 'Wang Shouhua zhuanlüe' [Short biography of Wang Shouhua], *Jindai shi yanjiu*, 1, 1983, 62–4.

Huang Meizhen, Shi Yuanhua, Zhang Yun. *Shanghai daxue shiliao* [Historical Materials on Shanghai University], Shanghai, 1984.

Huang Meizhen, Zhang Yun, Shi Yuanhua. 'Shanghai daxue – suo xinying de geming xuexiao' [Shanghai University, a revolutionary college of a novel type], *Dangshi ziliao congkan*, 2, 1980, 152–174.

Huang Songyi. *Zhonggong zhigong yundong zhi yanjiu* [Researches on the Chinese labour movement], Master's Thesis, Guoli zhengzhi daxue, Taiwan, 1975.

Huang Xiurong. *Gongchan guoji yu Zhongguo geming guanxi shi* [The history of the Communist International and the Chinese revolution], (2 vol.), Beijing, 1989.

Huang Zhenshi. 'Wo suo zhidao de Huang Jinrong' [The Huang Jinrong I knew], *Jiu Shanghai de banghui*, Shanghai, 1986, 167–194.

Huang Zhirong. 'Guanyu yijiuersan nian zhi yijiuerqi nian Shanghai daxue dangzuzhi de fazhan qingkuang' [Concerning the conditions of development of party organization at Shanghai University in the years 1923 to 1927], *Zhonggong dangshi ziliao*, 2 (11), 1982, 98–102.

Huang Zulin. *Liu Shaoqi qingshao nian shidai* [Chronicle of Liu Shaoqi's youth], Beijing, 1991.

Jiang Guangci. 'Duanku dang' [Party of the Sans-Culottes], *Shiwen xuanji*, Beijing, 1957.

Jiang Peinan, Chen Weimin. 'Shanghai zhaopai gonghui de xingwang' [The rise and fall of Shanghai's 'signboard' labour unions], *Jindai shi yanjiu*, 6, 1984, 45–78.

Jiang Peinan, Chen Weimin. 'Zhongguo laodong zuhe shujibu shimo kao' [An overview of the history of the Chinese Labour Organization Secretariat], *Dangshi ziliao congkan*, 3(4), 1980, 105–115.

Jiang Weixin. 'Huiyi Shanghai gongren sanci wuzhuang qiyi ji qita' [Reminiscences of the Shanghai workers three armed uprisings and other things], *Dangshi ziliao congkan*, 2 (3), 1980, 99–107.

Jiang Zhichan. 'Dageming shiqi de Shanghai xuelian' [The Shanghai Student Union during the Great Revolution], *Diyici guogong hezuo shiqi de Gongqingtuan zhuanti lun wenji*, Gongqingtuan zhongyang qingyun shi yanjiushi (ed.), Beijing, 1985, 96–120.

Jiangnan zaochuanchang changshi, 1865–1949.5 [The long history of the Jiangnan arsenal, 1865-May 1949] Shanghai shehui kexueyuan jingji yanjiusuo (ed.), Shanghai, 1983.

Jiu Shanghai de banghui [The secret societies of old Shanghai] Zhongguo renmin zhengzhi xieshang huiyi Shanghai shi weiyuanhui (ed.), Shanghai, 1986.

Ke Lao. *Yijiuerwu nian Shanghai rishang shachang gongren bagong zhi neimu ji shi-mo ji* [The inside story from beginning to end of the strikes in the Japanese cotton mills of Shanghai in 1925], Shanghai, 1926.

Kong Fanjun. 'Dang zai chuangli shiqi dui bangkou he huidang de zhengce yu celüe' [The strategy and tactics of the party towards the secret societies in its formative period], *Zhonggong dang shi yanjiu*, 4, 1990, 93–4.

Lao gongren hua dangnian [Old workers talk about those years], vol. 1, Beijing, 1962.

Li Da. 'Guanyu Zhongguo gongchandang jianli de jige wenti' [Several questions concerning the founding of the CCP], *'Yida' qianhou*, vol. 2, Beijing, 1980, 1–5.

Li Da. 'Huiyi dang de zaoqi huodong' [Recollections of party activity in the early period] *Dangshi ziliao congkan*, 1, 1980, 22–24.

Li Da. 'Huiyi lao yuyang li erhao he dang 'Yida' 'Erda" [Memories of No. 2 Old Yuyang Lane and the First and Second CCP Congresses], *Dangshi ziliao congkan*, 1, 1980, 17–21.

Li Da. 'Zhongguo gongchandang chengli shiqi de sixiang douzheng qingkuang' [Circumstances surrounding the ideological struggle at the time of the foundation of the CCP] 'Yida' qianhou, vol. 2, Beijing, 1980, 50–55.

Li Dazhao. 'Xinde, Jiude' [The new, the old], Li Dazhao Wenji [Collected works of Li Dazhao], vol. 1, Beijing, 1984, 537–40.

Li Hong. 'Dang de chuangli shiqi zhongyao de gongren baokan jieshao' [Introduction to the principal workers' periodicals at the time of the foundation of the party], Zhongguo gongyun shiliao, 2, 1958, 75–89.

Li Shiyu. 'Qingbang zaoqi zuzhi kaolü' [A consideration of the organizational origins of the Green Gang], in Jiu Shanghai de banghui, Zhongguo renmin zhengzhi xieshang huiyi Shanghai shi weiyuanhui (ed.), Shanghai, 1986, 29–50.

Lin Jianbai, Li Zhining. Li Qihan, Guangdong, 1984.

Liu Ding. 'Xuesheng yundong yu sanci wuzhuang qiyi' [The student movement and the three armed uprisings], Shanghai gongyun shiliao, 2, 1987, 40–5.

Liu Guanzhi. 'Guanyu 1924–1925 nian Shanghai gongren yundong de huiyu' [Recollections of the Shanghai labour movement during the years 1924–5], Zhongguo gongren yundong shiliao, 1, 1960, 34–81.

Liu Mingkui. '1912–1921 nian Zhongguo gongren jieji de zhuangkuang' [The condition of the Chinese working class, 1912–21], Zhongguo gongren yundong shiliao, 1, 1958, 82–114.

Ma Chaojun. Zhongguo laogong yundong shi [A history of the Chinese labour movement] Chongqing, 1942.

Ma Chaojun. Zhongguo laogong yundong shi [A history of the Chinese labour movement], Taibei, 1958.

Mao Qihua. 'Da geming chuqi Shanghai Zhonghua shuju zongchang de dang, tuan zuzhi yu gongren yundong' [Party and league organization and the labour movement at the Shanghai Zhonghua Book Company at the start of the Great Revolution', Shanghai gongyunshi yanjiu ziliao, 4, 1984, 2–5.

Mao Qihua. 'Da geming shiqi dang de dixia yinshua chang' [Underground print works of the party during the revolutionary era], Dangshi ziliao congkan, 3(4), 1980, 54–62.

Nanyang xiongdi yancao gongsi shiliao [Historical materials on Nanyang Bros. Tobacco Company], Shanghai shehui kexueyuan jingji yanjiusuo (ed.), Shanghai, 1958.

Qu Qiubai. Qu Qiubai xuanji [Selected works of Qu Qiubai], Beijing, 1985.

Qu Qiubai. 'Zhongguo guomin geming yu Dai Jitao zhuyi' [The Chinese national revolution and Dai Jitaoism], Zhongguo gongren yundong shiliao, 2, 1981, 12–25.

Qu Qiubai. 'Zhongguo geming zhuyi zhi zhenglun wenti' [Contentious issues concerning the Chinese revolution], Liuda yiqian dang de lishi cailiao, Beijing, 1980 (orig. 1927), 670–736.

Ren Jianshu. 'Chen Duxiu yu Shanghai gongren sanci wuzhuang qiyi' [Chen Duxiu and the Shanghai workers' armed uprisings], Zhonggong dangshi ziliao, 1982, 4 (13), 70–83.

Ren Jianshu. Chen Duxiu zhuan [Biography of Chen Duxiu] vol. 1, Cong xiucai dao zong shuji [From scholar to general secretary], Shanghai, 1989.

Ren Jianshu. 'Shanghai gongren wuzhuang qiyi yu shimin zizhi yundong', [The citizens' self-government movement and the Shanghai workers' armed uprisings], Dang'an yu lishi, 3, 1987, 56–63.

Ren Qingxian, Xie Qingzhai et al. 'Zhuiji 'Shangwu' jiuchadui de douzheng ji shimin zhengfu de jianli' [Remembering the struggle of the Commercial Press picket and the establishment of the citizens' government], Shanghai gongyun shiliao, 2, 1987, 10–15.

Ren Wuxiong. 'Shanghai gongchanzhuyi xiaozu de youguan jige wenti' [Several questions concerning the Shanghai Communist small group], *Dangshi ziliao congkan*, 1 (2), 1980, 49–59.

Rongjia qiye shiliao [Historical materials on the Rong family enterprises], Shanghai shehui kexueyuan jingjisuo jingjishi zu (ed.), vol. 1, 1896–1937, Shanghai, 1980 (orig. 1962).

Sha Jiansun (ed.). *Zhongguo gongchandang tongshi* [A comprehensive history of the CCP], vols. 1 and 2, Changsha, 1996.

Shanghai disanshiyi mian fangzhi chang gongren yundong shi [A history of the labour movement in the Shanghai No. 31 Textile Mill], Shanghai gongchang qiye dangshi gongyun shi congshu, Beijing, 1991.

Shanghai fangzhi gongren yundong shi, [The history of the labour movement among Shanghai textileworkers], Beijing, 1991.

Shanghai gangshi hua [Discussion of the history of the Shanghai docks], Shanghai, 1979.

'Shanghai gonggong zujie gongbuju jingwu ribao zhaize' [Extracts from the Shanghai IS Police Daily Reports, 1 March to 30 April 1927], *Dang'an yu lishi*, 1, 1987, 20–65.

Shanghai gongren sanci wuzhuang qiyi [The three armed workers' uprisings in Shanghai], Zhou Qisheng (ed.), Shanghai, 1983.

Shanghai gongren sanci wuzhuang qiyi yanjiu [Research on the Shanghai workers' three armed uprisings], Xu Baofang, Bian Xingying (eds.), Zhonggong Shanghai shiwei dangshi ziliao zhengji weiyuanhui (ed.), Shanghai 1987.

Shanghai gongren yundong shi [History of the Shanghai labour movement] Shanghai, 1935.

Shanghai gongyun zhi [Annals of the Shanghai Labour Movement], Chen Huili, Fang Xiaofen (eds.), Shanghai, 1997.

Shanghai haiyuan gongren yundong lishi [A history of the labour movement among Shanghai seamen], Beijing, 1991.

Shanghai jiqi ye gongren yundong shi [A history of the labour movement in the Shanghai machine trades], Beijing, 1991.

Shanghai juanyanchang gongren yundong shi [The history of the labour movement in the Shanghai Cigarette Factory], Beijing, 1991.

Shanghai lieshi xiaozhuan [Brief biographies of Shanghai martyrs], Shanghai, 1983.

Shanghai shangwu yinshuguan zhigong yundongshi, [The history of the labour movement at the Shanghai Commercial Press], Beijing, 1991.

Shanghai shi tongji [Statistics on Shanghai], Shanghai shi difang xiehui (ed.), Shanghai, 1933.

Shanghai shi zhinan [Guide to Shanghai], Shen Bojing (ed.), Shanghai, 1933.

Shanghai xuesheng yundong dashi, 1919.5 – 1949.9 [Chronicle of the Shanghai student movement], Wang Min (ed.), Shanghai, 1985.

Shanghai xuesheng yundong shi [History of the Shanghai student movement], Shanghai shi qingyun shi yanjiuhui (ed.), Shanghai, 1995.

Shanghai zhi gongye [Industry of Shanghai], Shanghai shi shehui ju (ed.), Shanghai, 1929.

Shanghai zilaishui gongren yundong shi [The history of the labour movement in the Shanghai Water Works], Beijing, 1991.

Shanghai zonggonghui baogao [Report of the Shanghai General Labour Union], Shanghai, 1927.

Shao Lizi. 'Dang chengli qianhou de yixie qingkuang' [Certain circumstances surrounding the founding of the CCP] *'Yida' qianhou*, vol. 2, Beijing, 1980, 61–70.

Shao Weizheng. 'Guanyu Zhongguo gongchandang diyici quanguo daibiao dahui zhaokai riqi de chubu kaozheng' [A preliminary investigation into the dates of the convocation of the first national congress of the CCP] *Dangshi ziliao congkan*, 1, 1979, 127–38.

Shao Weizheng. 'Jiandang qianhou de Shanghai gongren yundong' [The Shanghai labour movement at the time of the founding of the party], *Dangshi ziliao congkan*, 3, 1982, 64–84.

Shen Yixing. *Gongyun shi ming-bian lu* [Putting the record straight on the history of the labour movement], Shanghai, 1987.

Shen Yixing, Jiang Peinan, Zheng Qingsheng. *Shanghai gongren yundong shi* [A history of the Shanghai labour movement], vol. 1, Liaoning, 1991.

Shen Yu. 'Si yi er fangeming zhengbian de yunniang he fadong' [The concoction and mobilization of the 12 April counter-revolutionary coup], *Dang'an yu lishi*, 2, 1987, 75–83.

Shi Bing. 'Deng Zhongxia', *Zhongguo gongren yundong de xianfeng*, [Pioneers of the Chinese Labour Movement], vol. 2, Beijing 1983, 1–147.

Si Binghan. 'Li Qihan', *Zhongguo gongren yundong de xianfeng* vol. 2, Beijing, 1983, 149–87.

Su Zhiliang. 'Shanghai liumang shili yu 'Si yi er' zhengbian' [The forces of the Shanghai gangsters and the 12 April coup], *Jindai shi yanjiu*, 2, 1988, 212–25.

Su Zhiliang, Chen Lifei. *Jindai Shanghai hei shehui yanjiu* [Researches into the secret societies of modern Shanghai], Hangzhou, 1991.

Sulian yinmou wenzheng huibian [Collection of documentary evidence of the Soviet Russian Conspiracy], Peking Metropolitan Police Headquarters, Beijing, 1928

Sun Yutang (ed.). *Zhongguo jindai jingji shi cankao ziliao congkan: Zhongguo jindai gongye shi ziliao* [Series of reference materials on the history of the modern Chinese economy: materials on the history of modern Chinese industry], vol. 1, parts 1 and 2, Beijing, 1957.

Tang Chunliang. *Li Lisan zhuan* [Biography of Li Lisan], Heilongjiang, 1984.

Tang Hai. *Zhongguo laodong wenti* [Chinese labour problems], Shanghai, 1926.

Tang Zhengchang (ed.). *Shanghai shi* [History of Shanghai], Shanghai, 1989.

'Tao Jingxuan lieshi jieshao' [Introducing the martyr Tao Jingxuan], *Shanghai gongren yundong shiliao*, 3, 1987, 36–9.

Wang Guichang. 'Shanghai gongren sanci wuzhuang qiyi zhongde xuesheng' [Students in Shanghai's three workers' uprisings], *Diyici guogong hezuo shiqi de Gongqingtuan zhuanti lun wenji*, Gongqingtuan zhongyang qingyun shi yanjiushi (ed.), Beijing, 1985, 274–82.

Wang Jiagui, Cai Xiyao. *Shanghai daxue, Yijiuerer – yijiuerqi nian* [Shanghai University, 1922–1927], Shanghai, 1986.

Wang Jianmin. *Zhongguo gongchandang shigao* [A draft history of the CCP], (3 vols.), Taibei, 1965.

Wang Jianying (ed.). *Zhongguo gongchandang zuzhishi ziliao huibian* [Edited materials on the organizational history of the CCP], Beijing, 1982.

Wang Renze. 'Shanghai zhuming qiyejia – Yu Xiaqing' [Shanghai's famous entrepreneur, Yu Xiaqing] Xiong Shanghou (ed.), *Minguo zhuming renwu zhuan* [Biographies of Famous People from the Republican Period], vol. 3, Beijing, 1997, 516–37.

Wei Fang'ai. *Shanghai gongren sanci wuzhuang qiyi* [The three Shanghai armed workers' uprisings], Beijing, 1951.

Wusa yundong [The May Thirtieth Movement], (3 vols.), Shanghai, 1991.

Wusa yundong he Xianggang bagong [The May Thirtieth Movement and the Hong Kong strike], Jiangsu, 1985.

'Wusa yundong qijian Zhonggong Shanghai diwei huiyi jilu (xuanzai) (Yijiuerwu nian wuyue)' [Minutes of the CCP Shanghai regional committee meetings during the May Thirtieth Movement (selections)], *Zhonggong dangshi ziliao*, 22, 1985, 3–12.

Wusa yundong shiliao [Historical materials on the May Thirtieth Movement], Shanghai shehui kexueyuan lishi yanjiusuo (ed.), vol. 1, Shanghai, 1981; vol. 2, Shanghai, 1986.

Wusi shiqi qikan jieshao [Introduction to periodicals of the May Fourth Movement], (3 vols.), Zhongyang makesi engesi liening shidalin zhuzuo bianyi yanjiushi (ed.), Beijing, 1958.

Wusi yundong zai Shanghai shiliao xuanji [Selected historical materials on the May Fourth Movement in Shanghai], Shanghai shehui kexueyuan lishi yanjiusuo (ed.), Shanghai, 1960.

Xiandai shiliao [Historical materials for the contemporary period] (4 vols.), Shanghai, 1934.

'Xiao Jingguang huiyi lü E zhibu qianhou de qingkuang' [Xiao Jingguang recalls the branch that went to Russia and the surrounding circumstances] *Gongchanzhuyi xiaozu*, vol. 1, Beijing, 1987, 200–01.

Xiang Ying, Shi Zhifu, Sun Yan. 'Gongchan guoji daibiao deng renwu jieshao' [An introduction to the Comintern representatives], *Dangshi ziliao congkan*, 2, 1980, 182–97.

Xu Dingxin, Qian Xiaoming. *Shanghai zongshanghui, 1902–1929* [The Shanghai Chamber of Commerce, 1902–1929], Shanghai, 1991.

Xu Haojiong. 'Liu Hua', *Zhongguo gongren yundong de xianqu*, vol. 1, Beijing, 1983, 71–100.

Xu Meikun. 'Huiyi Shanghai gongren sanci wuzhuang qiyi de yixie qingkuang' [Reminiscences of some of the circumstances of the Shanghai workers' three armed uprisings], *Dangshi ziliao congkan*, 1981, 3 (8), 91–4.

Xu Meikun. 'Huiyi 'Xiangdao' de chuban faxing' [Remembering the production and distribution of 'Guide Weekly'], *Dangshi ziliao congkan*, 3, 1980, 63–5.

Xu Meikun. 'Jiang-Zhe quwei chengli qianhou de pianduan huiyi' [Extract from reminiscences of the time of the foundation of the Zhejiang-Jiangsu regional committee], *Dangshi ziliao congkan*, 1981, 2 (7), 24–28.

Xu Meikun. 'Yi qiyi qianhou' [Recollections of the uprisings], *Shanghai gongyun shiliao*, 2, 1987, 1–3.

Xu Zhizhen. 'Guanyu Xin Yuyangli liuhao de huodong qingkuang' [On the conditions surrounding the activity at No. 6 New Yuyang Lane], *Gongchanzhuyi xiaozu*, vol. 1, Beijing, 1987, 197–99.

Yang Tianshi. 'Beifa shiqi zuopai liliang tong Jiang Jieshi douzheng de jige zhongyao huihe' [Some important bouts in the war between Chiang Kai-shek and the left-wing forces during the Northern Expedition], *Dangshi yanjiu*, 1, 1990, 31–43.

Yang Yue et al. 'Nanshi qiangsheng' [Gunshots in Nanshi], Shanghai gongyun shiliao, 2, 1987, 25–8.

Yang Yunruo, Yang Kuisong. *Gongchan guoji he Zhongguo geming* [The Communist International and the Chinese revolution], Shanghai, 1988.

Yang Zhihua. 'Yang Zhihua de huiyi' [Reminiscences of Yang Zhihua], *'Yi da' qianhou*, vol. 2, Zhongguo shehui kexueyuan xiandai yanjiu she (ed.), Beijing, 1980, 25–30.

Yang Zilie. *Zhang Guotao furen huiyi lu* [Memoirs of the wife of Zhang Guotao], Hong Kong, 1970.

Yao Tianyu. 'Peiyang geming ganbu de honglu – Shanghai daxue' [Shanghai University – A mighty furnace for training revolutionary cadres], *Dangshi ziliao congkan*, 1980, 2, 72–79.

'*Yida' qianhou: Zhongguo gonchandang di yici daibiao dahui qianhou ziliao xuanbian* [Around the time of the First Congress: A selection of materials on the time around the First Congress], Zhongguo shehui kexueyuan xiandai shi yanjiu shi, Zhongguo geming bowuguan dangshi yanjiu shi (eds.) (2 vols.), Beijing, 1980.

Yijiuerqi nian de Shanghai shangye lianhehui [The Shanghai Commercial Association of 1927] Liu Pinggang (ed.), Shanghai, 1983.

'Yijiueryi nian zhi yijiuerqi nian Shanghai, Jiangsu, Zhejiang dang zuzhi fazhan gaikuang' [Survey of the development of party organization in Shanghai, Jiangsu and Zhejiang between 1921 and 1927], *Zhonggongdang shi ziliao*, 10, 1984, 181–244.

'Yu Xiusong gei Luo Zhixiang de xin' [Letter from Yu Xiusong to Luo Zhixiang], in *Gongchanzhuyi xiaozu*, vol. 1, Beijing, 1987, 63–4.

'Yuan Zhenying di huiyi' [Memoirs of Yuan Zhenying], *Gongchanzhuyi xiaozu*, vol. 1, Beijing 1987, 194–6.

Zhang Jungu. *Du Yuesheng zhuan* [Biography of Du Yuesheng], vol. 1,Taibei, 1980 (orig. 1967).

'Zhang Guotao huiyi Zhongguo gongchandang "Yida" qianhou [Zhang Guotao's memoirs about the First Congress of the CCP], "*Yida*"' *qianhou*, vol. 2, Beijing, 1980, 122–183.

Zhang Quan. 'Guangyu Huxi gongyou julebu' [Concerning the West Shanghai Workers' Club], *Dangshi ziliao congkan*, 1980, 3(4), 116–24.

'Zhang Weizhen tan Hunan zaoqi gongyun' [Zhang Weizhen talks about the origins of the labour movement in Hunan], *Danshi yanjiu ziliao*, 1, 1980, 236–41.

'Zhang Weizhen tongzhi tan Shanghai gongren sanci wuzhuang qiyi' [Comrade Zhang Weizhen discusses the three workers' armed uprisings in Shanghai], *Dangshi yanjiu ziliao*, 1, 1980, 313–17.

'Zhang Weizhen tongzhi tan Shanghai "Wusa" yundong' [Comrade Zhang Weizhen discusses the May Thirtieth Movement in Shanghai], *Dangshi yanjiu ziliao*, 1, 1980, 304–12

Zhang Xuexin (ed.). *Ren Bishi zhuan* [Biography of Ren Bishi], Beijing, 1994.

Zhang Zurong, Dong Tingzhi. 'Guanyu Zhonggong "Yida" daibiaoren shu de jige shuofa' [Some observations on the number of representatives at the First Congress of the CCP], *Dangshi ziliao congkan*, 1979, 1, 139–143.

Zhao Pu. 'Zhongguo gongchandang zuzhi shi ziliao' [Materials on the history of the organizations of the CCP] (6 parts): *Dangshi yanjiu*, 2, 1981, 65–71 (part 1); 3, 1981, 62–9 (part 2); 1982, 1, 52–5 (part 3); 3, 35–40 (part 4); 4, 30–37 (part 5); 1983, 2, 38–46 (part 6).

Zhao Yinong et al. 'Hudong gongren fenqi bodou', [The workers of east Shanghai rise up in struggle] *Shanghai gongyun shiliao*, 2, 1987, 32–3.

Zheng Chaolin. *Huai jiu ji* [Remembering times past], Beijing, 1995.

Zhonggongdang shi renwu zhuan [Biographies of past members of the CCP], Zhonggongdang shi renwu yanjiu hui (ed.), (55 vols. at time of writing), Xi'an, 1980–1994.

'Zhonggong Shanghai quwei youguan Shanghai gongren sanci wuzhuang qiyi de wenxian qi pian' [Seven documents from the Shanghai regional committee of the CCP concerning the third armed uprising], *Dang'an yu lishi*, 1, 1987, 1–15.

Zhonggong zhongyang qingnian yundong wenjian xuanbian [Anthology of CCP Central Committee documents on the youth movement], Tuanzhongyang qingnian yundong shi yanjiushi and Zhongyang dang'anguan (eds.), Beijing, 1988.

Zhonggong zhongyang wenjian xuanji [Selected materials of the Central Committee of the CCP], vol. 1, 1921–1925; vol. 2, 1926; vol. 3, 1927, Zhongyang dang'anguan (ed.), Hebei, 1989.

Zhongguo funü yundong lishi ziliao, 1921–1927 [Materials on the history of the Chinese women's movement], Zhonghua quanguo funü lianhehui funü yundong lishi yanjiushi Renmin chubanshe (ed.), Beijing, 1986.

Zhongguo gongchandang diyici daibiao dahui dang'an ziliao [Archival Materials on the First Congress of the CCP], Beijing, 1982.

Zhongguo gongchandang faqi ren fenlie shiliao [Materials on divisions between the founding membes of the CCP], Hong Kong, 1968.

Zhongguo gongchandang renming da cidian [Comprehensive dictionary of CCP members], Sheng Ping (ed.), Beijing, 1991.

Zhongguo gongchandang Shanghai shi zuzhishi ziliao, 1920.8 – 1987.10 [Historical materials on the organization of the CCP in Shanghai, 1920–87], Zhonggong Shanghai shiwei zuzhibu (ed.) Shanghai 1991.

Zhongguo gongchangdang tong zhi [The complete record of the CCP], (3 vols.), Zheng Hui, Zhang Jingru, Liang Zhixiang (eds.), Beijing, 1997.

Zhongguo gonghui lishi wenxian, 1921–27 [Documents on the history of the Chinese labour unions, 1921–27], Beijing, 1958.

Zhongguo guomindang dierci quanguo daibiao dahui huiyi jilu mulu [Reminiscences, records, lists of the Second GMD Congress], Guomindang zhongyang zhixing weiyuanhui, April 1926.

Zhongguo guomindang gesheng shi zong dengji he gedangyuan tongji [Statistics on Provincial and Municipal Registered Party Members of the GMD], Zhongguo guomindang zhongyang zhixing weiyuanhui tongji chu, Nanjing, 1929.

Zhongguo lici laodong dahui wenxian [Documents on all previous Chinese labour congresses], Zhonghua quanguo zonggonghui zhigong yundong yanjiushi (ed.), Beijing, 1957.

Zhou Enlai. 'Guanyu Shanghai de wuzhuang qiyi' [On the armed uprising in Shanghai], *Dang de wenxian*, 1, 1994, 75–80.

Zhou Enlai nianpu [Chronicle of Zhou Enlai's Life], Beijing, 1989.

Zhou Shangwen, He Shiyou. *Shanghai gongren sanci wuzhuang qiyi shi* [The Shanghai workers' three armed uprisings], Shanghai, 1987.

Zhou Yumin, Shao Yong. *Zhongguo banghui shi*, [History of secret societies in China], Shanghai, 1993.

Zhu Bangxing, Hu Linge, Xu Sheng. *Shanghai chanye yu Shanghai zhigong* [Shanghai industry and Shanghai labour], Shanghai, 1984 (orig. 1939).

Zou Yiren. *Jiu Shanghai renkou bianqian de yanjiu* [Research on population change in old Shanghai], Shanghai, 1980.

Books and Articles in Western Languages

A.A. (A.P. Appen). 'Tri shankhaiskikh vosstaniia', *Problemy Kitaia*, 2, 1930, 63–86.

Adibekov, G.M., Shakhnazarova, E.N., Shirinia, K.K. *Organizatsionnaia struktura Kominterna, 1919-1943* [Organizational Structure of the Comintern, 1919–43], Moscow, 1997.

Aho, James A. *This Thing of Darkness: A Sociology of the Enemy*, University of Washington Press, Seattle, 1994.

Akatova, T.N. 'Tsiui Tsiu-bo v rabochem dvizhenii Kitaia' [Qu Qiubai in the Chinese labour movement], *Gosudarstvo i obshchestvo v Kitae*, Moscow, 1978, 253–65.

Anderson, Marston. *The Limits of Realism: Chinese Fiction in the Revolutionary Period*, University of California Press, Berkeley, 1990.

Anderson, Perry. 'The Antinomies of Antonio Gramsci', *New Left Review*, 100, 1976–77, 5–80.

Anderson, Perry. 'Modernity and Revolution', *New Left Review*, 144, 1984, 96–113.

Benton, Gregor. *China's Urban Revolutionaries: Explorations in the History of Chinese Trotskyism, 1921–1952*, Humanities Press, Atlantic Highlands, N.J., 1996.

Bereznyi, L.A. 'Geroicheskoe vosstanie shankhaiskogo proletariata v marte 1927g.'[The heroic uprising of the Shanghai proletariat in March 1927], *Sovetskoe kitaevedenie*, 3, 1958, 97–107.

Bergère, Marie-Claire. 'The Chinese bourgeoisie, 1911–37' *Cambridge History of China*, vol. 12, J.K. Fairbank (ed.), Cambridge, 1983, 721–825.

Bergère, Marie-Claire. *The Golden Age of the Chinese Bourgeoisie, 1911–1937*, (Janet Lloyd trans.), Cambridge University Press, Cambridge, 1989.

Boorman, Howard L. and Howard, Richard C. (eds.). *Biographical Dictionary of Republican China*, (5 vols.), Columbia University Press, New York, 1967–79.

Brandt, Conrad. *Stalin's Failure in China, 1924–1927*, Harvard University Press, Cambridge, Mass., 1958.

Bush, Richard. *The Politics of Cotton Textiles in Kuomintang China*, Garland Press, New York, 1982.

Cadart, Claude and Cheng Yingxiang. *Mémoires de Peng Shuzhi. L'envol du communisme en Chine*, Gallimard, Paris, 1983.

Cai Hesen. 'Istoriia opportunizma v Kommunisticheskoi Partii Kitaia' [History of opportunism in the CCP], *Problemy Kitaia*, 1, 1929, 1–77.

Carr, E.H. *The Bolshevik Revolution*, vol. 3, Penguin, London, 1966 (orig. 1953).

Cavendish, Patrick. 'The "New China" of the Kuomintang', in Jack Gray (ed.), *Modern China's Search For a Political Form*, Oxford University Press, 1969, 138–86.

Chan, Ming Kou. 'Labor and Empire: the Chinese Labor Movement in the Canton Delta, 1895–1927', PhD, Stanford University, 1975.

Chang Chufang. 'Chinese Cotton Mills in Shanghai', *Chinese Economic Journal*, vol. 3, no. 5, 1928, 901–17.

Chang Kuo-t'ao. *The Rise of the Communist Party, 1921–27: Volume One of the Autobiography of Chang Kuo-t'ao*, University Press of Kansas, Lawrence, 1971.

Chatterjee, Partha. *Nationalist Thought and the Colonial World*, Zed Books, London, 1986.

Chen Yung-fa. *Making Revolution: the Communist Movement in Eastern and Central China, 1937–45*, University of California Press, Berkeley, 1986.

Chesneaux, Jean. *The Chinese Labor Movement, 1919–1927*, Stanford University Press, Stanford, Ca., 1968.

China Year Book, 1924–25, H.G.W. Woodhead (ed.), Tientsin, 1925.

China Year Book, 1926–27 H.G.W. Woodhead (ed.), Tientsin, 1927.

China Year Book, 1928, H.G.W. Woodhead (ed.), Tientsin, 1928.

China Year Book 1938, H.G.W. Woodhead (ed.), Shanghai, 1938.

Chow Tse-tung. *The May Fourth Movement: Intellectual Revolution in Modern China*, Harvard University Press, Cambridge, Mass., 1960.

Clifford, Nicholas R. *Shanghai 1925: Urban Nationalism and the Defense of Foreign Privilege*, Michigan Papers in Chinese Studies, no. 37, University of Michigan, Ann Arbor, 1979.

Clifford, Nicholas R. *Spoilt Children of Empire: Westerners in Shanghai and the Chinese Revolution of the 1920s*, Middlebury College Press, Vermont, 1991.

Cochran, Sherman. *Big Business in China: Sino-Foreign Rivalry in the Cigarette Industry, 1890- 1930*, Harvard University Press, Cambridge, Mass., 1980.

Connell, R.W. *Gender and Power*, Polity/Blackwell, Oxford, 1987.

Dalin, S.A. *Kitaiskie Memuary, 1921–1927* [Chinese Memoirs, 1921–27], Moscow, 1975.

Dalin, S. 'Na dalekom Kitae' [In far China], *Molodaia gvardiia*, 2, 1923, 306–9.

Dal'nevostochnaia politika sovetskoi Rossii, 1920–22gg.: sbornik dokumentov Sibirskogo biuro TsK RKP(b) i Sibirskogo revoliutsionnogo komiteta [The Far Eastern policy of Soviet Russia: collection of documents on the Siberian Bureau of the CC of the RCP(b) and the Siberian Revolutionary Committee], Novosibirsk, 1995.

Day, Richard B. *N.I. Bukharin: Selected Writings on the State and the Transition to Socialism*, M.E. Sharpe, Armonk, NY, 1982.

Dirlik, Arif. *Anarchism in the Chinese Revolution*, University of California Press, Berkeley, 1991.

Dirlik, Arif. 'Mass Movements and the Left Kuomintang', *Modern China*, vol. 1, no. 1, 1975, 46–74.

Dirlik, Arif. *The Origins of Chinese Communism*, Oxford University Press, New York, 1989.

Dittmer, Lowell. *China's Continuous Revolution: the Post-Liberation Epoch, 1949–1981*, University of California Press, Berkeley, 1987.

Dolezelova-Velingerova, M. (ed.) *A Selective Guide to Chinese Literature, 1900- 1949*, vol. 1, The Novel, E.J. Brill, Leiden, 1988.

Domes, Jürgen. *Vertagte Revolution: Die Politik der Kuomintang in China, 1923–7*, Walter de Gruyter, Berlin, 1969.

Drège, Jean-Pierre. *La Commercial Press de Shanghai, 1897–1949*, College de France, Institut des Hautes Etudes Chinoises, Paris, 1978.

Eng, Robert Y. 'Luddism and labor protest among silk artisans and workers in Jiangnan and Guangdong, 1860–1930', *Late Imperial China*, vol. 11, no. 2, 1990, 63–101.

Esherick, Joseph W. 'Revolution in a Feudal Fortress: Yangjiagou, Mizhi county, Shaanxi, 1937–48', *Modern China*, vol. 24, no. 4, 1998, 339–77.

Esherick, Joseph W. 'Ten Theses on the Chinese Revolution', *Modern China*, vol. 21, no. 1, 1995, 45–76.

Fairbank, John K. 'The Creation of the Treaty System', *Cambridge History of China*, vol. 10, part 1, J.K. Fairbank (ed.), Cambridge University Press, Cambridge, 1978, 213–63.

Feigon, Lee. *Chen Duxiu: Founder of the Chinese Communist Party*, Princeton University Press, Princeton, 1983.

Fewsmith, Joseph. *Party, State and Local Elites in Republican China: Merchant Organizations and Politics in Shanghai, 1890- 1939*, University of Hawaii Press, Honolulu, 1985.

Fitzgerald, John. *Awakening China: Politics, Culture and Class in the Nationalist Revolution*, Stanford University Press, Stanford, 1996.

Galbiati, Fernando. *P'eng P'ai and the Hai-lu-feng Soviet*, Stanford University Press, Stanford, 1985.

Gilmartin, Christina K. *Engendering the Chinese Revolution:Radical Women, Communist Politics and Mass Movements in the 1920s*, University of California Press, Berkeley, 1995.

Glunin, V.I. 'Grigorii Voitinskii, 1893–1953', *Vidnye sovetskie kommunisty – uchastniki kitaiskoi revoliutsii*, Moscow, 1970, 66–87.

Glunin, V.I and Grigor'ev, A.M. 'Komintern i kitaiskaia revoliutsiia', *Voprosy istorii KPSS*, 1989, 95–110

Goodman, Bryna. *Native Place, City and Nation: Regional Networks and Identities in Shanghai, 1853–1937*, University of California Press, Berkeley, 1995.

Grigor'ev, A.M. 'Bor'ba v VKP(b) i Kominterne po voprosam politiki v Kitae (1926–27gg.) [The struggle in the Russian Communist Party and the Comintern on problems of policy in China, 1926–7], *Problemy Dal'nego Vostoka*, part 1, 2 1993, 102–117; part 2, 3, 1993, 109–128.

Harrison, James Pinkney. *The Long March to Power: A History of the Chinese Communist Party, 1921–72*, Macmillan, London, 1972.

Henriot, Christian. 'Municipal Power and Local Elites', *Republican China*, vol. 11, no. 2, 1986, 1–21.

Henriot, Christian. 'La rupture entre PCC-GMD en 1927: suicide ou assassinat?', *Cahiers d'études chinoises*, 5, 1986, 45–99.

Ho, David Yau-Fai and Chiu, Che-Yue. 'Component Ideas of Individualism, Collectivism, and Social Organization: An Application in the Study of Chinese Culture', in Uichol Kim et al. eds., *Individualism and Collectivism: Theory, Method and Applications*, Sage Publications, Thousand Oaks, California, 1994, 137–156.

Honig, Emily. *Creating Chinese Ethnicity: Subei People in Shanghai, 1850–1980*, Yale University Press, New Haven, Conn., 1992.

Honig, Emily. *Sisters and Strangers, Women in the Shanghai Cotton Mill, 1919–49*, Stanford University Press, Stanford, 1986.

Huters, Theodore. 'Ideologies of Realism in Modern China: the Hard Imperatives of Imported Theory, in Liu Kang and Xiaobing Tang, *Politics, Ideology and Literary Discourse in Modern China: Theoretical Interventions and Cultural Critique*, Duke University Press, Durham NC, 1993, 147–73.

Il'in, M.V. *Slova i smysly: opyt opisaniia kliuchevykh politicheskikh poniatii* [Words and Meanings: An Attempt to Describe Key Russian Political Concepts], Rosspen, Moscow, 1997

Isaacs, Harold R. *The Tragedy of the Chinese Revolution*, Stanford University Press, Stanford, 1961 (orig. 1938).

Iur'ev, M.F. *Revoliutsiia 1925–27gg. v Kitae* [Revolution in China, 1925–27], Moscow, 1968.

Jordan, Donald A. *The Northern Expedition: China's National Revolution of 1926–28*, University of Hawaii Press, Honolulu, 1976.

Kartunova, A.I. 'Novyi vzgliad na vopros o razryve s Chan Kaishi: ianvar'–aprel' 1927' [A new view on the question of the rupture with Chiang Kai-shek in January to April 1927], *Vostok./Oriens*, 1, 1997, 37–46.

Kartunova, A.I. 'Kitaiskaia revoliutsiia: diskussii v Kominterne' [Discussions in the Comintern on the Chinese Revolution], *Voprosy Istorii KPSS*, 6, 1989, 58–72.

Kartunova, A.I. *Politika kompartii Kitaia v rabochem voprose nakanune revoliutsii, 1925–27gg.* [The policy of the CCP on the labour question on the eve of the revolution of 1925–7], Moscow, 1983.

Kataoka, Tetsuya. *Resistance and Revolution in China. The Communists and the Second United Front*, University of California Press, Berkeley, 1974.

Kitaiskie dobrovol'tsy v boiakh za sovetskuiu vlast' [Chinese volunteers in the struggle for Soviet power], Moscow, 1961.

Kommunisticheskii Internatsional i kitaiskaia revoliutsiia: dokumenty i materialy [The Communist International and the Chinese Revolution: documents and materials], Moscow, 1986.

Kotenev, A. *Shanghai: Its Municipality and the Chinese*, Shanghai, 1927.

Kuo, Warren. *Analytical History of the Chinese Communist Party*, Book One, Institute of International Relations, Taipei, 1968.

Kwan, Daniel Y.K. *Marxist Intellectuals and the Chinese Labor Movement: a Study of Deng Zhongxia, 1894–1933*, University of Washington Press, Seattle, 1997.

Lee, Leo Ou-fan. 'Literary Trends I: The Quest for Modernity, 1895–1927', in *Cambridge History of China*, vol. 12, Republican China, 1912–49, part 1, John

K. Fairbank and Albert Feuerwerker (eds.) Cambridge University Press, Cambridge, 1986 452–504.

Lee, Leo Ou-fan. *The Romantic Generation of Chinese Writers*, Cambridge, Mass., 1973.

Levenson, Joseph. *Confucian China and Its Modern Fate: the Problem of Intellectual Continuity*, University of California Press, Berkeley, 1958

Leung, John Kong-cheong. 'The Chinese Work-Study Movement: the Social and Political Experience of Chinese Students and Student-Workers in France, 1913–25', Ph.D., Brown University, 1982.

Levine, Marilyn A. *The Found Generation: Chinese Communists in Europe during the Twenties*, University of Washington Press, Seattle, 1993.

Li Yu-ning, *The Introduction of Socialism into China*, Occasional Papers East Asian Institute Series, Columbia, 1971.

Li Yuning and Michael Gasster. 'Chü Ch'iu-pai's Journey to Russia, 1920–22', *Monumenta Serica*, 39, 1970–71, 537–56.

Lih, Lars T., Naumov Oleg V. and Khlevniuk Oleg V. (eds.). *Stalin's Letters to Molotov, 1925–1936*, Yale University Press, New Haven, Conn., 1995.

Link, Perry. 'The Genie and the Lamp: Revolutionary Xiangsheng' in Bonnie S. McDougall, (ed.), *Popular Chinese Literature and Performing Arts in the People's Republic of China, 1949–1979*, University of California, Berkeley, 1984, 83–111.

Liu, Lydia H. *Translingual Practice: Literature, National Culture and Translated Modernity. China, 1900–1937*, Stanford University Press, Stanford, 1995.

Luk, Michael Y.L. *Origins of Chinese Bolshevism: An Ideology in the Making, 1920–28*, Oxford University Press, Hong Kong, 1990.

Mamaeva, N.L. *Gomin'dan v natsional'no-revoliutsionnom dvizhenii Kitaia, 1923–27* [The GMD in the national-revolutionary movement of China, 1923–7], Nauka, Moscow, 1991.

Mandalian, T. 'Pourquoi la direction du PC de China n'a-t-elle pas rempli sa tâche?' in Pierre Broué (ed.), *La question chinoise dans l'Internationale communiste (1926–27)*, Paris, 1965, 279–92.

Mao Tun. *Midnight*, Foreign Language Publishing House, Peking, 1957.

Martin, Brian G. *The Shanghai Green Gang: Politics and Organized Crime, 1919–1937*, University of California Press, Berkeley, 1996.

Mast, Herman and Saywell, William G. 'Revolution Out of Tradition: The Political Ideology of Tai Chi-t'ao', *Journal of Asian Studies*, vol. 34, no. 1, 1974, 73–98.

Meisner, Maurice. *Li Ta-chao and the Origins of Chinese Communism*, Harvard University Press, Cambridge, Mass., 1967.

Mif, Pavel. *Heroic China: Fifteen Years of the Communist Party of China*, Workers' Library, New York, 1937.

Mif, Pavel. *Kitaiskaia revoliutsiia* [The Chinese revolution], Moscow, 1932.

Mitarevsky, N. *World Wide Soviet Plots*, Tientsin, n.d. (1927)

Mitchell, B.R. *International Historical Statistics: Africa and Asia*, Macmillan, London, 1982.

Murphey, Rhoads. *Shanghai: Key to Modern China*, Harvard University Press, Cambridge, Mass., 1953.

North, Robert C. *Moscow and the Chinese Communists*, (2nd ed.), Stanford University Press, Stanford, Ca., 1963.

Ono, Kazuko. *Chinese Women in a Century of Revolution, 1850–1950*, Joshua A. Fogel (ed.), Stanford University Press, Stanford, 1989.

Pantsov, A. 'Stalin's Policy in China, 1925–27: New Light from the Russian Archives', *Issues and Studies*, 34, no. 1, Jan. 1998, 129–60.

Papers Respecting Labour Conditions in China No. 1 (Foreign Office Memorandum), HM Stationery Office, London, 1925.

297

Perry, Elizabeth J. *Shanghai on Strike: The Politics of Chinese Labor*, Stanford University Press, Stanford, 1993.

Pickowicz, Paul G. *Marxist Literary Thought in China: the Influence of Chü Ch'iu-pai*, University of California Press, Berkeley, 1981.

Pipes, Richard. *Russia Under the Old Regime*, Penguin Books, London, 1974.

Pipes, Richard (ed.), *The Unknown Lenin: From the Secret Archive*, Yale University Press, New Haven, Conn., 1996.

Price, Jane L. *Cadres, Commanders and Commissars: the Training of the Chinese Communist Leadership, 1920–45*, Westview Press, Colorado, 1976.

Radek, Karl. 'God kitaiskoi revoliutsii' [A Year of the Chinese Revolution], *Pravda*, 30 May 1926, 2.

Rigby, Richard W. *The May 30 Movement: Events and Themes*, Australian National University Press, Canberra, 1980.

Roux, Alain. *Grèves et politique à Shanghai: les désillusions (1927–1932)*, Éditions de l'École des Hautes Études en Sciences Sociales, Paris, 1995.

Roux, Alain. 'Le mouvement ouvrier à Shanghai de 1928 à 1930' (thèse à troisième cycle), Sorbonne, Paris, 1970.

Roux, Alain, *Le Shanghai ouvrier des années trente: coolies, gangsters et syndicalistes*, Éditions L'Harmattan, Paris, 1993.

Saich, Tony. *The Origins of the First United Front in China: the role of Sneevliet (alias Maring)*, (2 vols.) E.J. Brill, Leiden, 1991.

Saich, Tony. 'Through the Past Darkly: Some New Sources on the Founding of the Chinese Communist Party', *International Review of Social History*, vol. 30, part 2, 1985, 167–80.

Schoppa, R. Keith. *Blood Road: The Mystery of Shen Dingyi in Revolutionary China*, University of California Press, Berkeley, 1995.

Schram, Stuart R. (ed.). *Mao's Road to Power: Revolutionary Writings, 1912–1949*, vol. 2, National Revolution and Social Revolution, December 1920 to June 1927, M.E. Sharpe, Armonk, NY, 1994.

Schurmann, Franz. *Ideology and Organization in Communist China*, University of California Press, Berkeley, 1968.

Schwarcz, Vera. *The Chinese Enlightenment: Intellectuals and the Legacy of the May Fourth Movement of 1919*, University of California Press, Berkeley, 1986.

Schwartz, Benjamin I. *Chinese Communism and the Rise of Mao*, Harvard University Press, Cambridge, Mass., 1951.

Selznick, Philip. *The Organizational Weapon: A Study of Bolshevik Strategy and Tactics*, McGraw-Hill, New York, 1952.

Shaffer, Lynda Norene. *Mao and the Workers: the Hunan Labor Movement, 1920–23*, M.E. Sharpe, Armonk, NY, 1982.

Shevelyov, K. 'On the History of the Formation of the Communist Party of China', *Far Eastern Affairs*, no. 1, 1981, 126–138.

Smith, S.A. 'The Comintern, the Chinese Communist Party and the Three Armed Uprisings in Shanghai, 1926–27' in Tim Rees and Andrew Thorpe (eds.), *International Communism and the Communist International*, Manchester University Press, Manchester, 1998, 254–70.

Smith, S.A. *Red Petrograd: Revolution in the Factories, 1917–18*, Cambridge University Press, Cambridge, 1983.

Smith, S.A. 'Workers and Supervisors: St Petersburg, 1905–1917, and Shanghai, 1895–1927', *Past and Present*, 139, 1993, 131–177.

Smith, S.A. 'Workers, the Intelligentsia and Marxist Parties: St Petersburg, 1895–1917 and Shanghai, 1921–27', *International Review of Social History*, 41, 1996, 1–56.

Sokolsky, George E. 'The Kuomintang', *China Year Book 1928*, Tientsin, 1928, 1309–1401.

Spence, Jonathan D. *The Gate of Heavenly Peace. The Chinese and Their Revolution, 1895–1980*, Penguin Books, London, 1982.

Spence, Jonathan D., *The Search for Modern China*, W.W. Norton and Co., New York, 1990.

Stalin, J.V. *Works*, vol. 8, January – November 1926, Foreign Languages Publishing House, Moscow, 1954.

Stalin, J.V. *Works*, vol. 9, December 1926- July 1927, Foreign Languages Publishing House, Moscow, 1954.

Stranahan, Patricia. *Underground: The Shanghai Communist Party and the Politics of Survival, 1927–1937*, Rowman & Littlefield, Lanham, MD, 1998.

Strikes and Lockouts in Shanghai since 1918, Bureau of Social Affairs, Shanghai, 1933.

Tan, Chester C. *Chinese Political Thought in the Twentieth Century*, Doubleday, Garden City, N.Y., 1971.

Tsai Kyung-we. 'Shanghai's Foreign Trade: An Analytical Study', *Chinese Economic Journal*, vol. 9, no. 3, 1931, 967–78.

Van de Ven, Hans. 'The Emergence of the Text-Centered Party', in T. Saich and H.van de Ven (eds.) *New Perspectives on the Chinese Communist Revolution*, M.E. Sharpe, Armonk, NY, 1995, 5–32.

Van de Ven, Hans J. *From Friend to Comrade: The Founding of the Chinese Communist Party, 1920–1927*, University of California Press, Berkeley, 1991.

VKP(b), Komintern i natsional'no-revoliutsionnoe dvizhenie v Kitae. Dokumenty [The All-Russian Communist Party (Bolshevik), the Comintern and the National-Revolutionary Movement in China. Documents], vol. 1, 1920–1925; vol. 2 (in two parts), 1926–27. Rossiiskii tsentr khraneniia i izucheniiz dokumentov noveishei istorii, Institut Dal'nego Vostoka Rossiiskoi Akademii Nauk and Vostochnoaziatskii Seminar Svobodnogo Universiteta Berlina, Moscow, 1994, 1996.

Wakeman, Frederic. *Policing Shanghai, 1927–1937*, University of California Press, Berkeley, 1995.

Wakeman, Frederic and Wen-Hsin Yeh (eds.). *Shanghai Sojourners*, University of California Press, Berkeley, 1992.

Waldron, Arthur. *From war to nationalism: China's turning point, 1924–25*, Cambridge University Press, Cambridge, 1995.

Wang Fan-hsi. *Chinese Revolutionary. Memoirs, 1919–1949*, Gregor Benton (ed. and trans.), Oxford University Press, Oxford, 1980.

Wang Kewen. 'The Kuomintang in Transition: Ideology and Factionalism in the 'National Revolution', 1924–32, Ph.D., Stanford University, 1985

Wasserstrom, Jeffrey N. *Student Protest in Twentieth-Century China: The View from Shanghai, Stanford University Press, Stanford, California, 1991*.

Wasserstrom, Jeffrey N. 'Toward a social history of the Chinese Revolution: a review', Part 2: The State of the Field, *Social History*, vol. 17, no. 2, 1992, 289–317.

Whiting, Allen S. *Soviet Policies in China, 1917–1924*, Columbia University Press, New York, 1954.

Wilbur, C. Martin and How, Julie Lien-ying. *Missionaries of Revolution: Soviet Advisers and Nationalist China, 1920–1927*, Harvard University Press, Cambridge, Mass., 1989.

Wilbur, C. Martin. *The Nationalist Revolution in China, 1923–1928*, Cambridge University Press, Cambridge, 1984.

Wu Tien-wei. 'Chiang Kai-shek's April 12 Coup of 1927', in G.F. Chan and T.H. Etzold (eds.), *China in the 1920s*, New Viewpoints, New York, 1976, 147–59.

Yang Xiaoren. 'Shankhaiskie sobytiia vesnoi 1927g.' [The Shanghai events of spring 1927], *Materialy po kitaiskomu voprosu*, 13, 1928, 3–22.

Yeh Wen-hsin. *The Alienated Academy: Culture and Politics in Republican China, 1919–1937*, Harvard University Press, Cambridge, Mass., 1990.

Yeh, Wen-hsin. *Provincial Passages: Culture, Space and the Origins of Chinese Communism*, University of California Press, Berkeley, 1996.

Yip, Ka-Che. *Religion, Nationalism and Chinese Students: the Anti-Christian Movement of 1922–27*, Western Washington University Press, Bellingham, 1980.

Zheng Chaolin. *An Oppositionist for Life. Memoirs of the Chinese Revolutionary, Zheng Chaolin*, Gregor Benton (ed. and trans.), Humanities Press, Atlantic Highlands, N.J., 1997.

Subject Index

ABC of Communism 127
All-China Federation for the Progress
    of the Workers' Section of
    Society 34, 41, 43
Alliance Society (*Tongmenghui*) 12, 15,
    65, 109, 145, 273n60
anarchism 10, 13, 14, 16-7, 19, 24,
    25–6, 30
armed uprisings 7, 139, 140, 211
  first (24 October 1926) 147–52, 207
  second (22–3 February, 1927) 153,
    161–3, 207
    CCP bypasses GMD 161
    CEC procrastinates 161, 162
    CEC verdict on 166–7
    effect on CCP 165–6, 269n122
    GLU and strike 158, 159–161, 163,
      219, 274n82
    strikers' confusion about 167
  third (21–2 March, 1927) 7, 132,
    179–85, 207
    casualties in 184
    CEC plan for 173, 174, 177
    GLU and 173, 178, 219
    effect on CCP 189
    merchants and 274n77
    NRA irregulars in 181, 183–4, 189,
      197, 275n100
    secret societies and 180, 183, 184,
      189
    speaker teams in 173
    strikers and 179
    trials of 'running dogs' in 186–7,
      191
Anti-Christian Student Federation 46
anti-Communist labour unions 34–5,
    39, 41–3, 44, 70–1, 99–100,
    130, 218

April 12th coup (1927) 7, 21, 132, 134,
    141, 172, 199, 200–4, 280n88
  see also Shanghai General Labour Union
Association to Wipe Out the Disgrace of
    the Japanese Atrocity 86, 87
Awakening (Juewu) 13, 67

BAT strikes 1921 36, 40
Beijing-Hankou railway union smashed
    (7 February 1923 massacre)
    44, 53, 65, 66, 70, 72, 78
business community
  see Chinese Millowners' Association,
    Shanghai General Chamber of
    Commerce, Shanghai
    Commercial Association,
    Shanghai General Labour
    Union, Chiang Kai-shek

Changsha First Normal School 13, 20,
    61
Central Union of Consumer
    Associations (*Tsentrosoiuz*) 31,
    62
China Industrial Association 34
China Labour Union 99
China Relief Society 105, 201, 203
Chinese Communist Party (CCP)
  anti-imperialism of 5, 66, 81, 83,
    88–9, 136, 137, 138, 213, 217
  April 12 coup, effect on 203, 204,
    205–6
  army, lack of an 208, 215
  bureaucratization of 62, 126, 219,
    223–4, 244n83
  Central Executive Committee (CEC)
    5, 51, 52, 59, 60, 61, 62, 86,
    89, 118, 120, 123, 124, 126,

127, 145, 149, 153, 154, 156,
161, 162, 163, 166, 175,
188–9, 198, 200, 212
central bureau 32, 59
collective living arrangements 123–4
labour-movement commission 78,
79, 139, 254n110
military commission of 148, 156–7,
273n37
moves to Wuhan 172, 277n163
CEC plenums
Aug 1922 52
Nov 1923 55
Feb 1924 55
May 1924 56, 70, 71, 73, 74
Dec 1924 73
Oct 1925 62, 106, 111, 113
Feb 1926 116
July 1926 106, 110, 116, 118–9,
121, 127, 133, 146
Dec 1926 146, 147
Aug 1927 207
presidium 59, 61–2
salary of members 62
women's bureau 48, 121–2
congresses
First (1921) 14, 16, 26–9, 32, 33,
61, 235n116
Second (1922) 26, 28, 48, 51, 58,
59, 69
Third (1923) 32, 44, 53, 54, 58, 59,
60, 62, 69, 70, 73
Fourth (1925) 57, 58, 60, 61, 63,
74, 78, 112, 117
Fifth (1927) 157, 168, 169, 170,
212, 218, 224, 269n111
Confucian culture in 224–5
contribution to Chinese politics 226
evasion of Moscow 212–3
bourgeoisie, policy towards 106–7
branches, size of 86, 112, 168
cells, building 74–5, 127, 128, 169,
236n13, 250n103
Canton organization of 113, 114,
116, 123, 145, 146
Chiang Kai-shek, perception of 145,
146, 153, 156, 174, 206–7
Chiang Kai-shek, plan to resist 195,
196, 198, 199, 200, 205–6,
207–8, 281n133
common people's schools 22, 23, 48,
71–3, 75, 246n136

destruction of factories 142
feminism of 46–7, 48, 49, 69, 123–4,
217
financial problems of 27, 33, 62, 86,
121–2, 128, 255n146
foundation, Comintern initiative in
29–30, 209
Guomindang, mistrust of 28–9, 51, 52
Guomindang factions, analysis of 56,
57, 64–5, 113, 116, 146, 156,
174, 214
informal networks in 29, 214, 225
intellectuals in 24–5
repudiation of family 123
'romantic' character of 25, 123–6,
187, 220, 221
intellectuals and workers in 6, 25,
111, 125, 128, 220–3
July 1920 conference 14
male domination in 223
membership of 28, 33, 58–9, 86,
110–11, 143, 168, 220,
243n54, 256n21, 256n23,
271n1, 272n5
female 33, 58, 112, 169, 172
worker 33, 58–9, 106, 111–12, 125,
168, 169, 172, 244n59, 272n5
Beijing 33, 111
Canton 33, 111
Hubei 33
Hunan, 111
youthful character of 171
mobilization of merchants 5, 217
mobilization of peasants 49–50, 146,
155, 172, 240n136, 240n20
mobilization of soldiers 17
mobilization of students 5, 17, 65–9,
72, 87, 117–20, 168, 170
mobilization of women 5, 46–9, 50,
69–70, 120–2, 169–70, 217
mobilization of workers 5, 17, 19–24,
29, 35–40, 49, 70–3, 74–88,
111, 130–44, 146, 151, 213,
217
mobilization of youth 5, 45, 50, 170,
217
'Moscow branch group' 60, 61, 66,
122
national revolution
conception of 146, 148, 151,
154–5, 206, 216, 242n21,
243n52

proletarian hegemony in 54, 57, 74, 106, 149, 151–2, 155, 174, 206, 242n43, 243n47, 257n54
native-place organization
opposition to 37
use of 40, 141
political education in 127–8
proletarian revolution, early commitment to 28, 29, 50, 33, 209–10
Red Terror 140–2, 163–5, 166, 187, 203, 206, 207, 218
regulations of 26, 128
revolutionary bureau (1920) 16, 17
secret societies and 6, 35–6, 39, 84, 97, 101, 103, 123, 134, 191, 214, 218
self-criticism in 225
self-government in Shanghai 147, 148, 149, 152, 159–60, 162, 174–7, 193, 198, 270n134, 273n53, 274n62
Shanghai 'small group' 16, 17, 19, 20, 21, 22, 23, 25, 27, 232n43
Shanghai regional committee 5, 7, 15, 60, 62, 66, 71, 78, 86, 87, 88, 89, 110, 117, 122, 137, 138, 139, 141, 142, 144, 147, 148, 149, 150, 157, 160, 163, 164, 175, 191, 196, 198, 199, 200, 204, 205, 206, 212, 219, 229n25
conference Feb 1927 155, 156, 172, 223
district committee secretaries of 150, 165
military commission 139, 140, 148, 163, 266n22
structure 32, 61, 69, 121, 122–3, 126, 127
'signboard' labour unions, opposition to 42–3, 71
shortage of activists 27, 86, 126, 171
special committee 172, 175, 178, 188, 195
military commission 172, 173
strike to regain foreign settlements 188–9, 198, 277n162
undemocratic character of 26, 32, 215, 216, 217, 219, 223–4
underestimation of rivals 215

united front policy 6, 51, 113–4, 116, 145–6, 162, 173, 174, 199, 207, 213, 226
'bloc within' 52, 55, 56, 58, 66, 73, 107, 209, 213, 215, 216
'bloc without' 51, 112, 115, 208
labour movement and 53, 54, 56, 73, 74, 111, 144
opposition to 6, 27, 51, 52, 54, 56, 107, 112, 115–6, 215
practical reality of 214
workplace branches 41, 86, 112, 169
see also armed uprisings, citizens' assemblies, Shanghai General Labour Union, pickets
Chinese Millowners' Association 81, 82, 95, 103
Chinese-Russian Press Agency 16, 17
Chinese Women (Zhongguo funü) 121
Chinese Worker (Zhongguo gongren) 45
Chinese Youth (Zhongguo qingnian) 66, 67
citizens' assembly 90, 159, 160, 169, 173, 174, 175, 176–7, 178, 185, 194, 273n53, 274n62
CCP advocates sovietization of 175–6, 207
district assemblies 154, 173, 180, 185
Nanshi 185, 201
Zhabei 152, 185, 201, 203, 280n91
Comintern, 17, 24, 206, 209–13
Executive Committee (ECCI) 5, 31, 33, 49, 50, 57, 86, 113, 116, 120, 133, 145, 147, 156, 172, 207
ambiguities of policy 211
'Bolshevization' of CCP 126–9, 220
CCP seen as weak, 'petty-bourgeois' 25, 59, 126, 128, 210, 220
GMD's class character, analysis of 51–2, 54, 55, 58, 114, 155, 214–5, 241n12, 245n45
national revolution, conception of 57–8, 114, 154, 206
plenums
sixth (March 1926) 115
seventh (Dec 1926) 128, 147, 153, 196, 212
eighth (June 1927) 213
splits over united front 52–4, 55, 57–8, 210, 211

united front policy 52, 55, 113,
146–7, 156, 207, 209, 214
East Asian Secretariat (Shanghai)
17–18
Far Eastern Bureau (Shanghai) 116,
121, 126–7, 133, 139, 145,
148, 149, 151, 154, 155, 162,
175, 188, 195, 197, 198, 205,
206, 210, 212, 273n53
Far Eastern Secretariat (Irkutsk)
(FES) 18, 27, 31
Shanghai as nodal point 31
congresses
first (1919) 17
second (1920) 17, 28, 57
third (1921) 19
fourth (1922) 52, 253n48
fifth (1924) 57
delegation to China 1920 12
difficulties of communication 212
financing of CCP 30, 33, 62, 128–9,
209
financing of GMD 53, 62, 129, 209
inability to control CCP 210, 211–12,
213
language of 8, 230n38, 242n44
responsibility for failure of CCP
policy 7, 206–8, 210
Common People (*Pingmin*) 173, 199
Common People's Women School 48,
245n99
Common Progress Society 190, 191, 200
Communist (*Gongchandang*) 17, 27,
232n47
Communist Party of the Soviet Union
225, 245n87, 272n31
Far Eastern Bureau 12, 14
internal opposition to united front
policy 115, 210–11, 258n56,
281n3
Politburo 5, 7, 52, 53, 54, 93, 94, 95,
113, 114, 115, 119, 120, 126,
145, 146, 147, 156, 189, 198,
210, 212, 258n67
Siberian Bureau, 14, 17, 18, 231n13
Communist Youth International (KIM)
45, 51, 66, 117, 126, 155, 175
Communist Youth League (CYL) 5, 15,
66, 84, 117, 155, 176, 195,
199, 203, 206, 216, 217,
276n132
CEC criticises 118–9

CEC intensifies control of 118–9, 170
membership in Shanghai 112–13,
170, 257n39, 272n5
organizational structure 117
sends members to Soviet Union 119
shortage and quality of activists 170
working-class youth and 117, 118,
180, 217
see also Socialist Youth League
Congress of Toilers of the East (1922)
28, 34
cotton industry in Shanghai 1
cotton workers' union 82, 83–5, 93, 97,
101, 104, 131, 133, 134,
136–8, 140, 143, 165, 251n8

Daxia University 79, 80, 108, 183
dockers' union 84, 133, 134, 143

electricians' union 22, 34, 35, 41
Executive Committee of Shanghai
Syndicates 35, 39, 43

foreign employees' union 94, 95, 131
Foreign Languages School 15, 18, 19,
21, 22, 27, 30
foreign troops in Shanghai 154, 179, 198
French Concession 1, 154, 187, 188,
200, 201
police of 24, 27, 148, 167, 190, 191,
255n146
Fudan University 14, 182

guild socialism 10, 25
Guide Weekly (*Xiangdao*) 33, 48, 61, 62,
73, 116, 135, 136, 138, 187
gold- and silver-smiths' union 38–9,
218
Guomindang (GMD) 6, 11, 13, 14,
19–20, 22, 29, 37, 50, 108,
138, 152, 153
Borodin's reorganization of 55, 65,
110, 215
CEC plenums
August 1924 56
May 1926 115
Mar 1927 156
CCP fractions in 55, 56, 216
CCP representation in GMD organs
63, 73, 87, 109, 110, 113–4,
115, 121, 146, 156, 173, 214,
215, 216

city-district and branch organizations
in Shanghai 63–4, 72, 170, 195
congresses
first (1924) 55, 63, 64, 65
second (1926) 108, 109, 113
government in Canton 37, 147, 148,
213
government in Wuhan 123, 145, 153,
154, 156, 176, 178, 189, 193,
195, 202
opposition to 204, 205
informal networks in 171, 173–4,
214, 215, 246n111
Jiangsu provincial bureau 65, 87, 110,
161, 162, 173, 176, 177, 193
Jiangsu special committee 147, 149
left wing 55, 65, 108, 109, 110, 145,
146, 170, 193, 214, 281n130
mass mobilization efforts of 65, 216
members sent to Sun Yat-sen
University 119–20
membership 62, 63, 108, 111, 170–1,
245n96
youthfulness of 171
educated character of 171
inactivity of 171
merchant association of 176, 217,
274n62
national revolution, conception of
65
party-affairs department 64, 89
Political Council 56, 57, 193
Shanghai branch of 173, 174, 177,
189, 193, 194, 215, 278n34
right wing 56, 64, 65, 70–1, 86–7, 89,
130, 170, 187, 191, 193, 194
'old right' 87, 109, 114
'new right' 87, 108–9, 113, 116
Shanghai executive bureau of CEC
62–3, 65, 67, 87, 88, 89, 108,
152, 161, 162, 170, 173, 176,
177, 188, 191, 192, 193, 203
women's committee 69, 120, 121,
171
Shanghai party bureau 110
Shanghai party purification
committee 203
state socialism of 25
structure of 55, 156, 171
united front policy 6, 7, 52
opposition to 6, 56, 73, 109, 113–4,
191, 214

Western Hills group 109, 113, 130,
158, 170, 184, 193
workers and 70, 108
Xinhai comrades' club 87, 109
Zhejiang provincial bureau 108, 109
see also Alliance Society, Chiang Kai-
shek
Green Gang
see secret societies

handicraft workers' union 134, 153, 218
Hot-Blooded Daily (Rexue ribao) 91
Huangpu Military Academy 114, 125,
157, 202, 225
see also National Revolutionary Army

Industrial Workers of the World (USA)
21
intelligentsia in Shanghai 10, 25
International Class-War Prisoners' Aid
94, 105, 253n48
International Settlement 1, 89, 138,
167, 188, 200
foreigners fear seizure of 154, 178–9,
183, 187
Mixed Court 87, 90, 91
Municipal Council 111, 179, 186
by-laws 87, 88, 90, 91
Chinese representation on 90, 91
police 77, 78, 79, 80, 81, 83, 85, 89,
102, 135, 138, 139, 140, 164,
179, 184, 190, 201, 202, 203–4
police harry CCP 24, 43, 44, 69, 82,
111, 118, 200, 255n146

Japanese Chamber of Commerce 85
Japanese Millowners' Association 83,
85, 95, 102–3, 137, 143
Jun'an seamen's guild 37, 38

Karakhan Declaration (1919) 11
KUTV see University of the Toilers of
the East

Labour Federation 34
Labour Organization Secretariat (LOS)
33–5, 45, 46
Shanghai section 34, 37, 38, 44
demise of, 40, 43–5
failed attempt to set up GLU 34
Labour Weekly (Laodong zhoukan) 33–4
Labour World (Laodongjie) 17, 19, 27

Male and Female Labourers' Anti-
    Communist Alliance 130
marxism in China, 11–12, 17, 27
Marxist Research Society 13, 14, 15,
    231n19
March 18th Massacre (1926) 119
March 20th Incident (1926) 114, 116,
    208, 215
May Fourth Movement (1919) 3, 4,
    9–10, 15, 18, 22, 23, 29, 34,
    47, 97, 126, 209, 214, 217
  workers in 10, 19, 77, 160
May Thirtieth Movement (1925) 21,
    86, 89–107, 108, 109, 110,
    117, 119, 120, 122, 130, 133,
    138, 140, 141, 144, 153, 189,
    213, 217, 221
  boycott 93
  CCP and 7, 89, 93, 95, 96, 106–7,
    111, 214
  demands of 90, 91, 92, 95
  demonstration on 30 May 87–8, 89
  leadership of 106
  Municipal Council severs electricity
    94, 103
  relief fund (ji'anhui), 93, 94, 99–100,
    101
  strike 93, 95, 160
  strike pay 93–4, 100
  strike settlement 95–6
  strikers fired 105
  triple stoppage (sanba) 90, 107, 160.
mechanics' club 70
mechanics' union 16, 20–2, 34, 35, 71

nation, representations of 10
Nanyang tobacco workers' friendly
    society 42, 43, 70, 71, 166
national assembly 67, 70, 147, 152
  campaign for women's representation
    in 70, 120
National General Labour Union 79,
    104, 134
  national labour congresses
  first (1922) 38, 44
  second (1925) 45, 71, 99, 134, 251n9
  third (1926) 130, 133, 134, 135
  fourth (1927) 139
National Revolutionary Army (NRA) 7,
    105, 111, 114, 115, 116, 145,
    148, 152, 153, 156, 159, 161,
    189, 214–5

arrival in Shanghai 168, 183, 194, 195
corps (army), first 172, 190
  first division 195, 196, 197
  second division 195, 196, 197
corps, second 115, 195
corps, sixth 115, 149, 195
corps, twenty-sixth 172, 196, 197,
    201, 202, 203
division, twenty-first 195
delays entry to Shanghai 161, 167,
    174, 178, 182, 183
nature of 196, 197
number of troops 196, 198, 279n60
political bureau of eastern route army
    194
popularity of 160, 167, 185, 187
Soviet military advisers to 114, 145
workers and 155, 195, 196–7
see also Huangpu Academy, Northern
    Expedition
National Student Union (NSU) 14, 66,
    67, 89, 90, 91, 111, 117, 185,
    215
Nechaev brigade 172, 181–2
New Culture Movement 9, 19, 25, 46,
    47, 125, 221, 224
New Youth (Xin Qingnian) 2, 9–10, 12,
    13, 17, 27, 33
Northern Expedition 7, 145
  CCP and 116, 212–3, 258n67

peace committee (heping weizhihui)
    148–9
pickets 5, 139–40, 146, 148, 150,
    156–9, 162–3, 167, 173,
    179–85, 189, 192–3, 197, 198,
    269n111, 269n112, 279n61
  CCP's resistance to disarming 188,
    197–8, 198–200, 207
  elimination of 187, 190, 200–2
  shortage of arms 140, 148, 157, 173,
    180
  see also Shanghai General Labour
    Union, CCP
Pioneer (Xianqu) 45, 66
postal employees' union 70, 131–2,
    133, 134, 160–1, 166, 218
Profintern 27–8, 31, 34, 62, 80
printers' union 22, 34, 35, 40–1, 133,
    134, 218, 221, 251n8
Protect-the Party Journal (Hudang tekan)
    64, 82

provisional municipal government
(1927) 177, 185, 186, 187,
188, 189, 193, 194, 195, 198,
203, 274n63
Pudong Industrial Society for the
Advancement of Morality 40,
43
Pudong weavers' union 35, 38–9, 40,
131

railway workers' union 133, 134
Republican Daily 23, 34, 46, 47, 64, 67,
69, 97, 124, 257n51
Russian Revolution, Chinese response
to 11–12, 18–19

St John's University 117–8
seamen's union 37, 38, 70, 94, 95, 96,
101, 133, 134, 143, 166, 202,
218, 251n8
secret societies 77, 80, 91, 100, 157,
278n6
'Big Three' 6, 190, 205, 218
Chiang Kai-shek, deal with 190, 218
Green Gang (*Qingbang*) 5, 35, 39, 89,
100, 101, 123, 133, 134, 142,
184, 190, 191, 200, 205, 214,
254n117
Japanese employers and 102–3, 141
labour contractors and foremen in 5,
36, 102, 141–2
Niu Yongjian and 148, 150, 161, 163
Red Gang (*Hongbang*) 5, 133, 134,
142, 184
see also CCP, Shanghai General
Labour Union, Common
Progress Society
Self-Government Guild (*zizhi gongsuo*)
147
Shamian massacre (Canton) 93
Shanghai
Chinese-administered districts 1, 66,
139
police in 24, 44, 46, 78, 80, 87,
102, 104, 111, 132, 139, 150,
163, 179–82, 186
under Fengtian clique 92, 94–5,
105, 172, 181, 249n53
Sun Chuanfang's forces in 105,
139, 161, 249n53
divided administration 1, 24, 213
hybrid culture 2

import-export trade 1
industrial centre 1
migrants to 2
population 1, 172.
symbol of modernity 1–2, 3
see also French Concession,
International Settlement
Shanghai All-University Association
(*Gedaxue tongzhihui*) 118
Shanghai Association of Women of All
Sections of Society (*Shanghai
gejie funü lianhehui*) 120, 121,
169
Shanghai Bankers' Association 192
Shanghai Commercial Association
(*Shanghai shangye lianhehui*)
153–4, 160, 185, 192, 192,
193, 197, 217
Shanghai Citizens' Association 81
Shanghai Federation of Street
Associations 85, 89, 90, 91, 92,
93, 104, 131, 138, 142, 153,
160, 217
Shanghai Federation of Syndicates
(SFS) 34, 71, 73, 82, 99, 100,
101, 130, 144, 218, 261n1
see also Shanghai General Labour
Union.
Shanghai Federation of Women's
Circles (*Shanghai nüjie
lianhehui*) 47
Shanghai General Chamber of
Commerce (GCC) 6, 82, 85,
89, 131, 136, 147, 153–4, 205
May Thirtieth Movement 90, 91,
92–3, 105, 106, 107
merchant militia 147, 148, 161, 163,
181, 182, 183, 204
Shanghai self-government 152
Zhabei chamber of commerce 147
Shanghai General Labour Union
(GLU) 90, 96–106, 130–144,
152, 158, 185, 192, 195, 199,
201, 203
abduction of strike breakers 93,
252n36
accused of corruption 100, 205
activists and officials 98–9, 102, 105,
143
affiliated membership 96, 105, 133,
143, 153, 186
anti-imperialism 96–7, 101

April 12 coup and 200, 202, 203
assistance to sacked workers 105, 143
business community and 85, 95, 103–4
Canton labour movement 262n31
closure of 104, 105, 106, 111, 132, 134, 135, 153
delegate meetings 106, 132, 134–5, 164, 166
friction with CCP 95, 139, 144, 159, 164, 188, 219
interference of CCP 219
leadership of 89–90, 135, 186, 251n8
May Thirtieth strike and 93, 94, 95
origins 34, 89–90, 251n8
promotion of class principles 97
'reformist' unions and 130–1, 144
reopens 1927 185–6
secret societies and 101–3, 133, 141, 144, 157, 191, 192, 204, 218, 219, 254n110
SFS attack on 99–100, 101, 103
underground existence 130, 132–5, 152–3
weakness of base unions 215, 217–8, 219
see also individual labour unions, armed uprisings, CCP, pickets
Shanghai Student Union (SSU) 67, 87, 89, 90, 91, 94, 118, 119, 138, 152, 185, 203, 276n132
Shanghai University 58, 63, 64, 65, 67–9, 72, 76, 84, 86, 88, 92, 108, 112, 117, 118, 120, 121, 124, 170, 182, 204, 259n126, 266n19
Shanghai Women's Industrial Progress Union (Shanghai nüzi gongye jindehui) 41, 43, 71, 132
Shanghai Women's Citizens' Assembly 70
Shanghai Worker (Shanghai gongren) 73
Shanghai Worker-Merchant Friendly Society (Shanghai gongshang youyi hui) 19–20, 34, 41, 99
Shanghai Workers' Recreation Club 23
shop employees' union 134, 153, 164, 166, 218
silk workers 132, 160, 166 see Shanghai Women's Industrial Progress Union.
social democracy 17, 26, 30

Socialist Youth League (SYL) 5, 16, 23, 25, 55, 65–9, 112, 117, 121, 217
anti-Christian movement 45–6, 67, 117–18, 217
congresses
first (1922) 45
second (1923) 65, 66
third (1925) 117
disbandment and reorganization 26, 45
foundation 14–15
members go to Russia 19, 30, 61, 233n61
membership 45, 65
bigger than CCP 66
workers in 66
Moscow branch 15
'petty-bourgeois' character of 24, 45
Shanghai regional committee 66
united front policy of 66, 67
Voitinskii on aims 14
Zhejiang network and 15
see also Communist Youth League
strikes
Japanese mill strike 1925 76–85, 102, 131, 134
central strike committee 79, 80
pickets 80
strike pay 80–1
Japanese mill strike 1926 111, 135–9, 142–3
seamen's strike (1922) 37–8, 237n52
strike wave of 1922 35, 39–40, 43
Soviet Consulate Shanghai 31, 212
Sun Yat-sen Three People's Study Groups 118, 170
Sun Yat-sen University 119–20

textile union (1921) 34
tobacco workers' union 34, 35, 36, 40
Tongji University 119
tram employees' union 104, 143, 214, 251n8
Truth Daily (Gongli ribao) 107
Tsentrosoiuz see Central Union of Consumer Associations.

Union of Labour, Commerce and Education (Gongshangxue lianhehui) 90–1, 99, 104, 217
CCP influence in 91–2

GLU in 91
office closed 94, 95
University of the Toilers of the East
(KUTV) 19, 60, 76, 86,
119–20, 224, 225

war between Jiangsu and Zhejiang
militarists (1924) 1, 67, 249n53
Washington Conference (1922) 43
Weekly Review (*Xingqi pinglun*) 13, 14,
15, 27
West Shanghai Workers' Club (*Huxi
gongren julebu*) 75–6, 77, 78, 80,
84, 141
White Terror 158, 160, 163, 164, 223
Women and Labour (*Funü yu laodong*) 47
Women's Review (*Funü pinglun*) 47
Women's Rights Alliance 48, 49
Women's Suffrage Association 49
Women's Voice (*Funü sheng*) 47–8
Women's Weekly (*Funü zhoubao*) 69
work-study mutual aid corps 11, 14
workers 244n84, 270n136
clientelist ties of 5, 79, 217
gender divisions among 5, 40, 217

guilds 21
native-place networks of 5, 21, 36–7,
38, 77, 78, 79, 98–9, 136, 141,
211, 217
native-place labour unions 41
secret-society ties of, 5, 35, 211
Workers' and Merchants' Association
130
Workers' Moral Progress Society
(*Gongren jindehui*) 76, 79, 82
Workers' Section of Society Support
Association (*Gongjie weizhi hui*)
131
Workers' Thrift and Morality Society
(*Gongren jiande hui*) 131

Young China Party 118, 170
Young Men's Christian Association 117
Young Women's Christian Association
49

Zhejiang First Normal School
(Hangzhou) 11, 13, 14, 15, 41,
61, 98, 117, 225
Zhejiang New Tide Weekly 11, 13

Name Index

Albrecht, A.E. 155, 156, 175, 195, 273n37
An Ticheng 68.
Appen A.A. 148, 157, 273n37

Bai Chongxi 153, 159, 167, 172, 178, 182, 183, 184, 186, 187, 193, 195, 200, 201, 202
Bao Huiseng 235n113
Bao Xiaoliang 141, 181
Bi Shucheng 178, 181, 182–3
Bliukher, V.K. 153, 281n133
Borodin, M.M. 54, 55, 56, 65, 110, 113, 115, 145, 146, 147, 153, 155, 174, 189, 199, 204, 210, 211, 212, 213, 214, 215, 216, 265n5
Brandt, C. 3
Bu Shiji 72
Bubnov, A.S. 114
Bukharin, N.I. 52, 53, 127

Cai Hesen 20, 29, 33, 49, 54, 59, 61, 62, 68, 123, 124, 225
Cai Yuanpei 12, 173, 174
Cai Zhihua 76, 79, 82
Cavendish, P. 214
Chang Yuqing 102
Chen Anfen 269n112
Chen Atang 137, 138, 142, 143
Chen Bilan 63, 121
Chen Boyun 180, 204
Chen Chengyin 118
Chen Guangfu 186, 193, 194
Chen Guoliang 99
Chen Duxiu 9, 16, 17, 19, 20, 21, 24, 25, 27, 29, 39, 41, 47, 49, 54, 58, 62, 63, 70, 78, 84, 86, 109, 110, 122, 123, 124, 127, 151, 152, 155,

156, 168, 169, 172, 173, 174, 188, 196, 197, 198, 199, 215, 221
  absent from First Congress, 28
  arrests of 12, 32, 44
  arrival in Shanghai 188
  background 12–13
  general secretary 32, 51, 59, 61
  illness of 114, 139, 212, 257n51
  'patriarchal' style 124, 224
  'right opportunism' of 54, 56, 116, 145, 146–7, 149, 207, 241n21, 243n52
  united front, calls for withdrawal from 52, 54, 113, 115–6
Chen Qiaonian 62
Chen Qicai 194
Chen Qun 190, 200, 203, 204, 277n3
Chen Wangdao 13, 16, 32, 68, 236n12
Chen Xinglin 90, 251n8
Chen Yannian 114, 206
Chen Youren 193
Chen Yun 221–2
Chesneaux, J. 43, 217, 218, 219
Chiang Kai-shek 3, 7, 21, 110, 111, 114, 115, 116, 123, 134, 155, 167, 173, 174, 178, 193, 195, 196, 197, 198, 199, 204, 205, 206, 215
  accumulation of power 156, 258n62, 269n103
  arrival in Shanghai 188, 190, 194
  business community and 153, 192, 267n80
  opposes Wuhan government 145, 146, 153, 192, 204
Chicherin, G.V. 53, 55
Clifford N.R. 268n84, 279n63

Dai Jinan 101
Dai Jitao, 11, 13, 14, 29, 63, 90, 108–9, 113, 118
Dai Pengshan 193
Dai San 79, 249n42
Dalin, S.A. 51, 59
Deng Zhongxia 44, 63, 66, 68, 71–2, 78, 79, 82
Ding Ling 48, 245n99
Ding Xiaoxian 177, 274n63
Dirlik, A. 4, 10, 30
Dong Chuping 38, 239n103
Dong Yixiang 41, 119
Du Yuesheng 89, 131, 160, 167, 180, 183, 190, 191, 200, 201, 205, 217, 270n141
Duan Qirui 70, 91, 105, 106, 119, 249n53
Duanmu Kai 118
Duncan, J. 196, 197

Fairbank, J.K. 1
Fang Jiaobo 83, 90
Fan Jiebao 125
Feng Shaoshan 89
Feng Ziyou 87
Fessenden, S. 167
Fitzgerald, J. 216
Fokin, N.A. 126, 127, 175
Fromberg M. 235n111
Fu Xiaoan 95, 140, 154, 160, 205
Fu Yuanxiong 90

Gao Erbo 193
Gao Junman 47, 124
Geller, L.N. 126, 127
Gilmartin, C. 6
Gu Shunzhang 139, 142, 164, 173, 200–1, 221, 264n101
Gu Xueqiao 103
Gu Zhenghong 86, 87, 88, 102, 103, 222
Gu Zhuxuan 142
Gui Xinqiu 116
Guo Bohe 67, 117, 182
Guo Jianxia 84, 90, 140
Guo Jingren 40
Guo Taiqi 173
Guo Yuheng 161, 162

Han Buxian 204
Hao Huoqing 136
He Baozhen 69, 123

He Chang 117
He Chengxiang 67
He Chengyi 88
He Jingru 139
He Luo 121, 274n63
He Shizhen 68
He Yingqin 167, 184
Henriot, C. 274n63, 278
Hou Shaoqiu 147, 173, 193, 266n19, 274n63
Hu Shi 123
Hua Gang 150
Hua Lin 19
Huang Jinrong 148, 190, 191, 205
Huang Zonghan 47
Hu Hanmin 63

Ibsen, H. 123
Isaacs, H.R. 167, 211

Ji Zhi 75
Jiang Guangci 124, 125, 187, 259n127, 276n128, 277n150
Jiang Weixin 75, 141, 42
Joffe, A.A. 52

Kang Sheng 223
Karakhan, L.M. 11, 55, 95, 115, 128
Kong Dezhi 120
Kong Yannan 84
Kuang Gongyao 42
Kuibyshev, N.V. 114
Kun, B. 17
Kuznetsova, M.F. 12, 14, 16

Lampson, M. 154
Lei Rongpu 92
Leng Xin 205
Lepse, I.I. 94
Li Baizhi 135
Li Baozhang 148, 149, 150, 152, 158, 159, 161, 163, 164, 167, 170
Li Da 16, 27, 32, 47, 48, 68, 234n104
Li Dazhao 2, 12, 28, 68, 72
Li Fengchi 101
Li Hanjun 16, 17, 26, 27, 28, 30, 234n104
Li Ji 68.
Li Jianru 141
Li Lisan 61, 62, 63, 72, 78, 79, 89, 90, 91, 92, 93, 95, 98, 100, 101, 102, 105, 122, 124, 125, 130, 135, 137, 142, 206, 218, 251n8

Li Qihan 16, 17, 22–3, 24, 25, 34, 36, 39, 44, 218
Li Ruiqing 84
Li Shiliang 99
Li Shixun 67
Li Shizeng 49
Li Shuoxun 117
Li Weihan 60
Li Yichun 61, 68, 124, 125
Li Yushi 181
Li Zhengyu 131
Li Zhenying 34, 237n31
Li Zhong 16, 20–1, 35, 233n71
Li Zongren 195
Liang Botai 98
Liao Zhongkai 63
Lidin, V.V. 31, 33, 46, 50
Lin Boqu 16
Lin Jun 91, 92, 148, 185, 188, 191, 193, 274n63, 277n162
Lin Weimin 38, 238n58
Liu Bolun 63
Liu Bozhuang 258n71
Liu Dabai 13, 17
Liu Guanzhi 79, 84, 90, 105
Liu Hua 75–6, 79, 83, 84, 86, 105–6, 221
Liu Huaiqing 141
Liu Luyin 89
Liu Qi 196, 197
Liu Renjing 28, 66
Liu Shaoqi 19, 62, 69, 90, 94, 98, 105, 123, 135, 251n9
Liu Yazi 110
Liu Yijing 67
Liu Zerong 17, 232n53
Liu Zhongmin 140
Liu Zunyi 121
Lockhart, W. Bruce 154
Lu Xun 226, 283n60
Luk, M. 4, 211, 220
Luo Yinong 19, 60, 110, 121, 122, 123, 127, 137, 148, 149, 150, 151, 159, 162, 172, 174, 191, 198, 199, 200, 206
Luo Zhanglong 59, 63

Ma Chaojun 89
Ma Lianghui 102
Malraux, A. 7
Mamaev, I.K. 12, 14
Mandalian, T.G. 154, 155, 175, 273n37

Mao Dun see Shen Yanbing
Mao Qihua 221
Mao Zedong 8, 13, 20, 23, 59, 61, 63, 64, 208
Martin, B.G. 190, 270n141, 277n3
Mei Dianlong 91
Meisner, M. 3
Molotov, V.M. 210
Mu Zhiying 41, 132

Nasonov, N.M. 155, 175
Ni Tiansheng 254n117
Nikol'skii, V.A. 27, 28, 31
Niu Yongjian 147, 167, 173, 175, 186, 192, 194, 266n24
    and first armed uprising 148, 149, 150, 151, 184, 266n39
    and second armed uprising 161, 162, 163
    and third armed uprising 174, 176, 178, 182, 183

Ou Shengbai 26

Pan Donglin 85, 130, 131, 142
Pan Yizhi 201
Perry, E.J. 254n90
Piatnitskii, I.A. 133
Peng Shuzhi 16, 19, 57, 60–1, 62, 63, 68, 116, 121, 123, 124, 145, 149, 151, 152, 162, 172, 174, 175, 188, 197, 212, 243n47, 268n88, 277n163

Qian Yongning 194
Qu Qiubai, 15, 18–19, 25, 56, 60, 61, 62, 68, 72, 109, 116, 124, 125, 128, 152, 162, 166, 172, 174, 212, 221, 224, 242n44, 243n47, 268n88

Radek, K.B. 53, 115, 119, 120, 257n54, 281n3
Rafes, M.G 126, 127, 133, 148, 149, 151, 152, 261n143, 267n63
Ren Bishi 19, 66, 68, 117, 123, 152, 220
Roux, A. 280n.95, 280n110
Roy M.N. 155, 172, 207, 212, 213, 224

Safarov, G.I. 53
Saich, T. 5
Sakh'ianova, M. 12

Schurmann, F. 4
Schwartz, B. 3
Shao Bingsheng 40
Shao Lizi 13, 16, 39, 63, 68, 123
Shao Yuanchong 109, 110, 113, 115
Shen Jianlong 124, 259n126
Shen Junru 152
Shen Lianfang 160
Shen Mengxian 222, 225
Shen Xuanlu 13, 15, 16, 63, 108, 109, 121, 124, 240n136, 259n126
Shen Yanbing (Mao Dun) 13, 16, 32, 41, 47, 68, 120, 125, 222
Shen Zemin 16, 17, 41, 47, 68, 69
Shen Zhongjiu 13
Shen Zitian 225
Shi Cuntong 13, 17, 45, 63, 66, 68, 69, 124, 245n99
Shi Jinkun 102, 103, 141
Shi Liqing 139, 191, 264n85
Shi Zhiying 124
Shumiatskii, B.Z. 18, 27
Sneevliet, H. 5, 27, 28, 31, 32, 33, 34, 37, 44, 50, 51, 52, 53, 54, 58, 62, 209
Sokolsky, G. 178, 222
Song Qingling 120
Song Ziwen 193
Stalin, I.V. 54, 57, 115, 210, 214
Stranahan, P. 4
Su Zhaozheng 38
Sun Chuanfang 84, 105, 111, 134, 139, 148, 149, 152, 153, 154, 163, 172, 196
Sun Guangren 101
Sun Jiefu 183
Sun Jinchuan 180
Sun Ke 113, 193
Sun Lianghui 75, 79, 82, 84, 86, 98
Sun Yat-sen 11, 12, 13, 14, 16, 21, 29, 37, 52, 53, 54, 55, 56, 62, 63, 65, 87, 108, 109, 113, 119, 127, 176, 186, 273n60
Sun Zongfang 130

Tan Yankai 156
Tang Jicang 193
Tang Jinda 131.
Tang Shaoyi 87, 109
Tao Jingxuan 84, 150
Tao Yihe 141
Teichman, E. 158

Tong Lizhang 20, 34, 99, 130
Trotsky, L.D. 53

Van de Ven, H. 3, 4, 13, 30, 103, 208, 220, 235n122, 282n30
Vil'de, S.L. 31, 62, 236n7
Vilenskii-Sibiriakov, V.D. 12, 14
Voitinskii, G.D. 14, 16, 17, 18, 19, 29–30, 51, 52, 53, 54, 55, 56, 57, 67, 78, 110, 113, 114, 115, 116, 121, 128, 139, 146, 151, 154, 155, 189, 198, 206, 210, 212
  background 12, 30
  FEB and 126, 127, 156, 212, 267n63
  foundation of CCP 13, 209, 231n13
  leaves Shanghai 1920 26, 27
  opposition to Borodin 145
  sent to direct May Thirtieth Movement 93, 94, 95

Wang Bian 122
Wang Fanxi 283n35
Wang Guanghui 130
Wang Hanliang 193, 274n62, 274n63
Wang Hebo 59
Wang Huafen 259n126
Wang Huiwu 47, 48
Wang Jingwei 63, 145, 199, 201, 207
Wang Jingyun 132, 134
Wang Ruqing 165
Wang San 141
Wang Shouhua 19, 98, 123, 133, 135, 137, 147, 148, 186, 187, 191, 192, 193, 197, 200, 201, 218, 274n62, 278n6
Wang Shouqian 193
Wang Si 141
Wang Xiaolai 147, 176, 188, 193
Wang Yanxia 151, 181, 204
Wang Yazhang 121
Wang Yifei 15, 117
Wang Yizhi 63, 66, 69, 124, 245n99
Wang Zhenyi 32
Wang Zhongyi 63
Wasserstrom, J.N. 6
Whiting, A. 3
Wu Min 90, 98
Wu Peifu 44, 53, 147
Wu Shuwu 32
Wu Tiecheng 115
Wu Xianqing 76, 78, 82, 222
Wu Yuanli 201

Wu Zhihui 67, 109, 147, 173, 175, 193, 194

Xi Zuoyao 150
Xia Chao 147, 148, 149
Xiang Jingyu 48, 59, 61, 62, 63, 68, 70, 72, 120, 121, 123, 124, 223, 240n134, 245n99, 247n141
Xiang Ying 78–9, 84, 97, 137
Xiao Asi 142
Xiao Jingguang 19
Xiao Zizhang 155, 162, 172, 225, 268n92
Xie Chi 64, 109
Xie Dejin 141
Xie Fusheng 193
Xie Wenjin 98, 122
Xing Shilian 94–5, 97, 103, 104
Xu Langxi 184, 276n120
Xu Meikun 2, 25, 32, 40, 139, 181, 202, 221, 239n79, 259n126
Xu Wei 75
Xu Xilin 39
Xu Zaizhou 98
Xu Zhimo 60
Xue Yue 183, 195, 196, 197

Yan Fangong 106
Yan Huiqing 132
Yang Damei 131
Yang Fulin 141
Yang Hu 190, 200, 203, 204, 277n3
Yang Huaping 34
Yang Jianhong 98, 105
Yang Mingzhai 16, 21, 23, 25
Yang Peisheng 169
Yang Shannan 117
Yang Shuzhuang 163
Yang Xianjiang 41, 110
Yang Xingfo 110, 173, 176, 193, 273n60
Yang Zhihua 15, 48, 49, 63, 69, 72, 79, 121, 124, 169, 223, 247n141
Yang Zilie 123, 240n136, 259n126
Yao Zuobing 14
Ye Chucang 63, 64, 89, 109, 110, 113, 115, 147, 173
Ye Dagong 135
Yeh Wen-hsin 3
Yin Kuan 122, 127, 172
Yu Rizhang 89
Yu Xianting 98

Yu Xiaqing 90, 91, 95, 96, 99, 104, 107, 123, 131, 136, 142, 146, 148, 149, 151, 153, 154, 155, 161, 162, 175, 176, 186, 192, 193, 194, 217, 223, 252n17, 263n57, 266n24, 267n80
Yu Xiusong 11, 14, 15, 16, 17, 41, 45, 98, 119
Yu Youren 63, 68
Yu Zhenhong 67
Yuan Dashi 38, 44, 139, 238n60
Yuan Youcai 101
Yuan Zhenying 16
Yun Daiying 10–11, 63, 66, 68, 87, 88, 105, 117

Zeng Fugen 165.
Zhang Dongsun 13, 14, 25, 234n94
Zhang Guotao 25, 27, 28, 32, 33, 34, 51, 54, 59, 62, 78, 81, 89, 93, 98, 123, 156, 224
Zhang Ji 64
Zhang Jingjiang 109, 147
Zhang Jingsheng 127, 261n153
Zhang Jingxuan 38
Zhang Jinqiu 69
Zhang Liang 199
Zhang Qiuren 15, 41, 45, 66, 67, 98, 117
Zhang Ruixian 35
Zhang Shuping 125, 180
Zhang Shushi 193
Zhang Tailei 15, 18, 45, 66, 68, 117, 124, 156
Zhang Taiyan 87, 109
Zhang Weizhen 97, 102, 186
Zhang Xiaolin 89, 190, 205
Zhang Xueliang 92
Zhang Yinglong 84
Zhang Yizhang 39
Zhang Zongchang 152, 172, 181
Zhang Zuochen 134, 135, 140
Zhang Zuolin 106, 163
Zhao Pu 168
Zhao Shiyan 117, 121–2, 134, 135, 136, 137, 138, 140, 159, 172, 173, 182, 204, 206, 263n47
Zheng Boqi 126
Zheng Chaolin 61, 62, 117, 127, 170, 224
Zheng Futa 41, 239n81
Zheng Yuxiu 193

Zheng Zhenduo 68
Zhou Deming 101
Zhou Enlai 61, 114, 157, 160, 163,
    167, 172, 173, 174, 182, 198, 199,
    201, 202, 206, 225, 273n37
Zhou Fengqi 196, 200, 203
Zhou Jinjiang 76
Zhou Zhonghua 101
Zhu Baoting 37, 38, 140
Zhu Dingyi 34

Zhu Guoping 90
Zhu Huaishan 119
Zhu Jixuan 147
Zhu Yingru 132, 262n19
Zhu Yiquan 87
Zhuang Wengong 15, 61, 122
Zinoviev, G.E. 52, 115
Zou Jing, 194
Zou Lu 109
Zuo Shunsheng 118